# Public Sector Employment in the Twenty-First Century

# Public Sector Employment in the Twenty-First Century

Marilyn Pittard
Phillipa Weeks

EDITORS

ANU
THE AUSTRALIAN NATIONAL UNIVERSITY

E PRESS

ANU
E PRESS

Published by ANU E Press
The Australian National University
Canberra ACT 0200, Australia
Email: anuepress@anu.edu.au
This title is also available online at: http://epress.anu.edu.au/public_sector_citation.html

---

National Library of Australia
Cataloguing-in-Publication entry

Public sector employment in the twenty-first century.

ISBN 9781920942601 (pbk.)
ISBN 9781920942618 (online)

1. Civil service - Australia. 2. Labor contract -
Australia. 3. Privatization - Australia. 4. Contracting
out - Australia. 5. Labor laws and legislation - Australia.
6. Industrial relations - Australia. 7. Civil service -
New Zealand. 8. Civil service - Great Britain. I. Pittard,
Marilyn J. (Marilyn Jane). II. Weeks, Phillipa.

351.60994

---

Cover design by ANU E Press
Cover image used by permission of Bruce Moore

# Table of Contents

# Phillipa Weeks 1953–2006

# A Tribute[1]

Phillipa Weeks spent much of her life being too young. She won her first major scholarship in 1963, a Canberra-Goulburn Archdiocese Bursary to enter first year of high school as a boarder at Our Lady of Mercy College Goulburn, but had to forfeit it because she was only 10! Six years later, having completed her schooling at Harden Catholic Primary School, Cootamundra Catholic High School (to year 10), and Cootamundra High School (to year 12), she won a prestigious National Undergraduate Scholarship to attend The Australian National University at the age of only 16 — too young even to have a drink, legally, at the University Union bar. And on 4 August 2006, she died of cancer at the age of only 53 — far too young for a person whose outstanding achievements to that point, and whose remarkable impact on those around her, only underlined how much more she still had to give.

Phillipa was born in Sydney in 1953, the oldest of four children. The family moved to Harden, in country New South Wales, when she was two, and later to Cootamundra. Her secondary school final year results in 1969 were brilliant: 1st in the State in Modern History, 5th in French, 16th in English, and School Captain to boot. Taking up the scholarship that led her to the ANU, she graduated in 1974 with a Bachelor of Arts, with first class honours in history, in the course of which she clearly made a considerable impression on Professor Manning Clark, who later mentioned her in his autobiography in the company of Geoffrey Blainey and Ken Inglis.[2] After a brief stint with the Department of Foreign Affairs in 1975, Phillipa turned to the law in 1976, embarking on a graduate-entry law degree at ANU.[3] She graduated in 1979 with first class honours and a swag of prizes, including the Supreme Court Judges Prize for the best honours result on graduation. Her talent, and her potential for an outstanding academic career, were quickly spotted, and she was recruited, when she was but a student in Family Law in 1978, to teach that subject in 1979.

A tenurable position in the Faculty became available in 1982 for a specialist in property law, one of the few subjects which Phillipa had not been called upon to teach in her four years of temporary teaching appointments. The selection committee wisely invested in her potential, and she turned herself into a leading property lawyer, though the scholarship for which she is best known is her work in the area of labour law. She won the ANU's prestigious Crawford Prize in 1987 for her LLM thesis on trade union law, and subsequently earned a well-merited reputation as one of Australia's leading labour lawyers. She was appointed as a Professor of the ANU in 2001, and in her Inaugural Professorial Lecture in early 2002 spoke on 'Fairness at Work', a subject on which she was not only an incisive and insightful scholar, but also, in her capacity as Associate Dean and Head of School from 2000 to 2005, a masterful exponent.

Phillipa's scholarship made a significant contribution to our understanding of labour law, particularly in the areas of trade union security, freedom of association, and public sector employment. The last topic is of course the subject of this book, Phillipa's final work, published posthumously; indeed, checking the proofs was the last work-related thing that Phillipa did before she died. She also made a significant contribution as a teacher, and not just because of the clarity of her exposition and the sweep of her erudition. Generations of students attest to the personal interest she took in them, citing in particular her practice of writing personal notes of congratulation and encouragement; this in an era in which teachers of larger and larger classes are hard-pressed to know their students by name, let alone to have a meaningful relationship with them.

If her contributions to scholarship and teaching were significant, her contributions to the university and the wider community were astonishing: Director of the Credit Union of Canberra, Member of the Social Security Appeals Tribunal, Chair of the ACT Sex Industry Consultative Group, and a plethora of like offices and activities. Although quite ill, she was fittingly honoured for her service to the university community at an ANU graduation ceremony in December 2005, when a packed Llewellyn Hall rose to its feet as one and movingly paid tribute — a magical moment that will live in the memory of those present.

It is not these contributions, however — significant as they are — for which Phillipa Weeks will be primarily remembered. Every now and again, a person comes along with personal qualities that (if we assume, as we must, that they are capable of acquisition rather than simply part of our genetic inheritance) are truly inspirational. A mere catalogue cannot do Phillipa justice, but these are some of the values and qualities with which she was typically identified: grace, empathy, generosity, integrity, compassion, courtesy, kindness, modesty, collegiality, humanity, commitment, honesty, respect, wisdom, warmth, positiveness, unaffectedness, courage, gentleness, good humour and a good sense of humour — and yet, amidst these saintly characteristics, an indelible professionalism, even a certain toughness when the situation required it. She was, most of all, a refreshing and powerful antidote to cynicism, an awesome role model, and incontrovertible, though regrettable, evidence of the truth of the aphorism that it is indeed the good who die young.

A measure of the affection and esteem in which Phillipa was held is that, at the ANU College of Law Annual Alumni Dinner on 25 August 2006, a group of Phillipa's former students spontaneously initiated a fund-raising campaign for a scholarship in her name. Accordingly, the Phillipa Weeks Scholarship in Law has been established at the ANU, and will assist students who have a country or regional background not dissimilar from Phillipa's own formative experiences in Harden and Cootamundra and who display similar academic and leadership qualities.[4]

Phillipa Weeks was a wonderful colleague and a very special person, and is sorely missed. Her presence defined the spirit of collegiality that pervades the ANU College of Law. Her memory will continue to do so.


Professor Michael Coper
Dean of Law and Robert Garran Professor
The Australian National University

## ENDNOTES

[1] This is an edited version of the obituary that first appeared in *The Canberra Times* on 16 December 2006. A more comprehensive and personal eulogy, delivered by the author at Phillipa's funeral on 9 August 2006, is published in (2006) 34 *Federal Law Review* iii, together with the proceedings of a memorial gathering for Phillipa held at the ANU on 31 August 2006.

[2] Manning Clark, *The Quest for Grace* (Viking, 1990) 212, and see SG Foster and Margaret M Varghese, *The Making of The Australian National University 1946-1996* (Allen & Unwin, 1996) 209.

[3] Phillipa's husband Ian Hancock, also then an ANU historian, has remarked that Phillipa's abandonment of a career in Foreign Affairs meant that, rather than have them wasted on the Russians, the ANU was to become the beneficiary of her considerable skills of tact and diplomacy.

[4] Intending contributors to the scholarship fund should contact Michelle Mabille at the ANU College of Law, Canberra, ACT 0200, Australia.

# Preface

For many decades the role of the public servant in common law jurisdictions had been well established but, as with many other aspects of the working world, a gradual evolution of the recognised models commenced towards the latter part of the twentieth century. In the 1990s and for the first few years of this century, the area of public sector employment law was undergoing substantial changes, as exemplified by the reform ideas and developments in the *Public Service Act 1999* (Cth) and the new corporate model of the Commonwealth public service.

The idea for this book of essays, to examine and analyse these changes, came out of the public sector employment project for which Phillipa Weeks and I were awarded an Australian Research Council Large Grant.

Phillipa and I enjoyed countless academic discussions and a similar approach to the scholarship in the field. Her debilitating illness and untimely death were tragic blows, both personally for me in the loss of a friend and academic colleague for whom I had the utmost respect and for the book project of which she was an integral part. The loss of an esteemed co-editor and contributor during the production of the book meant that, for me and the other contributors, the project became tinged with real sadness.

There are many people who deserve our grateful thanks — Professor Michael Coper for his generous personal and institutional support (as Dean of the College of Law at The Australian National University) and for his tribute to Phillipa Weeks published in this book; research assistants Emma Pelka-Caven and Vidal Vanhoof; external style editor Phillip Litchfield; Peter Kennedy and Paul Munro for early input on themes and scholarly exchanges; the Australian Research Council for its grant funding; and of course the contributors themselves - all experts in their areas, willing participants in the project and very supportive colleagues. There are others to whom I am sure Phillipa would wish to have conveyed her grateful thanks, including her husband Ian Hancock who provided continuing support for Phillipa and the book project.

The ANU E Press and staff also deserve our sincere thanks for their support; and thanks, in particular, are due to Lorena Kanellopoulos, of ANU E Press, for her cheerful and professional assistance. Thank you to Vic Elliott, Director of Scholarly Information Services and University Librarian for his assistance in organising the approval of this book.

Bruce Moore, my husband, provided his painting to which Teresa Prowse of the ANU E Press applied her inspiration to create the cover design — thank you!

It is to Phillipa Weeks that this book is dedicated, with grateful appreciation.

Marilyn Pittard
Professor of Law
Monash University
Clayton

June 2007

# Contributors

**Gordon Anderson** is Professor of Law at the Victoria University of Wellington and a barrister of the High Court of New Zealand. He has taught labour law for many years, is the author of numerous academic articles on various aspects of the law and is joint author of the leading New Zealand text, *Mazengarb's Employment Law*.

**Jane Bryson** is a Senior Lecturer in the Management School at Victoria University of Wellington, New Zealand. She is an organisational psychologist, and prior to joining the University staff she worked for 15 years as a consultant in organisation development and HRM in both the public and private sector. Her research interests focus on the investigation of HRM, organisational and individual capability; and on professionals, managers and occupational change.

**Keith D Ewing** was appointed Professor of Public Law at King's College London in 1989. He held previous academic appointments at the University of Edinburgh and Cambridge University and visiting professorial positions in Australia and Canada. He has published extensively in the fields of labour law and public law, including *The Cost of Democracy: Party Funding in Modern British Politics* (2007); *Constitutional and Administrative Law* (14th ed 2006, with A W Bradley); and *Labour Law Text and Materials* (2nd ed 2005, with Hugh Collins and Aileen McColgan). He is President of the UK Institute of Employment Rights and together with John Hendy QC edited *A Charter of Workers' Rights* on behalf of the Institute. He is also Vice President of the International Centre for Trade Union Rights, and legal editor of International Union Rights. As an authority on labour law he is called upon regularly to advise trade unions in the United Kingdom and elsewhere.

**Peter Gahan** is Associate Professor in the Department of Management at Monash University. He has held previous academic appointments at the University of New South Wales and Deakin University. He lectures in industrial relations policy and human resource management. He has published widely in the field of public sector management and is undertaking a project on women and equity in the Victorian public service. He was formerly Director, Workplace Innovation in the Victorian Department of Industry, Innovation and Regional Development.

**Mark Molloy** is a Senior Executive Lawyer with the Australian Government Solicitor in Canberra and is currently 'outposted' as the in-house counsel to the Department of the Treasury. Mark was admitted to practice in August 1993 after a career of nearly 20 years as an administrative and senior policy officer in the Australian Public Service. He obtained a Masters Degree in Law (with specialisation public law) from The Australian National University in 2001. Mark's administrative, academic and legal background has had a particular focus on public sector employment law as well as industrial and workplace relations law in general. He has had extensive experience in advising public sector clients in the context of the recent changes in this area of the law, beginning with the *Workplace Relations Act 1996* up to the most recent amendments of the 'Workchoices' legislation.

**John R Nethercote** edited the *Canberra Bulletin of Public Administration* from 1980 until 2000. In three decades in the Australian public service his assignments included the Royal Commission on Australian Government Administration, the Public Service Commission of Canada, the Defence Review Committee, the National Inquiry into Local Government Finance as well as the Public Service Board. He was also secretary to the Senate Standing Committee on Finance and Public Administration, 1987-88. Research for his chapter was funded by the Australian Research Council.

**John O'Brien** is Associate Professor in the School of Organisation and Management at the University of New South Wales. He has researched and published in Australia and internationally in a broad range of areas including public sector management and industrial relations, union strategy and organisation; and employment relations in the education sector and on industrial relations legislation. He currently holds ARC Grants on public sector industrial relations in the United Kingdom and Australia and on executive remuneration and organisational performance. He is a member of the Advisory Committee to the Federal Privacy Commissioner

**Michael O'Donnell** is Reader in the School of Management, Marketing and International Business at The Australian National University. He has written extensively in the field of public sector employment relations and workplace bargaining and on topics ranging from performance-based pay to the management of change and leadership in the public sector. Recent research includes an ARC funded comparative study of changes in employment relations in public service agencies in Australia and the United Kingdom. A monograph exploring research findings from this project will be published by Routledge in 2008.

**Marilyn Pittard** is Professor of Law at Monash University and formerly Associate Dean in Research and Postgraduate Studies. She has written numerous book chapters, articles and papers on labour and employment law and co-authored the books *Industrial Relations in Australia: Development Law and Operation* (Longman) and several editions of *Australian Labour Law: Cases and Materials* (LexisNexis). With Philippa Weeks, she was chief investigator for an ARC grant on public sector employment. She is editor of the *Employment Law Bulletin,* and is on the editorial board of the *Australian Journal of Labour Law.* She is also a member of numerous professional law organisations, including the executive committee of the Australian Labour Law Association, convenor of the Victorian chapter of that association and the advisory board of the Institute of Employment Rights. She is consultant to Clayton Utz, a national law firm.

**Robert G Vaughn** is Professor of Law and A Allen King Scholar at the American University Washington College of Law in Washington DC. He has held visiting appointments at many universities including King's College London and Ritsumeikan University School of Law in Kyoto, Japan. His extensive publications of books and articles include the areas of public information law, public employment law, consumer law, whistleblower protection, and federal open government laws in the United States. He has testified before committees of the United States Congress on whistleblowers, freedom of information and civil service reform and consulted with organisations, such as the World Bank, the Treasury and Civil Service Committee of the House of Commons, and the Office of Legal Cooperation of the Organization of American States.

**Phillipa Weeks** was Professor of Law and employment law specialist at the College of Law, The Australian National University. She researched and published widely in the field including *Trade Union Security: A Study of Preference and Compulsory Unionism* (The Federation Press, 1995). She was a founding member of the editorial board of the *Australian Journal of Labour Law* and was called upon to speak at many conferences in her legal fields of expertise. With Marilyn Pittard, she was chief investigator for an ARC grant on public sector employment. The Tribute to her by Professor Michael Coper in this book contains more information.

# Chapter One

# Public Sector Employment in the Twenty-First Century: Themes and Introduction

## Marilyn Pittard and Phillipa Weeks

Employment in the public sector has been caught up in the winds of change which have radically reshaped the legal environment for labour relations more generally in the last two decades. It has not been immune from the pressures for change in the private market sector.

In Australia, the United Kingdom and New Zealand — to name but three jurisdictions which have shared a common approach in the past to employment in the public service, and in the public sector more broadly — legislation and practice has reformed and revised the concepts and structures which govern the employment relationship in the public arena. These changes demonstrate a number of common influences and themes but with several variations in timing and content. There have even been some revisions to new concepts, as governments of various political persuasions come and go in the political cycle and as they adjust and 'fine tune' or modify earlier reforms.

The contributions in this book weave together the themes of, and influences on, public sector employment in contemporary Australia, whilst exploring parallels and differences between public sector employment in the United Kingdom and New Zealand, with some discussion of whistleblowers' legislative protection, including developments in the United States.

## Themes

This introductory chapter identifies the common threads of these themes and influences which are analysed and emerge in the other chapters. The themes include:

- the processes of changing industrial relations and legislative frameworks, both general industrial relations legislation and specific public sector legislation, and the influences exerted by those processes themselves;
- the move to individual contracts and more general individualisation in public sector employment, with impact on the rights and obligations of public sector employees and of their government employers;

- the trend to outsourcing of functions previously undertaken by government workers and the associated diminution of the size of the public sector;
- changes in the nature and approach of the role of government generally;
- the influence of general labour market reform on Australian public sector employment relations and changes in the nature of the employees engaged in the public sector in terms of gender and level of education;
- the move to decentralised and agency-based bargaining and the problem of the maintenance of centralised control over public servants;
- the impact of accountability mechanisms, such as whistleblowers on the public sector, and the role of unions in bargaining; and
- parallel influences in some other countries.

Each chapter, then, deals with a separate but linked aspect of employment relations in the contemporary public sector.

## The Scope of the Chapters

One of the major effects of change has been upon the legal framework of the relationship of the government employee to the government employer, with consequential significant transformation in that relationship. In her chapter, Phillipa Weeks analyses the transformation from a relationship governed largely by statute to one in which the contract plays a far greater role. Both the legal and political implications are drawn out and explored.

The chapter identifies and examines the traditional model of public sector employment, with its historical origins providing for dismissal at pleasure and a limited role for the contract and the implications arising from administrative law principles. By way of contrast, as it reviews the contemporary model which provides a different structure for the employment relationship, the chapter considers the impact of the changes in engagement, in tenure and in termination of employment, as well as methods of review of employment decisions. A number of these changes have evolved through vehicles such as Australian Workplace Agreements, with their consequential impact on the individualisation of the public service. The courts have of course been required to review the operation of many of these changes. How have they done so in cases such as *Jarratt's case*,[1] and what attitudes have been evinced by them to the employment of public servants in the new legislative environment? How have the courts treated these changes to the notion of tenure of public servants and the move to employment more akin to that in the private sector? Phillipa Weeks concludes that one of the major changes is the diminution of the size of the public sector engaged directly by government, therefore bringing with it a reduced number of employees who are affected by, or subject to, the *Public Service Act 1999* (Cth). The legal consequences of these changes are identified and explored. The contractualisation of the public service has brought public sector employees closer to their private sector counterparts in terms of rights and remedies for any breach of contract or detrimental treatment during the employment relationship.

Public administration does not stand still; the matrix of underlying administrative structures and arrangements has evolved and developed as part of the context for employment. John Nethercote[2] identifies, and traces historical changes in the broad administrative and governance arrangements underlying Australian government employment — in particular the matters of Ministerial control, statutory regulation, central management functions, the form and values of 'career service' and 'merit', and the management of workplace relations. He argues that the post war years have seen enormous changes in the institutions and structures and administrative arrangements of government. The role of government has expanded significantly in Australia, and Commonwealth administration has been consolidated, along with the transformation of the workforce from one with a clerical, less-educated emphasis to one substantially of a graduate character. At much the same time, the public sector has experienced other changes in workforce composition, such as increased employment of women and persons from non-English speaking backgrounds, whilst simultaneously adjusting to the centralisation and computerisation of the administration.

At the national level, some of the changes have been reflected in, or brought about by, the *Public Service Act 1999* (Cth) which John Nethercote examines in illustrating the statutory, doctrinal and institutional arrangements for government; the position before the enactment of the *Public Service Act 1999* (Cth) is contrasted and compared to highlight the changes arising from it.

Whilst much was done through non-legislative means, of course the legislative framework remained (and remains) critical to the implementation of particular public sector employment policies. The *Public Service Act 1999* (Cth) and the *Workplace Relations Act 1996* (Cth), and the contesting forces for continuity and change, are analysed in the chapter by Mark Molloy as he sets out the regulatory frameworks for the collective and individual environment in which public sector employees work and negotiate their terms and conditions of employment.

The context of new structures for dispute resolution and agreement-making for the workforce are generally set out in the *Workplace Relations Act 1996* (Cth). Nonetheless the *Public Service Act 1999* (Cth) as the major formal vehicle for the modernisation of the Australian Public Service ('APS'), amongst other changes, called for the embodiment of the values and codes of the APS in the APS Values and the APS Code of Conduct. But did these formal changes do more than give a 'seal of approval' to developments which were already in train? Molloy's thesis is that:

> the APS did not undergo revolutionary change as a result of the PSA 1999. As a practical matter for APS employees, the passage of the [*Public*

*Service Act 1999* Cth)] presented no great change to the way they were engaged and rewarded or how they went about their business. The substance of the matters dealt with by the new framework had already been substantially put in place under the framework of the [prior legislation, the *Public Service Act 1922*] PSA 1922 (albeit in a more convoluted way). As such, the new Act really represented a step closer to the end of a journey of reform, rather than the beginning of another.[3]

The author espouses the view that the *Public Service Act 1999* fitted better and worked better with the *Workplace Relations Act 1996*. More recently, however, the *Workplace Relations Amendment (Work Choices) Act 2005* ('the Work Choices Act') has drastically amended the *Workplace Relations Act*. The author argues the Work Choices Act should have the result that making collective or individual agreements will be easier because, when either form of agreement is made, only one of them will apply to a particular employment at a time. Mark Molloy concludes by saying that:

> The Work Choices legislation further entrenches agreement-making arrangements at agency level across the APS. However, particular provisions have the potential to have significant effects on the environment in which those agreements are reached, including by further regulation of the formal role of unions in the process.[4]

Despite the increased emphasis on individual work arrangements and agreements, collective bargaining in the public sector remains alive, as is analysed fully by John O'Brien and Michael O'Donnell in this volume. Contemporary case studies (including Centrelink collective agreements from 1997 to 2009) demonstrate the implications for workplace relationships in the context of policy changes. Via the case studies, the authors explore and reveal the 'the contradictions faced by a government that wished to pursue its overall policy agenda while espousing an industrial relations policy that provides for a significant degree of managerial autonomy'.[5]   John O'Brien and Michael O'Donnell conclude that the implementation of a policy for 'a comprehensive performance-related pay system' and marginalisation of unions in the agreement-making process was of varied success in different departments.[6] However, whilst the public sector unions were able to modify some of the impact of management's agendas where they were present, they 'could not impose a template across the APS'.[7]

Whilst governments create environments for the conduct of industrial relations, for example in which employers and employees negotiate suitable arrangements for their organisations, the authors argue that:

> In the APS, however, the government is the ultimate employer: it cannot be indifferent to the outcomes achieved in particular agencies. Moreover, as the financial guardian of the nation it must be mindful of the costs of

its own employees. Government control of budgets places considerable constraint on the capacity of any agency to offer generous remuneration.[8]

In exploring the role of the government in negotiations, the authors note that there has been a movement away from the APS as 'the monolith' since the service-wide framework for employment no longer prevails. Nonetheless, whilst pay diversity has occurred, the authors note that many APS agreements use similar terminology, despite some variations and diversity in implementation within an agency. However the authors are careful to caution that:

> it would be misleading to conclude that the APS employment arrangements have been radically altered in the direction of a series of quasi-independent agencies. In the end, public service departments and agencies are instruments of government.[9]

They conclude as follows:

> In the existing bargaining environment management has been endowed with more 'choices' albeit within tighter parameters set by government, while the CPSU and other public unions face even more challenges to their capacity to organise their members and to preserve their employment conditions.[10]

Can employees keep their government employers honest and accountable by 'blowing the whistle' with impunity? Robert Vaughn analyses legal frameworks to protect and control whistleblowers. In drawing conclusions from a survey of such laws, and from undertaking a comparison with the United States, a legal revolution has arguably occurred in whistleblower protection. Further the chapter argues that

> An examination of how the principles and precepts of whistleblower protection challenge public employment law also exposes the similarities between public and private employment law. In discounting the distinctions between the two, whistleblower protection ironically poses perhaps its greatest challenge, a challenge to the very notion of a distinct public employment law.[11]

Traditional areas of public sector employment have been challenged by the trend to outsourcing — the delegation of functions which were previously performed by government to the private sector. This change in thinking about how some services for the public generally are to be provided has paralleled developments in the private sector in respect of services required by private businesses for them to function. In the public sector context, what are the implications for government employees? Can their negotiated or award terms and conditions carry over to the private sector when there is outsourcing? What effect does such outsourcing have on employment rights and duties? Can outsourcing be seen purely as cost-cutting and avoiding public sector award or collective agreement obligations and therefore might it fall foul of the freedom of association provisions in the *Workplace Relations Act*? In considering another dimension of the privatisation of activities formerly directly carried out by the public sector, Marilyn Pittard's chapter examines the framework of the *Workplace Relations Act* and assesses the potential impact of revolutionary reforms made by the Work Choices Act in Australia's national labour relations law generally and in connection with transmission of business in particular.

Can we learn from other or innovative models for public sector employment? Some other models of public sector employment are explored in three other chapters:

- Peter Gahan examines the evolution of a partnership approach to industrial relations in the public sector which occurred in Victoria under the State Labor government.
- In New Zealand, dramatic deconstruction of traditional public sector structures took place in the late 1980s and early 1990s: the employment and management aspects of these reforms are analysed and evaluated in the chapter by Jane Bryson and Gordon Anderson.
- The modern transformation of the United Kingdom civil service is examined by reference to the theme of privatisation in Keith Ewing's chapter, which pursues the theme in relation to focus, structure, values, employment practices and employment regulation. Perhaps counter-intuitively, the influence of contract as opposed to traditional judicial review is identified as leading to diminution of individual employment rights. The proposal to enact a Civil Service Act and its purported and real potential impact are explored.

The chapter by Peter Gahan outlines the implementation of the reform of the Victorian industrial relations and workforce-planning framework covering public sector employees. Privatisation of government functions occurred against the background of the sweeping changes which had occurred in the 1990s when the Victorian Liberal government had introduced changes to the public sector which not only 'challenged traditional principles of public sector administration'[12] but also reflected the view that the private sector should be performing most of the functions previously performed by the public sector. During this era, management and organisational changes occurred with increased decentralisation of bargaining and delegation to agencies and individualisation of the agreements between public sector employees and government employers. There were positive implications but also negative aspects as outlined by the author which included:

> unsustainable pressures on employment arrangements, the capacity of public organisations to recruit and retain capable employees, and wage

anomalies which did not reflect market conditions. This was particularly evident in relation to a number of key occupational groups where labour shortages had emerged due to demographic shifts in the workforce and world-wide shortages.[13]

The Bracks Labor government, which succeeded the Kennett Liberal government, introduced a 'partnership approach' between government and unions whereby some of the reforms of the 1990s were retained but with a change in the returned emphasis on collective labour relations. Essentially unions were recognised for collective bargaining in relation to employment conditions with the concomitant arrangement with unions that they were committed to understanding and taking account of the fiscal realities of government. The decentralised approach was retained so that ministerial responsibility was delegated to agency level. Peter Gahan's chapter outlines the challenges this partnership approach posed for the unions and for government and assesses and evaluates, to the extent possible, the successes and tensions in the system. It also gives the flavour of the further memorandums of understanding and new versions of the partnership agreement that have been entered into, in an attempt to continue the arrangement and make it workable for the future.

The reversal of the individualisation approach of the Liberal government and the return to the collective approach to industrial relations and public sector employment is a model which is novel.

In the chapter 'The Privatisation of the Civil Service', Keith Ewing analyses how corporate values have 'penetrated the public sphere' in the United Kingdom as seen by:

- first, 'the privatisation of the process of government' not via outsourcing or privatising government functions but rather through adoption of private sector values and methods and what the author calls 'private sector similes';[14] and
- secondly, the adoption by government of what the author labels 'private sector legal forms' to provide the civil servants with some degree of protection which was previously lacking in the context of their employment under the royal prerogative.

The chapter points to the paradox that, despite the addition of some protections in this way, the use of private sector legal forms actually *removes* some of the protections which would otherwise be available through judicial review. How has this approach affected collective bargaining? It appears at least that 'collective bargaining was at its most effective' when the civil servants had little protection (as they were engaged under the royal prerogative and could be hired and fired at will).[15]

Although the evaluation of the draft Civil Service Act suggests that it is a potential source of more scrutiny by Parliament of the government's conduct in relation to civil servants, it is argued that this legislation is not likely to make any real practical difference to public sector employees in the United Kingdom.

In an antipodean experience influenced by the changes in the United Kingdom under the Thatcher government, in the chapter 'Restructuring State Employment in New Zealand', Jane Bryson and Gordon Anderson review and analyse the reforms in New Zealand in the late 1980s and early 1990s which:

> introduced a comprehensive legislative base as a catalyst of change, and as a reflection of the strategic direction of government. In the employment setting the role of law as a protector of rights was down-played.[16]

The authors argue that, as New Zealand entered the first decade of the twenty-first century, the 'big' reforms have been achieved in such a way as to remain embedded for the long term as indeed are 'the legislative framework and the supporting culture'. However, are there undesirable 'costs' of these reforms? The authors suggest that one of those costs is that private sector values and methodologies may not be the most suitable values and methodologies for meeting the objectives of and carrying out a range of government functions. An adverse consequence is the resulting segmentation of the public sector — with an impact on public service culture. The changes are further analysed by reference to industrial relations and human resource management. In exploring further recent changes, the authors put the argument that the role of law is no longer to be the vehicle for major change but is rather directed to 'achieving normative and cultural evolution within the state sector'. Further they argue in their chapter that the:

> push for change will come from the 'structural' mechanisms: the committees, boards and project teams established to implement aspects of the Review of the Centre and the teams, networks and organisational consolidation that emerge as new ways of working.

In addition there is a new lexicon — the authors label this 'the new state sector lexicon' — which is emerging in the words 'co-ordination'; 'capability'; 'sustainability'; 'leadership'; 'values', and 'outcomes'. They argue this new lexicon indicates cultural changes. They conclude by posing the question as follows:

> as governments worldwide grapple with skill shortages, particularly in the health and education sectors, will a joined up/reconstructed state sector be enough to meet the potential labour market and employment relations challenges that face a small economy such as that of New Zealand?[17]

Industrial relations in Australia today is at the cross roads: the path is deregulation as exemplified by the *Workplace Relations Amendment (Work Choices) Act 2005* (Cth) amending the *Workplace Relations Act 1996* (Cth), exposing employees to greater market forces in the negotiation of their terms and conditions of employment. In the concluding chapter, the radical reforms at federal level and the move to a 'freer' labour market are explored and their likely impact on public sector employment is debated. This final chapter by Marilyn Pittard examines the impact of changes to date and the likely impact of the new industrial relations policies contained in the Work Choices as well as overall future directions for public sector employment in Australia.

## Overview

A dramatic contractualisation and individualisation of the public sector has occurred within the last decade and a half in Australia, New Zealand and the United Kingdom. Values relating to management prerogative, privatisation, and corporate values and corporatisation of the public sector, which are studied in this book, continue to be influential on contemporary public sector employment. These developments are against a backdrop of changes in the industrial relations regulatory framework, particularly in the mid-1990s and well into the twenty-first century. This book explores this transformation of public sector employment.

## ENDNOTES

[1] *Jarratt v Commissioner of Police for New South Wales* (2005) 221 ALR 95; [2005] HCA 50 (8 September 2005). See Phillipa Weeks, this volume, Chapter 2.

[2] See John Nethercote, this volume, Chapter 3.

[3] See Mark Molloy, this volume, Chapter 4.

[4] Ibid.

[5] See John O'Brien and Michael O'Donnell, this volume, Chapter 5.

[6] Ibid.

[7] Ibid.

[8] Ibid.

[9] Ibid.

[10] Ibid.

[11] See Robert G Vaughn, this volume, Chapter 6.

[12] See Peter Gahan, this volume, Chapter 8.

[13] Ibid.

[14] See Keith D Ewing, this volume, Chapter 10.

[15] Ibid.

[16] See Jane Bryson and Gordon Anderson, this volume, Chapter 9.

[17] Ibid.

# Chapter Two

# The Reshaping of Australian Public Service Employment Law

## Phillipa Weeks

There is a bundle of components constituting the legal regulation of public sector employment. To a large extent, these are the same components that regulate private sector employment: contract (both express and implied terms), awards and agreements made under industrial/workplace relations legislation, other specialist and general statutes (for example, occupational health and safety, and anti-discrimination laws), and general law (such as tort and criminal law). There have always been, however, some distinctive components and weightings in respect of public sector employment, such as the dismissal at pleasure principle, the application of administrative law, and a more prominent role for specialist, detailed legislation. At any time or place, the precise mix of employment law components in both the public and private sectors varies. Different mixes of these components affect the complexion and character of the employment relationship, and produce different patterns of power, protection and accountability.

The civilian public sector in Australia is complex and diverse. Across the three levels of government there are nine separate public services; eight police services; state and territory based public education and health systems; thousands of statutory authorities and government business enterprises conducting activities ranging from insurance to broadcasting, postal services to research, electricity generation and distribution to the running of cultural and arts institutions. The organisational diversity is matched by variations in the legal framework for employment. This chapter focuses on the Australian Public Service ('APS') as a core segment of the public sector. Occasionally examples are drawn from other areas to illustrate principles that have broad application and to provide comparisons.

The chapter depicts the legal framework of contemporary APS employment by charting changes that have occurred in the past 40-odd years. The APS of the 1970s was in the traditional mould of Australian public service employment but was on the brink of substantial reform. It had been subjected to a comprehensive review by the Coombs Royal Commission in 1974–76;[1] the Commonwealth's 'new administrative law' implemented between 1975 and 1977 was to affect not only the interaction between government and citizens but also employment within the Service; and pressures were building for fundamental restructuring of the economy, including the public sector. The first part of this chapter gives an overview of the shape of Australian public sector employment law at that time, highlighting some contentious issues and showing how the legal framework worked to serve the 'constitutional' function of public services in a Westminster-derived system — a function of providing policy advice to the government of the day and implementing the government's policies and programs. The second part analyses the changes that followed, in particular changes in the nature and content of specialist public service legislation and the decentralisation of employment responsibilities, and explores the potentially adverse impact on the APS's constitutional function.

Awards and agreements made under the industrial/workplace relations legislation have for most of the past century set rates of remuneration and conditions such as hours and various forms of leave. These mechanisms are covered in Chapters 4 and 5, and there is only limited discussion in this chapter.

## The Traditional Model of Australian Public Service Employment

## Contract

In contrast to the traditional position in England, where the relationship between public servants and the Crown was generally regarded as non-contractual until the late twentieth century,[2] in the Australian colonies from the nineteenth century there was no doubt that a public servant's contract is 'his chief right, the very corner-stone of all his rights and privileges'.[3]

There were two principal concerns that influenced the English position:[4] while ordinary contract involves mutually binding obligations, not until 1970 was it settled that civil servants had an enforceable right to pay,[5] and secondly, the dismissal at pleasure principle (to be discussed below) gave the Crown a unilateral power not possessed by private contracting employers. Thus the civil service has been regulated under Crown prerogative by way of Orders-in-Council, which authorise the making of regulations and instructions about employment in the civil service by the relevant Minister.[6] This 'internal' regulation[7] is not legally enforceable, though the practical implications have been limited, given the conventions of the model 'good' employer, and especially as in the latter part of the twentieth century, general employment legislation on matters such as unfair dismissal has been made applicable to public sector as well as private sector employment.[8]

After Federation, there was a series of High Court decisions affirming that the relationship between public servants and the Crown in Australia was contractual.[9]  In the leading case, *Lucy v Commonwealth* (*'Lucy'*), a public servant's appointment had been invalidly terminated according to the terms of the *Commonwealth Public Service Act 1902* and the *Commonwealth Constitution*, and he succeeded in obtaining damages for wrongful dismissal, that is, for repudiation of the contract of employment.[10] Knox CJ explained the relationship between statute (in this case the *Constitution* as well as the public service legislation) and contract:

> [I]t is admitted, that the plaintiff was wrongfully dismissed or removed from the Public Service of the Commonwealth. In so dismissing him, the Commonwealth committed a breach of the contract of employment into which it had entered with the plaintiff, it being a term of that contract, by virtue of sec. 84 of the *Constitution* and sec. 60 of the *Commonwealth Public Service Act*, that the plaintiff should preserve all his existing and accruing rights, including the right to remain in the Public Service during his life or until dismissal or removal for some cause specified in the South Australian Acts...[11]

The analysis of Knox CJ in *Lucy* reveals that while public and private sector employees share a contractual basis for their employment, the public sector version is shaped by legislation. The role of special legislation has been a distinguishing feature of Australian public service regulation since the colonies gained self-government in the mid-nineteenth century,[12]  and in the Commonwealth one of the Parliament's first priorities was a public service Act, which resulted in the *Public Service Act 1902* (Cth). So entrenched did the legislative model become that it might have appeared to be a legal necessity. But it was policy rather than law that generated the dependence on legislation for employment regulation in the public service. That is, there is no legal requirement — constitutional or otherwise — for a statutory framework.[13]

The legislation in the Commonwealth and the states followed a more or less standard pattern of substantial prescription. For example, the *Public Service Act 1922* (Cth) (the 'PSA 1922'), which operated until 1999, detailed substantive rules and processes for the structure of the service, job classifications, appointment of the majority of staff to 'offices', which amounted in practice to permanent employment subject to probation, promotion, transfer, discipline and termination, whether by retirement, redundancy or dismissal. Discipline and dismissal were subject to due process and a right of appeal, and there was also an appeal system for promotions. The bulk of the employment powers were exercised by a central body — the Public Service Board (a 'central personnel agency').[14]

The classic public service statutes also authorised the making of subordinate legislation in the form of regulations, and determinations, notices, instructions, directions and guidelines issued by the central body. By the early 1990s, in the

Australian Public Service, this tailor-made statutory regulation filled nine binders called the Personnel Management Manual.

Inevitably, this legislation impinged on the common law contract of employment. In a much-cited judgment in 1985, Brennan J in the High Court observed that

> [t]he relationship between a civil servant of the Crown and the Crown has often been described as contractual, though the civil servant has been appointed pursuant to statute ... If the relationship is contractual, the contract must be consistent with any statutory provision which affects the relationship. No agent of the Crown has authority to engage a servant on terms at variance with the statute. To the extent that the statute governs the relationship, it is idle to inquire whether there is a contract which embodies its provisions. The statute itself controls the terms of service.[15]

Thus, failure to comply with provisions in a statute about the appropriate appointing authority and procedure for appointment cannot be overcome by resort to an argument that a contract of employment has been formed in fact by offer and acceptance,[16] and conditions of employment prescribed in a statute cannot be changed simply on the basis of contract variation or implied contract, unless the variation or implication falls within the statutory scheme.[17]

An extreme view of the dominance of the legislation over the contract was that the legislation constituted a code, displacing the common law, including contract terms and principles altogether. There was a set of cases which tested this view in the 1980s.[18]

Rogers J in the New South Wales Supreme Court held in the first of the cases that the detailed provisions in the PSA 1922 on suspension of employees — which required 'cumbersome' procedures, conferred appeal rights, and limited the circumstances in which salary could be withheld — constituted a code. The context was an industrial campaign in which employees had imposed selective work bans, and the effect of the decision was to deprive the Crown of the option of invoking the contractual right of an employer to withhold pay from an employee who declines to carry out duties in full as instructed (the 'no work as directed-no pay' principle).[19] Six years later,[20] Rogers J modified his position. He recognised the distinction between validity of a suspension — a matter governed by the public service legislation — and the employee's right to pay, which at common law is dependent on having provided the services required under the contract. Rogers J found nothing in the legislation that displaced the operation of the common law principle.[21]

In *Australian Telecommunications Commission v Hart* ('*Hart*'),[22] the Federal Court was asked to find that the public service employer was not empowered to take statute-based disciplinary action against an employee for disobeying an instruction about dress standards because the instruction itself was not statutorily authorised. The argument was as follows: the employer had a statutory power to make by-laws determining the terms and conditions of employment in the agency; the employer had exercised the power, but its by-laws made no provision about standards of dress; there was no room for the term implied by common law in the contract of employment that the employee must obey lawful and reasonable instructions, in this case about dress. A majority in the Court rejected the code argument with minimal comment.

## Dismissal at Pleasure

The dismissal at pleasure power emerged in the context of the fundamental reforms of the English civil service that began in 1780 and continued into the second half of the nineteenth century, when public administration was transformed from decentralised, and often corrupt, office-holding, allocated by patronage, to a unified, professionalised career service. The courts looked for guidance to the law governing military servants of the Crown and adopted the principle that, like military service, Crown service was at the pleasure of the Crown.[23] Thus the Crown could dismiss without notice, without giving a reason, and for any reason, and the dismissed public servant had no redress, that is, no right to a hearing, no right of appeal and no entitlement to compensation on any ground including early termination of an appointment for a fixed term.

There has been some uncertainty about the juridical nature of the Crown power. In England, it was usually characterised as a Crown prerogative, so that the exercise of the power was unchallengeable.[24] Australian courts have tended to explain the power as an implied term of the contract.[25]

In *Dunn v R*, a leading case at the end of the nineteenth century, Lord Herschell set out the rationale for the principle:

> It seems to be that it is the public interest which has led to the term which I have mentioned being imported into contracts for employment in the service of the Crown ... [S]uch employment being for the good of the public, it is essential for the public good that it should be capable of being determined at the pleasure of the Crown.[26]

Initially the principle was adopted in the Australian colonies, where the colonial administrations were being established in the latter half of the nineteenth century, but then an important departure occurred when, as discussed above in the section 'Contract', the colonies opted for comprehensive legislative regulation of public service employment. It was common for these statutes to deal with dismissal, and often in detail. The legal issue thrown up was how the legislation interacted with the dismissal at pleasure principle. The general answer was straightforward: the dismissal power, being a common law power, was subject to modification or displacement by statute. The answer in a specific case was a matter of statutory interpretation: did the statute preserve, or abolish, or abrogate in part, the power to dismiss at pleasure?

Ideally, the statute would deal with the matter expressly. For example, the *Public Service Act 1979* (NSW) s 118 provided:

> Nothing in this Act shall be construed or held to abrogate or restrict the right or power of the Crown, as it existed immediately before the commencement of this section, to dispense with the services of any person employed in the Public Service.[27]

More commonly the courts were faced with non-express provisions. A statute would deal with some aspect of dismissal, such as grounds or procedure, leaving to implication the effect, if any, on the power to dismiss at pleasure. In the leading case of *Gould v Stuart* (1896) ('*Gould*'), the Privy Council held that the *Civil Service Act 1884* (NSW) had supplanted the power altogether.[28] The New South Wales *Civil Service Act* contained detailed provisions on removal, including removal for misconduct. It specified procedures, including initial suspension, a report to the Minister, and an opportunity for the suspended officer to show cause or make explanation, and a scale of penalties for different degrees of misconduct. The court construed the legislation generously:

> These provisions, which are manifestly intended for the protection and benefit of the officer, are inconsistent with importing into the contract of service the term that the Crown may put an end to it at its pleasure. In that case they would be superfluous, useless, and delusive. This is, in their Lordships' opinion, an exceptional case, in which it has been deemed for the public good that a civil service should be established under certain regulations with some qualification of the members of it, and that some restriction should be imposed on the power of the Crown to dismiss them.[29]

*Gould* stands out as a high-water mark for judicial willingness to find a legislative override of the dismissal at pleasure principle. Subsequently, courts — including the High Court which considered the matter on several occasions[30] — insisted on clear statutory expression of the intention to abolish or modify the power. It happened that later litigation tended to be concerned with legislation that made less detailed provision on dismissal than the *Civil Service Act 1884* (NSW) — the three High Court cases were concerned with state legislation for their police services — so that the case for override was more difficult to establish. For example, it was not sufficient for a statute simply to confer employment powers including dismissal on some person or body, such as the Governor,[31] or to provide an appeal process for employees aggrieved by their dismissal,[32] or to specify a procedure for dismissal.[33] In 2003, in *Commissioner of Police for New South Wales v Jarratt* ('*Jarratt*'), the New South Wales Court of Appeal pointed out that these authorities imposed the onus of proof on the party contending that the dismissal at pleasure principle had been displaced by the statutory scheme.[34]

The decision in *Jarratt* epitomised the traditional view of the relationship between the dismissal at pleasure principle and legislation. The statutory provision to be construed specified that certain senior police officers 'may be removed from office at any time' by the Governor on the recommendation of the Commissioner, with the approval of the Minister.[35] An officer who had been dismissed without notice and without notification of the reason, but in compliance with the stipulated formal procedures, sued for wrongful dismissal on the basis that the termination decision was invalid for failure to provide natural justice to which he was entitled because the legislation had displaced the dismissal at pleasure principle. He argued that the legislation, and in particular the words 'at any time', transformed the common law power into a statutory power that attracted the duty to provide natural justice. The Court of Appeal was unpersuaded, however, and accepted the Crown argument that the phrase was 'far too slender a raft upon which to find a statutory incorporation of the principle'.[36] The Court of Appeal decision was reversed by the High Court in 2005, as discussed under the heading 'Review of Employment Decisions' below.

As for the APS, because the federal Public Service Acts (1902 and 1922) were cast in the mould of the *Civil Service Act 1884* (NSW) that prevailed in *Gould*, it has long been assumed that the Crown in right of the Commonwealth had lost the power to dismiss at pleasure. This was confirmed by the Full Court of the Federal Court in *Dixon v Commonwealth* (1981) (*'Dixon'*).[37]

Another dimension to the traditional principle of dismissal at pleasure that was established in England by the end of the nineteenth century was that the Crown's freedom could not be fettered by contract. Thus a public servant could be removed from office notwithstanding express agreement that the employment was for a definite term.[38] The issue did not arise directly for consideration in Australia until the 1980s.[39] In *Scott v Commonwealth*, Kennedy J in the Federal Court, acknowledging long-standing criticisms of the rule, concluded that it 'is now too well established to be questioned in this court', and thus he rejected a claim of wrongful dismissal by a public servant whose five-year contract had been prematurely terminated.[40] The New South Wales Court of Appeal took a more robust approach to the ability of the Director General of Education to fetter by contract its right to dismiss at pleasure in proceedings brought by Suttling.

Suttling was a teacher employed under the *Education Commission Act 1980* (NSW). He successfully applied for a position advertised as a two-year secondment, and his letter of appointment specified a two-year period. During the first year, an administrative reorganisation made Suttling's position redundant and he was redeployed to another post at a lower salary. Suttling sued the Director-General of Education for a declaration that he was validly appointed for two years and that he was entitled to be paid the salary of that position. The trial judge dismissed Suttling's action, holding that by virtue of the Crown's prerogative to dismiss at pleasure, the Director-General's power to terminate a fixed term contract at any time included the power to change terms of employment short of dismissal.

Suttling successfully appealed to the Court of Appeal, which held that 'the Crown may contractually abridge its right to dismiss at pleasure'.[41] The Court found that there was no binding Australian authority, and that several factors weighed in favour of overturning the traditional view: there were suggestions in two Privy Council decisions that the prerogative could be restricted by means other than statute; there had been extensive academic criticisms of the principle; the rule often caused great injustice; 'in an age where a large section of the workforce [was] employed by the Government, there [was] no reason in principle or justice why the contractual rights of Crown (who are in reality government) employees should differ from those of private sector employees'; and the Crown was not bound to enter into fixed term contracts, and if it chose to do so, it should accept the ordinary rules of contract.[42] Consequently, the Crown retained the power to terminate the employment but would be liable in damages if it acted in breach of contract, 'just as other employers pay damages when they cannot justify the termination of employment'.[43]

Unfortunately, the High Court appeal did not engage with the issue of contractual overriding of the dismissal power.[44] The Court resolved the dispute by reference to the provisions of the *Education Commission Act 1980*.[45] The Court of Appeal decision has subsequently been followed in *National Gallery of Australia v Douglas*[46] and *Bryant v Defence Housing Authority*,[47] both cases involving the federal Public Service Acts.

## Administrative Law

One of the striking features of federal government employment law which gained prominence in the late 1970s was the role of administrative law — both the traditional exercise of judicial review, and novel mechanisms for overseeing the exercise of government power, including its power as an employer.

### Judicial Review

Judicial review refers to a body of law in which courts determine 'the legality of the act or omission of an official or other body or institution within the *public* domain'.[48] That is, the courts supervise the lawfulness of government decisions at the behest of aggrieved citizens: '[t]he overall ground of judicial review is that the repository of public power has breached the limits placed upon the grant of that power'.[49]

The specific grounds for review embrace both express and implied substantive and procedural restraints on decision-making: that the decision-maker breached the rules of natural justice, failed to comply with mandatory procedure, lacked jurisdiction to make the decision, made a decision not authorised by the enactment, failed to take account of a relevant consideration, took account of an irrelevant consideration, exercised the power for an extraneous purpose, exercised a discretion on direction, exercised a discretionary power in accordance with a rule or policy without considering the merits, made an error of law, made the decision induced or affected by fraud, or made the decision in the absence of justifying evidence or material; bad faith, unreasonableness, and uncertainty.[50]

The heartland of judicial review is the exercise by government officials and bodies of powers that are conferred on them by statute.[51] As has been noted, since the second half of the nineteenth century, public service employment in Australia has been subject to regulation by statute. These traditional public service statutes were couched in terms of specifying the powers of the government employer, from initial appointment of public servants to termination of appointment, and prescribing detailed procedures for the various employment decisions such as classification of positions, promotions, transfers, and dismissal, and other forms of termination. In theory, then, judicial review was available to public servants seeking to enforce their statutory rights.

A number of factors, however, militated against public servants resorting to judicial review: the rules of Crown immunity,[52] particular technical rules associated with the specialised remedies (called prerogative writs), the lack of a financial compensatory remedy for the complainant,[53] and the high cost of the specialised jurisdiction. Litigation was rare.[54] And there was an alternative avenue of redress. As noted in the section above under 'Contract', the colonial courts characterised the relationship between the Crown and public servants as contractual, and treated the provisions of the public service legislation as terms of the contract. Thus, public servants alleging breach of their statutory rights — in relation to such matters as pay, superannuation, and their procedural rights in relation to promotion and so on — could mount a claim for damages for breach of contract, so long as economic loss was suffered. In a case where the public servant claimed that a termination of employment was invalid for breach of statutory entitlements, the action was for wrongful dismissal.[55] Theoretically, the remedy of specific performance, that is reinstatement, was also available but until recent times the courts have been loath to grant that remedy for employment contracts, and there is the practical obstacle that it is available only if the contract has been kept on foot.

Judicial review became much more accessible to federal public servants, along with other citizens affected by federal government decisions, from 1977, with the enactment of the *Administrative Decisions (Judicial Review) Act 1977* (Cth) (the 'ADJR Act'). The Act conferred power on the Federal Court[56] to review decisions of an 'administrative character made ... under an enactment', including subordinate legislation,[57] and thus did not extend to exercises of prerogative or other non-statutory executive power, such as contractual decisions.[58] The ADJR Act's improvement of the arcane common law jurisdiction was substantial: it simplified and therefore reduced the cost of procedure, codified the grounds of review, and provided simpler, more flexible remedies.

One of the most facilitative features of the ADJR Act was the requirement that a decision-maker provide written reasons for a decision on request, but there were exemptions on grounds of practicality and third-party privacy for certain APS personnel decisions: decisions of a policy nature which did not relate to a particular person, appointment decisions, and promotion and transfer decisions.[59]

The ADJR Act, then, provided federal public servants with a new, accessible avenue for challenging employment decisions made under the PSA 1922, the regulations and determinations made by the Public Service Board. And there was a flurry of litigation. Williams notes that whereas there were 23 reported cases of judicial review of personnel decisions between 1901 and 1979, there were 39 in the five-year period 1980–84 and almost 20 in the period 1985–91.[60] Public servants successfully challenged decisions about promotion,[61] discipline,[62] re-appointment,[63] suspension,[64] and dismissal,[65] and across the range of the grounds of review.

## Other Review Mechanisms

While judicial review is concerned with lawfulness and power, other review mechanisms are concerned with the merits of decisions. There were both internal and external mechanisms available to members of the APS by the late 1970s.

## Internal Review

The earliest public service Acts in the colonies provided rights of appeal for certain grievances.[66] By the late 1970s, under the PSA 1922, there were Disciplinary Appeals Committees, Promotion Appeals Committees and Re-appointments Review Committees, comprising an independent chair appointed by the Public Service Board, a nominee of the government department or body, and a nominee of employees, and these bodies and their procedures were of course subject to judicial review. There had also been a Grievance and Appeals Bureau established within the Public Service Board in 1979.[67] Another statute had created the Commonwealth Redeployment and Retirement Appeals Tribunals.[68]

## External Review

The administrative law innovations of the late 1970s introduced new channels of review of employment decisions in the APS. The new Administrative Appeals Tribunal, a general merits review tribunal which commenced operation in 1976,[69] was granted jurisdiction over the public service superannuation scheme (1976),[70] the public sector workers' compensation scheme (1981),[71] and freedom of information (1982) (discussed further below).[72] The Office of the Commonwealth Ombudsman, created to investigate and make reports and (unenforceable) recommendations about 'matter[s] of administration',[73] and thus to investigate both the merits and legality of decisions, was expressly precluded from dealing with

> action taken by any body or person with respect to persons employed in the Australian Public Service ... including action taken with respect to the promotion, termination of appointment or discipline of a person so employed or the payment of remuneration to such a person.[74]

This exclusion did not, however, prevent the Ombudsman from investigating complaints about matters arising before employment or after termination of employment.

Public servants could also take advantage of the *Freedom of Information Act 1982* (Cth) to gain access to their personnel records from their government employer, subject to some exemptions, including material provided in confidence, and material the disclosure of which could reasonably be expected to have a substantial adverse effect on the management or assessment of personnel by the Commonwealth or by an agency and disclosure was not in the public interest. The Act also conferred a right of correction of personal records.

The role of administrative law provided a stark contrast between public and private employment. Public employers, by virtue of their governmental status, were subject to obligations that were far more onerous than those applying to their private sector counterparts. Through judicial review and merits review, public sector employees could seek enforcement of their rights and entitlements by means unavailable to their private sector counterparts.

## Conclusion on the Australian Traditional Model

It had long been established that the substantive legal relationship between Australian public servants and the Crown was contractual, as in the private sector. It had also long been recognised that the contract was special because of its unilateral character: the terms of the contract were almost wholly supplied by legislation that was effectively under the control of the employer party to the contract,[75] and the contract could be terminated by legislation.[76] However, the PSA 1922 appeared by the late 1970s so comprehensively to prescribe the powers of the government employer and the rights and duties of the employees that courts could even contemplate the view that the legislation constituted a code to the exclusion of common law.[77]

Contract, then, provided the underlying legal framework of the relationship, but the content of the relationship derived largely from legislation and from awards and agreements made under industrial relations legislation. (The latter aspect is covered in Mark Molloy's Chapter 4 in this volume.) An additional effect of the traditional form of public service legislation was to facilitate the application of administrative law to the government's employment decisions, giving public servants distinctive rights and remedies. Legislation was thus the dominant component in the architecture of Australian public employment law, with contract operating in the background. Indeed the practice of designating a public servant as an 'officer' in the traditional public service statutes tended to obscure the role of contract.[78]

Contract did have a role to play, however, even if generally low-profile. As discussed, it provided more accessible remedies than administrative law for public servants pursuing their statutory rights, at least until the late 1970s, and from the mid-1980s it provided a significant constraint on the Crown's common law power to dismiss at pleasure (though this had not been a significant issue for the APS). And, as reflected in the cases of *Hart* and *Csomore*,[79] it was working in the gaps left by the public service legislation, which could never be truly comprehensive in regulating the employment relationship. The interaction of contract and statute in particular situations was, of course, a matter of statutory interpretation.

The dominance of the statutory regulation of the traditional type forged a certain character of public service employment.[80] In the first place it created 'the structure of the APS as an entity, as distinct from an aggregation of separate employing bodies which would be the case if the common law was the only basis of employment'.[81] In the second place, it imposed certain characteristics of employment uniformly across that service. These characteristics were encapsulated in the notion of a 'career service' that was independent of government control, impartial, and merit-based, and infused with the values of probity and equity.[82] There were three key elements.

First, the service was insulated from political influence, patronage and corruption by the allocation of employment powers to a central Board/Commissioner and to a lesser extent to Department Secretaries, and by the detailed prescription of the criteria and the processes for merit-based decision-making about employment matters.

Secondly, the legislation imposed constraints on management prerogative and provided for fair and equitable treatment of public servants through uniform rules and standardised formalities, including merits review for many employment decisions. Government was thereby a 'good' or 'model' employer.

Thirdly, the legislation conferred security of tenure on public servants by requiring that termination be only for cause and by due process, and subject to appeal.[83]

The rationale for the 'career service' was to facilitate the carrying out of the public service's 'constitutional' function of providing policy advice to the government of the day and implementing the government's policies and programs. In the Westminster tradition, ministers were individually responsible to the parliament for the actions of their departments, but while both ministers and governments came and went, the function of the public service was to provide continuous, non-partisan, public administration. In Richard Mulgan's words, '[t]he public service always wears the colours of the government of the day'.[84] The employment conditions provided by the public service legislation — a combination of constraints on management and guaranteed entitlements and protection for employees — conferred on public servants conditions that were superior to those of their private sector counterparts, in particular security of tenure. The objective was to protect public servants against the risk of political pressure and to engender a commitment to service in the public interest, that is, service that was professional, expert, apolitical, and stable.[85]

Of course, the theory of this model was not always achieved: occasionally there appeared to be political factors influencing appointment of heads of department,[86] and there were times when senior public servants did not give frank and fearless advice to the government, such as the VIP Affair, when the Prime Minister's Department helped Prime Minister Harold Holt keep a secret from Parliament and were active participants in a damaging cover-up.[87] Overall, however, there appeared to be consensus that it was appropriate and efficacious for employment arrangements to serve the constitutional function of the public service.

## The Contemporary Model of Australian Public Service Employment

### Reform Context

The APS underwent fundamental organisational, structural and cultural change in the late twentieth century. Initial reforms were prompted by recognition that the traditional bureaucratic model of public administration could be 'cumbersome, inefficient, impersonal, wasteful, negligent and unresponsive'[88] — recognition that prompted the establishment of the Coombs Royal Commission 1974–1976.[89] Then through the 1980s and 1990s came changing philosophies about the role of government and management as part of the all-embracing program of microeconomic reform and deregulation pursued by governments, both Labor and Coalition. Like private enterprise, government became committed to enhancing productivity, competition and efficiency in its own sector. The story of this multi-facetted reform has been told in detail elsewhere,[90] and the following summary simply highlights the depth and breadth of formal change in the employment arena in the period to the early 1990s:

- creation of the Senior Executive Service in 1984, with management and policy responsibilities;
- conferral on the Public Service Board (1980) and then the Department of Industrial Relations (1987) of power to make determinations about terms and conditions of employment, so that changes could be made more expeditiously than the previous method of making regulations;
- creation of the Merit Protection and Review Agency ('MPRA') in 1984 to carry out independent appeals and grievance resolution independently of the government, the Public Service Board, and departmental management;
- express statement in the PSA 1922 that the merit principle applied in appointment, transfer and promotion, and incorporation of anti-discrimination provisions (1984);
- a changing role for the Public Service Board, with the shift of responsibility to Secretaries of Departments for creation, abolition and reclassification of most positions (1984) and for other powers relating to appointment, discipline and promotion (1987), and eventually replacement of the Board in 1987 by the Public Service Commission, led by a Commissioner;
- simplification and streamlining of provisions relating to discipline, redeployment and retirement procedures, promotion and higher duties, including withdrawal of appeal rights from executive employees (1987);
- introduction of performance pay for the Senior Executive Service (1990);
- tinkering with the tenure of departmental heads (1984).

In the early 1990s, there was a wave of further reviews both internal to the APS and external, culminating in the internal McLeod Report (1994), commissioned by the Labor government to recommend changes to the present legislative framework under which the APS operates, so that it will be able to operate in a flexible and responsive fashion, 'unhindered by excessive and unnecessary legislative provisions which are out of touch with modern public sector management philosophy'.[91] The report made substantial recommendations for transformation and simplification of the PSA. It envisaged an Act that emphasised values and principles, leaving the details to regulations, awards, agreements and central agency instructions and directions.[92] The Report was generally endorsed by the Government, but was overtaken by the change of government in March 1996. The Coalition embarked on its own reform path, which was not all that different from McLeod's.

The then Minister, Peter Reith, issued a Discussion Paper which contended that the existing employment framework was a major barrier to the necessary improvement of performance in the APS. He identified several problems.

The first was the complexity of the employment framework: there were statutes, associated delegated legislation, APS-wide awards plus agency-specific awards, APS-wide certified agreements and agency-specific certified agreements. In its totality, this regulation was outdated, rigid, and cumbersome: it tied management of the APS 'in red-tape', produced 'a process-driven culture' and 'an entitlement mentality', and inhibited innovation and best practice.

The second was 'unrealistic presumptions' that the APS was a uniform labour market, and that equity necessitated identical treatment of individuals. As a consequence, there had developed a preoccupation with prescribing universal and detailed employee rights, which generated 'a grievance mentality', and 'conservative and cautious management'.[93]

The Minister's vision was the replacement of a single Commonwealth-wide public service and its strong centralised control, uniform employment conditions and permanent appointment to a lifetime career, with industrial and staffing arrangements that were 'essentially the same as those of the private sector'. The effect would be to give management greater freedom and flexibility, and to give public servants more autonomy and the benefit of a more direct relationship with their employers, rather than being managed through rules, regulations and third party relationships.[94]

There was a two-fold strategy for achieving the transformation. The first was the application of the 'Workplace Relations' agenda of simplifying awards and promoting agency-specific enterprise bargaining, which is discussed in detail in this volume in Mark Molloy's Chapter 4.[95] The effect was a speedy break-up of the uniform APS labour market, with pay and conditions diversified both at agency level, through collective Certified agreements, and at individual level through Australian Workplace Agreements ('AWAs'). Some aspects of AWAs are discussed under the heading 'Implications of Reform' below. The second part of the strategy was radical revision of the APS legislation, which, as outlined in the first section of this chapter, had been the central and dominating feature of APS employment law. This development will now be examined.

## Changes in the Specialist Public Service Legislation

The Public Service Bill was first presented to Parliament in June 1997, when the government lacked control of the Senate, which pressed for unacceptable amendments.[96] The government proceeded to implement a number of aspects of the Bill by administrative means — amendment of the Public Service Regulations to incorporate components of the Bill, delegation by the Public Service Commissioner of many employment powers to Agency Heads, and the review and streamlining of voluminous instructions and determinations. Ultimately the government accepted many of the Opposition amendments to secure passage of the Bill, which became the *Public Service Act 1999* (the 'PSA 1999').

The PSA 1999 is vastly different from its predecessor. It comprises fewer than 50 pages and is written in lucid language and a simplified style. Key features, which will be elaborated below, are:

- a statement of 'the APS Values' and creation of a 'Code of Conduct';
- conferral on agency heads of all the rights, duties and powers of an employer;[97]
- the imposition of some constraints on agency heads, specifically that the usual basis for engagement would be as an ongoing employee, and that the only grounds for termination of ongoing employment contracts would be those specified in the Act;
- retention of the position of Public Service Commissioner, in the role of guide, mentor and monitor;
- limitation of review rights for staff aggrieved by personnel decisions to internal agency review and a recommendatory review by the Merit Protection Commissioner, which is an independent office in the Public Service Commission;
- supplementation of the slim Act with a considerable amount of subordinate legislation:
  - specific matters such as the process of review of personnel decisions are to be dealt with by regulation and there is a standard general regulation-making power for the Executive;
  - the Public Service Commissioner is charged with issuing Directions on the APS Values, procedures to be established by agency heads for possible breaches of the Code of Conduct, and SES employment;[98]
  - the Public Service Minister is charged with issuing service-wide Classification Rules, designed to facilitate the application of the merit principle and the operation of inter-agency mobility arrangements but not requiring parity of remuneration;
  - the Prime Minister is authorised to issue Directions on leadership and management.

## Values and Code of Conduct

The APS Values[99] articulate much that was taken for granted over the preceding century about, not only employment and management of the workplace, but also the role that the APS plays in the service of government and the public. The Values that address the latter, 'constitutional' role,[100] are that the APS is apolitical, impartial and professional; is accountable for its actions to the

Government, the Parliament and the public; is responsive to government in providing frank, honest, comprehensive, accurate and timely advice and in implementing government policy and programs; has the highest ethical standards; and delivers services fairly, effectively, impartially and courteously to the public.

Other Values clearly relate to employment in the service: that employment decisions are based on merit;[101] that equity in employment is promoted; that the workplace is discrimination-free and diversity among employees is recognised; that workplace relations value cooperation, consultation and communication; that the workplace is fair, flexible, safe and rewarding;[102] that the APS focuses on achieving results and managing performance; that there is a fair system of review of employment decisions; and that the APS is a career based service to enhance the effectiveness and cohesion of Australia's democratic system of government.[103]

Enforcement of the Values occurs by way of a Code of Conduct, another innovation in the PSA 1999. The Code is framed in terms of the obligations of 'an APS employee',[104] and breach renders an employee liable to discipline, including dismissal.

The obligations include honesty and integrity, care and diligence, compliance with laws and with lawful and reasonable directions by a superior, confidentiality of dealings with Ministers, avoidance of conflict of interest, and upholding the APS Values and the integrity and good reputation of the APS.

Heads of agencies are required to establish procedures for dealing with employee breaches of the Code, with due regard to procedural fairness and subject to the basic procedural requirements set out in the Commissioner's Directions. Sanctions for breach range from a reprimand to reduction in salary or classification to termination of employment.[105] Breaches by management of the Values concerning employment may also be checked by way of the reviewability of individual employment decisions, which is discussed further below.

The Values constitute a complex package, and there is potential for conflict:

> While the Values complement each other, there may be tensions between them ... For example, being apolitical does not remove an employee's obligation to be responsive to the Government and to implement its policies and programs, nor does responsiveness permit partisan decisions or decisions that are not impartial. Compliance with the law always takes precedence over a public servant's obligations to achieve results and be responsive. On occasions, dilemmas may arise and public servants need to make difficult decisions.[106]

## Employer Powers of Agency Heads

Section 20(1) of the PSA 1999 confers on agency heads 'all the rights, duties and powers of an employer', with the objective of 'ensur[ing] that at law an Agency Head will have all the powers of an ordinary employer recognising that the employment laws for the APS are to be aligned as far as possible with the private sector'.[107] Some powers are in fact specified: to engage employees and determine the category of employment,[108] to assign duties,[109] to determine remuneration and other terms and conditions of employment subject to awards and agreements made under the WR Act 1996,[110] to suspend employment[111] and to terminate employment.[112]

The government explained its purpose in specifying some of the agency head's powers: it wanted to emphasise the change of the employment framework, where such matters had previously been controlled or overseen centrally or had been subject to statutory restriction.[113] In addition, the government had to accept the imposition of some restrictions on some of the powers, particularly engagement and termination, as part of the price of securing passage of the Act.

The general power conferred on Agency Heads by s 20 enables them to deal with unspecified matters such as underperformance, training, resignations, creation of new positions and grievance mechanisms, without separate statutory authority.[114]

## Engagement and Termination

The government's policy was to give the agency heads unfettered powers of hiring and firing. The Bill originally put no constraints on engagement,[115] and would have given the heads the right to terminate any contract by giving notice, whatever the duration and terms of the contract, subject only to the right of employees other than SES appointees to seek redress for unlawful or unfair dismissal under the WR Act 1996.[116] The WR Act also prescribes minimum periods of notice. The proposed right to terminate a fixed-term contract by notice is not available at common law to 'ordinary' employers, and has echoes of the dismissal at pleasure principle.

This policy of freedom to hire and fire would undermine the expectation that employment was 'permanent' and sought to emulate the private sector's flexibility, especially increased use of fixed term contracts. It generated controversy around the question of whether the traditional 'career service' and tenure of employment were essential characteristics of the impartial, apolitical public service giving frank and fearless advice to government, as required by the APS Values.[117] Competing views were expressed to parliamentary committees that reviewed the 1997 Bill, in the press, and in seminars and meetings about the proposed legislation. Former senior public servants voiced concerns that the loss of tenure and the consequent insecurity would tempt public servants to tell

Ministers what they wanted to hear, and would deter young staff from staying in the public sector.[118] They highlighted the effects of perception and fear in the workplace. On the other side, the then Secretary of the Department of Prime Minister and Cabinet, Max Moore-Wilton, observed:

> I do not believe that loss of tenure per se really should or needs to impact upon professional advice in the public sector. I think that tenure ... has very little to do with intelligence or honesty.[119]

The critics, including the Opposition, prevailed. The government accepted amendments that:

- set out the categories of employment as 'ongoing', fixed term and casual, and specified ongoing employment as the usual basis for engagement;[120]
- added to the APS Values the proposition that 'the APS is a career-based service';[121]
- specified — and thereby restricted — the grounds on which an ongoing contract could be terminated;[122]
- required that a notice terminating an ongoing contract specify the ground or grounds for the termination;[123]
- allowed SES employees to pursue relief under the WR Act against unfair or unlawful termination;
- allowed for regulations to limit the circumstances in which contracts may be made for a fixed term or on a casual basis, and to prescribe grounds or procedure applicable to the termination of non-ongoing contracts.[124]

These amendments, while retaining essential aspects of the traditional tenure, nonetheless streamlined the termination process. The concept of tenure is further discussed in the context of tenure of agency heads (see section 'Agency Heads' below).

## Review of Employment Decisions

The government's policy of radical pruning of staff appeal and review rights had two aspects.[125] First, all rights under the PSA 1922 were to be repealed and the independent Merit Protection and Review Agency was to be abolished. Agencies were to be required to resolve grievances at the workplace level, and external merits review (except for contract termination decisions, which would remain within the exclusive jurisdiction of the Australian Industrial Relations Commission and the Federal Court under the WR Act 1996) would be conducted by or through the Public Service Commissioner and would be limited to recommendatory rather than binding decisions.

The government accepted the suggestion of the Joint Committee of Public Accounts in 1997[126] that it should retain an independent body to exercise external merits review, and it substituted a Merit Protection Commissioner (within the Public Service Commission) for the Public Service Commissioner in the scheme. Under the PSA 1999 and the *Public Service Regulations 1999* (Cth), the Merit Protection Commissioner has primary jurisdiction over review of decisions about breaches of the Code of Conduct and secondary jurisdiction (that is, second tier review, after primary review by the Agency Head) over other employment decisions other than termination of employment. The jurisdiction is recommendatory only, except in the case of promotions, where the decisions of Promotions Review Committees that are established by the Commissioner are binding on Agency Heads.

The second part of the government's policy was to reduce, if not eliminate, judicial review of APS employment decisions by ensuring that the decisions did not have the necessary 'public' character. It was envisaged that the removal from the PSA of substantive and procedural prescription for decisions such as engagement, probation, promotion, transfer, redeployment, retirement, suspension, termination, leave of absence, mobility and re-integration, together with the conferral on Agency Heads of employer powers in the broadest terms, would render the staffing decisions contractual rather than statutory in character, and therefore immune from judicial review.

There was support for this strategy in a decision of the Federal Court in 1982, *Australian National University v Burns* ('*Burns*').[127] Burns had sought a statement of reasons under s 13 of the ADJR Act for the University's decision to terminate his employment on the ground of permanent incapacity. The question for the Court, then, was whether the termination decision was made 'under an enactment' for the purposes of the ADJR Act. The *Australian National University Act 1946* (Cth), which established the University, expressly conferred on the Council of the University the power to appoint staff, to make statutes on a range of matters including dismissal of staff (but no such statute had been made), and to 'have the entire control and management of the affairs and concerns of the University'. At the time of Burns' appointment, the University had provided him with a document called 'Conditions of Appointment', which included a provision dealing with termination of the contract by the Council on the ground of permanent incapacity. The majority found that the contract rather than the enactment was the basis of the termination decision.[128]

More recently, the High Court has given guidance on the principles to be applied. In a joint judgment in *Griffith University v Tang* ('*Tang*'), Gummow, Callinan and Heydon JJ held that

> a statutory grant of a bare capacity to contract does not suffice to endow subsequent contracts with the character of having been made under that enactment. A legislative grant of capacity to contract to a statutory body will not, without more, be sufficient to empower that body unilaterally to affect the rights or liabilities of any other party. The power to affect

the other party's rights and obligations will be derived not from the enactment but from such agreement as has been made between the parties. A decision to enter into a contract would have no legal effect without the consent of the other party; the agreement between the parties is the origin of the rights and liabilities as between the parties ... The determination of whether a decision is 'made ... under an enactment' involves two criteria: first, the decision must be expressly or impliedly required or authorised by the enactment; and, secondly, the decision must itself confer, alter or otherwise affect legal rights or obligations, and in that sense the decision must derive from the enactment. A decision will only be 'made ... under an enactment' if both these criteria are met.[129]

Thus, if the government had secured the bare-bones version of the PSA that it desired, so that employment decisions could be attributed to the contract of employment, it is conceivable that staffing decisions would not have been reviewable under the ADJR Act, and also would lack the 'public' quality necessary for review at common law. But the government did not secure the bare-bones version, and there remains extensive legislative prescription in the PSA 1999 and subordinate legislation that constrains management substantively and procedurally in making staffing decisions. The restrictions on engagement and termination have been outlined above, and the government has conceded that public servants may still resort to 'administrative law' in respect of termination decisions.[130]

There is a hard question, however, as to whether all APS employment decisions are made under an enactment for ADJR purposes, or raise issues of public law so as to attract the common law prerogative procedures. It could be argued that decisions that are regulated in some detail by the PSA 1999 and the Regulations and Directions — for example promotion, suspension and a determination that an employee has breached the APS Code of Conduct[131] — do meet these tests and are therefore amenable to judicial review. Other decisions, however, are unspecified and fall within the general remit of employer powers to agency heads (s 20 PSA 1999), and could be construed as non-statutory and not 'public' in character, as in the cases of *Burns* and *Tang*. On the other hand, all employment decisions are explicitly subject to the APS Values in s 10 of the PSA 1999,[132] including the merit principle, equity and fairness, and s 33 of the Act entitles APS employees to review of any action that relates to his or her APS employment.[133] In this light, all staffing decisions could be said to be sufficiently infused with a statutory flavour to be amenable to judicial review under either the ADJR Act or the common law.

As yet, there is no clear guidance from the courts. In only a handful of cases have APS employees sought judicial review of decisions made under the PSA

1999, and while all have been concerned with interlocutory matters, there has not been any dispute about the availability of judicial review. Three of the cases concerned decisions about termination of employment, a category of decision which is clearly amenable to judicial review.[134] The others dealt with suspension[135] and determination of a breach of the APS Code of Conduct,[136] matters that are regulated in some detail in the PSA (Code of Conduct breaches) or the Regulations (suspension) and are therefore analogous to termination.

The decision of the High Court in 2005 in *Jarratt v Commissioner of Police for New South Wales*,[137] while not concerned with the ADJR Act, nor the APS, is another straw in the wind. The Court showed an inclination to take an expansive view of jurisdiction to review employment decisions in the public sector. The overturned decision of the NSW Court of Appeal is briefly outlined in the section 'Dismissal at Pleasure' above.

The *Police Service Act 1990* (NSW) ('*Police Service Act*') provided that senior police officers could be removed from office 'at any time' by the Governor on the recommendation of the Police Commissioner as approved by the Minister. Deputy Commissioner Jarratt's five-year appointment had been prematurely terminated in accordance with these statutory procedures, without a reason and without an opportunity to be heard. Jarratt's case was that in the exercise of the statutory power the Crown was required to accord him natural justice on the principle formulated by the High Court in *Annetts v McCann* ('*Annetts*'), that is, 'when a statute confers power upon a public official to destroy, defeat or prejudice a person's rights, interests or legitimate expectations, the rules of natural justice regulate the exercise of that power unless they are excluded by plain words of necessary intendment'.[138] It followed that the denial of natural justice made the termination decision invalid, thus constituting a repudiation of the contract and entitling Jarratt to substantial damages for wrongful dismissal. The Crown's case was that it had exercised the power of dismissal at pleasure, which had not been displaced by the *Police Service Act*, and therefore natural justice was not applicable.

The six members of the High Court delivered four separate judgments in favour of Jarratt's right to natural justice and damages for breach of contract. Callinan J took the most traditional approach, similar to that in the NSW Court of Appeal, focussing on the question of whether the *Police Service Act* manifested an intention to displace the common law power of dismissal at pleasure. He reached a different conclusion from the Court of Appeal, however, influenced strongly by the *Annetts* principle. The other members of the Court — Gleeson CJ, McHugh, Gummow and Hayne JJ in a joint judgment, and Heydon J — gave short shrift to the dismissal at pleasure principle, emphasising that the power exercised by the Crown in Jarratt's case was statutory[139] and that there was no basis in the legislation for excluding the *Annetts* principle. Whereas the traditional approach was to require clear statutory language showing parliamentary intention to override the common law power to dismiss at pleasure, these judgments took the contrary approach of requiring clear statutory language to show parliamentary intention to preserve the common law power.[140] They were critical of the dismissal at pleasure rule, established in the nineteenth century in Britain, observing that it did not fit with 'modern conceptions of government employment and accountability',[141] with 'modern developments in the law relating to natural justice, and the approach to statutory interpretation dictated by those developments',[142] with modern authority on the reviewability of the exercise of prerogative and other non-statutory executive powers,[143] and with the different regulatory framework — that is, statute-based — for the public services in Australia.[144]

It is likely, then, that despite the government's commitment to removing its operation from the field of employment, judicial review remains a robust mechanism for enforcement of public servants' employment rights and for accountability of the government employer.

## Implications of Reform

The reform of the APS by the Howard government was designed to reshape the architecture of public service employment by reducing and changing the role of legislation and enhancing the role of agreements. The traditional public service legislation — and awards and collective agreements made under the industrial relations legislation — had provided universal and uniform pay and core terms and conditions of employment; decentralised agreement-making would provide flexibility and diversity. Thus the government aspired to changing the purpose and style of the public service legislation so that it would express general principle and leave detailed implementation to agencies, which would adapt the terms and conditions of employment to suit their needs. As outlined in the previous section, the government did not achieve its objective fully, as it was obliged to retain more detail in the PSA 1999 than it wanted. Despite this, agreements came to assume a dominant role in determining pay and conditions of employment from 1997. The primary vehicle for this change was not the common law contract of employment but agreements made under the WR Act 1996, both collective (certified agreements) and individual (Australian Workplace Agreements). In this volume, Mark Molloy's Chapter 4 examines these Agreements in detail and in Chapter 5, John O'Brien and Michael O'Donnell explore some case studies.

The shift towards agreements and a principles-based PSA with decentralised agency-based implementation was a departure from the traditional methodology for serving the constitutional function of the public service. Whereas in the past the objective of maintaining a professional, expert, apolitical, continuing and stable service was pursued *indirectly* by providing beneficial conditions of employment, notably tenure, the new approach *directly* articulated these attributes in the form of Values, which are enforceable by way of a Code of Conduct. Largely as a result of the political compromises needed to secure passage of the legislation in 1999, statutory employment conditions continued to play a role, but at a diminished level.

An important question is whether the new methodology matches the traditional approach in serving the constitutional function. By and large, judgments on the state of the APS have been positive. The combination of the new-style PSA 1999 and WR Act agreements has provided the flexibility needed for the modern economy and generated the higher degree of responsiveness sought by both Labor and non-Labor governments. There are however doubts persistently voiced about the cost paid for these gains, that is, the undermining of the non-partisan professionalism and stability that have been regarded as central to the constitutional function of the APS. Two problematic areas are the role and impact of Australian Workplace Agreements and the position of Agency Heads.

## Australian Workplace Agreements

Since late 1996, when the *Workplace Relations and Other Legislation Amendment Act 1996* (Cth) came into operation, the federal government has been able to make AWAs with its employees. The nature of, and legal requirements for, AWAs are outlined in Mark Molloy's Chapter 4. AWAs are entered into by agency heads (on behalf of the Commonwealth as employer)[145] and individual public servants. They are potent instruments providing for pay and conditions that override awards, certified/collective agreements, and determinations made by agency heads under s 24 of the PSA 1999, as well as any inconsistent contract terms.[146] They do not, however, override provisions of the PSA 1999, nor other federal statutes.

The government's policy has been that agencies should provide access to AWAs for all staff and in particular for the SES.[147] At 30 September 2005 there were 11,481 AWAs operating in the APS and the Parliamentary Service together, covering 1,966 SES and equivalent employees and 9,515 non-SES employees.[148] The total APS workforce at 30 June 2005, including 2,117 SES employees, was 133,596,[149] and the Parliamentary Service had 1,280 employees, of which 20 were in the SES.[150] Thus, almost all SES employees — 92 per cent — were parties to an AWA, and 7 per cent of non-SES employees. A factor leading to an increase in the number and proportion of AWAs is the trend of departments requiring new starters to sign an AWA as a condition of engagement. Indeed, as of 30 June 2007 there were 20,195 AWAs operating in the APS and Parliamentary Service covering approximately 2,445 SES and equivalent employees and 17,750 non-SES employees.

AWAs have been a distinctive tool for breaking down the traditional standardisation of pay and conditions in the APS.[151] Whereas certified agreements (collective agreements from 27 March 2006) operate on an agency-basis, that is, applying standardised pay and conditions across the agency, and until March 2006 have been published as a matter of course after approval in public proceedings by the Australian Industrial Relations Commission, AWAs have operated at the level of individual employees in the nature of a statutory but private contract, and have usually been kept confidential. The WR Act 1996 prohibits the official bodies (the Workplace Authority, and formerly the Employment Advocate; and, prior to March 2006, the Australian Industrial Relations Commission) from publishing the names of parties to an AWA. The legislation however prohibits the inclusion in an AWA of a provision that restricts disclosure by a party, so that either party has been free to disclose the fact and content of an AWA to whomever they choose.[152]

Generally, federal government agencies have not publicised their AWAs.[153] Aggregated information about the number of Agreements and remuneration patterns is made available by the Department of Employment and Workplace Relations,[154] and by the Public Service Commissioner in the annual State of the Service Reports.

The law and the practice of confidentiality of AWAs are problematic in the context of the APS Values of accountability, merit-based employment, and a fair workplace.[155] In 2000, a cross-party report of the Senate Finance and Public Administration References Committee criticised the lack of transparency of AWAs:

> AWAs are made between secretaries and public servants in their departments. The framework for establishing and approving these individual agreements involves no external scrutiny to ensure consistency with the APS Values or other ethical standards, or that the rewards to individuals are fair or within acceptable limits.[156]

The Committee was concerned equally with equity and fairness as between APS staff, and efficient and effective use of public resources.[157] A particular cause for disquiet was performance pay, which is a common feature of AWAs for SES employees:

> A system in which public servants are permitted to make payments of public money to each other based on subjective assessments of performance and without disclosure of the amounts paid, except in aggregate, is very difficult to reconcile with ... public accountability.[158]

Similar considerations underlie the long-standing concern of the Public Service Commissioner that the majority of APS agencies do not have policies that set out the criteria for determining remuneration for employees:

[I]t remains apparent that there are a substantial number of agencies that should undertake the development of robust remuneration policies that make clear the links between skills, performance and pay. Moreover, these policies should be transparent and available to all employees. This is important from an accountability perspective as well as for building and maintaining employee confidence in, and support for, individually based approaches to remuneration that are consistent with merit-based employment and a fair workplace (as required by the Values).[159]

By individualising pay and conditions, AWAs have taken the public service employment relationship out of the public into the private sphere. The development of differential pay and conditions and the secrecy of the Agreements pose risks of patronage, discrimination, and of undermining the cohesiveness of the APS. Without transparent policies and processes and comprehensive reporting, AWAs potentially compromise the core employment values of the APS and ultimately its constitutional function.

## Agency Heads

The issue of tenure of employment, already raised in the discussion of engagement and termination under the PSA 1999 (section 'Engagement and Termination' above), has been of particular significance for the heads of public service departments and other bodies, who must take responsibility for managing the tension between the traditional values of the APS being apolitical, impartial and professional on the one hand and being responsive to government on the other. Over the past 20 years, the tenure of departmental heads has been whittled away, so that today they have fixed term contracts that can be terminated at any time.

Prior to 1977, heads of department were appointed to permanent positions, and were called Permanent Heads. Apart from dismissal for misconduct, the only way to remove a head was to abolish the department, and then it was necessary to deploy the person's services.[160] In 1977, under the Fraser government, the PSA 1922 was amended to make the first inroad into tenure,[161] distinguishing between 'established candidates' — Permanent Heads who had previously been Permanent Heads, or were appointed by a procedure in which a committee comprising the Chairman of the Public Service Board and two other permanent heads nominated suitable names to the Prime Minister who recommended one to the Governor-General for appointment — and other appointees. A 'non-established' appointee was to be appointed for a fixed term of up to five years, and the appointment could be terminated early by the Governor-General on the recommendation of the Prime Minister, so long as the Prime Minister did not belong to the same political party as the Prime Minister who recommended the appointment.[162]

This scheme was recast under the Hawke Labor government in 1984.[163] Permanent Heads were renamed Secretaries of Departments and if not already 'officers' appointed under the PSA, they were appointed under fixed term contracts for a maximum term of five years. New provisions allowed for the Governor-General to terminate the appointment of a Secretary, whether fixed term or not, on a recommendation made by the Prime Minister after receiving a report from the Chairman of the Public Service Board (from 1987, when the Board was abolished, the report was to come from the Secretary to the Department of the Prime Minister and Cabinet[164]), and also for rotation of Secretaries between Departments. The presumption was that rotation would occur on a five-year cycle. Other new provisions addressed the relationship between Secretary and Minister. First, to emphasise 'the constitutional superiority of the Minister',[165] the words 'under the Minister' were added to the statement in the Act of a Secretary's responsibility for the general working and business of the Department and for advising the Minister. Secondly, the portfolio Minister was to be consulted on the appointment of a Secretary.[166]

The final step to abandoning tenure came in 1994.[167] The PSA 1922 was amended to allow for all Secretaries to be appointed on a fixed term. Thus, when a fixed term expired, there would be a vacancy to fill and no obligation to find another position for the former head who, in the absence of another appointment, was retired from the service. There was, however, no bar to reappointment or appointment to another position and in the majority of cases Secretaries have been retained. One notable exception was in 1996 when, immediately after the election that brought the Howard government to power, the contracts of six Secretaries were terminated.[168] To encourage existing Secretaries to convert their continuing appointments to a fixed term, the government offered a pay loading via a determination of the Remuneration Tribunal, which adopted the government's recommendation of 20 per cent.[169] The Remuneration Tribunal also determined that compensation payable for early termination would be one third of a month's salary for the balance of the term up to a cap of 12 months' salary.[170]

Under the PSA 1999, the appointment and termination powers were transferred from the Governor-General to the Prime Minister. The change simply reflected reality, as the Governor-General acted in accordance with advice based on the recommendation of the Prime Minister, but it was nonetheless symbolically important for articulating the very clear connection between Secretaries and the government of the day.[171] As before, the maximum period for the fixed term appointment was five years, and a report from the Secretary of the Department of the Prime Minister and Cabinet was a prerequisite for the exercise of the powers.[172]

The precarious tenure of Secretaries was revealed in 1999 when Paul Barratt contested the premature termination of his appointment as Secretary of the Department of Defence. The case was governed by the PSA 1922, but it is likely that the PSA 1999 would have yielded the same result.

Barratt first sought an injunction to restrain the imminent termination, contending that natural justice was required in the making of two decisions that were part of the process — the making of a report to the Prime Minister by the Secretary of the Department of Prime Minister and Cabinet (the 'Cabinet Secretary'), and the Prime Minister's making of a termination recommendation to the Governor-General. Barratt also contended that the power of termination could be exercised only for cause shown, that is for fault or incapacity of a fundamental nature that went to his fitness to continue for the remainder of the fixed term.[173]

On the first issue, Hely J found for Barratt on two bases: the *Annetts* principles of natural justice (discussed above in section 'Review of Employment Decisions'),[174] and the interpretive principles established by s 6 of the PSA 1922.

Section 6 of the PSA 1922 provided:

> The chief object of this Act is to constitute a public service for the efficient, *equitable* and proper conduct, in accordance with sound management practices (including personnel management practices), of the public administration of the Australian Government *and this Act shall be construed accordingly*. [emphasis added by Hely J]

Construing the provisions concerning termination of a Secretary's appointment, Hely J concluded:

> That factors such as fairness and justice are relevant, as well as those of efficiency, suggests a legislative intention that the Cabinet Secretary should afford the Secretary whose position may be affected with an opportunity to be heard if his report is to be adverse to the Secretary's position.[175]

On the content of the required procedural fairness, Hely J held that Barratt was entitled to be told by the Cabinet Secretary the grounds or reasons proposed for the report to the Prime Minister, to be given the opportunity to respond, and to have his response form part of the report. There was no right to an oral hearing, and no entitlement to make submissions to the Prime Minister as well as the Cabinet Secretary unless the Prime Minister proposed to formulate his recommendation to the Governor-General for reasons different from those comprised in the Cabinet Secretary's report.[176]

On the second issue of grounds of termination, Hely J found against Barratt. There was no basis in the legislation for an interpretation that the termination power could be exercised only for cause shown.

On the day after Hely J made his decision, the Cabinet Secretary informed Barratt that he was considering making a report to the Prime Minister proposing that Barratt's appointment be terminated on the grounds that the Minister for Defence had lost trust and confidence in his ability to perform the duties of Secretary, and that this lack of trust and confidence was detrimental to the effective and efficient operation of the Department. The Cabinet Secretary cited documentary and oral evidence from the court proceedings, and a recent statement by the Minister to the Cabinet Secretary about his loss of confidence in Barratt. Barratt requested details and when no further reasons were forthcoming, he returned to the Federal Court seeking a declaration that he was entitled to a statement of the grounds on which the Minister asserted that he had no trust and confidence in Barratt.

Hely J held against Barratt on this application.[177] Since the ground for the decisions was that the Defence Minister, 'rightly or wrongly and for whatever reason' had lost confidence in Barratt's ability to perform his duties as Secretary,

> considerations of procedural fairness do not require that [Barratt] be told why the Defence Minister has lost confidence in him, because this is not a matter which informs, or plays a part in, the decision making process of either the Cabinet Secretary or the Prime Minister.[178]

According to Hely J, neither the Cabinet Secretary nor the Prime Minister would be required to inquire into the reasons for the Minister's loss of confidence.

Barratt appealed unsuccessfully to the Full Court of the Federal Court against both decisions.[179] In a joint judgment, the three members of the Court substantively upheld the various conclusions Hely J had reached, although there were different emphases. Their key findings were:

- Barratt's fixed term appointment was not terminable at pleasure;[180]
- the PSA required that termination of a fixed term appointment be based on some ground or grounds;
- the range of grounds that could be relied on for the exercise of the power was governed by s 6 of the PSA (set out above), so that '[t]he discretion to terminate must be exercised to protect, maintain or advance the efficient, equitable and proper conduct, in accordance with sound management practices, of the public administration of the Australian government';[181]
- the range of permissible purposes of termination was not limited to considerations of management or administration, and 'political and policy considerations may be legitimate aspects of the basis upon which the power may be exercised';[182]

- there was nothing in the language of the PSA to suggest that termination could occur only when there had been serious fault on the part of the Secretary;
- the court's function did not extend to determining whether the ground of a proposed termination would or was likely to achieve the object set out in s 6, and it was sufficient that the court was satisfied that the ground relied upon was capable of being related to the object, and was not extraneous to it; and
- loss of the minister's trust and confidence was plainly capable of being related to the object in s 6.

The Court conceded that a recommendation for termination made purely on subjective grounds without any factual basis being ascribed to it would be inherently capable of being capricious and arbitrary and therefore extraneous to the object in s 6. Turning to the present case, the Court found that the ground relied on was not based purely upon subjective considerations and the material provided by the Cabinet Secretary to Barratt was sufficient to demonstrate the basis for the Minister's loss of trust and confidence. The Court made clear that the Cabinet Secretary and the Prime Minister would have to consider why there was a lack of trust and confidence and whether it was appropriate to take the formal steps of a report in the case of the Cabinet Secretary and a recommendation in the case of the Prime Minister. But neither was required to consider whether the reason for loss of trust and confidence was objectively well founded.

Despite Barratt's success in the first case in winning recognition of a Secretary's right to natural justice in the face of early termination of appointment, the government's response, sanctioned by the Federal Court, revealed that 'all that was legally needed for the [Secretary's] contract to be ended was for a minister, with or without a justifiable reason, to declare a lack of trust in their departmental secretary'.[183] Perhaps Weller overstates the case, as the Federal Court made clear that both the Cabinet Secretary and the Prime Minister must turn their minds to the reasons for the lack of confidence. Despite this, it is clear that the government can easily establish circumstances in which the natural justice to which a Secretary is entitled has very limited content and impact.

The Barratt episode crystallised questions about the relationship between tenure and the traditional public service qualities, in particular non-partisanship, responsiveness, frankness and fearlessness in giving advice, and the expertise and stability engendered by the operation of 'a career service'. Given the fixed term contracts, sometimes shorter than five years, with no guarantee of reappointment, and the ease of early termination at small cost and negligible accountability, would the Secretaries' attitude to advising Ministers be affected? In order to satisfy Ministers of their responsiveness, would Secretaries give precedence to short-term aspects over longer-term considerations? Would they pay more attention to political implications than other perspectives? Would public servants be willing to serve as Secretaries? Would able staff seek out the higher rewards of private sector employment with the consequence that their special skills would be lost to the public sector?

There are inherent difficulties in addressing these questions: Secretaries are unlikely to admit to experiencing problems, and staff are unlikely to comment on their interest in, or prospects of, appointment as Secretary. Patrick Weller and John Wanna have, however, endeavoured to gather empirical evidence by interviewing former and serving Secretaries.[184]

Secretaries interviewed in 1997 denied that loss of tenure had deterred them from giving frank and fearless advice to ministers, which they regarded as a matter of professional duty and integrity. They did, however, acknowledge some changes in the relationship: some ministers were more distrustful of anyone they inherited, particularly from a previous government, and wanted 'their' person for the job; while the substance of advice might not change, the style of presentation may, possibly emphasising the benefits for the minister; there was evidence of the erosion of a long-term view among Secretaries, with a new emphasis on short-term objectives, described as the 'parking meter view'; they feared that the greater vulnerability at the top meant that was different advice coming from within the department, based on the ethos that 'this is what they want to hear'.[185] Secretaries also reported that the lack of tenure at Secretary level was discouraging potential future appointees. While not the only factor involved in the loss of talented officers to the private sector, it was a symbol of the difficulties in keeping good people in the APS.[186] After more interviews, Weller wrote in 2001 that this range of concerns about the effect of insecurity of tenure persisted.[187] As Weller and Wanna observed, while the Secretaries' views were difficult to test, the frequency of such comments indicated that there were issues that needed to be taken seriously.

The legal framework for, and experience of, appointment and removal of agency heads has prompted some concerns about politicisation and the risk of compromising fundamental values of impartiality and non-partisanship. The concept of politicisation is not straightforward. The narrowest definition is that it involves appointment/removal on the basis of party political affiliation or association.[188] The few known examples are scattered over the last 30-odd years. Of more impact has been the replacement of Secretaries upon a change of government, as happened under the Whitlam administration and at the beginning of the Howard government, as an exercise in signalling a change and exerting control. Mulgan describes such appointments as politicised in the sense that the underlying assumption is that the government has the right to appoint their own people, undermining the concept of a politically neutral public service that is 'capable of professionally serving alternative governments' (and ministers).[189]

The principal risk, according to Mulgan, is not that advice will become less frank and fearless, but that professional experience and continuity, and thus efficiency and effectiveness, will be lost. Also there may be a demoralising effect on the ranks below secretary, and disincentives for able people to pursue careers in the public service. Mulgan also draws under the politicisation umbrella the appointment of Secretaries on the basis of their commitment to a particular policy or managerial direction favoured by the government.[190]

It is difficult to test the degree of politicisation of the public service, given these multiple layers of meaning. Clearly the APS has not moved very far along the spectrum towards the US model, where large numbers of senior civil servants are replaced when there is a new presidential administration. Despite this, by a series of changes and innovations over the past few decades, government has increased its capacity for, and its actual, control over the bureaucracy. The arrangements for appointment and termination of Secretaries are the most overt manifestation. Other practices include recruitment from outside the public service at all levels; the growth in numbers and influence of ministerial advisers as an alternative source of advice to ministers and as a filter for departmental advice; the creation of the SES as a more flexible and responsive managerial echelon in which positions are advertised within and outside the service, staff are expected to be mobile between departments, and promotion decisions are not reviewable; the utilisation of fixed term contracts and consultancies; the spread of confidential AWAs; the recognition of the Secretary of the Department of the Prime Minister and Cabinet rather than the independent Public Service Commissioner as Head of the Public Service.

Another recent development is the growth in the amount of interaction between Ministers and their staff and APS staff. Notably this contact extends well beyond senior staff levels. For example, in 2004–5 one in five APS employees had direct contact with Ministers or their advisers — 73 per cent of SES employees, 35 per cent of executive level employees and 15 per cent of APS 1–6 employees. One third of these employees believed they had faced a challenge in balancing the Values of being apolitical, impartial and professional, responsive to government and openly accountable, for example, being asked to change advice to reflect the political position of the Minister. Ten per cent had low levels of confidence that they could balance the values.[191]

The combined effect of these developments is to generate unease from time to time about how the balance is struck between the traditional 'constitutional' values of impartiality and non-partisanship on one side, and the greater emphasis on responsiveness to government on the other side. There are concerns outside and inside the APS that the Service is politicised and compliant in the sense that:

> public servants provide to government only the information and advice
> that it wishes to hear, either because political advisers let through only

that which they believe their Ministers want or because it is instructed to do so or because it is implicitly understood — if not explicitly stated — that certain facts or views will not be welcomed.[192]

In depicting this image of the Service in 2004, the Secretary of the Department of the Prime Minister and Cabinet was concerned to correct it, but there is no doubt that such views are tenacious. In 2003, a Senate Committee documented evidence from witnesses, including former senior public servants, and published commentaries about the 'erosion of public service advice'.[193] In a number of speeches in 2005, the Public Service Commissioner flagged politicisation as an issue to be addressed in the APS,[194] and describing the scope of a review of the PSA 1999, said:

> The areas that we will look at in particular ... are around whether or not the legislation needs an overriding statement about what binds the Australian Public Service together. Do we see ourselves as working in the public interest or the national interest; how do we fold in our responsibilities to the Government of the day — are the sorts of questions we're asking.[195]

## Conclusion

This chapter has canvassed the changing shape of APS employment law over the past 40-odd years, identifying the components and their interaction, and exploring their impact on the constitutional function of the Service.

For all the reform activity, there are marked continuities over the period: the substantive legal relationship between APS employees and the Crown is contractual; the content of the contract is largely supplied by the PSA and processes under the industrial/workplace relations legislation; the PSA remains a significant instrument for regulating APS employment, including engagement and termination; and administrative law continues to apply to employment decisions.

Yet significant changes have occurred. Whereas 30 years ago industrial awards and agreements operated Service-wide, agreements have almost completely displaced awards in the APS, and certified/collective agreements operate at agency level and AWAs operate at individual employee level. The specialist public service legislation has changed in substance and style, promulgating general principles rather than comprehensive prescription, and agencies fashion the detail to suit their needs. Substantive changes include loss of tenure for agency heads, who are appointed to fixed term contracts for up to five years and whose appointment may be terminated at any time; the contraction of employees' rights of review and appeal, with the withdrawal of promotion appeal rights from middle and senior management, the abolition of the independent review body and substitution of a body with recommendatory powers only;

and the removal of specialised procedures for discipline and dismissal matters. Thus, management prerogatives have been expanded and employee entitlements and protections have been reduced or modified.

A conspicuous aspect of the changes is the trend of devolution, that is, the abandonment of central structures, processes and control and transfer of responsibility to agency-level. Thus not only has the scope of industrial awards and agreements contracted over time to agency level, but the Public Service Board/Commission has lost its role as a central personnel administration, and agency heads exercise the powers of employer. This development parallels the displacement in general industrial/workplace relations law of national and industry regulation in favour of enterprise regulation. The transformation in the *modus operandi* of the APS has given agencies flexibility and choice, which are key virtues according to contemporary management theory and practice. The APS has not, however, been broken up. There is still a commitment to maintaining the Service as an entity, primarily through the shared Values that are articulated in the PSA 1999. As discussed in the section 'Values and Code of Conduct', these values encapsulate the characteristics considered necessary for fulfilling the Service's constitutional function as well as expressing in general terms the 'good' employer role of the Crown. One of the primary functions of the Australian Public Service Commission is to promote and 'embed' the Values by education and auditing.[196]

A major theme in this chapter has been the examination of the fit between the employment framework and the constitutional function of the Service. It has been argued that early in the twenty-first century, the fit does not appear as good as it was 30 years ago. Most of the contemporary concerns relate to the so-called phenomenon of politicisation, that is, an imbalance between being responsive to government and giving 'frank and fearless', impartial and professional advice. The problem can be manifest in various ways: telling the government what it wants to hear, withholding advice or information that the government does not want to hear, giving cautious or risk-averse advice, 'bend[ing] the rules around … perceptions of what the Government wants',[197] complying with instructions given by ministerial staff about the content of advice.[198] The incidence of these practices may be unmeasurable, and to the extent that they exist, they cannot be simplistically attributed to particular aspects of the employment framework. Rather, over-zealous responsiveness is likely to be a matter of culture that has evolved over time.

Nonetheless, there may be improvements to the employment framework that could signal the reassertion of the independence and impartiality of the public service without compromising the responsiveness that governments of all political hues want. In relation to appointment and termination of Secretaries, a Senate Committee recommended in 2003 that greater tenure be conferred on

Secretaries.[199] It is unlikely that the proposal would win political favour. There is more hope for an arrangement in which a panel or committee, or at least the Public Service Commissioner, is involved in making recommendations about appointment and termination.[200] In relation to the interaction of APS staff and the Minister and staff, formal guidelines have recently been published by the Australian Public Service Commission with a view to setting uniform standards and clarifying expectations.[201] This could well be complemented by a Code of Conduct for Ministerial advisers.[202] In relation to agency employment decisions, the merit principle would be served by the restoration of an independent review body with determinative powers. In relation to AWAs, much greater transparency and more extensive reporting would allay concerns about favouritism and discrimination. In relation to performance pay, clear policies on criteria and process would enhance fairness and equity as well as accountability. In relation to leadership, recognition of the Public Service Commissioner as the head of the APS, rather than the Secretary of the Department of the Prime Minister and Cabinet, would signify the independence of the Service.[203]

Prime Minister Howard set an admirable goal in 1998:

> No government 'owns' the public service. It must remain a national asset that services the national interest, adding value to the directions set by the government of the day. The responsibility of any government must be to pass on to its successors a public service which is better able to meet the challenges of its time than the one it inherited.[204]

# ENDNOTES

[1] Commonwealth of Australia, Royal Commission on Australian Government Administration, *Report* (1976).

[2] See ch 10, this volume [Ewing]. See also Graham Smith, *Public Employment Law* (1987) ch 3; Greg McCarry, *Aspects of Public Sector Employment Law* (1988) ch 2; Sandra Fredman and Gillian Morris, *The State as Employer* (1989) ch 3. The alternative analyses treated the relationship as one of status or office holding. In contrast to civil servants, other public sector employees, such as teachers and health workers, have been regarded as having contracts.

[3] *Browne v R* (1886) 12 VLR 397, 412 (Williams and Holroyd JJ). Paul Finn, *Law and Government in Colonial Australia* (1987) 107 explains that in Victoria public servants could not enforce their statutory rights (see below) against the Crown on account of Crown immunity, but could make claims in contract, and that the colonial courts yielded to 'this necessity' of treating the public service legislation 'as providing the foundation for a contract of service with the Crown — a contract which embodied the statutory rights'. For other colonial cases affirming the contractual relationship, see Finn 66.

[4] Ann Pickering, *Contract or Statutory Code? Private and Public Law Principles in Australian Public Service Employment* (LLB Honours Thesis, The Australian National University, 1984) 85.

[5] *Kodeeswaran v Attorney-General of Ceylon* (170) AC 1111.

[6] See ch 10 this volume [Ewing].

[7] Trevor C Hartley and John Griffith, *Government and Law: An Introduction to the Working of the Constitution in Britain* (2nd ed, 1981) 86.

[8] Chapter 10 this volume [Ewing]. See also Fredman and Morris, above n 2, 1.

[9] Other cases were *Williamson v Commonwealth* (1907) 5 CLR 174 (Higgins J) and *Carey v Commonwealth* (1921) 30 CLR 132 (Higgins J).

[10] *Lucy v Commonwealth* (1923) 33 CLR 229. Lucy was transferred from the South Australian public service, where his employment was subject to the state public service Act, to the Commonwealth service after Federation. Thereafter his employment was governed by the *Commonwealth Public Service Act 1902*. A provision of that Act, as well as s 84 of the *Commonwealth Constitution*, preserved all his existing and accruing rights, which would include the right to remain in the service during his life or until dismissal or removal for some cause specified in the South Australian Act. Lucy's service was terminated under a provision of the Commonwealth Act on the ground of age, which was not a basis for removal under the South Australian legislation. The case was argued on the basis that the removal was invalid, and the issues revolved around remedy, specifically, whether Lucy was entitled to damages for wrongful dismissal, ie wrongful termination of the contract of employment.

[11] (1923) 33 CLR 229, 237.

[12] Finn, above n 3, 15, 65.

[13] 'As a matter of law, each department could employ its own staff on its own terms and conditions, relying for its authority to do so on the executive power of the Commonwealth in the Constitution': Public Service Act Review Group, *Report* (December 1994) (known as the McLeod Report), para 2.4. The same reasoning applies for the states.

[14] Australian Public Service Commission, *The Australian Experience of Public Sector Reform* (2003) 35. See ch 3, this volume, section on 'The Central Public Service Management Agency' [Nethercote].

[15] *Director-General of Education v Suttling* (1987) 162 CLR 427, 437–8.

[16] *Chapman v Commissioner of Australian Federal Police* (1984) 50 ACTR 23. The person who purported to appoint Chapman was not authorised by the statute to do so. See also the later case of *Re Australian Industrial Relations Commission and Arends; ex parte Commonwealth of Australia* (2005) 145 FCR 277. The issue was whether a worker employed by the Department of Defence was 'a person in employment ... by authority of a law of the Commonwealth', which was the jurisdictional basis on which he could pursue relief against unfair dismissal under the *Workplace Relations Act 1996* ('WR Act 1996'). The Department conceded that the contract with the worker was an employment contract at common law, ie a contract of service, notwithstanding an express term describing him as an independent contractor, ie a contract for services. The relevant 'law of the Commonwealth' under which the worker was engaged was an instrument made pursuant to the *Defence Act 1903* (Cth) that provided only for contracts for services, and the Federal Court held that there was therefore no law of the Commonwealth that authorised the employment of the worker and he had no basis for an action under the WR Act 1996.

[17] *Keely v State of Victoria* [1964] VR 244. The employee was properly appointed under the statute, and subsequently carried out higher duties at the direction of a superior who had no authority under the

legislation to reclassify her position or approve payment of a higher salary. Her claim based in *quantum meruit* for services provided also failed because the superior officer did not have authority to request that the services be provided.

[18] Other cases: *Fowell v Iannou* (1982) 45 ALR 491; *Bayley v Osborne* (1984) 10 IR 5. Another case, often quoted in this context, *Australian Broadcasting Commission v Industrial Court of South Australia* (1977) 138 CLR 399, was about inconsistency between a Commonwealth statute and a state statute.

[19] *Bennett v Commonwealth* [1980] 1 NSWLR 581 ('*Bennett*'). One of the authorities on which Rogers J relied was *Gould v Stuart* [1896] AC 575, discussed below in section 'Dismissal at Pleasure'.

[20] *Csomore v Public Service Board (NSW)* (1986) 17 IR 275 ('*Csomore*').

[21] His Honour also held that on the facts there was no suspension.

[22] (1982) 43 ALR 165.

[23] B Beinart, 'The Legal Relationship between Government and its Employees' [1955] *Acta Juridica, Butterworths South African Law Review* 21, 24–5. Another principle applied from the military to the civil context was that Crown servants had no legally enforceable rights against the Crown — see section 'Contract' above.

[24] The traditional position was that the courts had jurisdiction to determine the existence of a prerogative power, ie whether or not the Crown was given the power by the common law, and its scope and extent, but the courts had no power to review or control the actual exercise of the power: *Attorney-General v De Keyser's Royal Hotel Ltd* [1920] AC 508. Recent developments are noted in section 'Review of Employment Decisions' below.

[25] In *Ryder v Foley* (1906) 4 CLR 422 ('*Ryder*'), 435–6, Griffith CJ said 'it is an implied term in the engagement of every person in the Public Service, that he holds office during pleasure, unless the contrary appears by Statute'. In *Fletcher v Nott* (1938) 60 CLR 55 ('*Fletcher*'), 68, Latham CJ said 'the contract between the Crown and a servant of the Crown is unilateral. The servant is bound to serve, and to continue to serve for the term for which he has undertaken to serve, but the Crown is not bound to continue to employ him and may determine the employment at any moment without cause, that is, simply at will. While the employment continues, the relations are contractual in character ... But there can be a contract which is determinable at will ...'.

[26] *Dunn v R* (1896) 1 QB 116, 120–1.

[27] Such provisions are not uncommon in state legislation.

[28] *Gould v Stuart* [1896] AC 575. The court described the dismissal power as 'a condition' that was 'imported into the contract' — [1896] AC 575, 577.

[29] [1896] AC 575, 578–9.

[30] *Ryder v Foley* (1906) 4 CLR 422; *Fletcher v Nott* (1938) 60 CLR 55; *Kaye v Attorney-General for Tasmania* (1956) 94 CLR 193 ('*Kaye*').

[31] *Ryder v Foley* (1906) 4 CLR 422; *Kaye v Attorney-General for Tasmania* (1956) 94 CLR 193.

[32] *Kaye v Attorney-General for Tasmania* (1956) 94 CLR 193.

[33] *Fletcher v Nott* (1938) 60 CLR 55. Other important factors were that the procedural provisions were in subordinate legislation rather than in the primary statute, and were in the nature of administrative machinery that was not mandatory.

[34] (2003) 59 NSWLR 87, 109–10.

[35] Section 51 of the *Police Service Act 1990* (NSW).

[36] (2003) 59 NSWLR 87, 112.

[37] (1981) 55 FLR 34, 39. Also by *obiter dicta* in *Bennett v Commonwealth* [1980] 1 NSWLR 581, 585 (Rogers J).

[38] *Dunn v R* [1896] 1 QB 116.

[39] The issue was conceded in *Carey v Commonwealth* (1921) 30 CLR 132.

[40] (1982) 64 FLR 89, 96.

[41] *Suttling v Director-General of Education* (1985) 3 NSWLR 427, 448 (McHugh JA with whom Glass JA concurred, Kirby P dissenting).

[42] Ibid 447.

[43] Ibid 446.

[44] *Director-General of Education v Suttling* (1987) 162 CLR 427.

[45] One other finding of note by the High Court was that this case did not involve an exercise of the power to dismiss at pleasure as the power does not extend to reducing the position and salary of a person whose services are retained: (1987) 162 CLR 427, 442 (Brennan J).

[46] [1999] ACTSC 79 (Unreported, Higgins J, 22 July 1999).

[47] [2002] ACTSC 43 (Unreported, Miles CJ, 24 May 2002).

[48] Mark Aronson, Bruce Dyer and Matthew Groves, *Judicial Review of Administrative Action* (3rd ed, 2004) 14 (emphasis added).

[49] Ibid 85.

[50] This list is taken from the *Administrative Decisions (Judicial Review) Act 1977* (Cth) s 5, which codifies the common law grounds.

[51] Other areas of operation are non-statutory government powers (such as the prerogatives, discussed above at section 'Dismissal at Pleasure' and later in section 'Review of Employment Decisions') and some decisions of some private bodies. See Aronson, Dyer and Groves, above n 48, ch 3.

[52] Finn, above n 3, 107 and ch 6.

[53] Broadly, the remedy is to treat the defective decision as a nullity or to compel the making of a decision. The equitable remedies of injunction and declaration are also available. Damages are not available.

[54] Finn, above n 3, 107 cites three 19th-century cases in Victoria, and Pickering, above n 4, 86 cites another 19th century case and one 20th century case. The High Court case of *Kaye*, discussed above in section 'Dismissal at Pleasure', was an administrative law action in which a dismissed police officer claimed a declaration that the dismissal was ineffective. On the inaccessibility of judicial review generally, see Harry Whitmore, 'Law and the Administration: Justice or Expediency?' in Richard Spann and Geoffrey Curnow (eds), *Public Policy and Administration: A Reader* (1975) 275, 275–7.

[55] Finn, above n 3, 66 (nn 46, 52) and 103 (n 87) cites numerous pre-Federation contract-based claims for wrongful dismissal, and two superannuation cases. The High Court cases of *Lucy*, *Ryder* and *Fletcher* — above section 'Dismissal at Pleasure' — were also framed as contract actions. Pickering, above n 4, 86 adds some Victorian and other High Court cases. See, generally, M Pittard and R Naughton, *Australian Labour Law: Cases and Materials*, (4th ed, 2003), ch 5 ; B Creighton and A Stewart, *Labour Law*, (4th ed 2005), 443–450; R Owens and J Riley, *The Law of Work*, (2007) 262–268.

[56] Also on the Federal Magistrates Court since 2000.

[57] Section 5 and definitions in s 3(1). There were also express exemptions in the Act: decisions taken by the Governor-General, and decisions listed in sch 1 of the Act, which include defence force disciplinary decisions and decisions made under the WR Act 1996.

[58] Review of prerogative powers and contractual decisions is further discussed below in section 'Review of Employment Decisions'.

[59] The to-ing and fro-ing on these exemptions is set out by Neil Williams, 'The ADJR Act and Personnel Management' (1991) 20 *Federal Law Review* 158, 159. There is no common law right to reasons for an administrative decision: *Public Service Board of New South Wales v Osmond* (1986) 159 CLR 657. See, generally, Marilyn Pittard, 'Reasons for Administrative Decisions: Legal Framework and Reform' in Matthew Groves and HP Lee (eds), *Administrative Law - Fundamentals, Principle and Doctrines*, (Cambridge University Press, 2007), ch 11.

[60] Williams, above n 59, 159. Included in the number were some common law cases, eg *Dixon v Commonwealth* (1981) 55 FLR 34 and *Ansell v Wells* (1982) 63 FLR 127. Some had been commenced before the enactment of the ADJR Act, or were taking advantage of provisions in the *Judiciary Act 1903* (Cth) which avoided the jurisdictional limitations of the ADJR Act, such as the requirement that the decision be made under an enactment and exemptions for decisions under the WR Act 1996 and the *Defence Force Discipline Act 1982* (Cth). Pickering, above n 4, Appendix A, 6, cites a report of the Administrative Review Council that in 1982 there were 19 applications made under the ADJR Act against the Public Service Board alone, and that there would have been more applications made against individual departments.

[61] Eg *Hamblin v Duffy* (No 2) (1981) 55 FLR 18 (breach of natural justice, and decision taken by an incompletely constituted body); *Bewley v Cruickshanks* (1984) 1 FCR 534 (taking into account an irrelevant consideration).

[62] Eg *Perkins v Cuthill* (No 2) (1981) 3 ALN N88 (an irrelevant consideration taken into account, unreasonableness, breach of natural justice, absence of evidence, excess of jurisdiction).

[63] Eg *Cole v Cunningham* (1983) 81 FLR 158 (breach of natural justice).

[64] Eg *Dixon v Commonwealth* (1981) 55 FLR 34 (breach of natural justice); *Schmohl v Commonwealth of Australia* (1983) 74 FLR 474 (breach of natural justice).

[65] Eg *Dixon v Commonwealth* (1981) 55 FLR 34 (breach of natural justice).

[66] Eg the *Civil Service Act 1862* (Vic) provided for a right of appeal in regard to classification and dismissal.

[67] Previous arrangements for dealing with grievances were ad hoc, and were criticised by the Coombs Royal Commission in 1976: above n 1, ch 8.

[68] *Commonwealth Employees (Redeployment and Retirement) Act 1979*.

[69] *Administrative Appeals Tribunal Act 1975* (Cth).

[70] *Superannuation Act 1976* (Cth). Under the *Superannuation Act 1922*, the appellate body was the High Court constituted by a single justice.

[71] *Commonwealth Functions (Statutes Review) Act 1981* (Cth). The AAT took over from the Commonwealth Employees Compensation Tribunals, which were created in 1971.

[72] *Freedom of Information Act 1982* (Cth). See, generally, Moira Paterson, *Freedom of Information and Privacy: Government and Information Access in the Modern State* (2005).

[73] *Ombudsman Act 1976* (Cth) ss 5(1), 15, 16.

[74] *Ombudsman Act 1976* (Cth) s 5(2)(d). In contrast, s 19C(3) of the Act gives the Defence Force Ombudsman power to investigate any matter 'that is related to the service of a member of the Defence Force'.

[75] Another reason for the distinctiveness of the public service contract was the Crown's common law power of dismissal at pleasure, which had more limited practical impact than the role of legislation.

[76] For example *Scott v Commonwealth* (1982) 64 FLR 89, discussed above in section 'Dismissal at Pleasure'.

[77] Commentators of the time highlighted this issue: Smith, above n 2, 189–90; McCarry, above n 2, 41; Finn, above n 3, 65; Pickering, above n 4, ch 8.

[78] The concepts of 'office' and 'officer' derive from the British background. For elaboration, see Finn, above n 3, ch 2; McCarry, above n 2, 11–22.

[79] See above section 'Contract'.

[80] This analysis was made in Phillipa Weeks, 'Reconstituting the Employment Relationship in the Australian Public Service' in Stephen Deery and Richard Mitchell (eds), *Employment Relations — Individualisation and Union Exclusion: An International Study* (1999) 69–87.

[81] See above n 13, para 2.10.

[82] For elaboration of the concept of 'career service', see Coombs Royal Commission, above n 1, para 8.1.12; McLeod Report, above n 13, para 1.20; Joint Committee of Public Accounts, Parliament of Australia, Report 323. *Managing People in the Australian Public Service — Dilemmas for Devolution and Diversity* (1993) paras 3.2–3.6; Gerald Caiden, *Career Service* (1965) 2–4. Patrick Weller, a political scientist, in *Australia's Mandarins: The Frank and the Fearless?* (2001) 50, identifies the core ideas of a career service as 'a single career, a commitment to public service, and the belief that officials would rise to the top and retire, or perhaps take another government position'.

[83] Greg McCarry, 'The Demise of Tenure in Public Sector Employment' in Ron McCallum, Greg McCarry and Paul Ronfeldt (eds), *Employment Security* (1994) 138 shows that, notwithstanding all the safeguards, termination was still possible but that there was an 'implicit contract' that the government employer would use the powers only in extreme circumstances (eg redundancy and abolition of agencies), or when there was demonstrated cause for dismissal on account of misconduct or incompetence. See Marilyn Pittard, 'The Age of Reason: Principles of Unfair Dismissal in Australia', chapter 2 in the same volume (McCallum, McCarry & Ronfeldt (eds), *Employment Security*, 1994, p.16) for common law and later unfair dismissal protection of private sector employees.

[84] Richard Mulgan, 'Public Servants and the Public Interest' (Australian Senate Occasional Public Lecture, Canberra, 11 August 2000) <http://www.aph.gov.au/Senate/pubs/occa_lect/transcripts/mulgan.htm> at 4 May 2006.

[85] An extreme version of this reasoning sees public servants being independent guardians of the public interest, ie independent of government. See Mulgan, above n 84; Michael Keating, 'The Public Service: Independence, Responsibility and Responsiveness' (1999) 58(1) *Australian Journal of Public Administration* 39; Peter Shergold, Secretary of the Department of the Prime Minister and Cabinet, 'Pride in Public Service' (Speech delivered to the National Press Club, Canberra, 15 February 2006) <http://www.pmc.gov.au/speeches> at 4 May 2006. This debate cannot be pursued here.

[86] Weller, above n 82, 23, 26.

[87] Ian Hancock, 'The VIP Affair 1966–67: The Causes, Course and Consequences of a Ministerial and Public Service Cover-Up' (2003) 18(2) *Australasian Parliamentary Review* (whole issue).

[88] Linda Colley, 'The Changing Face of Public Sector Employment' (2001) 60(1) *Australian Journal of Public Administration* 9, 10.

[89] See above n 1.

[90] Australian Public Service Commission, *The Australian Experience*, above n 14; Australian Public Service Commission, *A History in Three Acts* (2004) <http://www.apsc.gov.au/publications/index.html> at 4 May 2006.

[91] See above n 13, vii.

[92] Proposals of this kind had first surfaced in 1990 within the Public Service Commission: Australian Public Service Commission, *A History in Three Acts*, above n 90, 119.

[93] Hon Peter Reith, *Towards a Best Practice Australian Public Service — Discussion Paper Issued by the Minister for Industrial Relations and Minister Assisting the Prime Minister for the Public Service, November 1996* (1996) v–vi, 5–6, 15 <http://www.apsc.gov.au/publications96/apsreformdiscussionpaper.htm> at 4 May 2006.

[94] Ibid vii, viii, 5, 14.

[95] See also Weeks, above n 80.

[96] The Bill was again debated to an impasse in March–April 1998.

[97] As the Explanatory Memorandum, Public Service Bill 1999 (Cth) para 4.1 points out, the agency heads are not named as employers because constitutionally the ultimate employer is the Crown in right of the Commonwealth.

[98] The Directions are intended to specify minimum standards rather than to prescribe detailed requirements: Australian Public Service Commission, *A History in Three Acts*, above n 90, 152–3.

[99] Section 10(1).

[100] Described by the government in the Explanatory Memorandum, Public Service Bill 1999 (Cth) para 3.4 as 'the philosophical underpinning for the APS'.

[101] There is an extended definition of 'merit' in s 10(2); patronage and favouritism in employment decisions are expressly prohibited in s 17; and s 19 precludes Ministers from involvement in individual employment decisions.

[102] The Supplementary Explanatory Memorandum, Public Service Bill 1999 (Cth) paras 3.3.1–3.3.2 added a gloss of 'principles' including that the remuneration and conditions of employment will be fair and flexible, and that APS provides its employees with fair and flexible treatment, free of arbitrary or capricious administrative acts or decisions.

[103] The Values relating to equity, review of decisions, and career service were added to the 1999 Bill in order to secure Opposition support in the Senate. The Public Service Commissioner's Directions elaborate the minimum content of all the Values in terms of the separate obligations of agency heads and employees in relation to each Value, though in very general terms.

[104] Section 13, and s 14(1), extends the Code to heads of agencies.

[105] Section 15.

[106] Australian Public Service Commission, *APS Values and Code of Conduct in Practice: A Guide to Official Conduct for APS Employees and Agency Heads* (revised ed, 2005) ch 1 <http://www.apsc.gov.au/values/conductguidelines.htm> at 4 May 2006.

[107] Explanatory Memorandum, Public Service Bill 1999 (Cth) para 4.2.

[108] Section 22.

[109] Section 25.

[110] Section 24. This power is therefore designed to cover matters not dealt with in awards and agreements: Explanatory Memorandum, Public Service Bill 1999 (Cth) para 4.11.4. The Department of Employment and Workplace Relations advised agencies that the power should be treated as a 'reserve power' and used 'sparingly', in the main as an interim arrangement where a new agency is set up or where genuinely unforeseen circumstances arise during the life of an agreement: *APS Advice 09 of 2000* <http://www.workplace.gov.au/workplace/Organisation/Government/Federal/WRAdvices> at 4 May 2006; Department of Employment and Workplace Relations, *Supporting Guidance for the Workplace Relations Policy Parameters for Agreement Making in the Australian Public Service* (April 2006) 31–2

<http://www.workplace.gov.au/workplace/Organisation/Government/Federal/AgreementMaking> at 4 May 2006.

111 Section 28 and reg 3.10.

112 Section 29.

113 Explanatory Memorandum, Public Service Bill 1999 (Cth) paras 4.11.3, 4.12.

114 Explanatory Memorandum, Public Service Bill 1999 (Cth) para 4.3 and Attachment A.

115 Clause 22, Public Service Bills 1997 and 1999.

116 Clause 29(1), Public Service Bills 1997 and 1999. The PSA 1922 allowed for dismissal of officers only for cause and it specified exclusive grounds and mandatory procedure, and there was a right of appeal to the MPRA. These protections were abandoned by agreement between the government and the public sector unions in 1995. Although the provisions remained in the statute, they were superseded by a certified agreement made under the then *Industrial Relations Act 1988* (Cth) that limited review of termination to the grounds and procedures under that Act. The appeal of the IRA scheme to the unions at the time was that the remedy of compensation was available as an alternative to reinstatement, whereas the MPRA could not order payment of compensation.

117 The phrase 'frank and fearless' is a popular usage. The APS Values in s 10 of the PSA 1999 refer to advice that is 'frank, honest, comprehensive, accurate and timely'.

118 Submissions and evidence by Sir Lenox Hewitt (former head of the Department of Prime Minister), Denis Ives (former Public Service Commissioner), and Derek Volker (former head of several Commonwealth departments) to the Joint Committee of Public Accounts, Parliament of Australia, *Report 353: An Advisory Report on the Public Service Bill 1997 and the Public Employment (Consequential and Transitional) Amendment Bill 1997* (1997).

119 Evidence to Joint Committee of Public Accounts, Commonwealth of Australia, Canberra, 28 August 1997, 220 (Max Moore-Wilton).

120 Section 22(2)–(3).

121 Section 10(1)(n).

122 Section 29(3).

123 Section 29(2).

124 Sections 22(4)–(5), 29(4). Regulations have been made on the circumstances and time limits and extension of fixed term contracts, and on procedure for termination of non-ongoing contracts: *Public Service Regulations 1999* (Cth).

125 The policy was most fully articulated in a joint publication of the Public Service and Merit Protection Commission and the Department of Relations: *The Public Service Act 1997: Accountability in a Devolved Management Framework* (1997), which was published after consultations about the Minister's Discussion Paper, above n 93.

126 See above n 118, 112.

127 (1982) 64 FLR 166.

128 (1982) 64 FLR 166, 174 (Bowen CJ and Lockhart J).

129 (2005) 221 CLR 99, 129, 130-1. The other member of the majority, Gleeson CJ, applied the test of whether the statute gave legal force or effect to the decision. Gleeson CJ also made approving comments about *Burns*. These four members of the Court found that a decision of Griffith University to terminate Tang's PhD program was not made under an enactment.

130 Australian Public Service Commission, *Termination of Employment* (May 2004) section 1.4 <http://www.apsc.gov.au/publications02/terminations.htm> at 4 May 2006.

131 Section 15.

132 The Code of Conduct (s 13(11)) states '[a]n APS employee must at all times behave in a way that upholds the APS Values'. Section 14(1) provides that Agency Heads are bound by the Code of Conduct 'in the same way as APS employees'.

133 There are some exemptions: termination of employment (s 33(1)), and a number set out in sch 1 of the *Public Service Regulations 1999* (Cth) such as engagement of an APS employee, action of a Promotions Review Committee, promotion of an ongoing APS employee as an SES employee, and movement of an APS employee to another agency to give effect to an administrative rearrangement (ie machinery of government changes).

134 *O'Halloran v Wood* [2004] FCA 544 (Unreported, Selway J, 5 May 2004). See also *Anderson v Secretary of the Department of Veterans Affairs* [2004] FCA 1594 (Unreported, Hely J, 8 December 2004) paras 8-9

where the possibility of proceedings under the ADJR Act was noted, and *Twining v Australian Public Service Commission* [2005] FMCA 1738 (Unreported, Mowbray FM, 10 November 2005).

[135] *Sullivan v Secretary, Department of Defence* [2005] FCA 786 (Unreported, Stone J, 20 June 2005).

[136] *Mongan v Woodward* [2003] FCA 66 (Unreported, Finn J, 12 February 2003); *Sullivan v Secretary, Department of Defence* [2005] FCA 786 (Unreported, Stone J, 20 June 2005).

[137] (2005) 221 ALR 95.

[138] (1990) 170 CLR 596, 598 (Mason CJ, Deane and McHugh JJ).

[139] (2005) 221 ALR 95, 102 (Gleeson CJ), 105, 113 (McHugh, Gummow and Hayne JJ), 134–5 (Heydon J).

[140] (2005) 221 ALR 95, 98–9 (Gleeson CJ), 114 (McHugh, Gummow and Hayne JJ), 134–5 (Heydon J). McHugh, Gummow and Hayne JJ noted the views expressed in earlier High Court decisions that dismissal at pleasure was an implied term of the contract of employment (*Ryder, Fletcher* and *Kaye*, discussed above in section 'Dismissal at Pleasure'), but doubted that the modern test for implying terms at law (*Byrne v Australian Airlines Ltd* (1995) 185 CLR 410) would be satisfied.

[141] (2005) 221 ALR 95, 97 (Gleeson CJ).

[142] Ibid 98 (Gleeson CJ).

[143] Ibid 110 (McHugh, Gummow and Hayne JJ), citing the UK cases of *Council of Civil Service Unions v Minister for the Civil Service* [1985] AC 374 and *M v Home Office* [1994] 1 AC 377. Although the High Court has not had to consider these authorities, in obiter dicta in *R v Toohey; Ex parte Northern Land Council* (1981) 151 CLR 170, 219–21, Mason J expressed his view that the exercise of prerogative power was reviewable (although the exercise of some prerogative powers may not be justiciable), and Wilson J expressed agreement (282–3). In *Minister for Arts, Heritage and Environment v Peko-Wallsend Ltd* (1987) 15 FCR 274 the Full Court of the Federal Court adopted the *Council of Civil Service Unions* decision that judicial review was applicable to the exercise of a prerogative power. In *Macrae v Attorney-General for New South Wales* (1987) 9 NSWLR 268, the New South Wales Court of Appeal held that the prerogative power to make judicial appointments was reviewable in a situation where members of a court that had been superseded were invited to apply for membership of the new court. The ground of review was that they had a legitimate expectation of procedural fairness.

[144] (2005) 221 ALR 95, 111 (McHugh, Gummow and Hayne JJ).

[145] WR Act 1996 s 415 (s 170WK prior to 27 March 2006).

[146] WR Act 1996 ss 348–349 and *Workplace Relations Regulations 2006* (Cth) regs 8.2 and 8.3 (prior to 27 March 2006, ss 170VQ and 170VR and *Workplace Relations Regulations 1996* (Cth) reg 30ZJ(1)(a)(i)).

[147] A more definitive stand has been taken since the passage of the Work Choices legislation (the *Workplace Relations Amendment (Work Choices) Act 2005* (Cth)): SES employees should be covered by AWAs and excluded from collective agreements (Department of Employment and Workplace Relations (2006), above n 110, 19).

[148] The Department of Employment and Workplace Relations publishes statistics on agreement making in federal government employment at <http://www.workplace.gov.au/workplace/Organisation/Government/Federal/Reports/ProgressinAgreementMaking.htm> at 4 May 2006; and for 30 June 2007 data accessed July 2007.

[149] Australian Public Service Commission, *The Australian Public Service Statistical Bulletin 2004–05* (2005) <http://www.apsc.gov.au/stateoftheservice/0405/statistics/index.html> at 4 May 2006.

[150] Australian Parliamentary Service Commissioner, *Annual Report 2004–05* (2005), 7.

[151] And to exclude unions.

[152] WR Act 1996 s 165 and *Workplace Relations Regulations 2006* (Cth) reg 5.3 (previously ss 83BS, 83BT, 170VG(2), 170WHB, 170WHC, 170WHD). It is government policy that collective agreements (formerly Certified agreements) — now lodged with the Workplace Authority, formerly the Employment Advocates — will continue to be published.

[153] Two examples of disclosure are given in a report by the Senate Finance and Public Administration References Committee, Parliament of Australia, *Australian Public Service Employment Matters, First Report, Australian Workplace Agreements* (2000) paras 2.42–2.43.

[154] See above n 148.

[155] PSA 1999 s 10(1); see section' Values and Code of Conduct' above.

[156] See above n 153, para 2.73.

[157] Ibid para 6.1.

[158] Ibid para 1.13 (citing an earlier report by the Committee on performance pay). The government response was to disagree with the Committee, stressing the importance of performance pay for attracting and rewarding high-quality staff (Australian Public Service Commission, *A History in Three Acts*, above n 90, 191).

[159] Public Service Commissioner, *State of the Service Report 2004–05* (2005) 104. The Commissioner had previously raised the issue in the reports for 2002–03 and 2003–04.

[160] According to Weller, above n 82, 25, the power was rarely used before 1972. Then the Whitlam government, which came to power after 23 years of non-Labor administration, abolished several departments. Keating, above n 85, 42 notes that heads of departments ceased to be permanent from the Whitlam-era when more than half the heads were displaced in less than three years.

[161] *Public Service Amendment (First Division Officers) Act 1976* (Cth).

[162] Weller, above n 82, 27 reports that no 'non-established' candidate was selected

[163] *Public Service Reform Act 1984* (Cth).

[164] *Administrative Arrangements Act 1987* (Cth).

[165] Weller, above n 82, 80.

[166] Ibid 29, 65 points out that ministerial involvement varies with circumstances, including the timing of the change (distinguishing a one-off change of Secretary from the multiple changes flowing from changes to machinery of government), the influence of the minister, and their relationship with the Prime Minister.

[167] *Prime Minister and Cabinet (Miscellaneous Provisions) Act 1994* (Cth).

[168] Weller, above n 82, 33. Also, in 1998, a meeting of Secretaries was told that the Prime Minister was not satisfied with the performance of a number of them, and there would be a review. In the event, no changes were made.

[169] Weller, above n 82, 31 reports that the initiative for this reform came largely from within the APS and that the figure of 20 per cent for the pay loading was recommended by a committee of secretaries. Keating, above n 85, 42 reports that before the 1994 legislation, the majority of displaced secretaries were taking the offer of a financial package.

[170] In 1999, the Remuneration Tribunal's function changed from determining Secretaries' remuneration and allowances to providing advice on those matters: *Public Employment (Consequential and Transitional) Amendment Act 1999* (Cth) sch 1, clauses 778, 780.

[171] Submissions to the Joint Committee of Public Accounts, *Report* 353, above n 118, 117–9.

[172] In the case of the appointment or termination of the appointment of the Secretary of the Department of the Prime Minister and Cabinet, the report is to be provided by the Public Service Commissioner.

[173] *Barratt v Howard* (1999) 165 ALR 605. Factual background on the relationship between the Minister and Barratt is set out in the appeal case, *Barratt v Howard* (2000) 96 FCR 428, and more detail is provided by Weller, above n 82, ch 9.

[174] (1990) 170 CLR 596, 598 (Mason CJ, Deane and McHugh JJ).

[175] (1999) 165 ALR 605, 619.

[176] Ibid.

[177] *Barratt v Howard* [1999] FCA 1183 (Unreported, Hely J, 26 August 1999).

[178] Ibid para 7.

[179] *Barratt v Howard* (2000) 96 FCR 428.

[180] The Full Court did not cite any authority for the finding that the Act overrode the common law — (2000) 96 FCR 428, 448; Hely J (1999) 165 ALR 605, 609 cited *Dixon* and *Bennett* (discussed above in 'Judicial Review' and 'Contract').

[181] (2000) 96 FCR 428, 449.

[182] Ibid.

[183] Weller, above n 82, 35.

[184] In 'Departmental Secretaries: Appointment, Termination and their Impact' (1997) 56(4) *Australian Journal of Public Administration* 13, they report the results of a research project commissioned by the Institute of Public Administration (ACT Division) to evaluate the appointment, termination, and terms of engagement of federal departmental secretaries in the context of the move to fixed term appointments from 1994. Their research includes interviews with 20 past and serving secretaries. In the book *Australia's*

*Mandarins*, above n 82, Weller draws on a more extensive range of interviews of former and current Secretaries.

[185] Weller and Wanna, above n 184, 22.

[186] Ibid 23.

[187] Weller, above n 82, ch 5.

[188] Ibid 12.

[189] Richard Mulgan, 'Politicisation of Senior Appointments in the Australian Public Service' (1998) 57(3) *Australian Journal of Public Administration* 3, 5-6.

[190] Ibid 5–7. Weller, above n 82, 13 prefers to characterise these latter practices as 'personalisation' rather than 'politicisation'.

[191] Public Service Commissioner, above n 159, 35-43. There were similar figures reported in the 2003–4 Report. In the State of the Service Report 2005 -6 it was stated: 'There continues to be slightly lower levels of confidence that most senior managers act in accordance with the Values (73 per cent) although this has continued to increase from 63 per cent in 2003. The majority of employees in each large agency agreed that most senior managers act in accordance with the Values, with results ranging from 61 per cent to 86 per cent.' <http://www.apsc.gov.au/stateoftheservice/0506/fourembedding. htm> 30 July 2007.

[192] Peter Shergold, Secretary of the Department of the Prime Minister and Cabinet, 'Once was Camelot in Canberra? Reflections on Public Service Leadership' (Sir Roland Wilson Lecture 2004, Canberra, 23 June 2004) <http://www.pmc.gov.au/speeches> at 4 May 2006.

[193] Senate Finance and Public Administration References Committee, Parliament of Australia, *Staff Employed under the Members of Parliament (Staff) Act 1984* (2003) paras 7.9–7.16.

[194] Lynelle Briggs, Public Service Commissioner, 'Public service reform' (Speech delivered to SES Breakfast, 12 May 2005); Lynelle Briggs, Public Service Commissioner, 'Changes in the Australian Public Service' (Speech delivered to the Australian National Audit Office, 29 November 2005); Lynelle Briggs, Public Service Commissioner, 'State of the Service Report 2004–05, Launch Speech' (Speech delivered, 1 December 2005). All can be found at <http://www.apsc.gov.au/about/pscommissioner.htm#media> at 4 May 2006.

[195] Quoted in Karlene Sargent, 'Employer of Choice? Today's Australian Public Service', *Defence Magazine* (The Official Magazine, Department of Defence, Canberra) August 2005 <http://www.defence.gov.au/defencemagazine/editions/20050801/sections/bigpicture.htm> at 4 May 2006. Other issues flagged by the Commissioner were streamlining the APS Values, the inflexibility of the conditions for non-ongoing employment, management by agencies of review of actions and code of conduct issues, and whistleblowing.

[196] Australian Public Service Commission, *Embedding the APS Values* (2003) <http://www.apsc.gov.au/values/values.htm> at 4 May 2006.

[197] Briggs 'State of the Service Report 2004–05', launch speech, above n 194.

[198] Lynelle Briggs, Public Service Commissioner, 'Supporting Ministers, Upholding the Values: A Good Practice Guide, Launch Speech' (Speech delivered 9 March 2006) <http://www.apsc.gov.au/media/briggs090306. htm> at 4 May 2006.

[199] Senate Finance and Public Administration References Committee, *Staff Employed Under the Members of Parliament (Staff) Act 1984*, above n 193, recommendation 18.

[200] Supported by Weller, above n 82, ch 10; Australian Public Service Commission, *A History in Three Acts*, above n 90, 214–5; Mulgan, 'Politicisation of Senior Appointments in the Australian Public Service', above n 189, 11; Keating, above n 85, 42.

[201] Australian Public Service Commission, *Supporting Ministers, Upholding the Values: A Good Practice Guide* (2006) <http://www.apsc.gov.au/publications06/supportingministers.htm> at 4 May 2006.

[202] Recommended by two Senate committees: the Senate Select Committee, Parliament of Australia, *A Certain Maritime Incident* (2002) recommendation 11, and Senate Finance and Public Administration References Committee, *Staff Employed Under the Members of Parliament (Staff) Act 1984*, above n 193, ch 6.

[203] John Nethercote, 'Values in Contention: Some Key Administrative Issues in 2002' (2003) 62(1) *Australian Journal of Public Administration* 88, 91; Australian Public Service Commission, *A History in Three Acts*, above n 90, 225–6.

[204] Quoted in 'A Healthy Public Service is a Vital Part of Australia's Democratic System of Government' (1998) 57(1) *Australian Journal of Public Administration* 3, 11.

# Chapter Three

# The Australian Public Service: Statutory, Doctrinal and Institutional Arrangements for its Governance

## J. R. Nethercote

The sixty years since the Second World War have seen a marked transformation of the Australian Public Service ('APS'). Major changes have included a very substantial expansion of functions as the role of the Commonwealth within the federation has grown, particularly the emergence of a comprehensive welfare state; consolidation of Commonwealth administration, especially as a consequence of relocating it from Melbourne to Canberra; increasing educational standards such that what had been a largely (veteran) clerical workforce is now very much a graduate workforce; computerisation of administration; and a more diverse demographic composition in which women as well as many people from non-English speaking backgrounds are now employed at all levels of Commonwealth administration. This period also witnessed, in the first instance, increased centralisation of administration followed in the past two and a half decades with a new departmentalism in which the old goal of a unified service derived from the Northcote-Trevelyan report is mainly now manifested at senior executive levels.

This transformation of the APS is clearly manifest in statutory, doctrinal and institutional arrangements for its governance. This observation applies to both the basic legislation, invariably entitled the Public Service Act, and to the central institutions with responsibilities for APS policy and management. It is the purpose of this chapter to provide an account of the main features of these governance arrangements identifiable in the various statutes, doctrines and structures upon which the management and organisation of the APS are based. This account will centre on an analysis of contemporary arrangements as contained largely but not exclusively in the latest *Public Service Act 1999* (Cth) ('PSA 1999'). It is, however, an important goal of this chapter to place the 1999 settlement in context. Showing the similarities and differences between the 1999 regime and its predecessors assists both to illustrate the transformation of the APS and to provide important insights into the character of the changes.

In exploring the governance fabric of the APS, it is enlightening to observe both similarities and differences with the public service of other countries where government is based on traditions and practices which have evolved in Westminster and Whitehall. Australia, at both national and state level, has generally had a distinctive approach to questions of public service management. New Zealand, not unexpectedly, is the only other country with an essentially similar approach historically, but in recent decades the similarities have been less pronounced.[1] In a doctrinal sense, there are inevitably close affinities with the United Kingdom Home Civil Service. There are, however, marked differences as well, some of which will be highlighted in this chapter. Likewise, the national public service of Canada has important similarities with the APS, sharing many doctrines about the role and responsibilities of the public service in government which reflect in some measure their common derivation from, as well as deferral to, Whitehall. Again there are also conspicuous and overt differences.

In the century and more of its existence, it is possible to discern various features or properties which have characterised public service administration in Australian national government. To some extent, these might even be described as foundational 'principles', though this is misleading if it is taken to suggest some rule which is either immutable or a means of discerning a correct or preferred method of addressing a particular issue. A number of features of Australian public service development are creatures of a particular stage of growth in the history of the service, or of the nation. Their expression and even validity is essentially contingent upon the circumstances of a particular time. For the purposes of this chapter, the following features or properties have been identified as providing a framework for understanding the structure, development and contemporary mould of the APS:

- Ministerial (government) control of administration, including organisation and financing. In contemporary institutional terms, this places great power in the hands of the Secretary to the Department of the Prime Minister and Cabinet. It also means that the Department of Finance (since 1997, Department of Finance and Administration) is a pervasive presence in many matters of public service policy.
- The basic rules for managing the APS are embodied in Acts of Parliament.
- Within the framework of responsible government, management and control of the public service is vested in officials with statutory powers, namely, a commissioner (previously a board of commissioners), and the heads of departments. Historically, the commissioner/board of commissioners had comprehensive responsibilities and powers. Under the PSA 1999, central responsibilities are ostensibly limited as are the powers. Ministerial control has grown in the field of workplace relations; formerly an indirect, even latent influence, it is now direct and active.

- The ministerial department and other similar organisations such as the Australian Taxation Office, the Australian Bureau of Statistics and the Australian Customs Service are the basic units of administration and many powers and responsibilities are vested in their chief executive officers (department secretaries) — or, in the instances referred to above, the Commissioner for Taxation, the Australian Statistician and the Comptroller-General of Customs.

- A major objective of public service legislation has been insulation of individual personnel decisions from ministerial direction and influence. These decisions include appointments, promotions, transfers, terminations and, in some measure, classification of posts.

- Upon this foundation, the APS is a 'career-based service' in which 'employment decisions are based on merit'.[2]

- Since 1984, control and management of the size and cost of public service employment has been handled within the conventional financial and budgetary system. For a major part of its history, the major method of allocating and controlling personnel resources of the APS was establishment management, through creation, salary classification and abolition of 'offices', conventionally known as positions.

- Public service workplace relations are regarded principally as a field of industrial relations, not a matter of public budgeting. Thus, when the comprehensive central personnel agency — the Public Service Board — was abolished in 1987, central responsibilities for pay and conditions of employment were assigned to the new Department of Industrial Relations (now the Department of Employment and Workplace Relations), not to the Department of Finance.

- Values and standards of conduct are statutorily codified and prescribed.

- For almost its entire history, the APS has recognised the right of employee association. Workplace relations procedures have included an acknowledged role for unions, for long known as staff associations. Recognition of the right of employee association has not, however, extended to recognition of the right to strike, which has never been accepted and is invariably challenged.

- A corollary of the recognised right of association has been provision (at least until 2006) for third-party arbitration of disputes, either by the national arbitration tribunal or in a specialist public sector arbitration jurisdiction.

- From its earliest years, the APS has accorded rights of appeal and grievance to its staff.

- In defining the responsibilities, duties and obligations of staff, the APS has increasingly acknowledged their rights of citizenship.

It is not the aim of this chapter to deal comprehensively with all these essential features of the Australian approach to public service management. The focus here is the statutory, doctrinal and institutional framework of the APS, and each of the foregoing features is of major relevance in providing the framework for an exploration of the disposition of authority over and within the APS.

## Ministerial Control over Government Administration

In Australia, one of the least trammelled prerogatives of executive government — in this instance, the Prime Minister — is the creation and abolition of departments[3] and the allocation of functions to and between them. Although there are statutory limits on the number of ministers,[4] there are no limits on the number of departments nor any prohibition on the number of departments an individual minister may administer. The relevant information is contained in the Administrative Arrangements Order issued periodically by the Governor-General, often following general elections and the swearing in of a reshuffled or new ministry. It lists the legislation for which portfolio ministers are responsible, and the principal matters with which their departments deal. (It is rare for the principal minister in a portfolio to have responsibility for more than one department. The only occasion in recent times was when Laurie Brereton was Minister for Transport and Minister for Industrial Relations in the Keating Government, 1993–96.)

The greatest political significance attaches to the prerogative of deciding the functions of each department. The views of Prime Minister R G (later Sir Robert) Menzies in November 1957 have as much force today as they did half a century ago:

> It is only the Government, acting under the control of Parliament, which can decide what functions are to be performed by the various departments. The decision is a peculiarly political one, and is, of course, affected by the views which any Government may hold or the electorate may demand … Since only the Government can determine these matters, no Government can escape its responsibility for reviewing these functions to determine whether any of them are unnecessary or performed to an undue extent, or badly placed in the general departmental organization … I do not think it would be seriously said that such problems as these should be off-loaded by the Government on to some entirely non-political authority.[5]

Departments have been staffed almost exclusively by the APS since the inception of the Commonwealth. The APS is, in this sense, a general purpose workforce for government departments and kindred agencies (see below), although there have been several cases, mainly in the Defence field, where departments have had separate employing authority — for example, the Department of the Navy under the *Naval Defence Act 1910* (Cth) or the Department of Supply under the *Supply and Development Act 1939* (Cth). The various trade departments (currently the Department of Foreign Affairs and Trade) have also had separate employing authority under the *Trade Commissioners Act 1933* (Cth).

Successive Public Service Acts have always assumed that government agencies other than departments of State will be staffed by the APS, for example, the Audit Office (now known as the Australian National Audit Office) or the Australian Taxation Office. In these two cases (and several others), the *Public Service Act 1922* (Cth) included a provision vesting the chief executive, respectively the Auditor-General and the Commissioner for Taxation, with the powers of a permanent head (subsequently designated departmental secretary). In other cases, legislation establishing a statutory authority staffed by public servants would include a provision vesting the chief executive officer (however designated) with secretary powers. For example, when the Australian Bureau of Statistics, previously the Statistician's Branch of the Treasury, was established as a statutory authority in 1974, the legislation stated that the Australian Statistician had the powers of a permanent head under the *Public Service Act 1922* (Cth). During the mid- and late 1970s, and for much of the 1980s, there were more than 50 statutory officials with department head powers.

The PSA 1999 specifically includes provision for a secondary agency, namely Executive Agencies, which like departments themselves are established by the Governor-General (s 65).

A final component in a government's control of the machinery of government, though one requiring parliamentary approval, is its prerogative to establish organisations in varying degrees outside the departmental/public service system. These have long been a feature of Australian Government. Some examples are the Commonwealth Bank, established in 1911 and privatised progressively by the Hawke-Keating Labor governments in the late 1980s and early 1990s; the Reserve Bank (1959); Trans-Australia Airlines (later Australian Airlines); and the Australian Law Reform Commission (1974). Conditions of employment in many bodies, such as the CSIRO and administrative posts at the Australian Broadcasting Commission ('ABC'), have at various times been subject to the approval of an APS employment authority, usually the Public Service Board.

Such bodies may move in or out of the departmental system. The Repatriation Commission, for instance, was created as a statutory body in 1921. In 1947, it was brought within the departmental system, though it was not until 1974 that the position of the chief executive (the President of the Repatriation Commission) was fully regularised. Conversely, the Postmaster-General's Department, long known as the Post Office, was one of the founding departments of the Commonwealth. Commencing 1 July 1975, it was separated entirely from the APS and replaced by the Australian Telecommunications and Postal commissions. Telecom, now known as Telstra, has since been semi-privatised by the Howard Government.

Responsibility for the machinery of government is one of a Prime Minister's most crucial strategic roles, and one with a huge bearing on the place of the APS in government. As a consequence, it means that in such matters, the Department of the Prime Minister and Cabinet is a major part of the institutional structure. Historically this has been exemplified, for instance, in its secretary's membership of the Permanent Heads Committee, together with the head of the Treasury and the Chairman of the Public Service Board. Its task was to advise the Higher Salaries Committee of the Cabinet on top salaries and related matters.[6] These tasks have been handled by the Remuneration Tribunal since 1974.

The Prime Minister's power over the APS is now underwritten by the PSA 1999. It authorises the Prime Minister to 'issue general directions in writing to Agency Heads relating to the management and leadership of APS employees'.[7] It requires the Secretary of the Department of the Prime Minister and Cabinet to report to the Prime Minister before any appointment to a secretary vacancy is made.[8]

This responsibility of the Secretary of the Department of the Prime Minister and Cabinet is of recent origin; it dates from amendments in 1987 to the *Public Service Act 1922* (Cth) following abolition of the Public Service Board. Previously, from 1976 until 1987, the statutory duty of reporting to the Prime Minister on secretary appointments was in the hands of the Chairman of the Board, assisted by a committee from 1976 until 1984. In earlier times, the Chairman of the Board had often but by no means invariably performed the role of advising on top appointments by administrative arrangement. Until at least the mid-1960s such appointments usually involved the departmental minister more than the Prime Minister; it is unclear when the Prime Minister became the lead figure, but it had certainly become the case by the time the Whitlam Government took office on 5 December 1972.

The current arrangement at both ministerial and official levels reflects declared practice in Whitehall since 1983 (effectively 1981) and Ottawa since the mid-1960s. It is nevertheless contentious. It concentrates the advisory role in a single individual, one who is more actively involved with ministers than officials. There has been a good deal of criticism, much of it focussed on the high probability that appointees would be drawn from the deputy secretary ranks of the Department of the Prime Minister and Cabinet. Given that the Secretary of the Department would in any case be involved, it would be preferable for responsibility for advice to rest with the Public Service Commissioner, particularly having regard to the Commissioner's role in all appointments to and within the Senior Executive Service.

## Statutory Regulation of the Australian Public Service

The earliest appointments to the APS, apart from those State public servants transferred to the national government under the *Australian Constitution* when the Commonwealth was formed on 1 January 1901, were made under s 67 of the *Australian Constitution*:

> Until the Parliament otherwise provides, the appointment and removal of all other officers of the Executive Government of the Commonwealth shall be vested in the Governor-General in Council, unless the appointment is delegated by the Governor-General in Council or by the law of the Commonwealth to some other authority.

Section 67 is still occasionally used, but it was not very long before the inaugural government of the Commonwealth introduced a Public Service Bill which was adopted in 1902. It was overtaken by another Act in 1922. As already noted, Australia's third and latest *Public Service Act* dates from 1999; like the 1902 Act, it had a long journey through Parliament. Like the 1922 Act, there was a long hiatus between the time when it became apparent that new legislation was highly desirable and its eventual realisation. First mooted during the early 1990s, a bill was finally introduced in June 1997. It was subject to detailed inquiry by the Joint Committee of Public Accounts, most of whose recommendations for amendment were incorporated. A revised bill was reintroduced following the 1998 elections and eventually passed the Senate after much debate, which included provisions relating to staff appeal rights and procedures.

The PSA 1999 is the statutory basis for Australia's now highly departmentalised public service in which centralisation is minimised but hardly eliminated; in which ministerial control in most fields is reasserted except in individual personnel decisions[9] and in which public service workplace relations are largely re-integrated with the national system.[10] Articulation of APS Values[11] and the APS Code of Conduct[12] give effect to the current approach to public service identity based on values rather than, as has been claimed, a unified pay and grading system. According to s 3, the objects of the Act are:

a. to establish an apolitical public service that is efficient and effective in serving the Government, the Parliament and the Australian public; and
b. to provide a legal framework for the effective and fair employment, management and leadership of APS employees; and
c. to define the powers, functions and responsibilities of Agency Heads, the Public Service Commissioner and the Merit Protection Commissioner; and
d. to establish rights and obligations of APS employees.

This statement is a reflection of legislative drafting practice in the past decade and a half. There is no comparable statement in either of the predecessor Acts as it was not then the fashion to include declarations of this character. The 1902 Act was designed for a Commissioner-managed public service. The first purpose was to bring some order (commonality) to the disparate assortment of organisations — the Post Office, Defence, Trade and Customs — inherited from the colonies on or shortly after establishment of the Commonwealth. It also entailed fostering some commonality of practice in the four, very small departments the Commonwealth created for itself: External Affairs; Attorney-General's; Home Affairs; and the Treasury. General management power was comprehensively vested in the commissioner, appointed for a seven-year term, though 'Chief Officers' had authority for a range of day-to-day decision-making.

Although not explicitly stated, chief officers were conceptually the heads of State branches of departments; this level of management may also have been recognised as a form of delegation within departments themselves. In cases of departments inherited from the States, it was a means of assuaging injury to pride of former department heads now subordinate to the head of the department at the new Commonwealth level of government. There was a certain irony in the largely successful attempt to bring the whole public service, wherever people were actually employed, within a single system in that it remained in terms of career paths a basically departmentalised and, indeed, State-based, service. There was practically no inter-departmental mobility.

Following election of a Labor Government led by Andrew Fisher in 1910 — the first government in the history of the Commonwealth to have majorities in both Houses of the Parliament — the first circumscription of the Commissioner's powers was effected. By separate legislation, public service unions won access to the Commonwealth Court of Conciliation and Arbitration for settlement of disputes about pay and employment conditions.[13]

The wide-ranging statutory powers of the Commissioner can be explained in a number of ways. The most obvious was simply emulation of recent State public service legislation designed to promote efficiency, economy and competence, and to eliminate corruption, in New South Wales and Victoria (72 of its 80 sections had counterparts in the legislation of those States).

The major weakness of the 1902 Act was its completely inadequate treatment of the departmental side of public administration. Illustrative of this deficiency was its failure to provide a clear procedure for appointment of department heads. Nor did it clearly set out their powers, or the procedures by which the system was to work.

The 1922 Act replaced a commissioner-centred public service with one supervised by the Public Service Board but with a high level of definition of the department head role in establishments and, after 1925 amendments, promotions and transfers. The move towards the departmentalised service embodied in the PSA 1999 was under way. One explanation for these particular characteristics of the new public service regime is that its major architect was a department head, Sir Robert Garran, Secretary to the Attorney-General's Department, Solicitor-General and parliamentary draftsman. The Board's exclusive role in recruitment and appointment remained. The wide-ranging central powers of determination of pay and employment conditions were now subject to a Public Service Arbitrator, created in 1920 also by separate legislation.[14]

The 1922 Act, amended substantially from time to time — notably in 1935 (graduate recruitment), 1946 (promotions appeals) and 1960 (general recruitment) — remained viable until the early 1970s. Thereafter, it became increasingly unwieldy and prone to additions of a most detailed kind, partly a consequence of union demands that changes be incorporated in legislation and partly in an effort to cope with the unstable departmental structure of the period from 1972 to 1987. Important statutory changes such as winding back the traditional tenure of public servants were sensibly addressed in separate legislation;[15] such legislation (like that removing the prohibition on permanent employment of married women in 1966[16] ) had application to other areas of public sector employment, not simply the APS alone.

The law covering public service employment is thus found in many other Acts as well the Public Service Act for the time being.[17] Public Service legislation also includes rule-making authority for the major agents. The 1922 Act empowered the Board to make regulations and determinations;[18] for administrative convenience, it also issued General Orders, which had the effect of law. The Public Service Arbitrator made determinations; these became awards when the jurisdiction was merged with that of the Conciliation and Arbitration Commission in 1984.

The PSA 1999 is buttressed by Commissioner's Directions issued under ss 11, 15 and 36 (see also s 42). In length these already rival the Act itself. The Act also authorises the Prime Minister to issue general directions to Agency Heads. Similarly, the Act authorises the 'Public Service Minister … by notice in the Gazette, [to] make rules about classifications of APS employees'.[19]

In an abstract sense, management of a public service in Australia by means of legislation is a matter of choice: indeed, the 1994 Review of the Public Service Act was advised by the Attorney-General's Department that the decision to have a new Act was 'a policy decision not a legal requirement'.[20]

That great source of wisdom on public service management, the 1853 report on *The Organisation of the Permanent Civil Service* by Sir Stafford Northcote and Sir Charles Trevelyan, concluded with a strong recommendation in favour of legislation:

> It remains for us to express our conviction that if any change of the importance of those which we have recommended is to be carried into effect, it can only be successfully done through the medium of an Act of Parliament. The existing system is supported by long usage and powerful interests; and were any Government to introduce material

alterations into it, in consequence of their own convictions, without taking the precaution to give those alterations the force of law, it is almost certain that they would be imperceptibly, or perhaps avowedly, abandoned by their successors, if they were not even allowed to fall into disuse by the very Government which had originated them. A few clauses would accomplish all that is proposed in this paper, and it is our firm belief that a candid statement of the grounds of the measure would insure its success and popularity in the country, and would remove many misconceptions which are now prejudicial to the public service.[21]

Legislation was promised by the Queen in a Speech from the Throne in 1855 but, in the event, the mid-nineteenth century reformers had to make do with an Order-in-Council. The Home Civil Service, in the subsequent century and a half, has occasionally been touched by legislation but there has never been anything approaching antipodean public service legislation.[22]

The Canadian public service has had a different experience with legislation. In its first four decades, there were several ineffectual pieces of legislation designed to bring a measure of direction to the development of the infant public service, mainly elimination of patronage in recruitment. Early in the twentieth century (1908) there was a concerted effort to improve efficiency through central recruitment. This early effort was followed a decade later at the end of the Great War with a comprehensive *Civil Service Act 1918* similar to the 1902 Australian Act rather than the later 1922 legislation. Being Commission-centred, it was deficient (like the 1902 Australian Act) in omitting to define the respective roles and powers of the central agency and department heads (deputy ministers). In 1967, a package of three laws was enacted, providing detailed regulation of the staffing (merit) system and the newly-introduced public service collective bargaining regime, but with only minimal coverage of the preponderant administrative power located in the Treasury Board, a statutory committee of the Cabinet, and its Secretariat.[23] Once again, the legislation failed (and did not overtly seek) to capture the dynamics of the relationship between the central agencies on one hand and the departments on the other.

The 1994 Review Group in Canberra concluded that there were 'sound policy and practical reasons for having a Public Service Act' and stated that 'it is essential that there continue to be an Act'.[24] Its reasons for this recommendation included various distinctions between public sector and private sector employment practice, including requirements of loyal and impartial service to ministers and of 'merit-based selection of staff for appointment and advancement which excludes nepotism, favouritism and unfair discrimination,' and of '"best employer" practice in the application of equal employment opportunity and social justice policies and practices laid down by the [then Labor] Government'.[25] According to the Review Group:

> The Public Service Act creates the structure of the APS as an entity, as distinct from an aggregation of separate employing bodies which would be the case if the common law was the only basis of employment. It provides a legal basis for the Parliament to express the important values and culture it wants in the Public Service.[26]

Another important advantage of legislation, the Review Group continued, was that it established 'the roles and powers of secretaries and their relationship with ministers in a clear, unambiguous and public way (an aspect of public accountability)'. Furthermore, '[i]f there were no Act, there would be no Public Service Commissioner (or equivalent office) and the underlying APS policy framework would be an amalgam of decisions of Executive Government, of the industrial relations system and of the courts'.[27]

## The Central Public Service Management Agency

A major rationale for a Public Service Act is the constitution of a central non-ministerial public service management agency. The PSA 1999 states that one of its objects is 'to define the powers, functions and responsibilities of ... the Public Service Commissioner and the Merit Protection Commissioner'.[28] Two of Australia's Acts have created an office of Public Service Commissioner; in the 1902 Act, a mighty figure with comprehensive powers over recruitment, promotion, classification, discipline, dismissal, pay and employment conditions; the Commissioner in the PSA 1999 has a range of operational responsibilities for management of the Senior Executive Service but is otherwise charged with fostering the professional and ethical character of the APS, particularly by enhancing observance of the merit principle and by upholding and promoting the APS Values.[29]

The Commissioner under the 1902 Act was only appointed for a prescribed period (seven years) — it was the only post in government at the time for which there was a statutory term of office. By contrast, under the original *Audit Act 1901* (Cth), the Auditor-General, like a judge, was appointed without any limit, even that of retirement at age 65 (a provision of this sort was later inserted after the first Auditor-General remained in office until death at age 76). This early distinction between the Commonwealth's first two statutory officers is readily explained. The Public Service Commissioner, though vested with an array of powers under statute and with an obligation to report annually to the Parliament, is unequivocally an officer of the Executive Government. The Auditor-General is a public officer, plainly not part of the Executive Government, with statutory reporting duties to the Parliament on the performance of Executive Government in the management of public finances.

In Britain, the executive (though not necessarily ministerial) character of all powers relating to the working of the Home Civil Service is never questioned;

powers thought inappropriate for ministers, mainly initial selection and appointment, are in the hands of the Civil Service Commission appointed by the Crown. In Canada, by contrast, the Public Service Commission is often seen as an agency of the Parliament; this role is not explicitly stated in the legislation. This conception is erroneous; it fails to distinguish between a body derivative of parliamentary functions (which do not include appointments or other staffing actions) and one which performs executive functions under statute; a responsibility to report to parliament does not, of itself, take an organisation beyond the pale of the Executive branch.

The founding Commonwealth Public Service Commissioner served two terms of seven years. The post was then filled on a temporary basis for a further seven years until the three-commissioner Public Service Board took office on 1 July 1923. The board created by the 1922 Act inherited the Public Service Commissioner's comprehensive responsibilities but in a supervisory rather than operational mode, thus explicitly incorporating department heads in the management system. The new Act also included a charter for the Board to review administrative activity with a view to achieving efficiencies and economies.[30] The new charter gave a greater sense of purpose to the Board's regular duties as much as acting as a basis for discrete reviews and investigations which it carried out from time to time.

It was not long before the three-member board fell victim to economies brought on by the Depression of the early 1930s. Apart from the chairman, commissioners were not replaced on retirement. There were nevertheless a few important developments during the 1930s of which the quest for recruitment of graduates for general administration is the most well known. It was only as the Second World War was drawing to a close that the composition of the Board was reappraised in the context of preparing the APS for the post-war world. The Chifley Government decided to reconstitute the three-member board from 1 January 1947. Pressure for a step of this kind came, inter alia, from the unions; one of their purposes, briefly accomplished, was to secure appointment of a commissioner with a staff association background.

Until its abolition in July 1987, apart from the inaugural chairman, chairmen were either drawn from the ranks of department secretaries or departmental officers effectively of deputy secretary rank. Those in the first category were W E (later Sir William) Dunk (External Affairs); A S (later Sir Alan) Cooley (Supply); R W (later Sir William) Cole (Finance); and Dr P S Wilenski (Labor and Immigration, later Education and Youth Affairs). Those of deputy secretary rank were F H (later Sir Frederick) Wheeler (formerly Treasury, returning to the APS after eight years as Treasurer of the International Labour Organisation); and K C O (later Sir Keith) Shann (Department of Foreign Affairs, upon return to Australia after several years as Australian Ambassador to Japan).

Of the seven chairmen, all but Cole were reappointed if available. Three retired from the post — Thorpe (1947); Dunk (1960); and Shann (1978). Four subsequently took department secretary posts — Wheeler, the Treasury, 1971; Cooley, Productivity, 1977; Cole, Defence, 1984; and Wilenski, Transport and Communications, 1987–88 and later, Foreign Affairs and Trade, 1992–93 (after a posting as Australian Representative at the United Nations in New York). Commissioners were mainly drawn from the ranks of department heads (1948–68), senior departmental officers (1974–86) and senior Public Service Board staff (1947–81). Two commissioners were drawn from the staff associations, one for a short period in 1947, and another from 1973 until 1977. Until 1975, all commissioners available for reappointment were, with one exception, reappointed; the exception moved to a post in a government company. With that exception, all indeed retired from the APS upon ceasing to be commissioners although one undertook a review of Australia House before actually leaving. After 1977, only one commissioner retired; the remainder were appointed to various senior government posts including departmental headships and one as Auditor-General; another became Auditor-General after an interval, first as a department head and then as consul-general in New York.

Abolition of the Public Service Board in 1987 saw revival of the post of Public Service Commissioner. The new post was not in any sense a recreation of the earlier office with the same designation. The new commissioner's responsibilities were mainly staffing in character; in an operational sense, concerning mainly the Senior Executive Service, which had been created in 1984.

Since 1987, there have been six commissioners, only one of whom has served a full term. Three were department secretaries prior to appointment — John Enfield, Helen Williams and Andrew Podger. Lynelle Briggs, Commissioner since 2004, was a deputy secretary prior to apppointment. One was subsequently appointed as a department head — Peter Shergold — and another was so reappointed — Helen Williams. Three have effectively retired from the post — Enfield, Denis Ives, and Podger.

The office of Public Service Commissioner as created under the PSA 1999 is unusual. It is located within the Prime Minister's portfolio and in a number of respects is a subordinate agency of the Department of the Prime Minister and Cabinet. The Commissioner's performance is not, however, subject to review for performance pay purposes. On the other hand, the independence of the post has, in the case of the last two appointments, been qualified by terms of office of three years; in the first case, the three-year appointment dated from the period immediately following the 2001 general elections; his successor was likewise appointed for a three-year term immediately following the general election of October 2004.

An important justification in the past for a statutory officer/board structure lay in divorcing the Government collectively and ministers individually from decisions relating to pay and conditions of appointment. This justification was supported by a view that it was beneficial to separate the Government's national roles in industrial relations from its role as employer (indeed, one of the largest employers in the country). A similar division of role had occurred in various Australian states and in New Zealand, for similar reasons. From 1917 until 1967, there was a comparable division in the Canadian civil service, but for partially different and complex reasons concerning the perceived impossibility of negotiating with the Crown over remuneration.

In Britain, civil service pay has always fallen directly under the responsibility of ministers and for most of the time, the Treasury. Likewise, since 1967, public service pay in Canada, under a collective bargaining structure, is a Treasury Board (that is, ministerial) responsibility.

When the Australian Public Service Board was dismembered in 1987, the pay and conditions role was vested in the new Department of Industrial Relations and not the Department of Finance. The role has changed in the subsequent two decades, as departments and agencies have been vested with greater autonomy in remuneration matters but general policy has remained with the various successor departments of Industrial Relations, currently Employment and Workplace Relations. Notwithstanding the historical rationale, actual settlement of pay matters does not appear to have become a major preoccupation of ministers.

## Departments and Agencies as the Basic Unit of Management

The basic unit of management in the APS is the department, or a comparable body such as an executive agency or statutory authority staffed with APS employees.[31] The essential manifestation of this principle is s 57 of the PSA 1999, which addresses the 'Responsibilities of Secretaries'. It states, inter alia, that '[t]he Secretary of a department, under the Agency Minister, is responsible for managing the Department and must advise the Agency Minister in matters relating to the Department'. This provision is a successor to s 25(2) of the 1922 Act, which stated that 'The Secretary of a Department shall, *under the Minister*, be responsible for its general working, and for all the business thereof, and shall advise the Minister in all matters relating to the Department'. The words in italics were added by the *Public Service Reform Act 1984* (Cth).

In the 1922 Act, department heads were expressly vested with powers regarding establishments and classification, and promotions and temporary transfer (after 1925). Curiously, under the earlier *Public Service Arbitration Act 1920* (Cth), it was ministers rather than department heads who were respondents to determinations, though they rarely played any role, most matters being handled by the Board. Under the 1999 legislation, the Secretary is the principal actor subject to the provisions of legislation itself.

## Individual Personnel Decisions

It was a cardinal principle of the Northcote-Trevelyan report that ministers should not be involved in initial appointments to the civil service. This was the core procedure designed to rid the civil service of the evils of patronage. Otherwise, in the British civil service, all questions of personnel management remained, so far as these matters were clear at law, ministerial powers. In fact, from a relatively early stage they were exercised by permanent secretaries.

One effect of Australia's approach of embodying the system of public service management in statutory form has been to locate most personnel powers clearly in the hands of relevant authorities. Under the 1902 regime, all such powers resided in the Public Service Commissioner. The powers would normally be exercised on the basis of departmental head recommendations, but there was no formal requirement to that effect.

Under the 1922 Act, the Public Service Board retained powers of appointment after a probationary period, and of dismissal. Apart from recruitment, these powers were invariably exercised on the basis of departmental recommendation. From the 1970s, the Board would only be involved if an appointment were to be annulled. In the case of disciplinary matters, including dismissal, any action by the Board followed a hearing by a tripartite disciplinary appeal board.

From 1925, powers of promotion and transfer of staff were vested in department heads, with a right of appeal to the Public Service Board. After 1946, appeals were heard by tripartite committees composed of an independent chair, a departmental nominee and a staff association nominee. In the case of middle-ranking and senior posts, the Board acted on the basis of recommendations from the committee; in other cases, the committee made the decision.

The only individual personnel decisions actively involving ministers were those concerning the department heads and the small number of others, practically always former department heads, in the first division. Appointments and dismissals were matters for the Governor-General, acting on the advice of ministers. In the case of appointments, it was usually the case that the Board would be involved in the recommendation; in other matters, especially disciplinary in character, there would be recommendations from an adjudicatory body.

The principle that ministers do not become involved in individual personnel decisions is clearly stated in s 19 of the PSA 1999. Certain procedures are contained in subordinate documentation reinforcing this prohibition. In recent years, however, there have been a number of public claims of ministerial interventions in the personnel process, mainly at Senior Executive level.

## A Career Service

The PSA 1999 states that 'the APS is a career-based service' in which 'employment decisions are based on merit'.[32] The APS has always described itself as a career service although this has never previously been articulated in legislation; the provision in the PSA 1999 is essentially a statement rather than an articulation. It has been taken to mean competitive appointment, promotion largely on merit, and security of tenure in the sense that termination may occur only for cause. In practice, it took the form of young people joining at junior levels of the hierarchy and working their way up until retirement between ages of 60 and 65. This conventional picture fitted very few staff and was, historically, heavily qualified by veterans' preference[33] and the various prohibitions on women.[34]

The APS still has a career framework but entry is possible at any stage in the hierarchy; employment on a fixed-term contract basis is increasingly used, often in association with individualised Australian Workplace Agreements; and there are now well established procedures for redundancy on a voluntary and involuntary basis.

An important purpose of the career service was development of an impartial workforce able to serve any government irrespective of which side of politics it was drawn from, and equipped to give impartial advice frankly and fearlessly to ministers. This aspect of the career service has been hotly debated for many years and the outcome is a provision in the APS Values that 'the APS is responsive to the Government in providing frank, honest, comprehensive, accurate and timely advice and in implementing the Government's policies and programs'.[35]

## Establishment-Based Rather than Financial Control of Staffing: A Major Change in Culture

Until 1984, the central mechanism for staff control was control of establishments — the authority over the creation, salary classification and abolition of 'offices' (positions) in which staff were employed. 'Offices' were central to the definition and allocation of work, assignment of duties, location in an organisation, and pay. This establishment work was governed by s 29 of the *Public Service Act 1922* (Cth). Formal action, except reclassification, was in the hands of the Governor-General, thus providing ministers with a role which likewise was largely formal though potentially burdensome in terms of paperwork. They acted on the basis of approvals by the Public Service Board of reports submitted by department heads.

Control of establishments was the principal method whereby, within the frameworks of the first two Acts, it was possible to develop a relatively cohesive APS-wide grading system. By the early 1970s, the system was increasingly controversial and increasingly ineffective as the numbers of authorised positions greatly exceeded the number of staff and the funds available for paying staff. From the early 1970s, the Public Service Board developed a series of systems under which classification decisions were effectively delegated to departments and agencies. By the mid-1970s, with the numerical size of the public service, a recurrent topic of contention politically and with the unions, establishment control had essentially collapsed and been taken over by direct staffing controls under various names, the most usual being 'staff ceilings'.

Establishment and classification control was itself perhaps the clearest manifestation of the scientific management methods which underlay the first two Public Service Acts. It was explicitly used in all antipodean public services and, until 1967, in the Canadian public service. In the British civil service, staff costs were always regulated by conventional Treasury control of public expenditure. However, internally in departments, and in reviews of staff costs, similar classification techniques were employed, partly because of the connection to pay.

Canada abandoned this method of staff control in 1967 and integrated management of staff costs into the program budgeting system adopted in that year. Again, because of the connection with the pay system, monitoring of gradings was fairly active, but not especially effective. Throughout the 1970s, several of the Australian states abandoned central classification systems and absorbed staffing costs in the general financial management system.

The 1984 reforms of the APS tried to preserve a central classification system but ended the separate system of staff control. Henceforth, staff costs were controlled by the Department of Finance and formed part of the general expenditure system. The framework for maintenance of a central classification system has been maintained but little has been done to activate it.

The demise of establishment-based staff controls at the end of the 1970s and early 1980s is perhaps the most substantial change in the management practices of the APS in its century-long history. It brought a significant reduction in central interventions in the way departments and agencies organised themselves and operated, and thereby increased departmental autonomy in management.

## Workplace Relations

This matter is addressed in Chapters 4 and 5 in this volume. Historically, industrial relations have been separated from expenditure management and seen as part of personnel management. In 1987, with the abolition of the Public Service Board, this feature was retained, the function being vested in the (then)

Department of Industrial Relations. It was not assigned to the Department of Finance as it would have been had the ruling philosophy been one of fully integrating or consolidating staff management. This has largely been the pattern in Australian States. In Britain and Canada, key industrial relations matters such as pay and employment conditions have been dealt with respectively by the Treasury (except for the Civil Service Department interregnum, 1968-81) and the Treasury Board since its establishment as the general manager of government in 1967.

## Conduct and Ethics

The PSA 1999 has, as centrepieces, a statement of Values and a Code of Conduct. Hitherto, statutory codification of ethics and conduct matters has usually been avoided, although these subjects have continuously been addressed on an ad hoc basis, including in the context of discipline.[36] The original legislation dealt with certain values of the nineteenth and early twentieth century, such as prohibitions on employment of bankrupts. The inaugural Public Service Commissioner used his annual reports to expound his extensive views about how officials should conduct themselves, not least his hostility to political and union activity. Even in this era, any statements emanating from Britain were given very close attention, the currency case of the 1920s being a leading example. British expositions, among them major addresses by Sir Edward (later Lord) Bridges, Head of the Home Civil Service from 1945 until 1956, concerning behaviour, conduct and ethics, from the mid-1940s to the 1960s were studied very closely, and frequently repeated. Bridges' influence was also considerable in Canada where, after retirement, he was invited to deliver the prestigious Clifford Clark lectures for the Institute of Public Administration of Canada. Statements by ministers where relevant were also seen as major sources of guidance on conduct and ethics. The leading instance of this type of contribution is Sir Paul Hasluck's Sir Robert Garran Memorial Oration in 1968, 'The Public Servant and Politics'.

Australian views about ethical practice were always distinctive and did not necessarily follow the British path. For instance, from the 1930s, rules relating to engagement in political activity were liberalised; in 1945 arrangements were made to allow staff who resigned to contest an election to be reappointed if they were not successful.[37] The prohibition on public comment was also relaxed to allow staff to comment on local matters after an embarrassing case where a temporary employee of the Department of Post-war Reconstruction had criticised the Department of the Interior concerning facilities in Canberra.[38] The guiding principle was usually that any conduct should not be related to the duties of staff, should not be based on or use information obtained in the course of employment, nor should it affect the confidence which ministers, from either side of politics, had in the public service.

In the 1970s, the Public Service Board increasingly adopted a more direct approach to conduct and ethical matters. This approach was reinforced by the Report of the Royal Commission on Australian Government Administration. In general, it preferred an advisory to a prescriptive approach.[39] When the prohibition on public comment was repealed in 1974,[40] it was replaced by guidelines in the then General Orders. In addition, a booklet on the subject was published. A broadly similar approach was adopted in addressing acceptance of business appointments on resignation or retirement. This more systematic approach culminated with publication of *Guidelines on Official Conduct of Commonwealth Public Servants* in 1979. Several new editions were published by the Public Service Board in succeeding years, and, in dramatically shortened form, by the Public Service Commissioner subsequently.[41]

## Right of Employee Association

For most of its history, staff of the APS have been permitted to join unions, usually referred to as staff associations. The unions, moreover, have been part of the statutory structure for deciding pay and other conditions of employment. Indeed, access to various arbitral tribunals, in particular the Public Service Arbitrator, until abolished in 1984, was virtually only possible via a union or staff association registered under the legislation. An individual case over, say, a classification, could only be arbitrated if the union supported the officer's case.

One of the initiatives of the Chifley Government was establishment of a Joint Council chaired by the Public Service Board with representatives of departments and staff associations. Although apparently modelled on the National Whitley Council established in Britain following the Great War, it was different in major respects. In the first instance, it did not become involved in pay matters; more generally, it became the forum for dealing with matters upon which there was broad agreement between management and the unions. During the 1970s, it became a useful vehicle for handling important revisions and innovations such as overhaul of the disciplinary system, arrangements for officers who resigned to contest elections, and facilitating increased employment of women. Reassertion of management prerogative during the 1980s and 1990s saw the Council decline in significance and disappear. Another major difference with the Whitley system was that it convened. Unlike the Whitley system, the Joint Council never had formal departmental or agency counterparts.

Unionism however, has never been compulsory. There were periodically attempts when Labor governments have been in office to confine certain benefits negotiated by unions to members of unions, especially when arbitration was involved.[42] The last significant attempt to apply union preference came during the early days of the Whitlam Government. On that occasion, the aim was to restrict extension of annual recreation leave entitlement from three weeks to four weeks, accomplished by determination of the Arbitrator, to paid-up members of unions. The determination, however, was disallowed in the Senate on the basis that the Government, in its election platform, had not given any warning that the extended entitlement would be confined to unionists. The matter was settled by amendment of the *Public Service Act 1922* (Cth) extending the benefit to all staff irrespective of whether they were members of a union.

In recent decades, by contrast, there have been sustained endeavours by non-Labor governments to reduce the role of unions and to foster direct links between management and individual employees.[43] A major means for achieving these goals has been by use of Australian Workplace Agreements negotiated under the *Workplace Relations Act 1996* (Cth).[44]

Acquiescence in, even sympathy for, unionism has never extended to recognising a right to strike. The *Public Service Act 1922* (Cth) expressly forbade strikes on pain of automatic dismissal.[45] During the late 1960s and early 1970s — the last years of the near quarter century long Liberal-Country Party Coalition Government — there were strikes of various kinds, mostly in the Postmaster-General's Department. The draconian provision of the Act was never invoked, the industrial action itself being deemed to be 'stoppages' rather than 'strikes'. There were more stoppages from the mid-1970s to the mid-1980s as well, for example, by air traffic controllers, but tactics generally switched to various forms of 'work to regulation', for example, among staff of employment offices, and also customs staff. New legislation was passed to cover such industrial action.[46] The common law rule of 'no work as directed, no pay' was also activated.[47]

These measures marked an important change in the balance of power between management and unions. The progressive expansion of the union role which had been evident since the end of the Second World War with very little interruption had been challenged. The immediate reaction was to challenge revival of management power in the tribunals. This counter-attack met with some success, but it was only brief as the Hawke Labor Government repealed the legislation.[48]

In the contemporary public service, the basic policy is that as much as possible workplace relations in the public service should be on the same footing as those in the wider workforce and that except for clearly specified reasons public service employees should not have any rights different from those of the workforce in general. Many distinctive features of the public service workplace derive from application of the merit principle and other, often related matters, addressed in the *Public Service Act*. The role of unions is examined in more depth in Chapter 5 this volume.

## Third Party Arbitration

A corollary of the right of association has been the long-standing existence of third-party arbitration especially for the settlement of disputes (though, unlike the private sector jurisdiction, the absence of a dispute did not rule out invoking an arbitration). The role of third-party arbitration was sharply reduced under the new legislative structure, as it has been within the workforce in general, and virtually eliminated by the *Workplace Relations Amendment (Work Choices) Act 2005* (Cth). But from 1911, when public servants first won access to the then Court of Conciliation and Arbitration, until adoption of the *Workplace Relations Act 1996* (Cth) in 1997, arbitration was a major feature of public service workplace relations. From 1920 until 1984, the public service even had its own discrete arbitral jurisdiction under the *Public Service Arbitration Act 1920* (Cth). From the early 1950s, there have been several changes to the legislation designed to integrate public service workplace relations with that of the workforce in general.[49]

Historically, the Australian practice of having a specialised industrial relations system for the public services has been in accord with arrangements in comparable public services in the Australian States and in the UK (the Whitley system) and Canada (the collective bargaining regime established in 1967). Australian practice developed ahead of most other jurisdictions, largely as a consequence of early election of Labor governments, which usually took the lead in providing a statutory basis for union activities. As already observed, the Home Civil Service did not recognise the union role in the sense of instituting formal procedures for handling management-staff relations until 1919; Canada did not move until the mid-1960s.

## Rights of Review

A long-standing feature of the APS personnel system has been a general right of review of decisions. The PSA 1999 lists among the APS Values that 'the APS provides a fair system of review of decisions taken in respect of APS employees'.[50]

This is a successor provision to a line of regulations and legislation dating back to the 1920s. For most of that time, appeals or other applications by staff concerning their employment were usually but not invariably decided by the Public Service Board. In 1979, the Board itself created within its own establishment an autonomous body to handle grievances and appeals. This task was separated from the Board in 1984 and vested in the newly created Merit Protection and Review Agency.[51]

In 1987, after the Board had been abolished, and following creation of the post of Public Service Commissioner, the MPRA was progressively integrated with the Commissioner's operations in what eventually became a body administratively known as the Public Service and Merit Protection Commission. Under the PSA 1999, the role is now vested in the Merit Protection Commissioner who is administratively part of the Australian Public Service Commission.

Apart from the general avenue of appeal, there have also been specialist review bodies, both ad hoc and permanent. The longest standing ad hoc bodies have been in the disciplinary field. From inception of the promotions appeal system there have always been a range of promotions appeal committees. Both are tripartite in composition — an independent chair (with the qualifications of a stipendiary or police magistrate in the case of a discipline board) together with a nominee from the department or agency, and a nominee from the union with majority coverage of the staff concerned.

With the decline of union power in the personnel system, the promotions appeal system has also been wound back. At its inception after the Second World War, all officers except the small number in the First Division, where appointments were made by the Governor-General, had a right of appeal. The case would almost invariably be heard by a promotions appeal committee; those concerning posts in the higher levels of the Third Division, and in the Second Division, were referred to the Board for decision. But since 1986,[52] promotion appeal rights have been progressively wound back and do not now exist beyond the middle ranks of what was formerly the Third Division,[53] and review committees no longer involve union representatives.

In the meantime, the growth of avenues for redundancy has seen emergence of some new but limited rights of appeal under the jurisdiction of the Merit Protection Commissioner.

## Citizen Rights

As has already been observed in connection with matters of conduct and ethics, the APS has long recognised the citizen and political rights of its employees. There have never been any statutory or regulatory barriers to political participation. The principal inhibitions basically felt by employees at higher levels — chief executives and senior executives — have been the conventions about impartiality and the need for governments from both sides of politics to have confidence in the APS. The Chifley Government amended the *Public Service Act 1922* (Cth) to allow officers who resigned to contest elections (as required in the case of national elections by the *Australian Constitution*, s 44) to be reappointed at the level they held prior to resignation if they were unsuccessful at the polls. This practice is now covered by s 32 of the PSA 1999, which states, inter alia, that a person who resigns to contest an election, but is unsuccessful, 'is entitled to be again engaged as an APS employee ...'[54]

Also, in contrast to counterparts in many other public services, APS employees since 1973 have been permitted to comment publicly on policy subject to various restrictions such as not using information obtained in an official capacity which is not otherwise publicly available.[55]

And although there have been guidelines and provision for counsel about employment upon retirement or resignation from the APS, there has never been either a prohibition or provision for a quarantine period. Procedures adopted in the early 1980s following the inquiry into Public Duty and Private Interest[56] are dealt with on the basis that neither the staff member nor the new employer should gain an advantage from the former's previous employment.[57]

## Conclusion

The evolution of the APS throughout its history since 1901 is an important case study in administrative change and it is very unfortunate that alone among the four national Westminster/Whitehall public services, it has not been the subject of a commissioned history. The occasion of its centenary on 1 January 2001 was merely marked by a celebratory, albeit informative, publication.

What preliminary study suggests is the extent to which so much change depends on external circumstances. The increased educational standards of APS staff in the post-war era depended significantly on rising educational standards in the community, themselves a consequence of expansion of the universities from the late 1950s. The increasing role of women was also heavily influenced by broader community development. But no factor in recent administrative change has been so significant as information technology, both in making desirable change possible and in otherwise forcing change. This, however, is rarely mentioned in studies of change in the APS.

Internal considerations are often portrayed as central to administrative change. This is probably erroneous, the product of narrowly focussed analysis, and, to a degree, the partially autobiographical character of many accounts emanating from individuals and institutions involved. Notwithstanding, such considerations do have their importance, though perhaps more in shaping the timing and extent of change than its actual occurrence. Key figures in a history of change are very significant in mediating application of ideas current in a general environment within the public service itself.

This chapter is partly based on a view that any major transformation experience is as interesting for the continuities with the past as for actual innovations and new directions. Particularly in the past generation, much change has been less important for its own inherent quality than for what may be called counter-inertia tactics, the fight against complacency and stagnation. Transformation is thus a diverse phenomenon (or, rather, a mixture of diverse phenomena), and much of interest would emerge from a deep, systematic and comprehensive study of the matters touched upon in this chapter.

# ENDNOTES

1   See ch 9 this volume, Bryson and Anderson, 'Reconstructing State Employment in New Zealand'.

2   PSA 1999 s 10(1)(n) and (b).

3   *Australian Constitution* s 64.

4   *Australian Constitution* s 65; *Ministers of State Act 1952* (Cth).

5   Gerald Caiden 'The Commonwealth Public Service Board' in Henry Mayer (ed), *Australian Politics: A Second Reader* (1969) 589, 593–4.

6   Gerald Caiden, *The Commonwealth Bureaucracy* (1967) 172.

7   PSA 1999 s 21. These must be published in the *Gazette* within fourteen days. The Prime Minister may also make rules about classifications of APS employees (s 23(1)).

8   PSA 1999 s 58(3). This role is fulfilled by the Public Service Commissioner when there is a vacancy in the post of Secretary of the Department of Prime Minister and Cabinet (s 58(2)).

9   Section 19 of the Act states that an Agency Head is not subject to direction by any Minister in relation to the exercise by the Agency Head of powers under the Act in relation to employment of particular individuals.

10   PSA 1999 s 8(1) stipulates that the PSA 1999 has effect subject to the *Workplace Relations Act 1996* (Cth). See ch 4 in this volume by Mark Molloy.

11   PSA 1999 s 10. See also the elaboration in the *Public Service Commissioner's Directions 1999* (as amended) ch 2.

12   PSA 1999 s 13.

13   *Arbitration (Public Service) Act 1911* (Cth).

14   *Public Service Arbitration Act 1920* (Cth).

15   See, eg, *Commonwealth Employees (Redeployment and Retirement) Act 1979* (Cth).

16   *Public Service Act (No 2) 1966* (Cth).

17   See ch 4 in this volume [Molloy].

18   PSA 1999 ss 97, 82D.

19   PSA 1999 s 23(1).

20   Public Service Act Review Group, *Report* (December 1994) (known as the McLeod Report), para 2.7.

21   Sir Stafford Northcote and Sir Charles Trevelyan, 'The Northcote-Trevelyan Report' (1854, reprinted) (1954) 32 *Public Administration* 1, 16.

22   See ch 10 [Ewing] on proposals for a Civil Service Act.

23   *Public Service Employment Act*, SC 1966-67, c 71; *Public Service Staff Relations Act*, SC 1966-67, c 72; *Financial Administration Act, an Act to Amend*, SC 1966-67, c 74.

24   McLeod Report, above n 20, para 2.14.

25   Ibid para 2.9.

26   Ibid para 2.10.

27   Ibid paras 2.11–2.12.

28   PSA 1999 s 3.

29   The Commissioner's functions are set out in s 41 of the Act.

30   PSA 1999 s 17.

31   PSA 1999 s 9 and definitions in s 7.

32   PSA 1999 s 10(1)(n) and (b).

33   First implemented by amendment of the 1902 Act in 1915.

34   Notably differential pay rates (until the *Equal Pay* cases beginning in 1968) and, until 1966, the marriage bar, according to which married women could not be permanent officers of the APS, and were thus unable to compete for promotion and did not have access to superannuation.

35   PSA 1999 s 10(1)(f).

36   See, eg, *Public Service Act 1922* (Cth) s 55(1), which specified disciplinary offences, including wilful disobedience, negligence or carelessness in the discharge of duties, use of intoxicating liquor or drugs to excess, disgraceful or improper conduct.

37   Caiden, above n 6, 397. See also *Public Service Act 1922* ss 47C, 82B.

38 *Public Service Regulations 1935* (Cth) reg 34 prohibited the use of information gained by or conveyed through an officer's connection with the Service other than for the discharge of official duties and prevented public comment about 'any administrative action or upon the administration of any Department', except for residents of Commonwealth Territories, who were permitted to comment on Territory civic affairs (an exception applying from 1947).

39 Commonwealth of Australia, Royal Commission on Australian Government Administration, *Report* (1976) [2.4.16].

40 *Commonwealth Statutory Rules 1974* No 98.

41 *Guidelines on Official Conduct of Commonwealth Public Servants — A Summary* (1996). The current version is Australian Public Service Commission, *APS Values and Code of Conduct in Practice. A Guide to Official Conduct for APS Employees and Agency Heads* (revised ed, 2005).

42 Phillipa Weeks, *Trade Union Security Law* (1995) 37–40.

43 Ibid 40 for efforts of the Fraser government; see ch 4 [Molloy] on the Howard Government. See also Phillipa Weeks, 'Reconstituting the Employment Relationship in the Australian Public Service' in Stephen Deery and Richard Mitchell (eds), *Employment Relations — Individualisation and Union Exclusion* (1999) 69, 75–6 on the early years of the Howard government.

44 See chs 4 and 5 in this volume [Molloy; and O'Brien and O'Donnell].

45 *Public Service Act 1922* (Cth) s 66.

46 The *Commonwealth Employees (Employment Provisions) Act 1977* (Cth) (not proclaimed until July 1979) gave Commonwealth employing authorities the power of unilateral suspension and stand-down, ie independently of arbitration. Arbitral powers of suspension and stand-down were confirmed by the *Public Service Arbitration Amendment Act 1978* (Cth).

47 Eg *Briers v Australian Telecommunications Commission* (1979) 36 FLR 375. In response to the decision of Rogers J in *Bennett v Commonwealth* [1980] 1 NSWLR that suspension without pay of Commonwealth public servants could be carried out only in accordance with the *Public Service Act 1922* (Cth), the Commonwealth government procured passage of the *Public Service and Statutory Authorities Amendment Act 1980* (Cth), which added s 32A to the *Public Service Act 1922* (Cth) to give the Commonwealth as employer the common law power to withhold pay when employees refused to work as directed.

48 The *Public Service and Statutory Authorities Amendment Act 1983* (Cth) (repealed s 32A of the *Public Service Act*) and the *Commonwealth Employees (Employment Provisions) Repeal Act 1983* (Cth).

49 Caiden, above n 6, 233, 236.

50 PSA 1999 s 10(1)(o).

51 *Merit Protection (Australian Government Employees) Act 1984* (Cth).

52 *Public Service Legislation (Streamlining) Act 1986* (Cth).

53 *Public Service Regulations 1999* (Cth) reg 5.6.

54 See also *Public Service Regulations 1999* (Cth) div 3.2 (time limits etc).

55 Australian Public Service Commission, above n 41, ch 3.

56 Committee of Inquiry Concerning Public Duty and Private Interests, *Report* (1979).

57 Ibid ch 16.

# Chapter Four

# A Revised Legislative Framework for Australian Public Service Employment: The Successive Impacts of the *Workplace Relations Act 1996* (Cth) and *The Public Service Act 1999* (Cth)

## Mark Molloy[1]

This chapter considers the successive changes to the legislative framework governing employment in the Australian Public Service ('APS')[2] that have occurred since the election of the Coalition Government in 1996 to the present. In particular, it discusses the successive effects of:

a.   the *Workplace Relations and Other Legislation Amendment Act 1996* (Cth) (which introduced the *Workplace Relations Act 1996* (Cth));
b.   the *Public Service Act 1999* (Cth); and
c.   the *Workplace Relations Amendment (Work Choices) Act 2005* (Cth) (which significantly rewrote the *Workplace Relations Act 1996* (Cth)).

A major focus of the chapter is the legislative framework that provides for the determination of the terms and conditions of APS employment.

The chapter concludes that, significant as they have been, the above changes largely represent a continuation of the direction of change in APS employment culture that has been taking place since the early 1980s. However, some important new aspects have been introduced by the Work Choices legislation, including:

a.   the legislation has become more prescriptive in terms of the content required to be, or that may be deemed to be, included in industrial agreements and what is 'prohibited content' which cannot be included in agreements; and
b.   the introduction of the Australian Fair Pay and Conditions Standard that applies as a 'safety-net' for all employees under the *Workplace Relations Act 1996* (Cth) (including Commonwealth employees).

## The Position to 1996

In order to properly appreciate the nature and extent of the changes to the APS employment framework since 1996, one needs to commence with an analysis of the legal framework that had come to exist prior to 1996. The following provides a brief overview.

## Sources of Public Sector Employment Law

By 1996, the laws governing APS employment were sourced from an interaction of:

a.  laws enacted pursuant to the Commonwealth constitutional powers in relation to the public service,[3] (including by the application of general industrial relations legislation to its own employees); and

b.  the common law of employment.

It is important to note that the working relationship between the Commonwealth and its public servants may be characterised as an employer/employee relationship. This was the case even when, under the *Public Service Act 1922* (Cth), there was a distinction between 'officers' permanently appointed to the service and 'employees' (who were usually engaged for short or fixed terms).[4]

At common law, there were historical distinctions between a person who held an office and a person who was an employee. For example, salary may be payable to a person on the basis of holding an office for a particular period of time, whereas wages are payable to an employee on the basis of work performed (and may be withheld if work is not performed).

McCarry has discussed the difficulties of distinguishing between an 'officer' and an 'employee' in the public sector context. Given that the manner of the performance of work by officers was subject to control by the APS hierarchy, this meant the major indicium of the common law employment relationship was present.[5] McCarry notes the possibility of a 'pure' officer who has a lawfully imposed independent function which is not the subject of control by an employer.[6] In the public sector context however, there were very few 'pure' officers, so described, who had such an independence of function. Therefore, McCarry concludes that the common law criteria for the existence of an employment relationship would exist regardless of whether a statute referred to public servants as 'officers' or 'employees',[7] and early High Court observations seem to confirm the contractual nature of the relationship.[8]

Hence, public servants are engaged under a contract of employment. This contract of employment will therefore be a source of conditions of service, including terms implied by the common law. However, in the context of the APS, the overwhelming source of employment obligations has been legislation of the following types:

*   general public service legislation such as the *Public Service Act 1922* (Cth) ('PSA 1922') and the *Public Service Act 1999* (Cth) ('PSA 1999') (together the 'Public Service Acts');

- general industrial relations legislation such as the *Conciliation and Arbitration Act 1904* (Cth), the *Industrial Relations Act 1988* (Cth) and the *Workplace Relations Act 1996* (Cth); and
- legislation directed at specific conditions of employment (see later list).

## General Public Service Legislation

Although it has been noted that the Commonwealth could establish a public service without a general legislative framework,[9] the Public Service Acts have in fact provided one since 1902.[10] These Acts provide a common framework for public service employment and allow for the Parliament to express the values and culture it wishes to see in the public service. Moreover, legislation means that the Parliament can entrench principles and bestow rights and obligations which would be unavailable at common law (eg impartiality, appointment and promotion on merit, disciplinary and appeals processes).[11]

## The General Industrial Relations Framework

The general industrial relations framework has become an increasingly important source of employment rights and obligations in the public sector. For some time, industrial relations matters were dealt with by a public service arbitrator.[12] With the repeal of the relevant legislation,[13] Commonwealth public servants were brought under the then *Conciliation and Arbitration Act 1904* (Cth). With some express exceptions, awards made under general industrial relations legislation could prevail over conditions otherwise deriving from the general public service legislation.[14]

Awards historically applied across industries, and the APS was regarded as an industry for this purpose. However, since the early 1980s the APS has undergone a series of reforms, both in terms of its internal structure and because of other changes within the industrial relations system (see below from 1.2).

## Specific Legislation

The final and important source of APS employment rights and obligations has been the various statutes directed to specific aspects of the employment relationship and which includes:

- *Long Service Leave (Commonwealth Employees) Act 1976* (Cth);
- *Maternity Leave (Commonwealth Employees) Act 1973* (Cth);
- *Merit Protection (Australian Government Employees) Act 1984* (Cth);
- *Occupational Health and Safety (Commonwealth Employment) Act 1991* (Cth);
- *Safety, Rehabilitation and Compensation Act 1988* (Cth); and
- the various Superannuation Acts.

The focus of the following discussion, however, will be on changes to the employment conditions which have resulted from changes to the general APS and industrial relations legislative frameworks since 1996. The above specific legislation has undergone relatively little change and is in fact 'quarantined' from the effect of workplace agreements made under the *Workplace Relations Act 1996* (Cth) ('WRA').[15]

## An Environment of Reform

The legal framework governing APS employment had been undergoing significant changes since the early 1980s. The reform agenda involved both the revision of public service legislation as well as the application of industrial relations reform to the APS.

In 1983, the then Government produced a White Paper entitled Reforming the Australian Public Service.[16] The White Paper proposed a number of changes to management arrangements, including:

- the transfer of staff allocation and financial responsibilities from the Public Service Board ('the Board') to the Department of Finance;
- devolution of responsibility for personnel matters from the Board to agency heads (although the Board retained responsibility for overall APS staffing policy);
- establishment of the Senior Executive Service ('the SES'); and
- entrenchment of merit and equity principles in employment.[17]

Key elements of the White Paper were implemented by the *Public Service Reform Act 1984* (Cth).

In 1986, there was further devolution of personnel functions to departmental heads and streamlining of appeals processes.[18] This was followed in 1987 by the replacement of the Board by the Public Service Commission and machinery of government changes that provided for so called 'mega-Departments'.[19]

In the late 1980s and early 1990s, enterprise bargaining came to be adopted in the Australian industrial relations system. International economic pressures were forcing the private and public sectors to examine their international competitiveness. Fundamental changes in the community wage-fixing and the industrial relations environment were a response to these pressures, linking future pay rises to improvements in productivity at the enterprise level.

Enterprise bargaining was embraced as a micro-economic reform, aimed at achieving increases in productivity and efficiency in individual workplaces.[20] Wages outcomes were increasingly based upon structural adjustments and efficiency gains.[21] In the APS context, the Second Tier Agreement of 1987 provides an early example of a wages/productivity bargain which provided for workplace restructuring.[22]

Enterprise bargaining was adopted as a general wage-fixing principle in the 1991 'National Wage Case'. In 1992, the *Industrial Relations Act 1988* (Cth) was amended to provide for certified agreements, with compulsory union involvement, at the workplace (rather than industry) level.[23] These certified agreements prevailed over inconsistent provisions in industrial awards. In March 1994, the *Industrial Relations Reform Act 1993* (Cth) moved the emphasis further in favour of enterprise bargaining by including provisions for enterprise flexibility agreements which could be negotiated without union involvement. The policy approach was that a major certified agreement would cover the APS as a single workplace, but with provision for further agreements of some matters to be negotiated at agency level.[24]

In 1994, the McLeod Report recommended a new and simplified Public Service Act which emphasised the role, standards and values of the APS and with agency heads being primarily responsible for employment matters within their agencies.

Aside from the legal changes, there were also changes being implemented in APS management policy. In particular, there were changes being implemented to financial management practices. Managers were being expected to manage for results or 'outcomes'. There was devolution of management and financial accountability to line management, which was also accompanied by a concomitant accountability for the outcomes actually achieved.

Therefore, by 1996, the APS had undergone a number of cultural changes, both of a legal and policy character. This chapter however has its focus on the changes to the legal framework affecting APS employment, and so it would be appropriate to have a more detailed regard to the legislative framework as it had come to exist in 1996.

## The Legislative Framework of the PSA 1922 and the *Industrial Relations Act 1988* (Cth)

Prior to the advent of the *Workplace Relations Act 1996* (Cth), employment rights and obligations in the APS were generally determined within the framework provided by the PSA 1922 and the *Industrial Relations Act 1988* (Cth), although this framework had itself undergone recent reforms.

### *Public Service Act 1922* (Cth)

By 1996 the PSA 1922, with a large number of amendments over the years, had come to represent a patchwork of provisions rather than a structured framework for regulating APS employment arrangements. Indeed, as will be seen, a significant amount of the rights and obligations in APS employment derived from the industrial relations legislative framework. Nevertheless, the PSA 1922 contained important provisions in the areas set out below.

## Appointment and Promotion

The PSA 1922 provided for the creation and abolition of offices, for appointment to and transfer and promotion within the APS, and for the application of the merit principle in relation to appointments, transfers and promotions.[25]

The PSA 1922 also provided for appeals against promotion decisions on the grounds of superior efficiency. However, by 1996, such appeals were limited to promotions below the senior officer grades. Persons who unsuccessfully applied for promotions at or above the senior officer grades could apply to the Merit Protection and Review Agency ('MPRA') on the grounds that there had been a breach of the merit principle (including by some form of discrimination).[26]

Joint Selection Committees that included a union representative were also provided for and the decisions of such committees were not subject to appeal or review by the MPRA.[27] The PSA 1922 also provided for employment equity issues through a requirement for agency equal employment opportunity plans and industrial democracy plans.[28] It allowed for permanent part-time work[29] and for the engagement of temporary and fixed term employees.[30]

## Discipline

The PSA 1922 provided the framework for making inquiries into misconduct and for taking disciplinary action, including fines, reductions in salary, demotions and dismissals. Recent reforms had meant that these powers were generally exercisable by the Secretary of a department.[31]

## Redeployment, Retirement and Redundancy

The PSA 1922 contained relatively complex provisions dealing with retirement and redeployment of officers who had been declared excess to requirements.[32] For officers below the Senior Executive Service ('SES') level, the Australian Public Service General Employment Conditions Award 1995 (see below) operated to require certain procedures to be followed before a Secretary could take action to retire or redeploy excess staff.[33]

The terms of the PSA 1922 allowed for appeals against redundancy decisions to be taken to the MPRA, however this avenue of review was blocked from 1995 because of the operation of the APS Enterprise Agreement (discussed below). By 1996, the sole avenue of review had come to be the unfair dismissal provisions of the *Industrial Relations Act 1988* (Cth).

## Mobility

Complex mobility provisions dealt with the situation of former officers whose functions had recently been transferred outside the service. These provisions were the product of structural reforms in the public sector whereby some functions had been transferred (or outsourced) to either a public authority or private concern. The mobility provisions gave former officers certain rights to return to the service or to apply for jobs back in the service, and preserved long service leave rights.[34]

## Determinations under the PSA 1922

One of the most important provisions of the PSA 1922, in terms of the employment framework, was s 82D. It provided for the Public Service Commissioner to issue written determinations in relation to terms and conditions of employment for officers and employees. These determinations dealt in detail with a large variety of terms and conditions of employment including allowances, leave and other benefits. Such conditions were often settled as a result of the industrial process, either in settlement of disputes or as an outcome of consultative processes.

### Public Service Regulations

Discussion of the PSA 1922 should not ignore the regulations made under that Act. These regulations also contained important provisions for officers and employees. For example they:

- specified the duties of officers, a breach of which might have been the subject of disciplinary action; and
- contained secrecy provisions,[35] the grievance procedures and higher duties arrangements for non-SES officers.

There seems to have been little reason, except historical preferences and the relative ease of passage into law, as to why some provisions were included in the regulations and why some were included in the PSA 1922 itself. Like the 1922 Act, the regulations had come to resemble a patchwork of provisions which had evolved over the previous decades.

### Industrial Relations Act 1988 (Cth)

At the beginning of 1996, the *Industrial Relations Act 1988* (Cth) (the 'IRA') provided the framework for many of the terms and conditions applying to employment in the APS. It did this through two main instruments:

- the Australian Public Service General Employment Conditions Award (the 'GECA');[36] and
- the Continuous Improvement in the Australian Public Service Enterprise Agreement: 1995-96 (the 'APS Enterprise Agreement').

The arrangements between the operation of the GECA, the APS Enterprise Agreement and the PSA 1922 (and regulations) were complex and there was overlap in subject matter in a large number of areas.

The GECA was an award relating to Commonwealth public sector employment and prevailed over inconsistent provisions of the PSA 1922 (including s 82D determinations and regulations). This is because the then s 121 of the IRA permitted the Australian Industrial Relations Commission ('AIRC') to make awards that were inconsistent with certain laws affecting public sector employment.[37]

The APS Enterprise Agreement was a certified agreement under Part IVB of the IRA. As such it was regarded as an 'award' for the purposes of that Act and so would also prevail over terms and conditions of employment deriving from the PSA 1922.[38] Taken together, in relation to non-SES personnel, GECA and the APS Enterprise Agreement dealt with (and prevailed over) many of the conditions of employment set out in the PSA 1922, the s 82D determinations and in the regulations.

The relationship between GECA and the APS Enterprise Agreement was that the latter prevailed over the former to the extent of inconsistency.[39]

## Outline of GECA

GECA was a relatively recently made award which resulted from award restructuring and rationalisation efforts in the early 1990s. It represented the consolidation of a number of awards covering APS employment and dealt with matters such as:

- payment of wages and related matters such as incremental advancement (although it did not specify the base rates of pay);
- hours of work and overtime rules;
- leave (such as annual leave, public holidays, sick leave, and other miscellaneous leave types);
- redeployment, retirement and redundancy; and
- various allowances.

GECA included award flexibility provisions to allow for variation of the award by an agency agreement (ie an agreement at department level rather than at service wide level). However, GECA provided that agency agreements could not affect base rates of pay and essential standards of employment conditions, namely hours of work, public holidays, recreation leave, sick and long service leave, maternity leave, parental leave, redeployment and redundancy arrangements.[40]

In terms of its interaction with the PSA 1922, perhaps the key provisions of GECA were the redeployment, retirement and redundancy provisions which effectively controlled the manner in which the relevant provisions of the PSA 1922 actually operated.[41] It provided for union involvement, processes for voluntary retrenchment, income maintenance, and retention periods for those being considered for involuntary retrenchment.[42]

## APS Enterprise Agreement

The APS Enterprise Agreement was the latest in a series of service-wide certified agreements under the IRA framework. It was a certified agreement under the then s 170MC of the IRA. As such, its provisions prevailed over both GECA and the PSA 1922.[43]

Among other things, it provided for:

- base rates of pay for the various classifications;
- certain non-salary allowances;
- removal of certain MPRA appeals rights;
- the IRA to be sole right of review of termination of employment decisions; and
- performance appraisal arrangement for senior officers and the Senior Executive Service.[44]

The APS Enterprise Agreement also provided for a continuing commitment to workplace reform and improved productivity and flexibility in the public service.[45] It provided that agencies 'may agree to reflect improved productivity outcomes from workplace reforms in benefits to staff and clients, but excluding pay increases and alterations to service-wide classification structures and the formal framework of the Public Service Act and Regulations.'[46] This was an important departure (and reversal) from the immediately preceding certified agreements covering the APS, which had allowed for base rates of pay to be supplemented by agency agreements.[47]

## Agency Agreements

Since 1992, certified agreements under the IRA had also provided a limited opportunity for agency bargaining. A typical example was the then Department of Human Services and Health Agency Bargaining Agreement 1994, which provided for such things as flexible leave arrangements, selection procedures and supplementary pay.[48]

## Developments since 1996 Leading into the Twenty-First Century

In 1996, the Coalition Government came to office with a policy that continued the approach of taking APS management and employment practices closer to those of the private sector. The strategy basically centred on an expanded approach to bargaining at the agency level (and the rejection of APS-wide agreements), the use of AWAs, and greater regulation of the role to be played by unions in negotiating agreements. There have been three major legislative developments since 1996:

a. the introduction of the *Workplace Relations Act 1996* (Cth);

b.  the passage of the *Public Service Act 1999* (Cth); and

c.  the significant rewriting (and constitutional rebasing) of the *Workplace Relations Act 1996* by the Work Choices legislation.[49]

These legislative developments in (a) and (b) will be considered in the following sections; and the development in (c) will then be examined.

## The Introduction of the *Workplace Relations Act 1996*

The *Workplace Relations and Other Legislation Amendment Act 1996* (Cth) ('WROLA') was passed by the Commonwealth Parliament in November 1996 and commenced at the end of that year.

WROLA changed the name of the *Industrial Relations Act 1988* (Cth) to the *Workplace Relations Act 1996* (the WRA).[50] It pushed further down the road of enterprise bargaining by continuing to shift the emphasis from industry-based awards to bargaining at the workplace level. For the APS, this meant a shift from APS-wide agreements to agreements concluded at an agency level.

The new arrangements were to have a significant effect on the manner in which APS terms and conditions of employment were negotiated and settled.

### Awards

A new s 89A of the WRA provided that, after an interim period, awards would only be allowed to deal with certain 'allowable matters'.[51] Other terms and conditions of employment could be included in certified agreements or Australian Workplace Agreements ('AWAs'). This is what was known as the award 'simplification' process.

The 20 award matters allowed by s 89A included classifications of employees, hours of work, rates of pay, public holidays, certain types of leave (including annual leave, sick leave, but not including union leave), penalty rates, redundancy and termination, stand-downs, dispute settlement and superannuation. Significantly, and in keeping with the safety net approach to awards, the Australian Industrial Relations Commission ('AIRC') could specify only minimum rates of pay, ie paid rates awards, could no longer be made.[52]

### Certified Agreements

WROLA repealed the former Part VIB of the IRA and substituted a new Part VIB of the WRA.

The former Part VIB, which had been inserted by the *Industrial Relations Reform Act 1993* (Cth), had provided for two types of enterprise bargains or agreements: a 'certified agreement' and an 'enterprise flexibility agreement'. The former Part VIB had relied upon the existence and settlement of an industrial dispute for the ability to make certified agreements (ie s 51(xxxv) of the Constitution). The making of enterprise flexibility agreements did not require the existence of an industrial dispute and instead relied upon the corporations power (ie s 51(xx) of the Constitution) in that the corporation could reach an agreement with employees whether or not a dispute or a union was involved.[53] This was the first significant step down the path of reliance on the corporations power, which ultimately led to the Work Choices legislation (discussed later).

The new Part VIB substituted two new categories of certified agreements:

a. Division 2 provided for certified agreements to be made between an employer and employees where the employer was a 'constitutional corporation',[54] or was the Commonwealth;[55] and

b. Division 3 provided for certified agreements in settlement of industrial disputes.

As to Division 2, the constitutional underpinning was the corporations power (s 51(xx)) and the executive power combined with the express incidental power (ss 61 and 51 (xxxix)). Although WROLA represented an expanded reliance by the WRA on the corporations power, that aspect is not directly relevant to the APS employment aspects which fall under the executive and express incidental heads of constitutional power.[56]

As to Division 3, the constitutional support was the industrial relations power (s 51(xxxv)). This power had been, of course, the traditional constitutional basis for Commonwealth non-APS industrial relations legislation.

Division 2 provided for two types of agreement. Section 170LJ provided for agreements to be made between an employee and a union that represented employees in the workplace, while s 170LK provided for an employer to make an agreement directly with employees.[57]

Both ss 170LJ and 170LK required the agreement to be approved by a majority of the employees proposed to be covered. They must have had at least 14 days to consider the agreement before voting and the employer was required to explain the terms of the agreement.[58]

An agreement with employees had to be made in such a way that there was no discrimination between union members and other employees.[59] If an agreement was being made under s 170LK, a union member had the right to ask for union representation in meetings and confer with the employer on the proposed agreement.[60]

Before commencing operation, an agreement was required to be certified by the AIRC.[61] A certified agreement also had to satisfy the 'no-disadvantage test' (see below). Certified agreements commenced when they were certified by the AIRC and continued until terminated, or replaced by another certified agreement after their nominal expiry date.[62]

## Australian Workplace Agreements

A new Part VID was inserted into the WRA that provided for the making of AWAs. The AWA provisions provided a specific statutory framework for an individual form of employment contract. Unlike a common law employment contract, the statutory framework within which AWAs were made, allowed the employer and employee to reach an agreement that prevailed over awards and certain State and Commonwealth laws.[63] In effect, they were able to contract out of certain obligations which would otherwise apply. Breach of an AWA also carried with it certain statutory penalties that would not apply at common law.[64]

AWAs were also subject to the same 'no disadvantage test' that applied to certified agreements (see below).

Generally speaking, an AWA was required to be approved by the (then) Employment Advocate[65] before it could come into operation. An AWA could not be approved unless there had been genuine agreement to the making of the AWA, and a person could not be subject to duress in the making of an AWA.[66] One of the other important approval requirements was that an employer was generally required to offer an AWA on similar terms to all comparable employees, unless it was reasonable not to do so.[67]

Although the essence of an AWA was that it was an individual agreement with an individual employee, the employee was able to appoint a bargaining agent[68] and a number of individual agreements could be negotiated collectively and included in the one document.[69]

## No Disadvantage Test

The new Part VIE of the WRA provided for a 'no disadvantage test'. In effect, the test generally required that a certified agreement or AWA could not be certified or approved (as the case may be) if it would result, on balance, in a reduction in the overall terms and conditions of employment applying to employees under relevant awards, and any relevant laws (ie legislation).[70]

## Protected Industrial Action

The WRA provided for limited immunity for employers and employees in relation to the taking of industrial action connected with the negotiation of a certified agreement or an AWA.[71] In certain circumstances, an employer or employees were able to take 'protected industrial action' (eg lock out or strike action) during a formal 'bargaining period'.[72] In certain circumstances, an employer or an employee would be able take 'AWA industrial action' during negotiations for an AWA.[73]

## Award Simplification

An award simplification process was undertaken as a result of joint working party arrangements between the Commonwealth and the APS unions agreed on 22 May 1997.[74] While some matters were agreed through a process of conciliation, other matters required arbitration.[75] The Australian Public Service Award 1998 (the 'APS Award 1998') was finally made on 29 September 1998. It replaced ten APS awards then in existence (in effect replacing the GECA, referred to above, and merging the provisions of the SES Award).[76] Through the progressive adoption of comprehensive certified agreements and AWAs across the APS, the contents of the award would largely become redundant: to the extent that it operated as a safety net in the APS, there would be few people to catch.

## Applying the New Arrangements in the APS: Initial Policy Approaches

The Federal Government announced its approach to agreement making in the APS, under the new WRA framework by stating that:

* certified agreements would be made subject to finalisation of Government policy parameters; and
* a framework for APS agency bargaining principles was to be negotiated with the public sector unions to assist in the progress of bargaining across the APS, but comprehensive agreements would be able to be made in advance of those principles being settled.[77]

The Government's initial policy parameters for agreement making were issued to APS agencies on 23 May 1997. The twelve parameters included requirements for agreements to:

* be consistent with the Government's workplace relations and wages policy;
* be funded from agency appropriations;
* retain portability within the APS of annual leave and sick leave entitlements;
* move to a rationalised classification structure; and
* provide for flexible remuneration on a salary sacrifice basis, as appropriate.[78]

The policy parameters on agreement making were published without formal union agreement.[79]

The policy parameters were supplemented by the Supporting Guidance for the Policy Parameters for Agreement Making in the APS, which, in fact, provided the detailed instructions for agreement making by agencies.

Draft certified agreements had to be cleared with the then Department of Industrial Relations.

The initial Government policy in relation to AWAs was that there was an expectation that members of the SES would enter into these agreements as a matter of priority.[80]

It was also government policy that certified agreements and AWAs were to be as comprehensive as possible in order to minimise the number of different instruments governing pay and conditions; ie they were to provide for terms and conditions of employment as far as possible to the exclusion of awards, determinations and, in particular, the APS Enterprise Agreement.[81]

## Certified Agreements in the APS Context

The experience of the WRA was that the Commonwealth, as employer, was most likely to make an agreement under the then Division 2 of Part VIB of the WRA, rather than under the then Division 3, which dealt with agreements in settlement of industrial disputes. Therefore certified agreements would usually be made with organisations of employees under the old s 170LJ or directly with employees under the old s 170LK.

Part VIB provided that certified agreements might be made at the level of a single business or part of a single business. Although the Commonwealth was defined as a single business,[82] Government policy was to make certified agreements only at the agency level (ie as part of a single business).

The framing of certified agreements under the old Part VIB of the WRA was initially complicated by the relationship between a certified agreement and other existing sources of APS terms and conditions of employment. In this regard, ss 170LY and 170LZ of the WRA relevantly provided that while a certified agreement was in operation:

- it prevailed over an award or order of the AIRC to the extent of any inconsistency between the two;[83] and
- it could displace conditions of employment in Commonwealth laws prescribed in the Workplace Relations Regulations 1996 (Cth).

### Certified Agreements and APS Awards

When the WRA commenced, the major awards in APS employment were the GECA and the SES Award (later replaced by the APS Award 1998). Certified agreements could therefore limit or exclude the operation of these awards.

### Certified Agreements and the APS Enterprise Agreement

The definition of 'certified agreement' in the WRA only applied to certified agreements made under the substituted Part VIB. WROLA did not include specific transitional provisions to cover the operation of certified agreements made under the IRA. However, the preferable view was that agreements such as the APS Enterprise Agreement continued to operate but that a new certified agreement, being made under a later law, prevailed over it to the extent of any inconsistency.[84]

## Certified Agreements and the PSA 1922

Section 170LZ(4) of the WRA provided that a (new) certified agreement prevailed over conditions of employment in a Commonwealth law prescribed by the regulations. The regulations initially prescribed:

- all determinations under s 82D of the *Public Service Act 1922* (Cth);
- directions and notices about retirement and dismissal under that Act and regulations; and
- classification of offices.[85]

Other specific legislation applying to APS employment (such as long service leave, maternity leave, superannuation, and safety, rehabilitation and compensation) was not prescribed and so could not be affected by a certified agreement.

## The Experience of Making Certified Agreements in the APS

Agencies began to make certified agreements under the WRA from May 1997 following the release of the Government's initial Policy Parameters for Agreement Making in the APS that have been referred to above.[86] By the advent of the Work Choices legislation, the original set of 12 parameters had been reduced by successive revisions to six parameters which required that:

1. agreements were to be consistent with the workplace relations policies of the Government;
2. improvements in pay and conditions were to be linked to improvements in organisational productivity and performance;
3. improvements in pay and conditions were to be funded from within agency budgets;
4. agreements were to include compulsory retrenchment, reduction and retrenchment provisions, with any changes not to enhance existing redundancy arrangements;
5. agreements were to facilitate mobility across the APS; and
6. agreements were to include leave policies and employment practices that support the release of Defence Reservists for peacetime training and deployment.[87]

A so-called 'first round' of certified agreements was negotiated between 1997 and 1999. Agreements typically ran for a two or three year period; hence successive 'rounds' of agreement making tended to occur at approximately two yearly intervals. By the time of the Work Choices legislation, many agencies had completed four or five rounds of agreement making.

Certified agreements have tended to include the following initiatives:

- a variety of pay outcomes and performance-linked salary progression;
- flexible use of the APS classifications structure and broadbanding of classifications;
- higher duties allowance only being payable after a minimum period of acting above level;
- more flexible working hours;
- streamlined leave provisions with generally three basic leave types:
  - annual leave
  - personal leave (which combines previous leave types such as sick, special, carers and bereavement leave); and
  - miscellaneous leave (which would cover leave such as for performance of jury duty, for approved study and other leave without pay); and
- streamlined allowances provisions.[88]

As noted above, it was Government policy that agreements were to be comprehensive in the sense that they stood alone and did not operate in conjunction with other instruments (such as awards or previous certified agreements). In the author's experience, this was achieved to varying degrees in the 'first round' of certified agreements negotiated between 1997 and 1999. However, many of the agreements either incorporated by reference, or continued in effect, the provisions of the PSA 1922, awards, and the APS Enterprise Agreement.[89] This was often for reasons of convenience in that such mechanisms avoided the sheer amount of detail of terms and conditions which would have to be repeated (if they were not to be renegotiated).[90] Concern over the possibility of breaching the 'no-disadvantage test' was also a motivation for not excluding the operation of certain of the then current employment conditions.

Of the 98 'first round' certified agreements at 30 June 1999, 54 were stand-alone agreements in that they did not operate in conjunction with other awards or certified agreements.[91] The subsequent rounds saw virtually all agreements move on to a standalone basis.[92] While this trend had been noted to reflect a growing 'maturity' in agreement making by agencies,[93] the author suggests that removal of the complexities in the legal framework referred to above, together with the passage of the PSA 1999, discussed below, also had a significant facilitating influence in that regard.

In time, there has also been a change in approach in terms of the amount of detail that might be expected in a certified agreement. It is now expected that certified (or collective) agreements will be 'simple principles based' agreements that are free from administrative and procedural matters; those matters being dealt with in policy or guidelines material to which the certified (or collective) agreement would make reference.[94] It remains to be seen how far this approach can be taken in terms of acceptance by employees. Many administrative and procedural matters actually involve important terms and conditions of employment which employees may wish to retain as the subject of a binding agreement.

Another interesting factor has been the trend in the number of agreements made with unions under the old s 170LJ, compared with those made directly with employees under the old s 170LK. As at 1 May 2006, there were 100 certified agreements covering APS and parliamentary service staff that were in operation under the old provisions of the WRA (ie as the WRA stood before the commencement of the Work Choices legislation on 27 March 2006). Of these, only 31 agreements (or 31 per cent) had been made directly with employees under s 170LK of the WRA.[95] In fact, the percentage of agreements made under s 170LK had dropped significantly since earlier rounds. As at 30 June 1999, of the 98 certified agreements then covering all APS and parliamentary agencies, 44 per cent of these had been s 170LK agreements.[96]

Although certified agreements no longer needed to be cleared with DEWR, agencies were still required to provide a draft of their proposed agreement to that Department before seeking their Minister's approval of the agreement. A requirement was imposed that any policy issues raised by DEWR should be brought to the attention of their Minister before he or she provided approval.[97]

## Australian Workplace Agreements in the APS Context

In relation to making AWAs with Commonwealth employees, the Secretary to a Department will represent the Commonwealth.[98]

In the APS, AWAs have represented a significant new policy direction consistent with a desire to have workplace bargaining arrangements reduced to the employer/employee level of direct negotiation. Although agency heads, and some SES staff, may have previously had individual contracts, introducing AWAs across the broader SES, and to lower levels, was a major step.

In the experience of the author, and in particular prior to the passage of the PSA 1999, the technical operation of an AWA depended a great deal on how it related to other instruments that set out terms and conditions of employment. The relationship between an AWA and these instruments in the APS context was complex, as will be seen in the following discussion.

As with certified agreements, it was Government policy that AWAs should be comprehensive agreements in that they would clearly provide for all the terms and conditions of employment and stand alone from other instruments such as awards and certified agreements. However, mainly for reasons of convenience, AWAs have often been framed on the basis of 'calling up' or incorporating by reference the content of more comprehensive instruments such as awards or certified agreements; ie they would incorporate or adopt the text of such instruments as terms of the AWA itself. There is now an expressed policy position to have AWAs as 'textually' comprehensive agreements, in that they should expressly contain all the employee's terms and conditions of employment (although, as is the case with certified agreements, they should now be 'simple principles based' agreements).[99]

## AWAs and Awards

The old s 170VQ(1) of the WRA provided that, during its period of operation, an AWA operated to the exclusion of any award that would otherwise apply to the employee. It is important to note that this effect was broader than for a certified agreement. A certified agreement merely prevailed over an award to the extent of any inconsistency; an AWA excluded the award entirely. If it was desired to continue the effect of certain provisions of an award, then the terms of the award needed to be incorporated by reference as part of the AWA rather than being referred to as continuing to have effect as part of the award.

## AWAs and Certified Agreements

The old s l70VQ(6) of the WRA provided for a complex relationship between an AWA and a certified agreement.

Generally speaking, a certified agreement which had not passed its nominal expiry date would prevail over an AWA unless the certified agreement allowed a subsequent AWA to operate to the exclusion of the certified agreement.[100] A certified agreement which came into operation after the nominal expiry date of an AWA would also prevail over the AWA to the extent of any inconsistency.[101] In all other cases, the AWA operated to the exclusion of a certified agreement.

As was the case with awards, AWAs did not prevail over a certified agreement to the extent of any inconsistency. Hence, if the terms of the certified agreement were to effectively apply, the drafting technique was to incorporate the relevant terms of the certified agreement as terms of the AWA.

## AWAs and the APS Enterprise Agreement

A further complexity was that the APS Enterprise Agreement was not a 'certified agreement' for the purposes of s 170VQ(6) of the WRA. Therefore, there were no express rules governing the relationship of an AWA and the APS Enterprise Agreement. However, as discussed above, for certified agreements made under the new Part VIB, the AWA, being made under a later law, would be taken to prevail over the APS Enterprise Agreement to the extent of an inconsistency. Hence, an AWA could expressly limit or exclude the operation of the APS Enterprise Agreement.

## AWAs and the PSA 1922

To the extent that it was relevant in the APS context, AWAs (like certified agreements) prevailed over conditions of employment in a Commonwealth law prescribed by the regulations.[102] Initially the regulations included:

- all determinations under s 82D;
- directions and notices about retirement and dismissal under the Act and regulations; and
- classification of offices.[103]

Other specific legislation applying to APS employment (such as long service leave, maternity leave, superannuation, safety rehabilitation and compensation) was not prescribed and so could not be affected by an AWA.

## The Experience of Making AWAs in the APS

The nature of AWAs is that, as individual agreements, they are not open for scrutiny in the manner of certified agreements. Although the WRA prevented AWAs including secrecy provisions,[104] the documents are usually covered by an agency's policy of protecting the confidentiality of its personnel records. Unless the parties agreed to the release of details of the AWA there would be implications under the *Privacy Act 1988* (Cth).

The following observations on AWAs are provided from the author's experience of drafting AWAs for many Commonwealth agencies. The observations are necessarily general in nature. Since 1996, there have also been other reports and publications dealing with the making of AWAs in the APS and these are also a source of confirmation of the nature of the matters that have been dealt with by these agreements.[105] As some of these publications have also acknowledged, the development of AWAs involved significant agency resources;[106] and, as may be gathered from the foregoing discussion, they have involved some complexity in their drafting.

Government policy after the commencement of the WRA was to offer AWAs to SES officers as a priority and to look to extend them to senior non-SES levels and specialist positions. By the time of the passage of the Work Choices legislation, it had got to the position where Agency Heads were required to put in place arrangements that enabled any employee in their agency to seek to negotiate an AWA.[107]

AWAs within the APS may be dealt with in two categories. Those involving:

- SES personnel; and
- non-SES personnel.[108]

These are considered in detail below.

## SES Personnel

The first phase of AWAs commenced operation in advance of the 'first round' agency certified agreements that were negotiated between 1997 and 1999. The policy was that AWAs should be comprehensive in their scope, in the same manner as was envisaged for certified agreements (ie they did not operate in conjunction with other instruments). However, especially in this first phase, it was not practical that each AWA expressly detail all the terms and conditions of employment, and in many cases it was legally necessary to continue the effect of other instruments.

At the time that the first AWAs were being negotiated, the terms and conditions of SES personnel derived from:

• the Australian Public Service, Senior Executive Service (Salaries and Specific Conditions) Award 1995;
• various s 82D determinations or provisions of the APS Enterprise Agreement (of general or specific application); and
• other provisions of the PSA 1922 that specifically applied to them.

The failure to maintain certain of these conditions could have raised issues about whether there would be a breach of the 'no-disadvantage test'.

AWAs for SES personnel tended to be relatively short agreements providing for:

a. general conditions of employment (such as hours of duty, leave and travel entitlements); and
b. the remuneration package (including base salary, bonus payments, salary reviews, private plated vehicles and flexible remuneration packaging).

AWAs were also required to include mandated content in relation to dispute resolution and anti-discrimination.[109] They also might typically include provisions dealing with termination of employment, resignation and termination or variation of the AWA (but these were often included as 'comfort' provisions that merely restated the legal situation in any event).

Generally speaking, agencies offered AWAs in similar terms to all SES employees, although there were cases where remuneration rates differed or where different terms were offered to specialist positions.[110]

SES AWAs were often drafted on the basis that the s 82D determinations and the APS Enterprise Agreement would continue to apply except to the extent that they were inconsistent with the particular terms of the AWA. Even where more comprehensive AWAs did generally exclude the operation of s 82D determinations and the APS Enterprise Agreement, it was a common requirement for them to, at least, continue the operation of the APS Enterprise Agreement provisions relating to salary regression for SES personnel and the prevention of appeal rights to the MPRA.[111]

As agencies negotiated certified agreements, the issue for SES AWAs was what, if any, should the relationship be with those agreements. As has been seen above, the technical legal relationship between an AWA and a certified agreement was complex, and depended upon the time the respective agreements were made, their nominal expiry dates and whether a certified agreement allowed a later AWA to operate to its exclusion. Along with this, the policy was that SES personnel should be covered by comprehensive AWAs rather than come under an agency's certified agreement. Therefore, it was generally the case that AWAs operated to exclude the formal application of a certified agreement to SES employment or the relevant certified agreement was expressed not to cover SES employees. This resulted in two basic approaches to AWA formulation:

1.  the AWA did not refer to matters included in a certified agreement but it may (or may not) have continued the operation of relevant s 82D determinations or the APS Enterprise Agreement; or

2.  the AWA recited, or incorporated by reference, terms of the relevant certified agreement (either on a general or selective basis) that were to operate as terms of the AWA.

With the passage of the PSA 1999, there was no longer the legal technical need to continue the operation of provisions of awards, s 82D determinations and the APS Enterprise Agreement which have been discussed earlier. This removed a great deal of the drafting complexity. Nevertheless, many AWAs still continued to 'call up' provisions of agency certified agreements, as terms of the AWA, rather than be 'textually' comprehensive documents in themselves.

## Non-SES Employees

In relation to non-SES personnel, the first phase of AWAs (ie those negotiated before an agency's certified agreement) involved different considerations. At that time, the relevant employment conditions were basically drawn from GECA and the APS Enterprise Agreement.

AWAs were generally offered to this group as a way of providing performance pay or retention bonuses (for example in relation to staff who might be tempted to go with an outsourced IT function). A typical early form of AWA for this class merely dealt with those special conditions but otherwise effectively continued the operation of the terms of the GECA or the APS Enterprise Agreement. As AWAs actually operated to the exclusion of GECA[112] the terms of that award had to be adopted as part of the AWA but without the technical overriding effect on the PSA 1922 that awards and the APS Enterprise Agreement could otherwise have.[113]

As agencies began to put in place their certified agreements, it became more common to offer AWAs to senior non-SES staff. Nevertheless, these AWAs almost invariably sat atop the certified agreement. Again, because the AWA generally operated to the exclusion of the certified agreement, the drafting technique was to incorporate the terms of the certified agreement as if they were terms of the AWA. Apart from the formal requirements in relation to anti-discrimination and dispute resolution, the balance of the substantive provisions of the AWA dealt with the special conditions to apply to the non-SES employee (e.g. retention and performance or skills bonuses).[114]

## The Extent of Use of AWAs

As at 1 May 2006 there were 13,390 AWAs in operation in the APS (and Parliamentary Service) out of a total workforce of around 134,000.[115] Of these, 2,131 related to SES employees and 11,259 to non-SES employees.[116]

The figures confirm the widespread practice of offering AWAs beyond the SES. While, non SES staff on AWAs are very much in the minority, even at the Executive Levels (ie those levels immediately below the SES), the numbers continue to grow, up from approximately 6,400 in November 2003. This would be primarily driven by the offer of performance bonuses and the like. It will be interesting to see how the trend continues under the Work Choices legislation.

## The Introduction of the PSA 1999

For a considerable period of time, there had been a general consensus that the PSA 1922 was in need of replacement. The McLeod Report of December 1994 had recommended a new Public Service Act that emphasised the role, standards and values of the APS and with agency heads being primarily responsible for employment matters within their agencies.

Until the passing of the new PSA 1999 in November 1999, the WRA operated in conjunction with the PSA 1922. Therefore the new agreement making arrangements under the WRA had to take account of the legislative provisions of the PSA 1922 which affected employment entitlements and obligations. As outlined above, certified agreements and AWAs could override determinations made under s 82D of the PSA 1922. This was necessary, from one policy perspective, given that those s 82D determinations provided for service-wide conditions of employment whereas the goal of the new WRA (as it was applied to the APS) was to move bargaining down to the agency level.

The PSA 1922 had an outward structure that did not fit with the new agreement making arrangements. However delegations of authority to Agency Heads had meant, in a practical sense, there were no great impediments to agency bargaining. Any minor difficulties with agreements not being able to override certain provisions of the PSA 1922 could have been resolved by amendment of the Workplace Relations Regulations 1996 (Cth). Nevertheless, change was desirable in order to make for a more coherent legislative framework.

Parliament failed to agree on a form of Public Service Bill that was presented in 1997. As an interim measure, the Public Service Regulations (Amendment-Interim Reforms) 1998 (Cth) were made. Those regulations provided for the APS Values and APS Code of Conduct that were to be included in a new Act.[117]

A revised Public Service Bill was passed by the Parliament in 1999 which is discussed below[118]

# Structure of the PSA 1999

The PSA 1999 presents a more simply drafted and up to date piece of legislation governing APS employment.

## The Australian Public Service

The APS is defined in s 9 as being comprised of Agency Heads and APS employees.

The culture of the APS is based upon the 'APS Values', which are set out in s 10. They are fifteen in number, with some notable ones being that the APS:

- is apolitical in the performance of its functions;
- makes employment decisions based upon merit;
- provides a workplace that is free from discrimination;
- provides frank, honest, comprehensive, accurate and timely advice to the government;
- establishes workplaces that value communication, consultation, cooperation and input from employees;
- provides a fair, flexible, safe and rewarding workplace;
- promotes equity in employment;
- is a career based service; and
- provides a fair system of review of decisions that affect employees.[119]

Section 10(2) provides a definition of 'merit' for the purposes of the PSA 1999.

The APS Code of Conduct is provided in s 13. This is essentially the same as that which operated under the Interim Reform Regulations from March 1998, and some of the more notable aspects are that an APS employee must:

- act with honesty and integrity, and care and diligence;
- treat others with respect and without harassment;
- obey lawful and reasonable directions;
- maintain appropriate confidentiality;
- disclose and avoid conflicts of interest;
- not make improper use of inside information or their position; and

- comply with other matter prescribed by the regulations (including the duty of non-disclosure).[120]

Failing to uphold the APS Values is a breach of the Code of Conduct. Agency Heads are required to establish procedures for deciding whether an APS employee has breached the Code of Conduct. These procedures must comply with the Public Service Commissioner Directions 1999 (Cth) (discussed below). The PSA 1999 sets out the sanctions which may be applied for a breach, ranging from a reprimand to termination of employment.[121]

## APS Employees

In terms of APS conditions of employment, the regulatory heart of the PSA 1999 is in Part 4.

Section 20 provides that the Agency Head, on behalf of the Commonwealth, has all the rights, duties and powers of an employer in relation to the APS employees in the relevant agency.[122] This formalised the trend which had practically occurred by way of the delegations to Agency Heads made under the PSA 1922.

Section 22 provides that Agency Heads have the power to engage persons on the following bases:

1. as an ongoing APS employee;
2. for a specified term or for a specified task; or
3. for duties that are irregular or intermittent.

The usual basis for engagement, however, is ongoing employment.[123]

Section 23 provides that the Public Service Minister may make rules about the classification of employees which have to be followed by Agency Heads. Moreover, an Agency Head may only reduce the classification of an employee, without consent, in specified circumstances.

Perhaps the most important formal devolution of powers achieved under the PSA 1999 is the power given to Agency Heads to determine terms and conditions for agency employees under s 24. This power corresponds to that which was previously formally held by the Public Service Commissioner under s 82D of the PSA 1922, although a s 24 determination cannot reduce the benefit of any condition of employment applying under the Australian Pay and Conditions Standard, an award, a workplace agreement, a pre-reform certified agreement or a pre-reform AWA.[124] Nevertheless, Agency Heads have been instructed that, as terms and conditions of employment should be established through agreements under the WRA, this determination power should be used sparingly, eg to deal with unforeseen or overlooked issues.[125]

Section 29 deals with termination of employment. Ongoing APS employees may only be terminated on grounds listed in s 29(3) including:

- being excess to requirements;
- loss of essential qualification; or
- breach of the Code of Conduct.

The unfair dismissal provisions of the WRA apply to the termination of employment of APS employees.

Section 33 provides for the review of APS actions other than termination of employment. Review procedures, including the role of the Merit Protection Commissioner, are set out in the regulations.

## Senior Executive Service

There are specific provisions which apply to SES employment, including that termination of employment must be certified by the Public Service Commissioner.

## Public Service Commissioner and Merit Protection Commissioner

Parts 5 and 6 respectively provide for the appointment and functions of the Public Service Commissioner and the Merit Protection Commissioner. The Public Service Commissioner has an important role to play in relation to APS terms and conditions of employment through the issuing of Commissioner's Directions (discussed below) and the Merit Protection Commissioner plays an important role in relation to the review of employment decisions (also discussed below).

## Secretaries of Departments

Part 7 provides for the appointment of Secretaries of Departments of State. A Secretary may be appointed by the Prime Minister for a period of up to five years, although the appointment may be terminated in writing at any time.[126]

## Management Advisory Committee

Section 64 continues the role of the APS Management Advisory Committee, although there is no longer any provision for formal union membership of that Committee.

## Mobility

In relation to machinery of government changes, s 72 of the PSA 1999 enables the Public Service Commissioner to move APS employees from one agency to another agency, or to move them outside the APS and into the employment of a Commonwealth authority, or to move them into the APS from other Commonwealth employment. As discussed below, the regulations provide for what happens to employee terms and conditions as a result of machinery of government changes.

## Subordinate Instruments under the PSA 1999

The PSA 1999 certainly does not contain the outdated detail and 'dead letters' of the PSA 1922. While the new Act provides a simplified statutory framework at the primary level, there are important matters of detail contained in a number of subordinate instruments made under the Act. These details fill out the framework provided by the Act and, in many respects, provide for service wide standards governing the activity of individual agencies.

## Commissioner's Directions

Various provisions in the PSA 1999 provide for the Public Service Commissioner to issue 'Commissioner's Directions', including for the purpose of:

- ensuring that the APS incorporates and upholds the APS Values;
- determining where necessary, the scope and application of the APS Values (in particular the merit principle as applied to engagement and promotion);
- procedures in an agency for dealing with breaches of the Code of Conduct; and
- the engagement, promotion, redeployment, mobility and termination for SES employees.[127]

## Prime Minister's Directions to Agency Heads

Section 21 provides for the Prime Minister to issue directions to Agency Heads relating to management and leadership of APS employees. At present, these directions deal with leave to undertake a statutory appointment or to work under the *Members of Parliament (Staff) Act 1984* (Cth) and with engagement of persons to take part in APS-wide training schemes.[128]

## Classification Rules

Section 23 provides that the Public Service Minister (presently the Prime Minister) may make rules about classifications of employees. The purpose of the Classification Rules is to provide a systematic mechanism for categorising employees for the purposes of facilitating the application of the merit principle and mobility arrangements.[129] The common service-wide prescription of the classification system is needed to distinguish clearly between promotions (subject to a merit test), assignment of duties at the same classification, and reductions in classifications (which are subject to restrictions).

## Regulations

The Public Service Regulations 1999 (Cth) contain much of the important detail of the subordinate instruments.

The Regulations contain rules in relation to the following matters:

- the Code of Conduct including the duty of non-disclosure (reg 2.1);[130]
- limitations on the employment powers of agency heads including the engagement and termination of non-ongoing employees and mobility (Part 3);
- Independent Selection Advisory Committees (Part 4);[131] and
- details of other functions of the Public Service Commissioner and the Merit Protection Commissioner (Parts 6 and 7).

Perhaps the most significant area in the regulations is Part 5, which deals with the review of APS actions. Division 5.2 provides for the review of promotion decisions up to APS Level 6. Application for a review on the ground of merit may be made to the Merit Protection Commissioner. The Merit Protection Commissioner is responsible for appointing a Promotion Review Committee ('PRC') to review the decision. The decision of the PRC is binding on the Agency Head.

Part 5 also provides for a two-tier level of review of APS actions other than promotion decisions. At the primary level are reviews conducted by the Agency Head, unless the APS action involves a determination relating to a breach of the Code of Conduct. The Agency Head may refer a primary level matter to the Merit Protection Commissioner.

The Merit Protection Commissioner considers primary level matters involving breaches of the Code of Conduct or those which have been referred by an Agency Head. The Merit Protection Commissioner may also conduct a secondary level review if a person is dissatisfied with the decision of the Agency Head at the primary level.

Part 8 of the Regulations also provides for employment conditions to apply when APS employees change agencies as a result of machinery of government or administrative rearrangements.

## Comparison with the PSA 1922

The major achievement of the PSA 1999 was to provide for a simpler and up to date piece of primary legislation which sets the framework for the detail in the subordinate instruments that have been discussed earlier. However, in reality, practically all of the employment reforms over the period discussed in this chapter had effectively been achieved within the old framework of the PSA 1922.[132]

In general terms it is accurate to summarise the PSA 1999 as having the following effects:[133]

- the primary legislation was simplified and updated (the old Act was some 245 pages, whereas the new Act is only 47 pages);

- it removed outdated detail and prescription, although there is much detail included in the subordinate instruments made under the new Act;
- the concept of 'merit' now has a specific definition;
- there was a change in employment categories, with the abolition of the notion of 'office';
- the maximum retirement age of 65 was removed;
- some review procedures have been changed although independent review of promotion decisions up to APS level 6 has been retained; other employment decisions may be subject to internal agency review prior to review by the Merit Protection Commissioner;
- complex Part IV mobility provisions were removed; and
- an Independent Selection Advisory Committee mechanism has replaced the old Joint Selection Committee Process, which is another instance of removal of a formal union function.

The PSA 1999 and its subordinate instruments do represent a significant rewrite of many of the pre-existing conditions of APS employment. In that regard, a new jurisprudence and practice has developed around the new framework. For example, agencies no longer need to consider concepts such as 'office' that employees no longer occupy particular positions, and references to 'temporary employees' are now altered to 'non-ongoing employees'. Nevertheless, the basic employment relationships operating under the PSA 1922 continue to operate under the PSA 1999.

## Relationship with the WRA

Section 8 of the PSA 1999 provides that the Act has effect subject to the WRA, and thus contemplates the agreement making and unfair dismissal provisions provided for by that Act. Shortly after its passage, a former Public Service Commissioner commented that the PSA 1999 is concerned primarily with the ethos, standards, accountability and key structure aspects of the APS while the WRA defines the employment relations framework.[134]

## Certified Agreements and AWAs

The Workplace Relations Regulations 1996 (Cth) were amended with effect from the commencement of the PSA 1999 to provide that a certified agreement or AWA could prevail over conditions of employment specified in a determination made under s 24 of the PSA 1999 (other than a determination made under s 72 in relation to machinery of government or other administrative changes).[135] This position can be equated with the previous position in which certified agreements and AWAs could prevail over determinations made under s 82D of the PSA 1922.

## Twenty-First Century Developments: The Work Choices Legislation

Since 1996, the third major change to the legislative framework governing APS employment has come with the passage of the Commonwealth *Workplace Relations Amendment (Work Choices) Act 2005* (the 'Work Choices legislation'). All of the relevant provisions had commenced by 27 March 2006.

The Work Choices legislation repealed and replaced a great deal of the WRA. Moreover, it effected a substantial constitutional 're-basing' of the WRA by expanding the Commonwealth's reliance on the corporations power in s 51(xx) of the Constitution. The reforms were stated to include:

- simplification of the inherent complexity in the existence of six separate workplace relations jurisdictions in Australia by creating a national workplace relations system based on the corporations power;
- establishment of the Australian Fair Pay Commission to set minimum wages;
- greater emphasis on direct bargaining and simplified lodgement processes for industrial agreements;
- direct legislation for certain minimum conditions of employment such as annual leave, personal/carers leave, parental (including maternity) leave and the maximum ordinary hours of work;[136]
- improved regulation of industrial action, including by requiring a secret ballot before the taking of 'protected industrial action';
- further simplification of awards that would provide a safety net; and
- the protection and preservation of certain award conditions.[137]

The Work Choices legislation has been the subject of much controversy. There was a challenge to its constitutional validity on a number of grounds in the High Court. In particular, the question was whether the legislation (dealing as it does with employment and industrial matters) went beyond a valid exercise of the Commonwealth Parliament's power to make laws with respect to trading and financial corporations. The principal arguments centre around:

- whether an employment relationship operating within a corporation is a matter with respect to its trading activities; and
- whether the Commonwealth's power with respect to corporations should be read down by reference to the conciliation and arbitration power in relation to interstate industrial disputes in s 51(xxxv) of the Constitution (ie that a valid law with respect to the industrial relations matters of corporations is also confined by the terms of that constitutional provision).

Whilst the High Court upheld the validity of the Work Choices legislation,[138] many of the controversial and constitutionally contentious matters are outside the scope of this chapter, dealing as it does with APS employment.[139]

Nevertheless, the Work Choices legislation, now declared valid and fully operative, together with the further changes brought about by the *Workplace Relations Amendment (A Stronger Safety Net) Act 2007* (Cth), have made significant changes to the arrangements for the APS introduced by WROLA at the end of 1996, particularly the arrangements for agreement making.

While it may still be too early to provide meaningful commentary on the practical effects of the changes for public sector employment, the Work Choices legislation does represent a further increment in the attempt to encourage agreements directly between employers and employees, and as well as further regulation of the role of unions in relation to that process.

## Workplace Agreements

Part 8 of the amended WRA now deals with what are known as 'workplace agreements'. It is sufficient to consider two basic forms of workplace agreements described in that Part, collective agreements; and AWAs.[140]

### Collective Agreements

Collective agreements now replace certified agreements.[141] For present purposes, we can consider two types of collective agreement:

- 'employee collective agreement';[142] and
- 'union collective agreement'.[143]

While both forms of collective agreement still require approval by a majority of the affected employees, there are some important changes:

- these agreements are no longer required to be certified by the AIRC in order to commence operation; rather they are merely required to be lodged with the Workplace Authority Director (formerly the Employment Advocate) within 14 days after approval;[144]
- except for checking some agreements as to whether they meet the fairness test, Workplace Ombudsman is generally not required to make a determination as to whether the agreement complies with the WRA;[145] and
- arrangements for the appointment of bargaining agents have been extended to individual employees, even in the context of the negotiation of collective agreements.[146]

### Australian Workplace Agreements

Part 8 of the WRA continues provision for the making of AWAs but with a number of changes:

- there is no longer a requirement to offer AWAs on similar terms to comparable employees; and

- there is no longer provision for multiple individual AWAs to be included in a single document.[147]
- Agency Heads continue to act on behalf of the Commonwealth in relation to the negotiation of AWAs.[148]

## Changes Common to Both Collective Agreements and AWAs

There are important new provisions that are common to the making of collective agreements and AWAs (as 'workplace agreements') which include:

- the period during which a proposed agreement must be available for an employee's consideration has been reduced from 14 days to seven days;[149]
- there is no longer an express requirement to explain the terms of a proposed workplace agreement to an employee;[150]
- the 'no-disadvantage' test in old part VIE of the WRA was repealed, effectively leaving the Australian Fair Pay and Conditions Standard and any 'protected award conditions' of the APS Award 1998 (see below) to operate as the 'safety net' for APS employees who ceased to be covered by a workplace agreement.[151] However the 'fairness test' later added by the *Workplace Relations Amendment (A Stronger Safety Net) Act 2007* now provides for compensation to be paid for any modification or exclusion of 'protected award conditions' in all collective agreements, and in AWAs involving an annual salary of under $75,000, made from 1 May 2007.[152]
- the nominal expiry date for workplace agreements may now be up to five years after the agreement has been lodged with the Workplace Authority Director;[153]
- a collective agreement or AWA is deemed to include 'protected award conditions' unless these have been specifically excluded by the agreement;[154]
- a collective agreement and an AWA are now expressly allowed to 'call-up' (ie incorporate by reference) the terms of another workplace agreement or industrial instrument (such as an award) that would otherwise apply to the employment of the employee(s);[155]
- 'protected industrial action' in relation to the negotiation of a collective agreement will now only be able to be taken following a secret ballot of the relevant employees.[156]

## Prohibited Content

A collective agreement or AWA will not be able to include 'prohibited content' which has been defined by the regulations to include terms relating to the deduction of union fees; leave to attend trade union training course or meetings; the renegotiation of the workplace agreement; restrictions on the engagement of independent contractors or labour hire workers; the encouragement or discouragement of union membership; the allowing of industrial action or dealing with unfair dismissal (except in relation to the management of underperformance);

restrictions on offering AWAs; excessive foregoing of annual leave and provision of employee information to trade unions.[157]

A workplace agreement cannot contain a term which would restrict or prohibit the disclosure of the content of a workplace agreement.[158] It is also 'prohibited content' to discriminate in an agreement on the basis of sex, sexual preference, age, disability, religion, marital status, etc unless inherent to the requirements of the position, or to include matters that do not pertain to the employment relationship.[159]

## Unilateral Termination

A party to a workplace agreement will now be able to unilaterally terminate that agreement after the nominal expiry date:

- if such termination is provided for by the agreement; or
- on the giving of 90 days notice.

On termination, an employee will not be covered by any other workplace agreement or award that might otherwise apply to the employee, except for any 'protected award conditions'.[160] Unless an employer gives undertakings about post-termination conditions under s 397 of the WRA, an APS employee who has, say, an AWA terminated, will fall back on the AFPC Standard and any 'protected award conditions' that apply.[161]

The effect of the above provisions is that the Commonwealth Parliament has now significantly expanded its direct legislation in relation to the content of APS workplace agreements, for example:

- it may have the effect of deeming that the terms of the 'protected award conditions' as set out in s354 of the WRA are taken to be part of the content of an agreement; and
- (conversely) it proscribes a range of matters as being 'prohibited content' in a workplace agreement.[162]

## The Relationship between AWAs, Collective Agreements, Awards and the PSA 1999

Many of the previously complex arrangements between the various sources of APS terms and conditions of employment have been addressed by more simplified arrangements to operate under the Work Choices legislation.

### AWAs and Collective Agreements

Section 348 of the WRA now makes it clear that only one workplace agreement can operate in relation to an employee at any one time. Further, a collective agreement has no effect in relation to an employee while an AWA is in operation.[163]

## Awards

Section 349 of the WRA makes it clear that an award has no effect in relation to an employee while a workplace agreement operates in relation to that employee.[164]

## PSA 1999

Section 350 of the WRA continues the arrangements whereby a workplace agreement may displace certain prescribed conditions of employment in prescribed Commonwealth laws. Consistent with the arrangements that applied prior to the Work Choices legislation, the new regulations made under the WRA specify that a workplace agreement may displace conditions specified in a determination made under s 24(1) of the PSA 1999 (other than certain determinations made in relation to 'machinery of government' changes pursuant to s 72 of the PSA 1999).[165]

# Transitional Arrangements

## Certified Agreements and AWAs

A certified agreement or AWA made before the commencement of the Work Choices legislation will be known respectively as:

- a 'pre-reform certified agreement'; and
- a 'pre-reform AWA'.

Generally speaking, pre-reform certified agreements and pre-reform AWAs continue to operate, in the same manner as under the old WRA, until they are replaced by a workplace agreement.

Once replaced by a collective agreement, a pre-reform certified agreement ceases to apply (and can never operate again). A collective agreement replaces a pre-reform certified agreement even if the nominal expiry date of the pre-reform certified agreement has not passed. Further, if an employee covered by a pre-reform certified agreement enters into an AWA, then the pre-reform certified agreement ceases to apply to that employee (and can never operate again in relation to that employee).[166]

A new AWA replaces a pre-reform AWA, even if it is made prior to the nominal expiry date of the pre-reform AWA.[167] The terms of a pre-reform certified agreement or a pre-reform AWA may be incorporated by reference into a new workplace agreement.[168]

## Awards

Awards made prior to the Work Choices legislation will continue to operate except that the number of allowable award matters has been reduced from 20 to 15. Any matter that is not one of the 15 matters listed in s 513 of the WRA ceased to have effect from commencement of the Work Choices legislation (ie from 27 March 2006) unless it is a 'preserved award term'.[169] Preserved award terms are those relating to:

- annual leave;
- personal/carers leave;
- parental, maternity or adoption leave;
- long service leave;
- notice of termination;
- jury service; and
- superannuation (until 20 June 2008).[170]

A preserved award term takes effect as part of the award. However, as noted, the award does not apply to any employee subject to a workplace agreement.[171]

In relation to the APS, the Australian Public Service Award 1998 continues in effect to the extent that it deals with the 15 allowable award matters and preserved award terms and does not include prohibited terms. However, apart from 'protected award conditions', its operation is entirely excluded by a new workplace agreement, and the 'protected award conditions' may themselves be entirely excluded.[172] Moreover, subject to the provisions of the previous WRA, the APS Award may also be excluded by the terms of a pre-reform certified agreement or a pre-reform AWA. As has been noted, the recent introduction of the 'fairness test' will mean that fair compensation may be required for modification of or exclusion of protected award conditions that occurs in collective agreements or AWAs involving an annual salary of less than $75,000 that are made from 1 May 2007.

Rates of pay are no longer to be matters dealt with as allowable award matters, nor are they to be 'preserved award matters'.[173]

## Early Experiences with Agreement Making in the APS under the Work Choices Legislation

In many ways, the Work Choices legislation has simplified arrangements for agreement making and clarified the position in relation to the operation of workplace agreements in relation to other industrial instruments. However, as agencies come to consider new AWAs and collective agreements the provisions of existing AWAs and certified agreements are being examined with regard to the following two subject matters:

- *prohibited content*: in order to ensure that new agreements do not restate or incorporate by reference provisions that would now be void if included and in order not to breach the legislation and be subject to civil penalties; and

- *the AFPC Standard*: in order to ensure that agreements do not carry forward terms that would now be less favourable than the standard. As noted, APS terms and conditions generally exceed the AFPC Standard but there are some aspects where adjustments are being required, for example, in relation to the accrual and crediting rules for leave.

As with WROLA, in 1996, it might be expected that there will be a period of adjustment for APS agencies in terms of aligning their agreement making arrangements with the latest changes to the legislative framework.

## Conclusion: A Comparison of the Present and Pre-1996 Frameworks

In the pre-1996 framework, APS terms and conditions of employment were sourced from: general public service legislation in the form of the PSA 1922; general industrial relations framework legislation that provided for awards; certified agreements (including some made at APS agency level); and public service legislation on particular matters.

In the present framework, APS terms and conditions of employment are sourced from: general public service legislation in the form of the PSA 1999; general industrial relations framework legislation that provides for awards, certified or collective agreements (routinely made at APS agency level); and AWAs; and public service legislation on particular matters.

The changes, since 1996, to the legislative framework for APS employment can be seen as forming part of a continuing process of reform to the manner and circumstances in which employment terms and conditions are determined. In devolving agreement making responsibilities to the agency level (subject to fairly comprehensive policy guidance) those changes parallel the approach that has been taken in relation to APS financial management reform since the 1980s. However, the Work Choices legislation, with the introduction of the AFPC Standard and 'prohibited content' adopts a position that has become more prescriptive about the matters which can and cannot be included in workplace agreements.

## WROLA and the Introduction of the *Workplace Relations Act 1996*

As discussed, the first major reform in terms of general industrial relations law was the introduction of the WRA.[174] That Act continued the then recent trend to emphasise workplace bargaining arrangements over industry awards, and the approach taken under the WRA has been to introduce comprehensive bargaining at APS agency level in place of service-wide agreements. It is true that comprehensive bargaining at the agency level was a significant step but, put in an historical context, the 1996 workplace relations reforms were carrying on a recent trend of change in the APS, rather than striking out in a new direction.

Agency level bargaining under the WRA has produced some variations in outcomes on pay and other conditions across the APS, although the Government maintains a significant degree of centralised control through its agreement making policy parameters and guidelines.

A significant new area of reform however was the introduction of individual bargaining to the APS in the form of AWAs. This form of agreement has provided some flexibility in terms and conditions and specific remuneration arrangements to apply in particular cases. AWAs have become standard for employees at SES level but, a decade or so later, it still remains to be seen how pervasive they will become at levels below the SES. For this latter group, AWAs are primarily used as a vehicle for performance pay and other specific benefits; otherwise there has been no real incentive for these employees to move out from cover under a certified agreement.[175]

The other significant change under WROLA was the winding back of a formal (or guaranteed) union role in negotiating agreements on a service wide or agency basis. Nevertheless, it is clear that unions have played a significant role in the negotiation of many certified agreements. The substantial majority of those agreements were made with unions under old s 170LJ of the WRA, and, it is probably the case that unions have also played a significant role in the conclusion of many of the agreements expressed to have been made directly with employees.[176]

The 1996 WRA regime, as applied in the APS, initially made the arrangements for determining terms and conditions of employment more complex. Certified agreements and AWAs were difficult to frame for the following reasons:

- the lack of clarity in transitional provisions concerning the status of old certified agreements;
- the continuing relationship of old awards and old certified agreements with the PSA 1922 and the determinations and regulations made under that Act;
- the different nature of the relationship between new certified agreements and AWAs on the one hand and the PSA 1922, its determinations and regulations on the other hand;
- the complex relationship between the new certified agreements, AWAs and existing awards;
- the effect of the 'no-disadvantage' test; and
- the different instruments which applied to SES and non-SES officers.

Nevertheless, it is fair to say that the 1996 WRA arrangements presented the opportunity for more simplified arrangements. As time progressed, certified agreements became more comprehensive in nature, meaning less reliance on the need to refer to awards and other instruments (and the 'no disadvantage test' became less significant as successive agreements were negotiated). Moreover, when AWAs were able to sit above (or call up) certified agreements, their operation also became clearer. Nevertheless, difficulties (both real but mainly in terms of presentation) remained with the continued operation of the PSA 1922. These were largely addressed with the passage of the PSA 1999.

## PSA 1999

The second major initiative affecting APS employment since 1996 has been the passage of the PSA 1999. This Act ultimately had bipartisan support and completed the work to modernise the legislation that had commenced with the McLeod Report in 1994.[177]

As has been noted, the PSA 1999 represented a welcome rewrite and modernisation of the old legislative framework. In particular, it works better with the WRA.[178] While the PSA 1999 is shorter and simpler, the detail has been moved to an increased number of subordinate instruments which keep in place a measure of control of employment policy and practice, especially with the continuing roles of the Public Service Commissioner and Merit Protection Commissioner.

A key design aspect of the PSA 1999 is that it embodied the relatively recent reforms in relation to the APS Values and the APS Code of Conduct. The APS Values provide an express statement of the principles of the APS which previously had to be derived from the prescriptive duties of officers formerly contained in the old Public Service Regulations.

Nevertheless, the APS did not undergo revolutionary change as a result of the PSA 1999. As a practical matter for APS employees, the passage of the PSA 1999 presented no great change to the way they were engaged and rewarded or how they went about their business.[179] The substance of the matters dealt with by the new framework had already been substantially put in place under the framework of the PSA 1922 (albeit in a more convoluted way). As such, the new Act really represented a step closer to the end of a journey of reform, rather than the beginning of another.

There was, however, a deal of activity required to adapt management systems to take account of the new legislative framework and terminology.[180] This seems to be confirmed by the State of the Service Report 1999/2000 tabled by the Public Service Commissioner. An entire section of that report is, not surprisingly, devoted to the experience of working with the PSA 1999 and it identified the major implementation issues for agencies as:

- dealing with the cultural effects of the removal of the concept of 'office' and updating delegations instruments;

- reviewing and revising recruitment and promotion arrangements to take account of legislative changes, including the new stricter requirements for engaging non-ongoing employees and application of the defined merit principle;
- creating agency procedures for dealing with breaches of the Code of Conduct and for review of employment decisions; and
- ensuring that changes to the legislative framework were properly factored into negotiations for 'second round' certified agreements.[181]

These issues were largely ones for organisations to deal with rather than being of practical day to day effect on employees. For example, for an employee, undergoing a promotion review process under the Public Service Regulations 1999 (Cth) is not unlike undergoing an appeals process under the provisions of the PSA 1922.

To reiterate, the above discussion is not to suggest the enactment of the PSA 1999 was not a significant and welcome step, for it was. It should however be seen for what it was: merely one of a series of steps in reform and not the entire reform agenda.

## Work Choices

Since 1996, the third significant change to the legislative framework for APS employment has, of course, been the Work Choices legislation. It is too early to discern the practical significance of the legislation in relation to the APS but the following aspects might be noted.

The Work Choices legislation further entrenches agreement making arrangements at agency level across the APS. However, particular provisions have the potential to have significant effects on the environment in which those agreements are reached, including by further regulation of the formal role of unions in the process.

It is not so much a change to the general framework of agreement making but rather a number of changes to the rules within that framework that have potential impact, including the following changes:

a.  the proscription of 'prohibited content' from workplace agreements removes the ability of agencies and, in particular unions, to come to their own agreement on that range of matters;

b.  the potential operation the AFPC Standard, and any 'protected award conditions' as terms of a workplace agreement, are key examples of the Commonwealth Parliament directly legislating for terms and conditions of employment;

c.  the requirements for 'protected industrial action' in relation to collective agreements now include a secret ballot;

d.  there are more express requirements placed upon the AIRC in relation to the termination of bargaining periods (and hence discontinuation of any protected industrial action); and

e.  the ability to unilaterally terminate a workplace agreement (especially an AWA) has the consequences that an affected APS employee will, unless undertakings are made, fall back upon the AFPC Standard and 'protected award conditions'.

Furthermore, the legislation now puts it beyond doubt that AWAs can be made a condition of engagement for new APS employees, with the potential to erode, over time, the numbers on collective agreements.

Obviously the issue of the ability of workplace agreements to modify or exclude the operation of award conditions has received some commentary and has prompted the recent introduction of the 'fairness test'. Nevertheless, this aspect of the potential operation of workplace agreements does not appear to have been an issue in the APS employment context.

The Work Choices legislation should generally make the framing of collective agreements and AWAs easier because it will be clear that only one instrument will apply to an employee at any one time. Nevertheless, there are initial complexities because of the need for new workplace agreements to pay appropriate regard to the AFPC Standard and to avoid the inclusion of any 'prohibited content'.

It remains to be seen how the other matters mentioned above will affect the way workplace agreements are made in the APS. The experience of the next couple of years will tell in that regard.

# ENDNOTES

[1] Mark Molloy is a Senior Executive Lawyer at the Australian Government Solicitor (AGS). The views expressed in this paper are Mark's personal views, and not necessarily the views of AGS.

[2] References to the Australian Public Service or APS throughout this chapter are references to the public service of the Commonwealth of Australia.

[3] The Commonwealth Constitution s 51(xxxix) combined with s 61 (the federal executive power) and s 52(ii) (the power in relation to departments transferred by the states).

[4] See Breen Creighton and Andrew Stewart, *Labour Law: An Introduction* (1990) 109.

[5] See *Stevens v Brodribb Sawmilling Company Ply Ltd* (1986) 160 CLR 16.

[6] G J McCarry, *Aspects of Public Sector Employment Law* (1988) 18.

[7] Ibid.

[8] *Williamson v Commonwealth* (1907) 5 CLR 174; *Lucy v Commonwealth* (1923) 33 CLR 229; *Fletcher v Nott* (1938) 60 CLR 55.

[9] This it could do by variously exercising powers under Constitution s 61 (executive power), s 64 (establishment of Departments of State) and s 67 (appointment of civil servants).

[10] Prior to the PSA 1922, there had been the *Commonwealth Public Service Act 1902*.

[11] See Public Service Act Review Group, *Report of the Public Service Act Review Group: December 1994* (1994) 13-15 (the 'the McLeod Report').

[12] *Arbitration (Public Service) Act 1920* (Cth).

[13] *Conciliation and Arbitration Amendment Act (No 2) 1983* (Cth).

[14] See, eg, *Industrial Relations Act 1988* (Cth) s 121 (and of the renamed *Workplace Relations Act 1996* (Cth)).

[15] See *Workplace Relations Act 1996* (Cth) s 350 and Workplace Relations Regulations 2006 (Cth) regs 8.2 and 8.3. The *Merit Protection (Australian Government Employees) Act 1984* (Cth) was repealed at the time of the passage of the PSA 1999; merit protection provisions are now contained in pt 5 of the Public Service Regulations 1999 (Cth).

[16] Commonwealth, *Reforming the Australian Public Service: A Statement of the Government's Intentions*, Parl Paper No 194 (1983).

[17] See also McInnes, 'Public Sector Reform under the Hawke Government: Reconstruction or Deconstruction?' (1990) 62(2) *Australian Quarterly* 108.

[18] *Public Service Legislation (Streamlining) Act 1986* (Cth).

[19] *Administrative Arrangements Act 1987* (Cth).

[20] Peter Punch, *Australian Industrial Law* (1995) 704.

[21] See, eg, *National Wage Case — March 1987* (1987) 17 IR 65 (Australian Conciliation and Arbitration Commission) ('The National Wage Case of 1987').

[22] This agreement provided for changes to office structures and classifications in exchange for a wage rise.

[23] *Industrial Relations Legislation Amendment Act 1992* (Cth); Punch, above n 20, 705.

[24] As will be seen, the WRA has continued the trend to enterprise bargaining, which is now completely conducted at the agency level in the APS.

[25] See PSA 1922 div 4 of pt III.

[26] See PSA 1922 subdiv D, div 4, pt III.

[27] See Ibid.

[28] See PSA 1922 pt IIA

[29] See PSA 1922 div 2B, pt III.

[30] See PSA 1922 div 10, pt III.

[31] See PSA 1922 div 6, pt III.

[32] See PSA 1922 divs 8A, 8B and 8C.

[33] See PSA 1922 s 76W(4) and *Industrial Relations Act 1988* (Cth) s 121

[34] See generally PSA 1922 pt IV.

[35] It is interesting to note that the general secrecy provision was recently held to be unconstitutional in the case of *Bennett v President, Human Rights and Equal Opportunity Commission* [2003] FCA 1433, but substantially the same provision is still retained as reg 2.1 of Public Service Regulations 1999 (Cth).

[36] In addition, the Australian Public Service, Senior Executive Service (Salaries and Specific Conditions) Award 1995 (the 'SES Award') dealt with rates of pay and some other issues for SES personnel. Clause 6.1 of that award also provided that SES officers were not covered by GECA and so most SES terms and conditions were actually those determined under s 82D of the PSA 1922 or those that applied by under the APS Enterprise Agreement.

[37] IRA s 121 continued as *Workplace Relations Act 1996* (Cth) s 116.

[38] See definition of 'award' in the then s 4(1) of the IRA.

[39] The then s 170MK of the IRA.

[40] GECA clause 17.

[41] PSA 1922 div 8C, pt III, which applies to non-SES officers.

[42] GECA clause 11.

[43] IRA ss 171 and 170MK.

[44] Unlike GECA, the APS Enterprise Agreement also covered SES officers.

[45] Clause 8 of the APS Enterprise Agreement.

[46] Clause 10(c) of the APS Enterprise Agreement.

[47] See *Improving Productivity, Jobs & Pay in the Australian Public Service: 1992-1994* (also known as the 'Framework Agreement'); see also Interim Framework Australian Public Service Agreement 1995 (the 'Interim Framework Agreement').

[48] Although the ability to negotiate for supplementary pay at the agency level was curtailed by the APS Enterprise Agreement.

[49] *Workplace Relations Amendment (Work Choices) Act 2005* (Cth).

[50] References to sections of the *Workplace Relations Act 1996* (Cth) are to section numbers prior to the amendments brought about by Work Choices legislation in 2005.

[51] See generally M Pittard, 'Collective Employment Relationships: Reforms to Arbitrated Awards and Certified Agreements' (1997) 10 *Australian Journal of Labour Law* 62.

[52] WRA s 89A(3). APS awards had traditionally been paid rates awards.

[53] See generally M Pittard and R Naughton, *Australian Labour Law: Cases and Materials*, 4th ed, 2003, ch 12.

[54] Defined by s 4 of the WRA to include foreign, trading and financial corporations within the meaning of s 51(xx) of the Constitution, a body corporate incorporated in a Territory or a Commonwealth authority.

[55] Division 2 also operated where the employer was an employer conducting business in a Territory; or an employer of certain employees such as waterside workers, maritime workers and flight crew officers engaged in interstate or overseas trade or commerce (see s 5AA of the WRA).

[56] Underpinning for additional operation of Div 2 was also provided by the Territories power (Constitution s 122) and the trade and commerce power (Constitution s 51(i)).

[57] It should be noted that employers could also make enterprise flexibility agreements directly with employees under the previous Part VIB of the IRA.

[58] WRA ss 170LJ(2), (3), 170LK(1), (2), (5).

[59] WRA s 170NB.

[60] WRA ss 170LK(4), (5).

[61] WRA div 4, pt VIB.

[62] WRA s 170LX.

[63] WRA div 6, pt VID.

[64] J Riley, G McCarry and M Smith, *Workplace Relations: A Guide to the 1996 Changes* (1997).

[65] An office established with the function of providing assistance to employers and employees about rights and obligations under the WRA, particularly in relation to AWAs: WRA s 83BB.

[66] WRA ss 170VPA, WG.

[67] WRA s 170VPA(1)(e).

[68] WRA s 170VK.

69 WRA s 170VE.

70 WRA s 170XA.

71 This limited immunity replaced the limited 'right to strike' in relation to the negotiation of certified agreements that had previously been included in IRA s 170VPA.

72 WRA div 8, pt VIB.

73 WRA div 8, pt VID.

74 DIR Workplace Relations Advice 1997/27, APS Agreement Making — Update, of 23 May 1997.

75 Department of Workplace Relations and Small Business ('DWRSB'), *Annual Report 1998* (1998) 55.

76 See clause 6.1.1 of the APS Award 1998 and Department of Employment, Workplace Relations and Small Business, *Annual Report 1999* (1999), 99.

77 DIR Workplace Relations Advice 1997/4, Agreement Making in the APS, 12 March 1997 (This and other DIR/DEWRSB/DEWR Advices are available at <http://www.workplace.gov.au> (Commonwealth Public Sector)).

78 DIR Workplace Relations Advice 1997/29, Policy Parameters for Agreement Making in the APS, 23 May 1997,

79 Throughout 1997, the Government and the ACTU (on behalf of public sector unions) conducted negotiations on an Agency Bargaining Framework. However, no framework agreement was concluded.

80 See, eg, 'Workplace Relations and Agreement Making in APS Agencies' a paper attached to DEWRSB Workplace Relations Advice 1997/33, Workplace Relations and Agreement Making in APS Agencies, 3 June 1997.

81 Policy parameter number 7 of the May 1997 Policy Parameters, however, for a number of reasons, this was difficult to achieve (see below).

82 WRA old s 170LB(1)(b) and now s 322(1)(b).

83 Except awards made under WRA s 170MX(3), which deals with arbitration in matters at the end of a bargaining period and 'exceptional matter' orders made after the commencement of a certified agreement.

84 So much would seem to follow from the effect of s *Acts Interpretation Act 1901* (Cth) s 8, which operates to preserve rights and obligations which have arisen under repealed legislation.

85 Then reg 30ZE of the Workplace Relations Regulations 1996 (Cth) and Sch 5 to those regulations. However, since the passage of the *Public Service Act 1999* (Cth), new regulations only refer to determinations made under ss 24 and 72 of that Act (which is discussed later).

86 At 16.

87 DEWR Workplace Relations Advice 2002/5, Policy Parameters for Agreement Making in the APS 2002, 7 June 2002; DEWR APS Advice 06 of 2003, Government Support for Defence Reservists, 3 December 2003. In April 2006, DEWR released revised policy parameters for the Work Choices legislation and these are discussed later.

88 See generally DEWRSB Agreement Making in the APS — The First Round (May 1997-June 1999), and the follow up Survey of Agreement Making in the APS (2001).

89 Although AWAs were to be as comprehensive as possible they also, at least initially, largely incorporated the terms of other instruments.

90 For example, a certified agreement could be drafted to exclude the legal operation of an award but to incorporate, by reference, the terms of that award as terms of the certified agreement. In a sense therefore, the agreement might legally have been a stand-alone agreement but it may not have been 'textually comprehensive'.

91 DEWRSB, *Annual Report 1998-99* (1999) 29.

92 DEWR Website figures as at 1 May 2006 record that 98 of the then 100 certified agreements were standalone agreements.

93 See DEWRSB, *Survey of Agreement Making in the APS* (2001) 9.

94 DEWR APS Advice 04 of 2005 (3 August 2005) and Supporting Guidance - Workplace Relations Policy Parameters for Agreement Making in the Australian Public Service (April 2006) 24.

95 DEWR figures at <http//www.workplace.gov.au>.

96 DEWRSB, *Annual Report 1998-99* (1999) 29.

[97] DEWRSB Workplace Relations Advice 1999/8, Policy Parameters for Agreement Making in the APS, 17 May 1999; and this will continue under the Work Choices arrangements: DEWR APS Advice 05 of 2006.

[98] WRA old s 170WK and now s 415.

[99] DEWR APS Advice 04 of 2005 (3 August 2005).

[100] And most certified agreements were drafted to so allow.

[101] These provisions are intended to reflect the primacy of operative certified agreements which are likely to contain more detailed provisions of benefit to the employee.

[102] WRA s 170VR(4).

[103] Then reg 30ZJ of the Workplace Relations Regulations 1996 (Cth) and Schedule 5 to those regulations. However, since the passage of the *Public Service Act 1999* (Cth), new regulations only refer to determinations made under ss 24 and 72 of that Act (discussed in a later section of this paper).

[104] WRA s 170VG(2).

[105] Reports and publications include: Department of Employment and Workplace Relations and Small Business, and the Office of the Employment Advocate, *Australian Workplace Agreements in the Public Sector: Early Experiences: Tips and Case Studies* (August 2000); The Senate Finance and Public Accounts Committee, Parliament of Australia, *Australian Public Service Employment Matters, First Report, Australian Workplace Agreements* (2000); and the Department of Employment, Workplace Relations and Small Business, *Survey of Agreement Making in the APS* (2001).

[106] Department of Employment, Workplace Relations and Small Business, *Survey of Agreement Making in the APS* (2001), 15.

[107] DEWR circular 13 April 2006.

[108] Prior to the passage of the PSA 1999, APS permanent APS personnel held an 'office', whereas they are now termed as (ongoing) 'employees'.

[109] WRA old s 170VG.

[110] On the basis that they were not 'comparable employees'; see WRA ss 170VA and 170VPA.

[111] To ensure that conflicting and outdated provisions of the PSA 1922 remained inoperative.

[112] WRA s 170VQ(1).

[113] See generally section 'Australian Workplace Agreements in the APS Context' above.

[114] See Department of Employment, Workplace Relations and Small Business/ Office of the Employment Advocate Booklet, 28; and Senate Committee: *Report on the Consideration of the Workplace Relations and Other Legislation Amendment Bill 1996*, commentary at 30-31.

[115] Total figure as at 30 June 2005 as per Australian Public Service, Statistical Bulletin 2002-05 (2005).

[116] <http://workplace.gov.au/workplace/Organisation/Government/Federal/Reports/Progressin AgreementMaking.htm>

[117] No. 23 — Reg 3: new regulations 5 to 11.

[118] As Act no 147 of 1999.

[119] PSA 1999 ss 10(1)(a), (b), (c), (f), (i), (j), (l), (n) and (o).

[120] PSA 1999 ss 13 (1) (2) (3) (5) (6) (7) (10) and (13); PS Regulations (Amendment-Interim Reforms) 1998 ss 7 (1) (2) (3) (5) (6) (7) (10) and (13).

[121] PSA 1999 s 15.

[122] PSA 1999 s 20.

[123] PSA 1999 s 22(3).

[124] This update list of instruments reflects amendments recently made by the Work Choices legislation (discussed below).

[125] DEWR, *Supporting Guidance: Workplace Relations Policy Parameters for Agreement Making in the Australian Public Service* (April 2006) 31.

[126] Subject of course to meeting the procedural fairness requirements described in *Barratt v Howard* (2000) 170 ALR 529, 543-46, and the reporting requirements of s 59.

[127] PSA 1999 ss 11, 15 and 36; Public Service Commissioner's Directions 1999 chs 2, 5 and 6.

[128] Prime Minister's Public Service Directions 1999 chs 2 and 3.

[129] Department of Employment, Workplace Relations and Small Business, APS Advice 1999/19, Classification Management Under the New Public Service Act, 18 November 1999.

[130] It would seem that the present form of the duty of non-disclosure provision is constitutionally invalid as a result of the decision in *Bennett v President, Human Rights and Equal Opportunity Commission* 10 December 2003 [2003] FCA 1433.

[131] An Independent Selection Advisory Committee ('ISAC') may be established to advise an Agency Head on selection decisions for up to APS Level 6. An ISAC will consist of a convener nominated by the Merit Protection Review Agency ('MPRA'), an agency representative and another APS employee nominated by the MPRA. An Agency Head is not bound to follow the recommendations of an ISAC but, if he or she does, then there is no right of review of that employment decision under pt 5 of the Regulations.

[132] In this regard, PSMPC Advice No 1 of 19 November 1999 included a comparison chart, which traces where particular subject matters were dealt with under the old and the new regimes. It reveals that the major impact of the PSA 1999 has been to change the location of the subject matters dealt with under the previous regime rather than remove those matters.

[133] Workplace Partners Update (2004) DEWRSB http://www.dewrsb.gov.au (at 29 August 2006).

[134] Denis Ives, 'Benchmarking the Issues', (2000) 95 *Canberra Bulletin of Public Administration* 31, 32.

[135] Now regs 8.2. and 8.3 of ch 2 of the Workplace Relations Regulations 2006 (Cth).

[136] Together with the minimum wages to be set by the Australian Fair Pay Commission, these entitlements are to be known as the Australian Fair Pay and Conditions Standard ('AFPC Standard').

[137] *Explanatory Memorandum*, Workplace Relations Amendment (Work Choices) Bill 2005 1-2.

[138] *New South Wales v The Commonwealth* [2006] HCA 52.

[139] As has been noted, the Commonwealth's constitutional power to legislate on APS employment matters is based on the executive power (s 61) and the express incidental power (s 51 (xxxix).

[140] The types of 'workplace agreements' are set out in WRA div 2, pt 8, and also extend to 'greenfields' agreements, which might apply in relation to new businesses and 'multiple-business' agreements, which might apply across a number of single businesses.

[141] There are transitional provisions to continue the operation of certified agreements until so replaced and these are discussed later.

[142] Provided for by WRA s 327, and which can be compared with old s 170LK certified agreements.

[143] Provided for by WRA s 328, and which can be compared with old s 170LJ certified agreements.

[144] WRA s 342.

[145] WRA ss 344(5) although s 363 provides for a power to make a variation where an agreement is considered to contain prohibited content.

[146] WRA s 355.

[147] A provision which was never availed of in the author's experience.

[148] WRA s 415.

[149] WRA s 337.

[150] Employers are required to provide 'information statements' about bargaining agents and how approval of the agreement is to be sought: WRA s 337(4).

[151] This is because a workplace agreement can 'switch off' the future operation of all but 'protected award conditions'. Although , as a practical matter, APS employees will continue to be covered by workplace agreements that provide for terms and conditions that are above the AFPC Standard, it has been noted that there is a lot of detail for agencies to examine to ensure that is the case — Richard Harding, Australian Government Solicitor Legal Briefing, *The Work Choices Act — How Will it Affect Commonwealth Employment?* (2006) 5.

[152] See WRA Part 5A.

[153] Increased from three years: WRA s 352.

[154] 'Protected award conditions' include those dealing with rest breaks, incentive-based payments or bonuses, annual leave loadings, public holidays, skills and expenses allowances, overtime and shift loadings, penalty rates and outworker conditions.

[155] WRA s 355.

[156] WRA div 4, pt 9: The ballot process is to be administered by the AIRC under detailed provisions provided for in the WRA.

[157] Workplace Relations Regulations 2006 (Cth) reg 8,5, ch 2.

[158] Workplace Relations Regulations 2006 (Cth) reg 8,5(4), ch 2.

[159] Workplace Relations Regulations 2006 (Cth) regs 8.6 and 8.7, ch 2.

[160] WRA s 399.

[161] See Harding, above n 151, 15.

[162] Previously, in relation to AWAs, there had been deemed inclusion of dispute resolution and anti-discrimination provisions under the old s 170VG.

[163] Nevertheless, the 'call up' provisions may be called in aid of the drafting exercise to effectively leave the AWA sitting on top of a collective agreement, however that would be contrary to DEWR policy discussed earlier in this chapter.

[164] However, 'protected award conditions' may be deemed to form part of the workplace agreement if they are not expressly excluded by the agreement.

[165] Workplace Relations Regulations 2006 (Cth) regs 8.2 and 8.3, ch 2. PSA 1999 s 24(1) has also been consequentially amended to provide that a determination cannot provide for terms and conditions less than those provided for under a relevant workplace agreement, award, pre-reform certified agreement or pre-reform AWA. As to the latter instruments see the following discussion on transitional arrangement.

[166] WRA clauses 3 and 7, sch 7.

[167] WRA clause 18, sch 7.

[168] WRA clauses 9 and 21, sch 7.

[169] WRA s 525.

[170] WRA s 527.

[171] Except that 'protected award conditions' are taken to be terms of a workplace agreement unless they have been expressly excluded: WRA s 354. See also above n 154.

[172] WRA s354.

[173] See Harding, above n 151, 9.

[174] By the *Workplace Relations and Other Legislation Amendment Act 1996* (Cth).

[175] The Work Choices changes, discussed below, may also have some impact upon the numbers of non-SES personnel signing up to AWAs.

[176] Again, the Work Choices legislation may also have further effects in this area.

[177] Although it is fair to say that a push for a modernised Public Service Act had been underway for some time before McLeod, see, eg, Ives, above n 134, 31.

[178] It removed the need to have regard to s 82D determinations and other outdated provisions of the PSA 1922.

[179] Also see comments to this effect in Podger, 'The New Public Service Act and the Commitment to Values' (2000) 97 *Canberra Bulletin of Public Administration* 22, 23.

[180] DEWRSB issued four advices and the then PSMPC issued 36 advices in the period immediately following the passage of the new Act.

[181] Public Service Commissioner, *State of the Service Report 1999-2000* pt 2, 'Implementation Issues'.

# Chapter Five

# From Workplace Bargaining to Workplace Relations: Industrial Relations in the Australian Public Service under the Coalition Government

## John O'Brien and Michael O'Donnell

The purpose of this chapter is to examine the implementation of the *Workplace Relations Act 1996* (Cth) (the 'WR Act') and the potential impact of the *Workplace Relations Amendment (Work Choices) Act 2005* (Cth) (the 'Work Choices Act') within the Australian Public Service ('APS') — where the Coalition government has the greatest opportunity to influence the working conditions of its own employees. The chapter argues that when governments seek to regulate the working conditions and wages of their own employees in a decentralising industrial relations environment, there is potential for tension between the roles of government as employer, as policy generator and financial controller. A government's financial and political responsibility requires that it control the cost of its own employees; its industrial relations policies may also require that more direct relationships between employers and employees be facilitated by the regulatory system. Nevertheless, as an employer, the government needs to retain ultimate control of its own employees. In the APS, the Coalition government attempted to resolve these tensions by providing policy 'parameters', via the Department of Employment and Workplace Relations ('DEWR'),[1] to its managerial agents within agencies and departments of state. These parameters devolved some autonomy to the government's managerial agents, but also required them to adhere to a process of centralised oversight of agency agreement-making by DEWR.

The principal public service union, the Community and Public Sector Union ('CPSU'), was compelled to respond to a process that was procedurally decentralised but where there was considerable potential for ongoing and substantial central intervention in workplace bargaining. For public sector unions, there are both threats and opportunities in this environment. The threat lies in the capacity of employers to minimise union involvement in the agreement-making process. The opportunity for unions is to counter this threat through organisation at the agency level and through efforts to increase union membership. The chapter explores the CPSU's attempts to retain its legitimacy at workplace level in three lowly-unionised agencies. These efforts are compared with union-management bargaining in an agency in which unions had a greater presence and organisational capacity.

## The Coalition's General Industrial Relations Policy

The key objective of the Coalition's industrial relations policies was to foster a more direct relationship between employers and employees at the workplace/enterprise level.[2] This involved reducing the power of 'outside bodies' that were said to interfere with or complicate the fostering of those direct relationships. In practice, this meant that the power of unions and of some (but not all) external regulatory bodies, such as the Australian Industrial Relations Commission ('AIRC'), would need to be reduced further. The first objective was to be achieved by removing the bargaining monopoly that had been exercised by unions. The second objective was to be achieved by reducing the powers of the AIRC to intervene in workplace-level negotiations and outcomes, to that of simply ensuring that the agreements met specified legislative requirements.[3] The reduction of the powers of the AIRC indeed had been begun by the previous Labor government, although it had been much more cautious about reducing the role of unions in a decentralised bargaining environment.

While the Coalition made some significant changes to the bargaining environment that had been established by the Labor government, it followed in the tradition established by the former government in using the APS as a testing ground for its general industrial relations policies. The Labor government needed to demonstrate that its approach to workplace bargaining was a fairer and more effective system than the Coalition model. The obvious place to conduct such an experiment was in the APS. There was some scepticism, however, that productivity-based bargaining could work effectively in a budget-funded environment. A study involving three academics, Professors John Niland, William Brown and Barry Hughes, considered the utility of a number of methods used in the APS to measure productivity and opted for a system of productivity measurement that combined general performance indicators and quality-focussed approaches to their development and application at the agency level.[4] They were of the view, however, that 'measures of APS wide productivity growth of an acceptable standard (were) ... not available and (were) ... unlikely to be so in the future'.[5] Productivity could only be regarded as a 'sub-set' of performance.[6]

The arguments about productivity measurement in the APS were in part designed to convince the unions that there could be workable agency-level bargaining that would not compromise the regime of service-wide wages and conditions.

Achieving the policy objective of introducing workplace bargaining for its own employees did not, however, sit comfortably with the desire of the unions to maintain a high level of common conditions. Moreover, a group of departmental secretaries had conducted a separate enquiry,[7] and the consultants agreed on one issue: that it was difficult to measure productivity in non-market environments.

In fact, the CPSU had no real choice but to accept some model of decentralised bargaining given that both the government and the ACTU wanted a shift in that direction. Of more immediate concern was the impending federal election. The government (and the unions) needed to demonstrate that its model of decentralised industrial relations could work more effectively and equitably than that proposed by the Opposition parties. In December 1992, the government and 27 public service unions signed an agreement on the introduction of agency-level wage bargaining. This agreement provided for the development of 'more flexible' employment conditions at the agency level to be achieved in agency-specific agreements provided that there was 'no overall disadvantage to employees'.[8]

During 1993 and 1994, most APS agencies either managed to negotiate an agency level agreement or gain access to a 'foldback' fund.[9] Among the agencies that relied on this latter arrangement were the Department of Finance and the Treasury. This was a considerable source of angst amongst the agencies that had reached agreements.[10] The central agencies were accused of being 'free riders' on the efforts of other agencies. An evaluation of the system conducted by the Department of Finance and the then Department of Industrial Relations confirmed this view, and also indicated that small agencies had experienced particular difficulty in identifying productivity savings.[11]

This episode of agency bargaining was followed by a return to a more centralised mode of bargaining and illustrates the conflicting objectives of governments in regulating their own employees. The government had a clear agenda to decentralise the wage bargaining system. The best way to do this was to demonstrate that it could work for its own employees. In the short term, there was an imperative to demonstrate its superiority over the more radical agenda of the opposition. On the other hand, the government needed to maintain control over the costs of such a system. Thus, the central agencies acted as the regulators on behalf of the government. In that sense, the system was not wholly decentralised. The government also needed to wrestle with the practical problems of productivity measurement and the expectation from the unions that all employees would receive a similar wage outcome. The solution to these problems through the 'foldback' mechanism meant that some public service managers, who had been able to bargain, had to finance the non-bargaining agencies or free-riders. Even for the bargaining agencies, it was difficult to see how productivity gains could be made without either continuing job losses and/or work intensification for the remaining employees. Nevertheless, the process facilitated further the incorporation of public sector unions into a recasting of the APS.

## The Coalition's 'Loose-Tight' Model

The incoming Coalition government, however, saw the process of decentralisation and then the subsequent recentralisation of industrial relations in the APS as a sham. The government declared itself determined to implement 'real workplace relations' in the APS.[12] The shift of discourse here is significant. Whereas the Labor government had talked about 'workplace bargaining', the Coalition preferred the term 'workplace relations', which did not necessarily envisage bargaining between public service unions and agencies, but rather more 'direct' relations between APS employees and managers.

Yet the Coalition government still faced the same dilemma faced by any business: the need to control the costs of its own employees. This could only be achieved through its control of budgetary arrangements. Departments and agencies needed to pay for the costs of their employees through their normal budget provision rather than to rely on supplementation from the government. Such an approach would have been less difficult to implement if the government had not also made it a policy objective to decentralise industrial relations and give greater autonomy to APS managers to organise their own employment arrangements.[13] How then could the government reconcile these two apparently contradictory objectives? The parameters for bargaining in the APS issued in 1997 in preparation for the next round of bargaining or agreement-making in the APS attempted to place the prime responsibility for bargaining on agency managers while maintaining a considerable degree of supervision of the process by the Department of Industrial Relations and the agent of the government in its role as the 'ultimate' employer.

The key provision of these guidelines, which have been re-issued periodically, was that any agency-level agreement must be consistent with government policy. Other principal 'parameters' were that:

- agreements were to be funded within agency appropriations;
- the accrual of sick leave and annual leave entitlements was to be portable across agencies;
- agencies were to introduce a rationalised classification structure linked to Service-wide benchmarks;
- flexible remuneration arrangements were to be permitted;
- redundancy provisions were to be cost-neutral to the agency;
- all certified agreements were to provide for the making of Australian Workplace Agreements (individual contracts);

- agreement-making be subject to coordination arrangements, including consultation with the (re-named) Department of Workplace Relations and Small Business ('DWRSB'); and
- agreements be subject to Ministerial clearance where significant policy issues were raised by the agreement.[14]

## Decentralising While Controlling: The Department of Workplace Relations and Small Business

The parameters for agreement-making provided a specific role for the (re-named) DWRSB to act as coordinator of agreement-making in the agencies. This continued a long-established tradition within the APS of central agency supervision of employment relationships. The Department was responsible for reviewing agreements at both the proposal and offer stages. The final draft would have to be cleared by the Department's staff against the government's policy parameters before agency management could put it to a staff vote. To ensure consistency, three policy sections within the department reviewed all draft agreements: pay, freedom of association and working conditions. Once this had taken place, the department would inform the agency whether the agreement met with its approval or whether changes were required to ensure it complied with the government's policy parameters. Clearly, the government was cautious about devolving too much responsibility to agencies as some might not abide by government policy or retain, from the government's perspective, too close a relationship with public sector unions.

Thus the central agency's oversight role remained necessary under the Coalition. For while there was considerable flexibility for agencies to vary some matters such as allowances, access to higher duties, span of hours and overtime arrangements to reflect their individual circumstances, ultimately all agencies had to comply with the policy parameters set down by the Department.[15] This was reflected in the Department's advice to agency management:

> Authority to make agreements now rests with agencies, within broad policy arrangements that recognise the Government's responsibility as the ultimate employer. This is consistent with the practice of other major employers. This framework balances the responsibility of an agency to conduct its own workplace relations with the requirements of public accountability of government bodies.[16]

There are clear limits to the devolution of employment relations in government agencies. While the heads of government agencies may be given considerable autonomy in making agency-specific arrangements, they are, in the end, agents of government in both its roles of employer and policy generator. This apparent contradiction was explained by a senior DWRSB officer as being akin to a large corporation with a number of enterprises within its structure.[17] While the corporation might allow its constituent enterprises considerable autonomy in its employment arrangements, they are formulated within the framework of overall corporate policy.[18] During interviews, agency managers conceded that the policy parameters set limits on their capacity to negotiate.[19] For instance, DWRSB examined the changes to the Centrelink classification structure carefully and expressed concern about its comparability with the APS structure and mobility between the two. Furthermore, the Freedom of Association provisions resulted in the Department revising the Centrelink agreement to omit specific mention of unions. To some extent, these tensions between DWRSB and line agencies reflected difficulties associated with the first round of a new system. In subsequent rounds, the role of DWRSB was confined to checking the final drafts of agreements. Indeed, it could be argued that the need to conform to government policy was sufficiently internalised by managers responsible for agreement-making so as to make close supervision by a regulating agency less necessary in subsequent rounds of bargaining.

The more important test, however, may be the degree to which the government's other agreement-making objectives were implemented in the various agencies and to what extent any variations were mediated by union action. The issue of remuneration systems provides a fruitful area of investigation in this context.

## Performance-Related Pay

Initial moves to introduce performance-related pay began under the former federal Labor government in 1992, and were restricted to members of the Senior Executive Service ('SES') and to senior officers, the next classification of APS employees below the SES. The Senate Finance and Public Administration Committee undertook an initial inquiry into the operation of this pay scheme in 1993 and received submissions noting the potential for performance-related pay to increase the politicisation of the public service.[20] Performance appraisal ratings were also viewed as being highly subjective and influenced by the biases of supervisors.[21] The committee therefore recommended that performance pay in the APS be abandoned.[22] Subsequent research into performance-related pay in the APS from 1992 to 1996 found that supervisors often rewarded their 'favourites' with the highest performance appraisal ratings, while senior managers and those working in high profile areas also tended to receive the highest ratings.[23]

Nevertheless, the Coalition government elected in 1996 was determined to introduce a rationalised classification structure linked to performance appraisal and pay. The new parameters for agreement-making consequently developed by DWRSB insisted that all agency agreements contain a commitment to develop flexible remuneration arrangements. Research into the effects of the performance-related pay schemes introduced into the APS from 1998 highlighted employee concerns over the potential for increased managerial discretion in the selection of performance criteria. Unless such criteria were specific and clearly linked to the major work tasks that employees undertook, there was the very real potential for supervisors to make arbitrary judgments regarding employee behaviour and work performance:

> You need to have specific responsibilities agreed/outlined to protect yourself from the possibility of supervisors coming up with various unrelated duties/expected outcomes at assessment time.[24]

Many APS employees also perceived the assessment of their performance by their supervisor to represent an inherently subjective process. For example, a number of employees pointed to favouritism in the performance appraisal system:

1.   Managers forget things you have done that meet the criteria.
2.   Personality differences and differences in style affect managers' decision-making regarding ratings.
3.   Sometimes [they] rely too much on hearsay and not evidence.
4.   Some managers lack the objectivity and intelligence to apply ratings fairly.[25]

There were also widespread concerns among employees that budgetary pressures were causing initial performance assessments provided by supervisors only to be moderated downwards by more senior management in order to increase the number of employees who were eligible for a bonus payment. There were also admissions by at least one departmental secretary that the payment of performance bonuses to some employees could result in other APS employees losing their jobs. The Secretary of the Treasury told the Senate Finance and Public Administration References Committee in 2000 that while he welcomed the new performance-based pay system in the Treasury, he noted that

> managers, in making assessments, were to be aware that there were budgetary considerations. If there were a clash, for example, if we paid more performance pay than we may have expected in designing the budget, we would operate with fewer numbers.[26]

He agreed with the comment of the Chair of the Committee, 'so in effect you could be trading off one person's job for one person's performance payment?'[27]

Nevertheless, for some managers, performance-related pay schemes have formed a central element of their agenda to inculcate a 'performance culture' within their organisations.[28]

Management efforts to introduce cultural change via performance-related pay represents an attempt to alter employee values, beliefs and behaviours and encourage increased commitment by individual employees to the goals of the organisation. It may also aim to weaken collective bargaining and the role of trade unions while strengthening the power of middle managers in decision-making over pay.[29]  A good example of such experimentation was in the Department of Finance and Administration ('DoFA').

## Implementing Performance Pay: The Department of Finance and Administration and the Department of Defence

The 1997 DoFA collective workplace agreement refers to a commitment to the promotion of 'a working culture based on high performance, quality outcomes and modern management and work practices'.[30]  Within DoFA, management adopted a very uncompromising approach to the promotion of this new high performance culture; and in staff newsletters, employees were encouraged to become 'action-oriented', to develop a 'will to win' and to be 'creative' in how they 'get the runs on the board'.[31]  The corporate culture orientation of the agency was also revealed in the principles and objectives of the agreement that were concerned to provide the environment where 'the employer and employees agree to work collaboratively and in consultation' to enhance a working culture based on high performance, quality outcomes and modern management work practices; and promote a performance culture by rewarding good performance and managing poor performance well and encouraging people to achieve their full potential.[32]

In addition, the performance management system in DoFA included a system for managing underperformance. Management used the performance rating scale to remove those staff who had not accepted the new culture by providing them with an 'unsatisfactory' assessment ('fundamental job requirements are inconsistently met') that resulted in the offer of a redundancy package.[33]  Even those staff who received a 'borderline' performance assessment ('fundamental job requirements are barely met') were also being sent a message that they did not fit into the new 'can do' culture of the department.[34]  Management was alleged to be adamant that it did not want 'closet cynics' who would be critical of the new culture.[35]  Such cynics were invited to accept voluntary redundancy packages while those who remained were expected to align themselves with the new culture.[36]  As a result of the pressure on staff to conform, a workplace culture of fear was alleged to be developing in DoFA.[37]  The very real threat of redundancy ensured at least behavioural conformity from the majority of staff to the new culture.[38]

The system established within DoFA, however, represented only one end of the spectrum of pay arrangements within the APS. At the other end was the Department of Defence that established a more rigorous system for movement through incremental scales and specifically rejected the notion of performance bonuses. Indeed the Secretary of the Department, Dr Allan Hawke, told the Senate Finance and Public Administration References Committee in 2000 that he did not believe in linking this sort of performance framework to performance pay or to any sort of model that involves notions like that — pay at risk, bonuses and the like. What we do is: at the end of the 12-month period it is simply a tick in the box if people have performed well, and if they have performed well then they go up to the next increment in the pay scale.[39]

He went on to insist the he did 'not approve of performance pay and do not have it in an organisation that I am in'.[40] He also expressed concern about the development of pay dispersion within the APS. As an experienced senior public servant, he had always subscribed to the notion of 'getting a fair day's pay for a fair day's work'; people therefore 'should get roughly equivalent to what they would get in a like job elsewhere in the Public Service'.[41]

The significance of these remarks is that one of the most senior members of the APS was taking issue with two central aspects of the government's pay agenda: performance-based remuneration and agency-specific pay rates. Yet the Department was allowed to establish a pay system that, while it had a performance element, fell far short of the government's objectives and stood in stark contrast with the pay system established in DoFA. Presumably, the government could have insisted on a much more performance-driven pay system, but accepted a system that was inconsistent with its overall objectives. This case illustrates one of the dilemmas of a decentralised mode of industrial relations. On the one hand, the government wanted to use the APS as a site for implementing its policies and enhancing agency-specific managerial prerogative. In the case of the Department of Defence, managerial independence was asserted at an apparent cost to government policy, while in DoFA managerial prerogative was used to implement government objectives in a manner that went well beyond the ambitions of the government.

## Union Response: Staying at the Bargaining Table

The Coalition's industrial relations policies envisaged a much less direct role for unions in the negotiation of agreements between employees and employers. In the APS, however, public sector unions had historically a strong presence, although its density in the APS in the early 2000s had fallen below 50 per cent.[42] The capacity of the public sector unions to influence industrial relations arrangements had been enhanced by the previously centralised employment arrangements within the APS. The Labor government had attempted to shift the focus of industrial bargaining towards the agency level in the face of strong opposition of the unions. Following the election of the Coalition government, the unions sought to negotiate a framework agreement with the government within which agency level negotiations would take place. The government resisted all attempts to negotiate such an agreement and so the unions in general

— and the CPSU in particular — were forced to accept that negotiations would take place agency by agency.[43] Moreover, the WR Act and more recently the Work Choices Act effectively removed unions from exercising a bargaining monopoly on behalf of APS staff. As a result, the first problem that the public service unions faced was to assert their rights to be at the bargaining table. Having established a right to be involved, then it was necessary for unions to demonstrate their capacity to modify the government's bargaining agenda and to restrict the capacity for agency level managements to further enhance their managerial prerogative.

Under the provisions of the WR Act, management representatives had no stronger an obligation than to 'meet and confer' with unions.[44] In agencies where unions had a strong presence, at the level of being the representative of a significant minority of staff, management could not really avoid dealing with relevant unions. Nevertheless, in agencies where unions had a significant, but minority presence, managements tried to establish bargaining arrangements where the union had to run candidates for positions as employee representatives.[45] In the Department of Employment, Education, Training and Youth Affairs, the union ran a ticket in the election for staff representatives and won all positions.[46]

In agencies where unions had a much stronger presence, the CPSU had less difficulty in asserting its claim to represent most staff. In DEWRSB, the Secretary attempted to establish an employee consultation mechanism that was designed to exclude union members.[47] Ironically, the Department found itself in breach of the 'freedom of association' provisions of the WR Act in attempting to use such a mechanism to marginalise unions.[48] Moreover, the secretary was forced to deal with unions who were able to insist that the final agreement would be with the unions rather than with employees: an option widely used in agencies where unions had a weak presence.

Indeed, in 2000 the CPSU complained to the Senate Committee on Finance and Public Administration enquiry on APS employment matters that it had been involved in the negotiation of most agreements even if it was not party to a significant number of them, particularly in smaller agencies.[49] While allowance must be made for a tendency to exaggerate its role, the CPSU's complaint indicates that it and the other public sector unions had not been excluded or marginalised in the overall process. Nevertheless, the fact that nearly half of the agreements in the first round were with employees, rather than with unions, indicated that the government had been successful in removing the unions' bargaining monopoly, particularly in smaller agencies.

In the bargaining round from November 2000 until July 2002, some 42 agreements were made. All but 13 agreements were made with public service unions rather than employees directly. The 13 agreements with employees covered some 3,300 employees. whereas the union-negotiated agreements covered some 55,000 employees.[50] On the face of it, the government had some success in de-legitimising the role of unions as the principal bargaining agent of APS employees during the first bargaining round. In subsequent agreements, however, the unions seemed to have made somewhat of a comeback with the CPSU claiming that it had negotiated on behalf of 80 per cent of APS staff. These raw figures, however, say nothing about the level of influence that the unions had on bargaining outcomes. All they do is illustrate that unions had not been rendered irrelevant to the bargaining process with the APS. It is instructive, therefore, to make some comparisons between the agencies where unions had a weak presence with those agencies where their capacity to organise was much stronger.

## Agreement-Making in Three Agencies

### The Guardian of Public Service 'Values': The Public Service and Merit Protection Commission

The strongest tests for the unions in 1997-8 were in agencies where they lacked numbers and organisational capacity. This was particularly the case in three agencies: the Public Service and Merit Protection Commission ('PSMPC'), DoFA and the Department of Foreign Affairs and Trade ('DFAT'). The PSMPC had the carriage of the government's changes to the *Public Service Act 1999* (Cth), replacing the *Public Service Act 1922* (Cth) and its public service reform agenda generally. Its agreement needed to be a 'best practice' instance of the government's approach to both industrial relations and public service reform. Notably, the agency was not a stronghold for public service unions, with union membership below 35 per cent.

The former Public Service and Merit Protection Commissioner, Dr Peter Shergold, was determined that the agreement in his agency would demonstrate the direction of the new public service environment.[51] In July 1997, Shergold told a gathering of public servants that there was a

> need to remove central controls that are premised on the false assumption that the APS is a single labour market and in which every employment decision is driven by the relentless pursuit of uniformity. We need to free ourselves from the red tape that binds our management decisions in layers of prescription. We need to wind back the cumbersome mechanisms of bureaucratic control.[52]

Moreover, the management of the PSMPC saw the explicit linkage between individual performance and pay as the crucial element in shifting the agency from a rule-bound 'red tape' culture to one of 'high performance' and 'continuous improvement'.[53] Therefore, a performance-based remuneration system was to be the centrepiece of the agreement; and the only means for receiving pay increases. The agreement outlined a new 'high performance culture' that would be promoted by:

- setting out individual responsibilities and the standard of performance expected from employees;
- providing regular feedback on performance;
- making decisions on salary advancement based on performance; and
- establishing a basis for managing poor performance.[54]

While the PSMPC management was not opposed to union participation in the process of achieving this 'culture', it saw the agreement as part of the transition from an 'industrial' relations model to a 'workplace' relations environment characterised by direct engagement with employees. The agreement was also to be consistent with other organisational changes such as a team-based structure and further 'de-layering' of the management hierarchy.[55] The Public Service and Merit Protection Commissioner moreover, had some success in extending the incidence of individual contracts within the agency in the form of Australian Workplace Agreements ('AWAs'). While all members of the SES were required to sign AWAs, the incidence of this arrangement also reached into middle management and AWAs were characterised by a 'much sharper performance edge' than the collective agreement.[56]

## 'Going the Extra Mile': The Department of Finance and Administration

DoFA is one of the key financial regulators of the public service. It seeks to bring 'best practice' in the private sector to bear on the 'business' of government. This disposition was reinforced when the new government appointed an 'outsider' from the private sector, Dr Peter Boxall, as its secretary. The DoFA management adopted a very uncompromising approach to the promotion of the new corporate culture. The department leadership extolled staff to become 'high performers', to be 'action-oriented', to develop a 'will to win' and to be 'creative' in how they 'get the runs on the board'. Indeed the organisation was said to need 'people who want to get things done and make a difference, working in a key agency at the centre of the business government'.[57]

The cultural orientation of the agency was revealed in the principles and objectives of the Department of Finance and Administration Certified Agreement 1997-1999 that were concerned to provide the environment where 'the employer and employees agree to work collaboratively and in consultation' to:

- foster corporate values and objectives;
- enhance a working culture based on high performance, quality outcomes and modern management and work practices;

- promote a performance culture by rewarding good performance and managing poor performance well and encouraging people to achieve their full potential; and
- promote self-management and flexibility by empowering people at the workplace level to work in a way which best suits them to support a work/private life balance.[58]

Indeed, the agreement gave prime attention to the performance management scheme, to the management of under-performance, and the new classification system that would underpin this performance culture.[59]

DoFA has a long history of hostility to unions.[60] The effect of this hostility had been lessened, however, by the existence of service-wide employment arrangements. The new regulatory environment enabled the management not only to break down these arrangements, but also further undermine union influence. Thus the DoFA management was empowered in its pursuit of broader government objectives, such as union marginalisation, in the new era of 'workplace relations'. So, while the PSMPC agreement was seen as a means of inculcating a new public management culture, DoFA saw the process as reinforcing already strongly held assumptions and practices. Agency management did not welcome union involvement in the agreement-making process, although it made a 'corporate decision' to consult the union.[61] The central propositions of the management agenda, including the introduction of performance pay and the abolition of overtime payments were not negotiable, although it was prepared to talk about issues of implementation. In the post-agreement environment, the union's role has been largely reduced to pursuing the personal grievances of an increasing number of members who were regarded as the casualties of the 'can do' culture of DoFA.[62] Indeed, the union marginalisation strategy has been compounded by a continuing refusal by the agency to negotiate with employees or their representatives in any manner in order to update the collective agreement. Individual contracts were now the only means of gaining pay increases.[63] By February 2004, there was still no collective agreement for the agency to replace the agreement made in 1997.[64] Indeed the DoFA Annual Report 2002-03 reported that 89.5 per cent of the staff of DoFA were covered by individual contracts in the form of Australian Workplace Agreements. Only 10.5 per cent of employees (excluding COMCAR drivers) were covered by a collective agreement that had not been updated since 1997.[65]

The agreement with staff legitimised the pursuit of the management's cultural agenda within the agency. The performance management system and the promotion of individual contracts by senior management were seen as central to the organisational life of the agency. If staff were aligned with the new corporate culture then, in management's view, they should be willing to sign an AWA. By December 1998, 211 of 1,082 staff covered by formal employment agreements were on AWAs.[66] By mid-2000, however, 56 per cent of staff had such arrangements — an increase from 32 per cent since mid-1999.[67] By mid-2002, the figure was 90 per cent and by mid-2004, it was 99 per cent of non-COMCAR staff.[68] The main difference between the agency agreement and an AWA was the offer of a performance bonus of up to 25 per cent compared to 15 per cent in the agency agreement.[69] Indeed, the management told an enquiry on APS employment matters conducted by a Senate Committee in 2000, that there was no formal limit on the amount of performance pay that could be available to 'high performers'.[70]

The unions were either unable to resist this agenda or to modify the management-determined processes that enforced its implementation. The CPSU was reduced to tending to the 'most seriously wounded' of its members. Nevertheless, the actions of the DoFA management provided a useful and continuing source of complaint for the unions.[71] Its actions were touted as what was possible when the position of unions were weakened by legislation and by a determination to limit the role of 'outside parties' in workplace agreement-making. In achieving the latter objective the DoFA management has had spectacular success.

## 'Turning Policy Officers into Managers': The Department of Foreign Affairs and Trade

DFAT places great store on its policy expertise, but it eschews the business orientation of Finance and Administration and is less of a generic public service department than many other agencies. It has a well-established and distinctive policy 'culture'. The requirement for overseas service also means that its detailed employment conditions, particularly relating to families, are the subject of considerable interest by staff.

The objectives of the management of DFAT in the agreement-making process were twofold. On a practical level, the agreement needed to take account of the fact that there had been considerable reductions in staff and in the running costs in the Department in the previous two and half years. There also needed to be greater flexibility in employment conditions to enable the agency to operate more efficiently and effectively. Second, the agreement needed to assist in the establishment of a new management culture within the Department, whereby managers could 'engage' with their staff more actively and effectively. Moreover, while the management recognised that employees had highly developed policy skills, their generic skills as managers, particularly in dealing with staff, needed to be enhanced.[72]

It was decided these objectives would be met through a performance management system that would include 'upward appraisal' mechanisms and through the devolution of responsibility for employment conditions to middle management.[73]

The allocation of staff to overseas postings would be more dependent on managerial performance than had been the case in the past.[74] Senior management was conscious of the need to provide significant family-related employment benefits for those serving overseas, particularly for the education of children. Thus, the traditional 'welfarist' orientation of the agency had to be integrated with a more explicitly managerial orientation, while maintaining the policy tradition central to the department's sense of itself. The new regulatory environment enabled DFAT management to attempt to graft a more explicit 'culture' of 'strategic people management' on to the existing policy and welfare 'cultures' of the department.

At the time the process was initiated, union density in the agency was below 40 per cent. Management was determined that it would only negotiate with employee representatives and not with union officials,[75] while the long-standing existence of an in-house staff association provided a structure for non-union negotiations. After some argument with the unions, it accepted a combination of union workplace delegates and representatives of the staff association as the employee bargaining team. The CPSU was able to coordinate its objectives and tactics with the non-union representatives. The unions used intranet communication systems and held regular meetings with both union and non-union staff. The management, however, was able to maintain communication with overseas staff in a manner not available to the unions. Senior management teams visited a number of overseas missions to explain the agreement-making process to staff. It was argued that this was necessary because the proposed agreement would involve the incorporation of overseas allowances into a more explicitly performance-oriented pay system.[76] The unions were confined to paper-based and electronic forms of communication. This lack of contact with overseas staff was reflected in the staff vote on the agreement. The unions organised a strong campaign against the draft agreement. In all, 58 per cent of employees who voted supported that agreement, but in Canberra — where the unions were most effectively organised — a majority of staff voted against the agreement.[77]

The experience in these three agencies makes an interesting contrast with the experience of the more unionised Centrelink agency.

## From a Welfare Culture to a Customer Service Culture: Centrelink

Centrelink is the largest agency in the APS, with approximately 25,000 employees, or about 25 per cent of all employees in the APS. It is significantly unionised and has a considerable history of industrial action that dates back to its former incorporation within the former Department of Social Security. It is one of the strongholds of the CPSU. In the 1980s, CPSU members made widespread use of selective industrial bans to preserve employment conditions. The long-standing industrial tradition within the agency significantly influenced the tactics of Centrelink management in the process of agreement-making.

Centrelink is a service delivery agency which had a formally devolved or indirect relationship with government, in that it was established by the *Customer Service Delivery Act 1997* (Cth) as a statutory authority with a Chief Executive Officer (CEO) and an independent Board. Under a series of Business Partnership ('Business Alliance') Agreements with 'client' agencies, Centrelink delivered services on behalf of departments such as Family and Community Services, Employment and Workplace Relations, as well as the Health Insurance Commission and the Australian Taxation Office. These services include transfer payments, the provision of jobseekers to Job Networks, and the implementation of regulations based on government policy decisions.

These arrangements placed continual pressure on Centrelink to provide services in a timely and cost efficient manner, and the CPSU conceded that negotiations with the agency took place within the context that services provided through Centrelink Call Centres could be provided more cheaply by similar operations located in the private sector.[78]

Centrelink was important to all sides in the industrial relations arena in the APS. The CPSU needed to illustrate that it was able to modify government and management agendas. The government and the Centrelink management needed to demonstrate that their agenda could be achieved in agencies where unions had a significant presence. The WR Act made that task easier. In the past, employees could impose selective industrial bans. Employers could invoke the 'no work as directed, no pay' remedy and stand down employees or dock full pay for the period in which the bans had been applied. Many employers chose not to take this course, preferring to resolve the dispute and resume normal operations rather than worsen the dispute. The WR Act however made it mandatory that employees not be paid if any industrial action were taken. Thus the weapon of selective bans, without cost to employees, which was widely used in the APS during the 1980s, was no longer available to unions. This resulted in the virtual absence of industrial action during the agreement-making period in 1997-1998 and during subsequent bargaining periods. In the view of a senior official formerly responsible for coordinating agreement-making in the APS, this provision in the legislation enabled quite 'significant structural change and downsizing' to be achieved in the APS 'without significant industrial disruption'.[79]

Throughout the negotiation of four Centrelink Development Agreements ('CDAs'), the union's role in the implementation of the agreements was recognised, although the hold of the union was loosened by the explicit recognition that any processes in which it was involved would be matched by parallel arrangements for non-union members. This was seen by management as important in shifting the consultative framework within the agency away from union domination towards direct employee consultation.[80] The management also saw the CDAs as an important initial step towards more fundamental changes in the agency along business-oriented and customer service lines. The CEO, Sue Vardon, saw workplace bargaining as a means of 'buying' a new organisation. Formerly the Head of Corrective Services and Public Service Commissioner in South Australia, she was, unlike most of her senior colleagues in the APS at that time, used to dealing with unions:

> I didn't want the unions to think that I was running the Reith agenda, I was appalled. Because what I was running was Sue Vardon's agenda for public sector reform. I knew what the government wanted, but I didn't have any problem with that as long as I could use this tool to buy a revolution (sic). I wasn't using this tool to impose the wish of the government upon the workers. It's very different. And I think the union understood that.[81]

She faced a well-organised CPSU division led by one of the union's most experienced industrial officers, Mark Gepp, who subsequently became National President of the union. Centrelink also inherited a strong tradition of militant rank and file organisation within the former Department of Social Security. In the words of Sue Vardon:

> Every time Social Security wanted to do something they took them to the cleaners. They had the strikes. The day the Prime Minister opened us the union tried to close every office. I was hysterical with rage. Because this is what you do, you protest by striking and so there was an incredible culture of striking … well I'd never seen anything like it in my life. Social Security was a hot bed.[82]

The WR Act however made it more difficult for unions to engage in industrial actions in the form of bans:

> I considered that our first agreement was a major success with the union because the union could see that their power was diminishing, they couldn't have all those strikes anymore because of the *Workplace Relations Act* which I must say I'm extremely grateful for that piece of legislation.[83]

Nevertheless, management conceded that the union has a considerable degree of influence in the organisation. There was also a large group of non-union staff who were keen for the union to negotiate on their behalf:

> I learnt a very important lesson. It doesn't matter how small they are, everybody who is not a union member wants to know that the union is

negotiating with management. At one stage I said we can get this through because there are hardly any union members. And something happened and the take home message to me was they don't want to be members of the union but they want to know they're there.[84]

## 1997 Collective Agreement

Vardon saw the negotiation of the first enterprise agreement in 1997 as 'establishing an environment that would enable the personalisation of our services to our customers' principally through greater flexibility in opening hours of Centrelink offices and shopfronts'.[85] The key objective of the agreement was to provide an 'efficient and cost effective service by committed and skilled employees'.[86]

While this first agreement, the Centrelink Development Agreement 1997-1998, concentrated on producing greater flexibility in the provision of services, the management had a longer-term agenda to align the remuneration system to the strategic objectives of the organisation. Some two per cent of the pay rise agreed in the first CDA was contingent on all Centrelink offices implementing customer service improvement plans and the organisation as a whole demonstrating improvements against a range of performance indicators. The first CDA delivered a comprehensive enterprise agreement overriding existing APS awards and bringing together into one document all employee pay, classifications and working conditions. Customer focus was to be achieved in the first instance by maximising access to Centrelink services through extended hours of opening. The first CDA involved substantial changes to opening hours, with staff losing the Wednesday afternoon office closure from 1.30pm. This time was meant to enable staff to hold meetings and to catch up on processes but the newly appointed CEO was opposed to this practice. Other managers though saw some value in providing staff with time to catch up on backlogs in work and with changes in social security legislation.

Other changes to hours included a broader span of hours, from 7am to 7pm. The former core hours were abolished and replaced with 'regular hours'. It was up to individual employees to negotiate their regular working hours with their supervisor over a four-week period. Nevertheless, Centrelink staff retained access to 'flex' time and to overtime payments when requested by management to work beyond their regular hours. Employees who worked beyond their regular hours voluntarily could accumulate 'flex' hours. On the whole, the outcomes negotiated in the first CDA were consistent with the promotion of a customer service agenda across Centrelink.

# Centrelink Development Agreement 1999-2002

The second CDA, the Centrelink Development Agreement 1999-2002, was certified in May 1999 and represented a three-year comprehensive agreement.[87] It introduced a Centrelink-specific classification structure in place of the APS-wide structure and linked employee advancement through this structure to the outcome of a performance assessment. Centrelink had to find much of the resources required to fund the second CDA internally. The organisation received merely 1.3 per cent in extra funding from the Commonwealth government as part of the safety net wage adjustment and found itself in the difficult position of making a trade-off between staff cuts and pay rises. Centrelink also identified a number of productivity measures that needed to be met before the pay rises could be paid. On the whole, Centrelink management believed that productivity across the organisation had improved with the introduction of new technology, the 'One Contact officer' approach, and the elimination of reworking and the establishment of customer service teams.[88]

# Centrelink Development Agreement 2003-2005

Substantive negotiations over the third agreement began in March 2002. By October, a preliminary agreement had been negotiated with the CPSU though this agreement was rejected by the union's Section Council. The management was concerned to secure an agreement with the minimum of industrial disruption. Vardon feared that there were members of the government who were not friends of Centrelink who would use significant industrial disruption to undermine the agency.[89] The CEO took the unusual step of attending the Centrelink Section Council meeting of the Employment Services Division to plead with the union to work with the management to preserve Centrelink. Nevertheless, negotiations proceeded without resolution and the union notified Centrelink of its intention to undertake industrial action in early December. On 2 December 2002, a stopwork meeting of CPSU members across Centrelink was organised and was followed by a half-day strike. In the aftermath of this industrial action, Centrelink decided to test the degree of support it had among Centrelink employees, and, in late December, the management put the draft negotiated to date to a ballot of staff in the form of a section 170 LK (non-union) agreement under the WR Act. The ballot was overseen by the Australian Electoral Commission and was held on December 19 and 20, 2002. Staff on leave at that time were given the opportunity to cast a postal vote.[90] Despite management's best endeavours to encourage a 'Yes' vote, the non-union agreement was overwhelmingly rejected by over 70 per cent of Centrelink staff who voted in the ballot. The union claimed that the timing of the issuing of the draft agreement had incensed a large number of staff.[91]

Following the rejection of the vote, management and the CPSU resumed negotiations in early 2003. By May 2003, the third CDA was certified for two and a half years until October 2005.[92] The pay rises comprised an initial $600 performance bonus, a four per cent pay rise in May 2003, a further four per cent pay increase in November 2003 and a final four and a half per cent pay rise in September 2004. The payment of the bonus on certification recognised that productivity improvements had been achieved since July 2002. The pay rises for November 2003 and September 2004 were 'linked to specific balanced Scorecard targets in relation to the number of correct payments made, improvements in customer satisfaction levels and reductions in the levels of unplanned leave'.[93] Centrelink management reported that, of those staff who voted, some 73 per cent voted in favour of accepting the agreement.[94] Overall, the agreement provided for: an extension of opening hours; the linking of accredited learning to advancement through Centrelink's classification system (which survived largely unchanged from the second agreement); the simpler performance assessment process outlined above; the establishment of senior practitioner roles; and the reclassification of team leader positions.[95]

## Centrelink Agreement 2006-2009

The fourth Centrelink Development Agreement was certified on 23 January 2006.[96] It covers a three-year period to January 2009 and provides for three guaranteed pay rises for Centrelink employees. The first pay rise of four per cent was made in January 2006. A second four per cent pay rise was made in December 2006, with a third four per cent payment due in December 2007. The agreement also provides for a conditional payment of half a per cent in September 2008 'if Centrelink's average unplanned absences figure does not exceed 11.53 days per full time equivalent employee for the financial year ending 30 June 2008'.

The negotiation of the fourth agreement highlighted tensions over the flexible scheduling of hours for Centrelink call centre employees. The agreement confirmed that employees were entitled to screen breaks of five minutes after 60 minutes of continuous work with screen-based equipment. The agreement also confirmed that Centrelink Call employees would be provided with ten minutes at the beginning of their shifts to review computer systems and five minutes to close down these systems at the end of their shifts.[97]

## Implications of Work Choices Legislation for Union Organisation within the APS

In December 2006, the Coalition government succeeded in legislating significant amendments to the WR Act that had considerable implications for most Australian workplaces and the APS, in particular. As far as public sector unions were concerned, union access to APS workplaces was further restricted; a strike could only occur during a bargaining period if a majority of voting employees supported the action; collective agreements were to be lodged with the Employment Advocate (later renamed the Workplace Authority), rather than certified by the Australian Industrial Relations Commission; the latter body, moreover, would be largely reduced to a conciliation role with the power to arbitrate on disputes only when all parties agreed. In addition, the Minister for Workplace Relations could veto any provision in agreements which he deemed opposed to government policy.[98] In some respects, these provisions were similar to those that had operated in the APS since 1997, except that they would have broader application. Indeed the Secretary of the Department of the Prime Minister and Cabinet, Dr Peter Shergold, considered that the provisions of the Work Choices legislation would have far less impact in the APS than in many other workplaces.[99]

This view was contested by the CPSU. It warned its members that it would find it more difficult to service its members in the workplace. Moreover, when access to a workplace is granted, employers will be able to exercise greater control when and how staff meet union officials.[100] Indeed, there was a fear that the union would need to rely on telephone, email and out-of-work meetings for communicating with them.[101] More significantly, the safety net is only five minimum standards set out in the Act (plus, where applicable, the recently introduced Fairness Test). To ensure that the agreements provided more comprehensive standards, members may be forced to bargain away some benefits or pay rise in exchange for maintaining other provisions, such as redundancy that was not one of the minimum standards and has been particularly important for the APS where restructuring of agencies often means loss of staff.[102] In agencies where there are low levels of unionisation and where agreements are made with employees directly, unions would have even more restricted access to workplaces and would not be bound by the agreements as had been the case previously, thus enabling the unions to pursue disputes arising out of these non-union agreements.

The greatest fear of the union, however, was that the government and agency managements would exploit this more difficult collective bargaining environment to promote individual Workplace Agreements. The worst-case scenario was DoFA where more than 95 per cent of staff were on individual agreements because the management had successfully refused to negotiate any kind of collective agreement since 1997. Although the CPSU had succeeded in thwarting a similar tactic being used by the management of the more highly-unionised environment of DEWR in late 2005, the greater restrictions on industrial action would make a similar campaign more difficult in the new environment. While the union had not given great priority to servicing members on individual contracts, it was concerned that a union official could only visit a workplace after such a member lodged a formal written request to the agency management for union access.[103]

It is too early to say how the CPSU will cope with this bargaining environment. It had spent much of the 1990s centralising the organising and financial resources of the union in order to be able to use them more flexibly. In the new bargaining environment, where access and bargaining would be more difficult, it would need to rely more heavily on its workplace delegates. The internal structure of the union was an issue in the CPSU elections in late 2005. The leadership group was faced with two dissident groups, CPSU Action and Members First. Both groups called for more activist-oriented approach by the union rather than a heavy reliance on the 'whole of union' approach espoused by the leadership. The CPSU candidate for National Secretary, Shane O'Connell, a long time activist in the Tax section and former national official, pledged 'to take the union back to its members, and away from the centralized union bureaucracy that has opened up such a lage gap between national officials and members and delegates'.[104] The leadership candidate won narrowly over the opposition candidates by 6,182 to 5,699 votes.[105] In so far as one can interpret union election results, these reveal the tensions between organisational effectiveness through centralisation on the one hand, and member activism on the other. The tension remains a live issue within the union.

## Conclusion

This account of three agencies with low union presence and an agency with a more significant union presence illustrates the contradictions faced by a government that wished to pursue its overall policy agenda while espousing an industrial relations policy that provides for a significant degree of managerial autonomy. In DoFA, DFAT and the PSMPC, the government's managerial agents were able to implement a comprehensive performance-related pay system and marginalise unions in the agreement-making process. On the other hand, in the Department of Defence and Centrelink much less progress was made in implementing the government's agenda.

The public service unions could not impose a template across the APS, although they could modify the impact of management agendas in particular agencies where they had both presence and organisational capacity on the ground. If nothing else, this reinforced the arguments of the proponents of delegate activism that 'union organisation and bargaining capacity, rather than management style, are decisive elements in maintaining and extending the union membership base'[106] and, as a consequence, a capacity for effective bargaining. Indeed, the newly elected National Secretary of the CPSU, Stephen Jones, told the governing Council of the union in May 2006 that:

We have 70 agreements to negotiate in the next twelve months. We will not be able to do this in areas where we have low density, low levels of membership activism and no delegates.[107]

The legitimacy of the government's industrial relations policy lies in its espousal of creating organisational environments where employers and employees negotiate arrangements that suit the particularities of the organisation. In the APS, however, the government is the ultimate employer: it cannot be indifferent to the outcomes achieved in particular agencies. Moreover, as the financial guardian of the nation it must be mindful of the costs of its own employees. Government control of budgets places considerable constraint on the capacity of any agency to offer generous remuneration. In the end, wage increases contained in agency agreements must fit within the overall budget provision. In the current environment, the government is insisting that any collective agreements be based on statements of principles, rather than setting out detailed entitlements. Their availability of entitlements is likely to be even more at the discretion of management than it has been in the past.[108]

On matters of employment conditions, the government clearly attempted to constrain the capacity of its agents to negotiate arrangements that fell outside its parameters. Even so, there was a degree of diversity in the performance-based remuneration arrangements from agency to agency, reflecting, in part, both management preference and union organisational capacity. Nevertheless, there is a remarkable sameness about the words used in many APS agreements, although there is clearly some diversity in specific implementation within any given agency.[109] While there may be some similarity in employment conditions across agencies, a degree of dispersion in salary rates has emerged after nearly ten years of the system's operation. In July 2006, at the middle range classification APS 6 (or equivalent) the dispersion was between $55,612 and $58,584 at the minimum point and between $63,110 and $67,214 at the highest point in the classification.[110]

The APS is not the monolith that it may have been when a service-wide employment framework prevailed. On the other hand, it would be misleading to conclude that the APS employment arrangements have been radically altered in the direction of a series of quasi-independent agencies. In the end, public service departments and agencies are instruments of government. The government's 'loose-tight' model of employment arrangements in the APS is tighter in some and looser in others: how loose and how tight is both a product of management preference and union organisational capacity. In the existing bargaining environment management has been endowed with more 'choices 'albeit within tighter parameters set by government, while the CPSU and other public unions face even more challenges to their capacity to organise their members and to preserve their employment conditions.

## Acknowledgement

Much of the research for this article was funded by an Australian Research Council Discovery Grant DP034439, *What does 'New Public Management' Look Like in the Public Sector Workplace: A Comparative study of Australia and the United Kingdom*: Researchers: John O'Brien, Michael O'Donnell, Anne Junor and Peter Fairbrother.

## ENDNOTES

[1] In the period covered by this chapter, the Department was variously named the Department of Industrial Relations until 18 July 1997, then the Department of Workplace Relations and Small Business until 21 October 1998, then the Department of Employment, Workplace Relations and Small Business until 26 November 2001, and then the Department of Employment and Workplace Relations.

[2] The Hon Peter Reith MP, *Better Work for Better Pay: The Federal Coalition's Industrial Relations Policy*, roneo, Canberra (1996).

[3] Ibid.

[4] John Niland, William Brown and Barry Hughes, *Breaking New Ground: Enterprise Bargaining and Agency Agreements for the Australian Public Service: A Report Prepared for the Australian Minister for Industrial Relations* (AGPS, 1991) 9-20.

[5] Ibid 61.

[6] Ibid. See also Graham Glenn, *An Approach to Workplace Bargaining in the Australian Public Service: A Paper Prepared by a Committee of Heads of Australian Public Service Agencies for the Minister for Industrial Relations* (1992).

[7] Department of Industrial Relations, *Improving Productivity: A Challenge for the Australian Public Service: A Discussion Paper prepared by a Committee of Heads of Australian Public Service Agencies for the Minister for Industrial Relations* (1991) 13.

[8] Department of Industrial Relations, *Improving Jobs, Productivity, Pay in the Australian Public Service* (1992) 4.

[9] John O'Brien, 'Employment Relations and Agency Bargaining in the Australian Public Service' in G Singleton (ed), *The Second Keating Government: Australian Commonwealth Administration 1993-1996* (1997) 175-192. The 'foldback' mechanism enabled agencies unable to negotiate an agreement to draw on a central fund created by the efficiencies return to government by agencies that had made agreements.

[10] John Halligan, Ian Mackintosh, and Hugh Watson, *The Australian Public Service: The View from the Top* (Coopers and Lybrand/ University of Canberra, 1996) 46.

[11] Department of Industrial Relations and Department of Finance, *Interim Evaluation of Bargaining in the Australian Public Service* (1994).

[12] Hon Peter Reith, *Towards a Best Practice Australian Public Service — Discussion Paper* issued by the Minister for Industrial Relations and Minister Assisting the Prime Minister for the Public Service, November 1996 (1996).

[13] Ibid.

[14] Hon Peter Reith, 'Agreement Making in the APS' (Press Release, 5 May 1997); Hon Peter Reith, 'Government Decision on Funding and APS Agreements' (Press Release, Department of Workplace Relations and Small Business, *Workplace Relations Advices 1997*, vol 1) 22.

[15] Interview with official in Australian Government Employment, Workplace Relations and Small Business, 6 August 1998.

[16] Department of Workplace Relations and Small Business 1998, *The Workplace Relations Act: A Pocket Guide for Australian Government Employment* 2.

[17] Bernie Yates, 'Workplace Relations and Agreement Making in the Australian Public Service' (1998) 57 (2) *Australian Journal of Public Administration* 82-90.

[18] Ibid.

[19] John O'Brien and Michael O'Donnell, 'Government, Management and Unions: The Public Service under the *Workplace Relations Act*' (1999) 41 *Journal of Industrial Relations* 446-467.

[20] Senate Finance and Public Administration Committee, Commonwealth Parliament, *Performance Pay* (1993) 22.

[21] Ibid 19-26.

[22] Ibid 65.

[23] Michael O'Donnell, 'Creating a Performance Culture? Performance-based Pay in the Australian Public Service' (1998) 57 (3) *Australian Journal of Public Administration* 28, 33-4.

[24] Comment by Administrative Service Officer, Department of Foreign Affairs and Trade, in CPSU 1999 Survey of members. See M O'Donnell and J Shields, 'Performance Management and the Psychological Contract in the Australian Federal Public Sector' (2002) 44 *Journal of Industrial Relations* 435.

[25] Comment by Administrative Service Officer, Department of Family and Community Services, in CPSU 1999 Survey of Members.

[26] Senate Finance and Public Administration References Committee, Commonwealth Parliament, *Australian Public Service Employment Matters*, Official Committee Hansard, (14 April 2000) 65. Access via <www.aph.gov.au/hansard/senate/commttee/s911.pdf> [July 2007].

[27] Ibid 66.

[28] Interview with Senior Manager, The Australian Bureau of Statistics, 25 February 1999; Statement by Barbara Sullivan, Manager, People Strategy Branch, Department of Finance and Administration, to Senate Finance and Public Administration References Committee, above n 26, (23 June, 2000) 198-202. Access via <http://www.aph.gov.au/hansard/senate/commttee/ s914.pdf>.

[29] I Kessler and K Purcell, 'Performance Related Pay: Objectives and Application' (1992) 2(3) *Human Resource Management Journal* 16-33.

[30] Department of Finance and Administration Certified Agreement 1997–99 2.

[31] John O'Brien and Michael O'Donnell, 'Creating a New Moral Order: Cultural Change in the Australian Public Service' (2000) 10 (3) *Labour and Industry* 66.

[32] Department of Finance and Administration Certified Agreement 1997–99.

[33] Interview with union delegates and DoFA, July 1998.

[34] Interview with two Industrial Officers, CPSU, August 1998; Interview with former manager, DoFA 25 June 2001.

[35] Ibid.

[36] Ibid.

[37] Ibid.

[38] O'Brien and O'Donnell, above n 31.

[39] Senate Finance and Public Administration References Committee, Commonwealth Parliament, *Australian Public Service Employment Matters*, Official Committee Hansard, (5 May 2000) 137. Access via <www.aph.gov.au/hansard/senate/commttee/s913.pdf>.

[40] Ibid 144.

[41] Ibid: 141.

[42] CPSU, *Annual Report 2001-2* (2002). In 2001, it claimed over 60,000 members. By 2005, membership had fallen to 57,803. During that period, the APS itself had between 123,000 and 128,000 personnel. See also CPSU, *Concise Financial Report for 2003-4* (2004) and *Financial Statement for 2004-5* (2005). The CPSU membership extends beyond the APS to entities such as Telstra and the ABC.

[43] Yates, above n 17.

[44] Unions are still able to serve logs of claims on management and open bargaining periods. These rights mean very little unless the union has the organisational capacity to enforce bargaining in 'good faith'.

[45] Interview with CPSU Industrial officer responsible for the Department of Education and Training and Youth Affairs, 23 February 1999.

[46] This has also happened in the two subsequent bargaining rounds. Arguably the propensity of the union team to win these elections has the effect of legitimising the union's role as bargaining agent on behalf of employees.

[47] Interview with union delegate, Department of Workplace Relation and Small Business, 25 February 1999.

[48] Ibid.

[49] Statement by Wendy Caird, National Secretary, Community and Public Sector Union to Senate Finance and Public Administration References Committee, Parliament of Australia, Canberra 14 April, 2000 78. (May be accessed via website, see n 26).

[50] Heaney and Associates 2002 *Agreements made in the Australian Public Service.*

[51] Dallys Bennett and Peter Shergold 'Commission Impossible? A New Approach to Workplace Relations in the PSMPC', (1998) 57 *Australian Journal of Public Administration* 91, 91-97.

[52] Peter Shergold, 'A New Public Service Act: The End of the Westminster Tradition', (Lunchtime Seminar Series, Public Service and Merit Protection Commission, 8 July 1997 <www.apsc.gov.au/media/shergold080797.htm>[July 2007].

[53] Ibid.

[54] Public Service and Merit Protection Commission, PSMPC Certified Agreement 1997-1999.

[55] Interview with senior manager, Public Service and Merit Protection Commission, 16 August 1999.

[56] Ibid.

[57] Via information through Department of Finance and Administration 1997 website.

[58] Department of Finance and Administration Certified Agreement D0776 Cas S Doc P 8746, Part A.

[59] Ibid.

[60] Interview with Industrial Officer, above n 34.

[61] Senate Finance and Public Administration References Committee, Parliament of Australia, *Australian Public Service Employment Matters*, 23 June 2000, Transcript, accessed via <www.aph.gov.au/hansard/senate/committee>.

[62] Interview with Organiser, CPSU, 23 August 1999.

[63] Senate Finance and Public Administration References Committee, Parliament of Australia, *Australian Public Service Employment Matters First Report, Australian Workplace Agreements*, 2000.

[64] There is, however, a certified agreement for the period 2002-2005 covering COMCAR drivers.

[65] Department of Finance and Administration, *Annual Report 2002-3* (2003). This report is available online at <http//:www.finance.gov.au/annual report>. There have been no certified agreements covering DoFA employees, other than COMCAR drivers, since 1997. As of June 2004, 99 per cent of all non-COMCAR staff are now on Australian Workplace Agreements: Department of Finance and Administration, *Annual Report 2003-2004* (2004) This report is available online at <:www.finance.gov.au/annual report>.

[66] House of Representatives, *Answer to Question from Mr Arch Bevis to the Minister for Finance and Administration, 8 February 1999*, question no. 351.

[67] Department of Finance and Administration, *Annual Report 1999-2000*. Accessed via <http://www.finance.gov.au/pubs/annualreport99-00/index1 .htm> [August 2007]

[68] Department of Finance and Administration, *Annual Report 2002-3* (2003), available http://www.finance.gov.au/annual report; *Annual Report 2003-2004*, available <http//:www.finance.gov.au/annual report>.

[69] Interview with union delegates, DoFA, (22 July 1998).

[70] Senate Finance and Administration References Committee, above n 26, (23 June 2000): 74, 77.

[71] Senate Finance and Public Administration Reference Committee, above n 26, (14 April 2000) 57-8.

[72] Interview with senior manager, Department of Foreign Affairs and Trade, 25 February 1999.

[73] Ibid.

[74] Ibid.

[75] Ibid.

[76] Ibid.

[77] Industrial Officer, above n 34.

[78] Interview with Mark Gepp, CPSU (13 July 1998). Even so, the Australian Electoral Commission has contracted Centrelink to provide an election information service in the 2004 federal election: Interview with Sue Vardon, Chief Executive, Centrelink, (10 October 2004).

[79] Yates, above n 17, 85.

[80] Interview with senior manager, Centrelink (25 February 1999).

[81] Interview with CEO, Centrelink (10 October 2002).

[82] Ibid.

[83] Ibid.

[84] Ibid.

[85] See Vardon 'Centrelink' in C Clark and D Corbett (eds) *Reforming the Public Sector: Problems and Solutions* (1999) 193.

[86] *Centrelink Development Agreement 1997-8* AG 774565, 2.

[87] *Centrelink Development Agreement 1999-2002* AG 776674; Centrelink, *Annual Report 1989-1999* (1999) 65.

[88] Ibid.

[89] Interview with Vardon, above n 78.

[90] Quality Committee, Centrelink, *Minutes of Meeting*, 10 December 2002 8-9.

[91] Interview with senior officials, CPSU (location/form of interview 19 August 2004).

[92] Centrelink Development Agreement 2003-2005 AG 824090 Print PR 931237. The agreement was with Centrelink, the CPSU, Professional Officers Association (Victoria), and the Media, Entertainment and Arts Alliance.

[93] Centrelink 2003 *Centrelink's Proposed Agreement Explained*, internal memorandum.

[94] Centrelink Quality Committee, *Minutes*, 8 April, 13 May and 10 June, 2003.

[95] Centrelink, *Annual Report 2002-2003*, chapter 7. The comprehensive agreement was 141 pages in length.

[96] Centrelink Agreement 2006-2009 AG 846162 Print PR 967825.

[97] Centrelink Agreement 2006-2009. Section 170LJ Agreement under the Workplace Relations Act between Centrelink and Media, Entertainment and Arts Alliance and Professional Officers Association (Victoria) and CPSU, the Community and Public Sector Union, 23 January 2006 (AG2006/2449).

[98] *Workplace Relations Amendment (Work Choices) Act 2005* (Cth). For a critique of the Act see Andrew Stewart, 'Work Choices in Overview: Slow Burn or Big Bang?' (2006) 16(2) *Economic and Labour Relations Review* 25, and all articles in issue: (2006) 19 *Australian Journal of Labour Law*.

[99] CPSU, *All Public Service Members: New IR laws to hit APS hard* (2005) News, 11 October 2005, <http://www.cpsu.org.au/news/1128983987_21577.html> [May 2006].

[100] Ibid.

[101] Terry Costello and Sue Bolton *Bunker Politics Prevail at CPSU Council Meeting* (2005) *GreenLeft Weekly* <http://www.greenleft.org.au/back/2005/622/622p10.htm> at 1 May 2006, reproduced in <http://www.members-first-org/news.html>.

[102] CPSU, *All Public Service Members: New IR laws to hit APS hard* (2005) News, 11 October 2005, <http://www.cpsu.org.au/news/1128983987_21577.html> [May 2006].

[103] CPSU, *Your Rights at Work: Fact Sheet 4 — Australian Workplace Agreements* (2005) <http://www.cpsu.org.au/campaigns/IRCampaign/resources/files/YRAWOCT4.pdf> at 1 May 2006.

[104] CPSU 2005, Candidates' statements, 1 November.

[105] CPSU *All CPSU Members: CPSU election — Jones/Gillespie Team Returned* (2005) News <http://www.cpsu.org.au/news/1134436139_18745.html> at 1 May 2006.

[106] Michael Alexander, Roy Green and A Wilson, 'Delegate Structures and Strategic Unionism: Analysis of Factors in Union Resilience' (1998) 40 *Journal of Industrial Relations* 663; A Morehead et all, *Changes at Work: The Australian Workplace Industrial Relations Survey* (1997) 142; Jeremy Waddington. and Allan Kerr 'Membership Retention in the Public Sector' (1999) 32 *Industrial Relations Journal* 164.

[107] CPSU *All CPSU members: Govt IR Campaign Not Working Says CPSU National Secretary* (2006) News <http://www.cpsu.org.au/news/1146804809_26969.html> at 1 May 2006.

[108] Department of Employment and Workplace Relations, *Supporting Guidance for the Workplace Relations Policy Parameters for Agreement Making in the Australian Public Service* (April 2006) 24 [Access via <www.workplace.gov.au>]. See also S Ramsay, 'Work Choices' (Presentation by Legal Officer, CPSU, seminar on Work Choices legislation, College of Law, Australian National University, 10 May 2006).

[109] One workplace consultant active in the APS who has spoken to the authors characterised the process as 'photocopy bargaining'.

[110] HBA Consulting, *Commonwealth Remuneration Guide, May 2005, Featuring Analysis in the Commonwealth by 1st Quartile, Median, 3rd Quartile and Average over a Three Year Period from January*

*2005 to January 2008* (2005) 2. The median for minimum point was $56,714 and average $57,270 and for the maximum point; $64,925 median and $65,231 average.

# Chapter Six

# Whistleblower Protection and the Challenge to Public Employment Law

## Robert G Vaughn

The last three decades have witnessed a dramatic but often unheralded revolution in the character of public employment law. Beginning with the federal government in the United States in 1978, protection of federal-employee whistleblowers has emphasised concepts of personal responsibility and accountability, long accepted in principle, but rarely implemented. The whistleblower provision of the *Civil Service Reform Act of 1978* [1] also marked the acceptance that disciplinary actions might be commenced against high-level government officials through an administrative process initiated outside an agency's chain of command. [2]

Subsequent amendments in federal law strengthened the enforcement of these whistleblower protections for federal employees. [3] These amendments also incorporated a right to disobey illegal orders, [4] a right previously recognised only by some state and federal courts. [5] The right to disobey also stressed the themes of personal responsibility and accountability. [6]

Since 1978, the vast majority of the US states has enacted statutes protecting whistleblowers who are public employees. [7] These statutes vary in scope and character but, like the federal statute, authorise employees to disclose information outside of the chain of command and under standards that replace internal agency rules or guidelines. [8] Like the federal law, these provisions articulate a concept of employee loyalty extending beyond an employee's agency or its managers. [9]

In the last decade or so, a number of countries, including Australia, New Zealand, Canada, South Africa, and the United Kingdom, enacted whistleblower statutes that protect public employees who disclose various types of misconduct or incompetence. [10] These enactments are striking not only because of their number, but also because they have been adopted in legal and cultural contexts seemingly inconsistent with them. For example, one of the more expansive whistleblower provisions may be found in Great Britain, a country with legal and cultural traditions supporting secrecy. [11] In Britain, one scholar had argued that whistleblowing by public employees was inconsistent with Britain's constitutional norms and parliamentary government.[12]

During this same period, a number of international treaties and conventions addressing governmental corruption have included provisions protecting whistleblowers.[13] Some international organisations, such as the World Bank and the European Commission, are developing internal standards and guides to protect employees who disclose corruption or wrongdoing connected with the activities of these organisations.[14] The recent spate of provisions protecting public sector whistleblowers, the strength of the international movements for transparency, for honesty in government, for human rights that support whistleblower protection, and the debates about the appropriate role of the public sector all counsel an examination of the challenge to public employment law evidenced in the legal protection of whistleblowers.

This chapter explores the implications of this legal revolution in the protection of whistleblowers. The first task of this exploration is to establish a framework into which the variety of laws may be placed. This undertaking begins with an analysis of the federal whistleblower law in the United States protecting federal employees, particularly the *Civil Service Reform Act of 1978*, a provision that stimulated subsequent legislation protecting public sector whistleblowers.[15] The background of this law and a review of its provisions and those of subsequent amendments establish themes to guide the subsequent analysis. These themes address concepts of employee loyalty, approval of individual responsibility in the face of hierarchical command, connection to information policy and access to government information, and empowerment of the right of freedom of expression as an underpinning of democratic accountability. These themes are developed in a review of state provisions protecting public sector whistleblowers.

Secondly, the chapter surveys the whistleblower laws of other countries. This survey permits a comparison of these laws with the themes developed with such public sector statutes in the United States. This comparison emphasises the many common themes as well as similar implications for public employment law drawn from these themes.

These tasks completed, the chapter considers the implications for public employment law. Whistleblower protection implements several principles and relies upon perspectives that challenge many concepts in public employment law. Whistleblower protection supports views of public employment that are not as fully recognised in public employment law but which amplify the effects of whistleblower protection on public employment law. Moreover, whistleblower protection blurs the distinctions between the regulation of public and private employment. The convergence of public and private sector employment law suggests that similar protections may apply to both, often under analogous justifications. This convergence offers some grounds by which to address a number of current phenomena including, as an example, the delegation of public functions to private organisations.

## Protection of Whistleblowers and Public Employment Law

Two pieces of United States legislation, the *Civil Service Reform Act of 1978* [16] and the *Whistleblower Protection Act of 1989*,[17] define the character of whistleblower protection for federal employees in the United States. In doing so, these statutes demonstrate how whistleblower protection challenges existing tenets of public employment law and show how whistleblower protection may transform public employment law. These statutes, particularly the *Civil Service Reform Act of 1978*, stimulated the enactment of other whistleblower provisions by the states.

## The US *Civil Service Reform Act of 1978* and the *Whistleblower Protection Act of 1989*

The *Civil Service Reform Act of 1978* ('Civil Service Reform Act') was the most extensive reform of the federal public service since the enactment of the *Civil Service Act of 1883*. Like the 1883 Act, the Civil Service Reform Act occurred in the shadow of national turmoil and a constitutional crisis. The violations of constitutional and civil liberties, the abuses of governmental power which forced the resignation, under threat of impeachment, of President Richard M Nixon in the view of some established a blueprint for executive tyranny. That blueprint relied heavily upon control of the public service and use of that control to evade legal and ethical restraints on executive power. That evasion permitted acts such as the ordering of illegal wiretaps, the improper award of grants and contracts, and the reduction of health and safety standards.[18] Particularly, loyalty to the president's 'team' replaced loyalty to agency, to law or to the public.[19]

The Vietnam War, which divided the American public, often along generational lines, legitimated dissent. This dissent included the release of the Pentagon Papers by whistleblower Daniel Ellsburg. Those confidential government documents that belied the government's own justifications for the war were published by the *New York Times*.[20] President Nixon's use of persons with connections to the Central Intelligence Agency to break into the Democratic National Committee's headquarters in the Watergate apartment complex and other violations of civil liberties, particularly the burglary of the office of Daniel Ellsburg's psychiatrist, suggested the importance of the First Amendment and the role of free speech and expression in supporting democratic accountability. Ironically, the Nixon cover-up of the Watergate break-in was motivated in part by the fear that exposure of that operation would lead to the discovery of Nixon's role in the Ellsburg burglary and other violations of civil liberties.

The Civil Service Reform Act pursued two, sometimes inconsistent, goals. The Act sought to make the public service more efficient by increasing the power of government managers to deal with poor performers, creating merit pay provisions, increasing the influence of political appointees over high ranking public employees, and regularising federal sector labor relations. Given the Nixon resignation and the national trauma surrounding the Vietnam War, the legislation also sought to protect federal employees from the abuse of the personnel authority, including that newly granted.

An important and revolutionary provision sheltered 'whistleblowers', employees who disclosed information that they reasonably believed evidenced a violation of law, rule, or regulation, a gross waste of funds, an abuse of authority or a specific and substantial danger to public health or safety.[21] The Act created an Office of Special Counsel to investigate violations of these protections, to represent whistleblowers, to examine allegations of misconduct, and to advocate for whistleblower protection.[22] Whistleblower claims could be pursued before a type of administrative court, the United States Merit Systems Protection Board, either as a defence to an appealable personnel action or in an action brought on behalf of the whistleblower by the Office of Special Counsel.[23]

The provisions pursuing the first goal of the Act assumed that employees are guided by command and motivated by fear.[24] The provisions implementing the second goal of the Act, including whistleblower protection, reflect a view that employees are also motivated by ideals and a desire to serve the public.[25]

These protections for whistleblowers can be seen as implementing principles already found in public employment law. For example, discipline of public employees rests on a concept of personal responsibility and accountability. Public employees are personally responsible for their misconduct or their failure to perform. Their conduct is evaluated by others and sanctions are applied based upon that evaluation. Depending upon the character of the position held, such an evaluation may be subject to judicial review or to independent adjudication.

Whistleblower protection can also be seen as departing substantially from existing provisions in public employment law. The protection of whistleblowers permits individual employees to call to account senior officials within a department or agency. The disclosure of information about misconduct or nonfeasance of others higher in the chain of command makes it more likely that the concepts of individual responsibility and accountability will be applied to all.

To the extent that whistleblower protection makes agency managers who retaliate against whistleblowers personally responsible for that retaliation through administrative discipline or through civil or criminal action, it radically alters the scope of persons within an agency to whom the traditional concepts of personal responsibility will apply. Indeed, the whistleblower provision of the Civil Service Reform Act permits the Office of Special Counsel to commence disciplinary actions against retaliating officials before the Merit Systems Protection Board.[26] This authority of the Special Counsel is one of the few instances in federal law that allows disciplinary actions to be commenced against high-level government officials by persons outside of the chain of command.[27]

The whistleblower provision of the Civil Service Reform Act can also be seen as implementing existing notions of employee loyalty. Although whistleblowing can appear to those superiors within an agency whose conduct is challenged as an act of disloyalty, federal employee whistleblowers had previously relied on the Code of Ethics for Government Service, a resolution passed by the United States Congress, as grounds for their disclosures. Among other provisions that code provided: 'Any person in government service should:

1. Put loyalty to the highest moral principles and to country above loyalty to persons, party, or government department …
2. Expose corruption wherever discovered
3. Uphold these principles, ever conscious that public office is a public trust'.[28]

This code was striking for the breadth of its definition of loyalty and for its imposition of an ethical obligation to expose misconduct.

This code, however, was hortatory. It failed to provide a basis in federal public employment for the protection of whistleblowers. The whistleblower provision was revolutionary because it provided legal protection for conduct that had previously been supported by mere admonitions. It permitted employees, quite properly, to expose the misconduct or nonfeasance of their superiors and to disclose information embarrassing or perhaps even harmful to the short-term interests of the agency for which they worked. By implication, it established, as did the code, a loyalty beyond persons, party or government department. That loyalty may be more circumscribed than loyalty to the highest moral principles or to the country, but remains a loyalty stretching far beyond that to an employee's immediate superiors and particular employer. An examination of protected disclosures suggests the character of this broader loyalty.

The protection of disclosures regarding the violation of law, rule or regulation describes a loyalty to the law, to the standards established by statute or by agency rule or other norms articulated and disseminated by a government agency. The rule of law, the concept that governmental power is limited by legal standards adopted either by Congress or by the Executive itself, is a premise underlying any democratic government seeking to protect the private sphere from improper interference by the government. Laws are approved by Congress and represent the articulation of standards by a democratically accountable body. Even agency standards rest upon the agency's perceptions of its legal powers deriving from statute or from the constitution. Because of its central place in the preservation of democratic government, loyalty to the rule of law encompasses a loyalty to the political and legal system which public employees ultimately serve. Because the legitimacy of a democratic government rests upon its authority rather than power alone, the government has an interest in ensuring that its agents act lawfully. Moreover, the specific agency for which the employee works also shares this interest in adherence to the law. Disclosures of abuses of authority address values likewise incorporated into the rule of law.[29]

Disclosures regarding a gross waste of funds acknowledge the interests of the government and taxpayers in the efficient use of resources in the implementation of government programs. The particular government program or agency also has an interest in the efficient use of those monies given it. Again, the loyalty implied by the protection of these disclosures encompasses a whistleblower's immediate employer but extends well beyond that employer.

In the sense that these disclosures protect the interests of the agencies, whistleblowers may be the most loyal employees even if loyalty focuses on the obligations of an employee to his or her employer. Whistleblowers are able to make this argument even in the narrow context of loyalty to the employer, because the Act implies a definition of loyalty to an organisation that extends beyond the interests of the managers who control that organisation at a particular time. Whistleblower protection separates loyalty to one's superiors from loyalty to one's employer. This separation, as does whistleblowing generally, challenges hierarchical command and gives to individual employees a role in the administration of government not previously countenanced.

Finally, disclosures regarding specific and substantial dangers to public health and safety concern the interests of the public generally. The employee loyalty implied by protection of such disclosures seems less clearly to encompass the employing agency or the government. Although government and individual agencies, particularly if they are charged with preserving health and safety, have an interest in the well being of the public, they do not implicate basic agency interests in legality or in efficiency.

There are perhaps reasons that explain this difference. Health and safety considerations are unique; for, injury to the person can never be fully compensated. Although we place a value on life and limb, the rationale for the disclosure of such risks, if they are specific and substantial, seems particularly strong. At the very least, such disclosures give responsible authorities and perhaps the public an ability to respond to them. Because of the strength of this interest, the Act protects these disclosures even if the risks do not flow from the violation of law, rule or regulation or the abuse of authority.

The whistleblower provision replaced a hortatory and abstract definition of employee loyalty with a practical and concrete one of legal effect. These changes in the concept of employee loyalty arise from whistleblower protection, but they can reverberate throughout public employment law.

These disclosures concern the activities of government.[30] Because they do so, protection of those employees who make these disclosures binds whistleblower protection in another way to the concept of democratic accountability. The ability of citizens to change government conduct, to require the redress of specific actions, to demand modifications in the powers or scope of government programs, or to insist on punishment or legal redress rely on the rights of freedom of expression, including the right of free speech and association. These rights are less meaningful without access to information about actions and procedures of government. Whistleblowers are an important source for such information.

This relationship of access to information to democratic accountability explains why whistleblower provisions are often connected to freedom of information and other open government laws. The passage of the federal *Freedom of Information Act* [31] in 1966 allowed whistleblowers to argue they simply provided the types of information to which the public would be entitled under a freedom of information law. One of the first state whistleblower laws was linked to the state's freedom of information law,[32] and the first attempt to enact whistleblower protection for federal employees likewise tied that protection to the federal *Freedom of Information Act of 1966.*[33] In a sense, both freedom of information and whistleblower laws statutorily empower the First Amendment.

The prohibitions against disclosure are limited. A disclosure is not protected if the disclosure is 'specifically prohibited by law' or if it is 'specifically required by an Executive Order to be kept secret in the interest of national defence or the conduct of foreign affairs'.[34] These prohibitions restrict the use of agency rules and regulations to limit scope of disclosure.

In enacting the whistleblower provision of the Civil Service Reform Act, Congress considered the First Amendment.[35] The whistleblower provision protected disclosures not protected, or ambiguously protected, under First Amendment law at the time.[36] For our purposes, one of the most striking distinctions was the protection under the statute of disclosures that might have been considered disruptive and not entitled to protection under the First Amendment. Congress legislated against weaknesses in the First Amendment and adopted a different approach to protection. The protection of employees who disclosed misconduct regarding their immediate superiors, with the attendant disruption, emphasises again how the enactment rejected a prevailing tenet in public employment law — the importance of hierarchical command. The Act and similar statutes create rights to freedom of expression not previously granted under public employment or constitutional law.

Moreover, when a legislative body weighs the disruption resulting from a whistleblower's disclosures and protects those disclosures, it reverses a judicial tendency to defer to a narrowly defined set of governmental interests focusing on efficiency and the chain of command. The judgment of a legislative body that the value of disclosures outweigh any resulting disruption enables the courts to act more boldly in applying constitutional restrictions. In another sense, such a provision is a redefinition of the character of public employment, which courts might appropriately incorporate into judicial development of that body of law.

A brief description of some of the principal provisions of the whistleblower provision of the *Civil Service Reform Act of 1978* supports the conclusion that the provision radically modified principal tenets of public employment law. Other parts of this provision buttress the view that whistleblower protection altered the scope of personal responsibility within government agencies, changed the character of employee loyalty, encouraged employee participation outside the chain of command, and rejected a view of government efficiency linked to preservation of the hierarchical control.

Of the important parts of the provision not previously discussed, three are particularly relevant to the themes already developed:

1.  protection of disclosures resting on reasonable belief;[37]
2.  approval of disclosures to persons and groups outside of the federal government;[38] and
3.  a provision directing that the Office of Special Counsel require federal agencies to respond to certain allegations of misconduct presented to the Special Counsel.[39]

The first of these protects an employee who has a 'reasonable belief' that a disclosure evidences one of the protected categories. The rejection of a more demanding standard, such as the requirement that the disclosure 'in fact' shows that there has been a violation of law, rule or regulation, a gross waste of funds, an abuse of authority, or specific and substantial danger to public health and safety exemplifies Congressional judgments about the value of these disclosures compared to the risk of disruption. That judgment relies on broad conceptions of employee loyalty and the importance of access to information to democratic accountability. The reasonable belief standard should encourage more disclosures, including some where there has in fact been no wrongdoing.

The language and legislative history of the whistleblower provision approves disclosures within government agencies and authorises them outside of the government as well.[40] Subsequently, Congress has made it clear that disclosures to the press are protected.[41] The protection of internal disclosures seeks to change the character of the workplace, making it more open to employee criticisms and participation. The protection of disclosures outside of government emphasises that the preservation of agency procedures and structures, including those regarding employee disclosures, do not justify limitations on the prerogatives of employees.

One of the most contentious provisions requires the Special Counsel to forward to an agency head for investigation and response those allegations which the Special Counsel believes demonstrate a substantial likelihood of agency misconduct.[42] The provision was contentious because it was a particularly clear embodiment of the tenet that an individual employee could bring the highest-ranking agency officials to account. Such accountability illustrates the practical expansion of the concepts of personal responsibility ingrained in whistleblower protection.

Subsequent changes in the whistleblower provision of the Civil Service Reform Act, particularly those contained in the *Whistleblower Protection Act of 1989*, addressed weaknesses in the enforcement structure, including the Office of Special Counsel, shortcomings in the drafting of the provision, and restrictive judicial interpretations.[43] A crucial change made it easier for a whistleblower to prove retaliation by stating that in order to meet the burden of demonstrating retaliation a whistleblower need only prove by a preponderance of the evidence the protected disclosure was a 'contributing factor' to the challenged agency action against the whistleblower.[44] If the whistleblower carried this burden, the agency must prove by clear and convincing evidence that it would have taken the same action absent the protected disclosure.[45]

For our purposes, the most important change was the recognition of the right of federal employees to disobey illegal orders.[46] Adoption of the right to disobey affirms many of the principles of the original Act that transform public employment law. The right to disobey illegal orders embodies the same concepts of employee loyalty incorporated in protection of disclosures of violations of law, rule or regulation. Those concepts of loyalty are broad ones encompassing more than loyalty to superiors or to a government agency but also a loyalty to the government and to the system of democratic government. Acceptance of the right to disobey contains similar judgments regarding the weight to be given to legality as opposed to the government's interest in preventing disruption of the workplace. Acceptance approves a concept of individual responsibility that allows an individual employee to act upon his or her own judgment about the legality of an order. Acceptance confirms that disobedience like criticism is a form of employee dissent appropriately protected not only because it preserves an employee's right of free expression but also because it vindicates the concept of democratic accountability.

## State Whistleblower Statutes

Following the *Civil Service Reform Act of 1978*, several states enacted laws protecting whistleblowers in public employment. An examination of these laws of general application illustrates the themes already developed and demonstrates how whistleblower protection has altered not only federal but also state public employment law. This examination also allows an assessment of how much the changes in public employment law follow the extensive protections provided in the federal provisions and how much the changes result simply from the acceptance of the concept of 'whistleblowing'. Such an assessment provides a basis for a discussion of whistleblower provisions applicable to public employees in other countries.

After 1978, statutes protecting whistleblowers in public employment swept the United States. At least forty-two states now have such statutes of general application to public sector employees.[47] In addition, several states have statutes applicable to specific areas of concern, such as health care, abuse of children and the elderly, foster homes, motor vehicle emissions, workers compensation and public utilities.[48] These statutes of general application vary in scope and in the character of protections provided but all accept whistleblowing by public employees.

A review of how these statutes resolve issues considered in the federal whistleblower law permits an appraisal of their implications for public employment law. The great majority of the state statutes protect disclosures regarding violations of law.[49] Most of the states that protect only one type of disclosure limit those disclosures to violations of law.[50] The substantial majority of these statutes protect disclosures regarding violations of federal as well as state law.[51]

No other category of protected disclosures is as common as the one regarding violations of law. The other most frequently protected disclosures regard, in order of frequency, governmental waste, substantial and specific dangers to public health or safety, and abuse of authority.[52] Another less commonly protected disclosure concerns mismanagement.

These categories of protected disclosures follow closely those articulated in the federal whistleblower provision. To the extent these categories track federal ones, the implications of the protection of these disclosures for conceptions of employee loyalty, described in regard to the federal provision, apply to these state laws. Indeed, this similarity in protected disclosures suggests that the federal law provided the basic model to which states made particular alterations. Such a reliance on the federal law, while probable, is not necessary to conclusions about the implications of these state provisions. This similarity, however, should not obscure two important differences relevant to the character of employee loyalty. First, the emphasis in the state statutes on violations of law occurs at the expense of the other disclosures which are less frequently included. Second, disclosures regarding violations of law encompass not only violations of state law but also violations of the law of another sovereign, the government of the United States.

The implications of whistleblower protection for the character of employee loyalty are not significantly altered by exclusion from the protection of some state statutes of all of the categories of disclosures except the violation of law. The majority of statutes contain most or all of the categories contained in the federal provision. Thus, the general implications of these whistleblower statutes for the field of public employment remain. Even if the analysis focuses on those states which protect only disclosures regarding violations of law, the implications of the character of employee loyalty in public employment law are still quite similar. The effect of the protection of disclosures of violations of law in federal law included above demonstrates that protection of that disclosure alone perceives an employee stretching beyond that to the employee's superiors or the agency in which he or she works. Rather, it describes a view of employee loyalty that includes the government generally, the system of democratic governance and those persons affected by such violations. Protection of such disclosures also sharply redefines the interests of the employee's own agency, separating loyalty to individual managers from loyalty to the agency. The analysis also asserted that same implications flow from protection of disclosures regarding an abuse of authority.

Although disclosures of waste or mismanagement concern interests in efficiency, the implications for conceptions of employee loyalty do not differ significantly from those applicable to the disclosures regarding violations of the law. Protection of these disclosures likewise suggests obligations beyond one's immediate superiors and a loyalty to others.

The effect of protecting disclosures regarding specific and substantial dangers to public health or safety does indicate that the exclusion of this protected disclosure might be relevant if we focus on a specific jurisdiction which does not protect such a disclosure. First, as noted in the discussion of the federal whistleblower provision, disclosures regarding specific and substantial dangers to public health and safety may not encompass the agency's own interests in the same way as the other protected disclosures. Arguably, the interest of a generic federal agency in the health or safety of the public does not implicate basic agency interests in legality and efficiency. Those agencies, however, with responsibilities for protecting public health and safety have a strong interest in ensuring that their mission is effectively accomplished. In this sense, the interests of some agencies are involved and like the other disclosures, this one includes a duty of loyalty to the agency.

Secondly, with those agencies having responsibilities for protecting public health and safety, these disclosures involve individual employees more directly in the administration of the agency's programs and the decisions applicable to them. This proposition relies on the premise that all agencies have a general concern for legality and efficiency in their operations and, while whistleblower disclosures regarding illegality or waste certainly become entangled with specific programs and policies (indeed, such entanglement may be the motivation for the disclosures), these disclosures are different in character and effect.

If this premise is accepted, it can be argued that the protected disclosures are less likely to be limited to activities in the workplace. A disclosure is more likely to concern the conduct of third parties that pose such a risk to public health or safety and such disclosures are more likely to enmesh employees in agency programs and policy making. For example, an employee identifies a private activity, involving the disposal of toxic chemicals in the course of mining, that the employee reasonably believes creates a specific and substantial danger to public health. The agency arguably has jurisdiction to regulate this conduct but is not legally required to do so. The agency is quite efficient in carrying out the regulatory responsibilities it has assumed. In effect, the employee's disclosure of a specific and substantial danger to public health challenges the agency's regulatory priorities.

If this line of argument is convincing, this type of protected disclosure gives individual employees an ability to participate in the development of regulatory policy, that may or may not occur in practice, beyond that approved in public employment law. Thus, the exclusion of this protected disclosure may have an impact on the principles of public employment in a particular jurisdiction. Perhaps the encouragement of employee participation lurking in the protection of this type of disclosure explains the requirement that the danger to public health or safety be 'specific and substantial'.

Providing protection solely of disclosures regarding violations of law can more generally be seen as an expression of hesitancy about encouraging independent judgment by individual employees concerning agency policy and practices. Disclosures regarding violations of law surely require judgment by an employee that addresses whether particular conduct reasonably can be seen as breaking established and articulated standards contained in laws, rules or regulations. The other types of disclosures draw upon less clear and established standards. For example, more employee discretion and analysis is involved in determining whether particular expenditures are a waste of funds or official action is mismanagement. Therefore, protection of these other types of disclosures may endorse more extensive judgments by employees regarding the propriety of the administration of an agency's programs.

A second important difference between these state statutes and the federal provision relevant to the character of employee loyalty pertains to the protection of disclosures of violations of federal law found in many state statutes. Certainly, this inclusion of violations of federal law reflects a judgment that the states' interests in the enforcement of these federal laws are viewed as significant enough to justify the extension of protection and the attendant costs. Conceivably, states could have a number of reasons for such an inclusion, but for our purposes, the more relevant question concerns implications for the character of employee loyalty of this protection of disclosures regarding violations of federal law.

The inclusion affirms the importance of legality in a democratic society. This affirmation stresses the larger obligation of every public employee to the concept of legality and to our political and legal system. That obligation overrides or replaces more narrow views of employee loyalty resting on the approval of supervisors, the convenience of agencies, or even the interests of state government. As a practical matter, the violators of federal law most likely identified by state employees are state officials or state agencies. At a time when many functions once performed by the federal government are 'devolved' to the states, this inclusion is also a reminder of the loyalty that state employees owe to the national government.

In contrast to the federal provisions which clearly protect disclosures to the press and to the public, 'the state statutes, with few exceptions, protect disclosures only to government officials and to public bodies'.[53] Although the overwhelming majority of the statutes broadly define public bodies 'often including state and local agencies and their employees, officials within the executive, judicial, and legislative branches, and federal agencies and officials',[54] this limitation does merit discussion. Many of the statutes do not specifically require that a public body have authority to regulate the conduct identified in a disclosure. A reasonable interpretation, however, would incorporate such a requirement. Even if this requirement is incorporated in the definition of a government body, a disclosure could still be protected when made to more than one agency.

In addition to the practical significance of this restriction on those persons and organisations to whom disclosures could be made, the limitation may alter the effect of a whistleblower provision on public employment law. Statutes which contain this restriction still reject the primacy of the agency structure of command. Many of these public bodies are separate from the public employer and some, at least, may not even be part of state government. Employees are permitted to make their own judgments about the conduct of agency officials and act in a way that may give those judgments legal effect. In this regard, the implications for whistleblower protection on public employment law do not seem altered.

This restriction on those to whom disclosures may be made, however, can alter the implications for public employment law in another way. To the extent that the close connection between whistleblower protection and public access to information links whistleblower protection to free expression and democratic accountability, the failure to protect public disclosures weakens this linkage. Arguably, such a restriction reflects different judgments about the weight given to the workplace disruptions likely caused by public exposures of official misconduct. In this sense, the statutes can be read, at least in part, as supporting a prevailing tenet in public employment law — the importance of workplace harmony sustaining hierarchical command.

Given the number of reasons for protecting internal disclosures, surprisingly few of the whistleblower statutes that are applicable to the public sector deal with this issue.[55] Of the statutes which address the issue, a good majority protect internal disclosures but require some type of internal disclosure before disclosures can be made to someone other than the employer.[56] Some of these statutes, however, incorporate exceptions that permit an employee to forego internal disclosures in certain circumstances often involving concern with delay, emergencies, reasons to believe that no action will be taken, and the fear of reprisal.[57]

At first glance, the requirement for internal disclosure stresses a narrow definition of employee loyalty. Several aspects of these statutes, however, caution against a characterisation of these statutes as a return to a view of employee loyalty traditionally contained in public employment law. Most of the statutes only require disclosure to the public employer not to specific individuals within an agency.[58] The authorisation to report to persons outside of the employee's chain of command thus can be seen as defining loyalty in terms of the public employer rather than the specific managers to whom an employee is responsible. Moreover, several of the statutes contain exceptions which permit an employee to forego the requirement. Finally, an employee who made an internal disclosure or who, under some provisions, has given the agency a reasonable time to address the allegations, may disclose them outside the agency. Although the internal disclosure has practical effects on the likelihood of disclosures, the requirement does not necessarily reject broader conceptions of employee loyalty.

Like the federal law, most of the state statutes only require a reasonable belief that the disclosures fall within those protected.[59] A few statutes only require that an employee act in good faith;[60] two statutes seem to require that a disclosure be true in order to be protected.[61] As noted, the reasonable belief standard relies on broad concepts of employee loyalty and the importance of access to information to democratic accountability by encouraging some disclosures which in fact are not accurate. The good faith standard should encourage a more substantial number of disclosures not in fact true. The true-in-fact standard will encourage the fewest of such unsustainable allegations but may also discourage the disclosure of many valid ones as well. The state provisions demonstrate that the state statutes overwhelmingly adopt the same expansive views of employee loyalty and the importance of public access to information contained in the federal law. Even the two states that adopt the most restrictive standard for disclosure accept that employees should act to expose misconduct if they are convinced that it has occurred.

The state laws, however, are more likely than the federal law to require a substantial connection between the protected disclosure and the challenged action taken against the whistleblower.[62] For example, whistleblowers may be required to prove by a preponderance of the evidence that the protected disclosure played a more substantial role in the challenged action.

Like the federal law, a substantial number of state whistleblower statutes include protections for employees who refuse to obey illegal orders.[63] These provisions vindicate the interests discussed previously with the federal statute and suggest the same types of revisions in public employment law created by protection of whistleblowers. The standard for disobedience is unclear under the federal statute.[64] The majority of the state laws adopt an illegal in fact standard of the right to disobey, but a significant portion of these laws embrace a reasonable belief standard.[65] Like the federal provision, these state laws have altered the landscape of public employment law.

The federal whistleblower law and the state statutes as a group contain many provisions that support and implement whistleblower protection. The discussion above demonstrates how these aspects of the whistleblower laws challenge public employment law by introducing principles and concepts that link whistleblower protection to innovative concepts of employee loyalty, to access to information and democratic accountability, and to free expression. These principles challenge in a number of ways a limited view of efficiency based on hierarchical command. It is useful to separate, however, the impact on public employment law of these relatively liberal statutes implementing whistleblower protection from the implications of the adoption of more restrictive whistleblower laws.

One way of accomplishing such a separation considers the implications for public employment law under a restrictive statute. The provision used for this purpose does not reproduce the terms of any statute thus far discussed, but rests on a hypothetical law that collects restrictive provisions from several state laws. In essence, this provision imagines the most limited law that still adopts, and presumably approves, the concept of whistleblower protection. That hypothetical law resolves the issues already discussed in the following manner:

1.  it only protects disclosures regarding violations of law that come to the attention of the employee in the course of his or her employment;

2.   it only protects disclosures to a particular public body, such as an ombudsman or auditor general;

3.   it requires internal disclosure prior to any other disclosure and contains no exceptions to this requirement;

4.   it imposes a standard for disclosure that requires wrongfulness in fact (reasonable belief is insufficient to provide protection);

5.   it only covers an employee who acts in the public interest without malice and without consideration for personal gain (it thus encourages an examination of the motives of a whistleblower); and

6.   it provides limited remedies and adopts a test for reprisal that compels an employee to prove that a protected disclosure was the primary reason for the challenged personnel action without the benefit of any presumption of retaliation.

From the discussion of the federal law and the state provisions, each of these resolutions of particular issues, as compared to those generally made in these provisions, are more supportive of traditional views of public employment and less accepting of the concepts behind whistleblower protection which challenge those views. However, that same discussion demonstrates that recognition of the legitimacy of whistleblower accepts concepts and values inconsistent with many of the assumptions regarding public employment on which legal regulation has relied. Of course, it is possible to argue that the combination of these choices in a single law renders application of the underlying principles so unlikely as to make the law a nullity. The ineffectiveness of the law can generate cynicism that undermines these underlying principles.

Despite this argument, the recognition of the legitimacy of whistleblowing is a powerful change in the view of public employment upon which legal regulation relies. Bureaucracies are not rigid and static, but dynamic. The behavior of employees is predicated in large measure by the perceptions of the types of conduct expected of them. Personal responsibility offers a fundamental way of controlling human conduct and behavior and provides an important principle by which large institutions may be limited by law. Articulations of employee loyalty which emphasise loyalty beyond the personal or institutional, support expectations of greater involvement by individual employees in protecting the public interest. Whistleblower protection expresses these values and brings them to bear on employee conduct. Whistleblower protection not only changes public employment law, but also alters the culture and character of public employment. Whistleblower protection, even in the most restrictive statute, can transform the character of the workplace.

## International Acceptance of Whistleblower Protection

International acceptance of whistleblower protection illustrates its power to transform legal regulation of public employment. The acceptance of whistleblower protection in countries with cultural and legal traditions inconsistent with the protection of whistleblowers offers a particularly clear illustration of this power. Great Britain's whistleblower law, enacted in 1998, provides a readily accessible example.

In the last decade or so, many national laws and international conventions have adopted whistleblower protection.[66] A general review of these laws permits comparison of them with those laws in the United States previously discussed, and allows speculation about the effects of their adoption on public employment law. This comparison shows many striking similarities in these laws as well as some important differences, differences explained in part by the background and context to some of them.

## The British *Public Interest Disclosure Act 1998*

The *Public Interest Disclosure Act 1998* (UK)[67] exemplifies the acceptance of whistleblower protection in a legal and cultural context antagonistic to it. It also demonstrates how the principles underlying such protection can transform the character of public employment law. It suggests how whistleblower protection subverts traditional rules regulating public employment.

The British public service, particularly the civil service, rested on centralised control, secrecy, and employee loyalty to the cabinet officer heading a ministry. By tradition and convention, civil servants were anonymous and silent. The character of public employment and premises of public employment law were antithetical to whistleblowing and offered whistleblowers little or no protection. Whistleblowing was an illegitimate act by any public employee.

The constitutional convention of parliamentary supremacy centralised control of a government ministry in the hands of the minister, who, as part of the cabinet, was directly accountable to Parliament for the administration of the ministry.[68] Loyalty to the minister was fairly conceived as satisfying loyalty to the government and to the democratic political system on which it rested. The conventions of ministerial responsibility and civil servant anonymity and supporting practices embodied this view of employee loyalty and of a circumscribed role for individual employees.[69] These conventions formed powerful arguments against whistleblowing, leading one commentator to conclude that a whistleblower commits a politically hostile act, and that an employee must make any complaints internally and may otherwise disclose concerns only after resigning from the public service.[70]

Public employment law reflected this antagonism to whistleblowing. The Official Secrets Acts imposed criminal penalties for the release of government information.[71] Civil service rules imposed discipline for the unauthorised release of information.[72] Because permission was required before a civil servant could release information, most disclosures that could be characterised as whistleblowing were unauthorised and punishable as such.

Although some justifications for whistleblowing could be constructed within this restrictive framework of public employment law,[73] such justifications were of marginal effect. As in the United States, these justifications relied upon ethical and professional standards. The culture of the civil service and the tenets of public employment law denied legitimacy to whistleblowing and punished any public employee who made unauthorised disclosures.

The British *Public Interest Disclosure Act* represents a striking departure from a restrictive view of whistleblowing. This departure challenges existing tenets of public employment law and seeks to create a different type of workplace.

The Act, being broad in scope, covers almost all employees in Britain, including civil servants and most categories of public employees.[74] It permits disclosures in circumstances in which public employees would previously have been compelled to remain silent. Although the Act does not authorise violation of statutory prohibitions against disclosure, such as the Official Secrets Acts, it provides that in order to be denied protection, a whistleblower must have been convicted of a violation of the Official Secrets Act, or that the adjudicatory tribunal hearing a claim of retaliation must be effectively satisfied 'beyond a reasonable doubt', that the whistleblower committed the offence.[75] This provision of the Act combined with the subsequent enactment of a freedom of information statute[76] in Britain reduces the legal demands for secrecy. Moreover, the Act voids contractual provisions that prohibit whistleblowers from disclosing any information or from exercising their rights under the Act.[77] In this sense, the Act protects disclosures 'whether or not the information is confidential'.[78]

The protection of whistleblowers alone undermines the legal and policy justifications for restrictions on the release of information by public employees. Such protection accepts and legitimatises such disclosures and implicitly rejects the arguments for restrictions which rest upon the premise that a public sector whistleblower commits a politically hostile act, both ethically and legally indefensible. On the contrary, the protection of whistleblowers is seen as so important that the Act deprives public employers of the ability contractually to limit disclosures protected by the Act.

The extent of the repudiation of tenets in public employment law illustrates the character of the challenge that whistleblower protection laws pose. The legal and cultural context in Britain starkly highlights this challenge. Advocates of whistleblower protection in Britain believed that a law was necessary to 'good governance and openness in organisations'.[79] The law seeks to change the character of the workplace making it more open and giving employees an important role in ensuring that administration followed the law and the standards for good governance.

The Act addresses internal and external disclosures in a way that emphasises how whistleblower protection serves to reform employment, including public employment and administration. Many whistleblower statutes authorise disclosures under a single standard whether the disclosure is internal, to another governmental body, to the media or to any other person. These 'single standard' statutes tend to treat internal disclosures like all others. In doing so, they can seem to underplay the value of internal disclosures and generate attempts to require internal disclosure often with restrictive or ambiguous exceptions. On the other hand, the British Act varies the standards for disclosure based upon the audience receiving the disclosure.

The Act protects disclosures of 'crimes, civil offences (including negligence, breach of contract, breach of administrative law), miscarriages of justice, dangers to health and safety or the environment and the cover up of any of these.'[80] Internal disclosures are protected under the most lenient standard, a reasonable belief and good faith belief that any of the covered misconduct has occurred or is threatened.[81]

A second type of disclosures, regulatory disclosures, may be made to prescribed persons, who are most likely to be health and safety or financial regulators.[82] The standard for regulatory disclosures is more demanding than the standard for internal disclosures. Regulatory disclosures must meet the standard for internal disclosures and, in addition, the whistleblower must also reasonably believe that the allegations are substantially true.[83]

Other disclosures, including disclosures to the media, must meet the test for regulatory disclosures, may not be made for personal gain, and must be reasonable under the circumstances.[84] In addition, the whistleblower must meet one of three preconditions for such disclosures:

1. reasonable fear of reprisal for the disclosure to the employer or to a prescribed person;
2. reasonable belief of the concealment or destruction of evidence relating to the misconduct; or
3. previous disclosure of the misconduct to the employer or to a prescribed person.[85]

The reasonableness of such disclosures depend upon the identity of the persons to whom the disclosure is made, the seriousness of the conduct reported, whether the conduct will continue or reoccur, and whether disclosure would require a breach of confidentiality.[86]

By treating internal disclosures under the most lenient standard for protection separately from other disclosures, the British Act emphasises the work environment as the principal venue of whistleblowing. As such, the British statute seeks to influence employment law and practices in order to change the character of the workplace. Thus, the British law clearly challenges the tenets of public employment. At the same time, it recognises the need for external disclosures and leaves the employee options to pursue such disclosures when necessary. Under the British statute, public employment law must recognise a loyalty of an employee beyond his or her supervisors or the management of the agency; public employment law must accept the involvement of individual employees in the affairs of the public employer in ways that may challenge unity of command; and public employment law must acknowledge that public employees may be an important source of information to other agencies and to the public.

The British *Public Interest Disclosure Act* represents the acceptance of whistleblower protection in what would seem an uncongenial legal and culture context. Because the character of the changes that the legislation wrought in public employment law are so stark, this acceptance demonstrates how whistleblower protection challenges public employment law.

## Whistleblower Protection as an Anti-Corruption Measure

Whistleblower protection is increasingly seen as an important part of international and national efforts to control corruption. Several national statutes emphasise this connection between whistleblower protection and anti-corruption efforts. The statutes of several Australian states illustrate this connection and allow an examination of the ways in which the ties to the control of corruption affect the arguments regarding the challenge that whistleblower protection poses to public employment law. This examination identifies some differences resulting from the connection of whistleblower protection to anti-corruption efforts but generally supports the analysis of the implications of whistleblower protection already presented.

As part of an international effort to control corruption, several international conventions, such as the European Union's Civil Convention on Corruption,[87] its Criminal Convention on Corruption,[88] and the Inter-American Convention Against Corruption,[89] contain provisions protecting whistleblowers. These provisions require implementing national legislation and the Organization of American States, Office of Legal Projects commissioned the draft of a model law to implement the section of the Convention protecting whistleblowers.[90]

The whistleblower laws of several Australian states are linked to anti-corruption provisions. These Australian laws often rely on anti-corruption commissions or similar offices for enforcement. Although these provisions vary, they reflect a concern with governmental corruption, misadministration and waste. Generally, but not exclusively, they protect disclosures regarding misconduct by public officials and seek to regulate governmental corruption.

The *Corruption and Crime Commission Act 2003* enacted in Western Australia[91] most clearly shows this link to anti-corruption efforts. This Act protects disclosures to the Corruption and Crime Commission regarding corrupt, criminal, biased or dishonest conduct by public officials.[92] The Act prohibits victimisation of persons making such disclosures and provides criminal penalties for violation of this prohibition.[93] In addition, persons making disclosures to the Commission are protected from private civil actions based on those disclosures.[94] Likewise, the New South Wales *Protected Disclosures Act 1994* [95] protects disclosures of corrupt conduct, maladministration or substantial waste by public officials.[96] Disclosures must be made by a public employee and it must not be part of the employee's official duties to report the misconduct.[97] The persons to whom disclosures may be made is limited and disclosures to the press or the legislature are protected but only in very limited circumstances.[98]

Other statutes, such as those of Queensland and South Australia, protect similar disclosures but also permit disclosures of official behaviour which poses a substantial risk to public health and safety.[99] The Queensland provision requires that the disclosure be made to an appropriate public body.[100] In certain circumstances, the South Australian law permits disclosures to others, including the media.[101] Some statutes, such as those of Victoria and the Australian Capital Territory, cover somewhat broader disclosures[102] but also limit disclosures to government agencies.[103]

The South Australian law, the first permanent provision protecting whistleblowers, was part of a group of measures designed to combat 'fraud and corruption'.[104] Other jurisdictions seem to have 'followed suit' in a number of ways, including an emphasis on controlling official corruption.[105] The South Australian law, even though extending protections to private employees, primarily sought to protect against corruption in government.[106]

Whistleblower laws linked to anti-corruption efforts may differ in some ways from the more general whistleblower provisions previously discussed. First, they are more likely to focus on disclosures to certain specialised bodies with responsibilities for punishing or preventing official corruption. Second, they suggest coverage of disclosures outside of the employment process. Undoubtedly many persons with knowledge of official corruption will be public employees, but it is easy to conceive that employees of private employers, employers who may be involved in corrupt practices with public officials, would be aware of these corrupt practices. In addition, persons not employed by the government or by those affected or involved with private employers may also have knowledge of official corruption.[107] Finally, it can appear that an anti-corruption rationale for these whistleblower laws is more limited than the rationale underlying many whistleblower statutes.

Together, these differences may suggest a more limited impact on public employment law. The reliance on specialised bodies, by reducing those persons to whom disclosures may be made, permits the argument that changes in concepts of employee loyalty are more modest and greater weight is given to institutional prerogatives. The extension of whistleblower protection beyond the employment context suggests that the character of employment is less a concern of these provisions. The more limited rationale for these anti-corruption provisions signifies concerns less drastically challenging the character of public employment.

The implications of the first of these differences regarding limitations on persons to whom disclosures may be made has, in fact, been explored in earlier discussions of the scope of disclosure. At the least, the challenge posed by approval of whistleblowing noted in those discussions supports the conclusion that this difference does not affect the implications for employee loyalty, personal accountability, and chain of command of the approval of whistleblowing. The second of these two differences is unlikely to alter the conclusions already reached because the overwhelming majority of whistleblowing is likely to be employment based. This difference also represents an aspect of many whistleblower statutes not simply those resting on an anti-corruption rationale — for many of these statutes cover both public and private sector employment. The implications of this coverage of public and private employment under the same law will be discussed in more detail below.

Finally, upon examination, the anti-corruption rationale is not limited and does not necessarily stand in contrast to other grounds for whistleblower protection. Anti-corruption provisions necessarily rest upon the importance of the rule of law and employees' loyalty to the law and the democratic system of which it is a part. Anti-corruption provisions recognise access to information regarding the activities of government officials as crucial to democratic accountability. In this way, anti-corruption provisions are also tied to the rights of free expression of citizens and of employees. Thus, anti-corruption provisions can challenge the tenets of public employment as do other whistleblower provisions.

The statutes of the Australian states make the anti-corruption rationale seem more restrictive than the analysis above suggests is justified. These statutes are more restrictive than some other whistleblower protection laws. For example, these statutes often limit disclosures external to the government, require internal disclosure before external disclosure and at least in one instance, require that allegations must be based not only on a reasonable belief but also must be determined to be substantially true. More restrictive statutes, however pose a challenge to public employment law similar to that of more liberal provisions.

The model whistleblower law drafted for the Organization of American States explicitly identifies the rule of law, democratic accountability, and free expression as supporting such a law.[108] This law represents provisions resting on the anti-corruption rationale that contains few of the restrictive provisions contained in the Australian anti-corruption statutes. Therefore, nothing in the character of the rationale for anti-corruption laws inherently reduces the challenge to public employment law.

A review of the types of whistleblower protections adopted internationally and in several countries supports the proposition that these protections challenge public employment law. The British *Public Interest Disclosure Act* clearly shows how the adoption of whistleblower protection modifies more general propositions in public employment law antagonistic to it. The Australian laws demonstrate that whistleblower statutes more closely tied to anti-corruption efforts present the same types of challenges to public employment law.

## Protection of Whistleblowers and the Implications for Public Employment Law

The challenge posed by whistleblower protection to public employment law helps to fashion a vision of public employment. This vision incorporates many of the concepts inherent in whistleblower protection. Although this vision challenges many of the principles of public employment law, it is a vision that draws upon theories of public employment, while not dominant, has coloured the discussion of public employment. The connection of whistleblower protection to a vision of public service may strengthen the challenge that whistleblower protection presents for public employment law. Because of this power to transform the law, whistleblower protection becomes more than simply an adjustment in practice and procedure.

Whistleblower laws vary in how they distinguish public and private sector employment. The federal whistleblower provisions in the United States, previously discussed, are limited to public employees with separate provisions addressing employees in the private sector. Likewise, many state laws distinguish between public and private employment. In countries other than the United States, whistleblower laws sometimes treat public and private employees differently, sometimes under separate laws. Even these separate statutes, however, often address identical issues, and some statutes cover both public and private sector employees. Despite treatment in different state statutes in the United States, there do not appear to be substantial and dramatic differences in the ways in which statutes conceive public and private sector protections. The similarities invite a reconsideration of distinctions between public and private sector employment and the significance of this reconsideration for public employment law.

## The Vision of Public Service

Thus far, this chapter has portrayed public employment law as a somewhat monolithic embodiment of a conception of public employment. It is true that public employment law stresses a narrow view of employee loyalty, efficiency supported by unity of command and restrictions on the rights of expression of public employees. Public employment law also rejects a significant role for public employees in democratic accountability. The conception of public employment, however, draws on a more complex set of theories than thus far presented. Within the confines of this chapter, the examination of these theories is necessarily cursory and intended only to identify strains of thought embedded in conceptions of public employment to which whistleblower protection relates.

An examination of some of these strains of thought show their relationship to whistleblower protection. For purposes of illustration alone, these strains of thought together can be conceived as a vision of public service. This vision has different views than the dominant view of public employment law of employee loyalty, efficiency, freedom of expression of public employees, participation by them in agency administration, and public employees' role in democratic accountability. This vision also assumes that employees are motivated by a morality of role that stresses the obligations to the public of those who exercise public power.

The strains of thought from which this vision of public service can be perceived reflect theories from different historical periods. The theories themselves are not always consistent with one another because they rest upon different views of the ideal character of administration.[109] For our purposes, however, it is sufficient to suggest how they form a reservoir of ideas and arguments which coincide nicely with the ideas and arguments regarding whistleblower protection. This coincidence of ideas and arguments allows whistleblower protection to draw on existing conceptions of public employment, conceptions which magnify the challenge of whistleblower protection to public employment law.

The admonition that a public office is a public trust describes public employment in terms of fiduciary duty, that is, the obligation of one person to act on behalf of another.[110] Conflict of interest provisions, in the United States, certainly support a duty to act on behalf of persons other than the management of an agency and, perhaps beyond a duty to act on behalf of the agency, to act on behalf of the government of which individual agencies are a part.[111] It is through this fiduciary duty that government employees act on behalf of the public.

This conception of loyalty reminds one of the Code of Ethics for Government Service discussed above. Like that code and the ethical standards contained within it, this conception of employee loyalty is a broad one. Unlike those ethical standards on which whistleblowers relied, this conception of employee loyalty has legal effect and status as an important principle of public employment law.

A concept of efficiency relying upon unity of command rests in part upon the need to legitimise administration. Administrators are generally unelected and exercise considerable discretion only loosely controlled by legislative enactments. Unity of command links the democratic accountability of the executive and of the legislature to public employees more generally and offers a narrative which subjects public bureaucracies to legal control.[112] The heads of administrative and executive agencies are chosen by the President and confirmed by Congress. These persons are responsible to these democratically accountable bodies. In turn, they have the power to control their agencies and the personnel authority to ensure compliance by the agency's employees. This support for unity of command was melded with views of administration which emphasised machine-like efficiency with each employee functioning almost as a small cog in a larger machine.[113]

The 'New Deal' concept of administration rejected this machine analogy and adopted a model relying on the expertise of public employees.[114] This emphasis on expertise provided not only a different view of efficiency — each employee now exercised considerable individual discretion and initiative within administration — but also a method of control of the bureaucracy — expertise and professional standards restrained the discretion of bureaucrats.

Beginning in the 1960s and 70s, public administration scholars also attacked the concept of efficiency arguing that centralisation and the control of information that it posited, reduced, rather than furthered, administrative efficiency.[115] Moreover, efficiency could not be isolated from the obligation of public employees to follow democratic and constitutional norms.[116] In a democratic society, these norms are inescapably incorporated into the role of the public employee. In becoming a public employee, one assumed an obligation to these norms.

With the demise of the view that public employment was a privilege, the grant of which could be conditioned on the surrender of an employee's constitutional rights, the courts began to apply constitutional protections, including freedom of expression, to public employees.[117] The key Supreme Court decision in the United States regarding the free speech rights of public employees linked that right to the public's access to information and to democratic accountability.[118]

As scholars conceived of administration as politics, employee participation in administration became a restraint on a political process which often operated to benefit special interests at the expense of the public interest.[119] An influential book on public administration argued that public bureaucracies should reflect the composition of the constituencies that they served.[120] These views of administration rejected a passive role for public employees and defined their role to include advocacy within administration for the public interest.

Because public employee ethics can be conceived of as a type of role morality where the assumption of a position carries with it the obligation to support certain values and to adopt particular perceptions of appropriate behavior, these strains of thought could be incorporated into this role for public employees. The above examination of those strains of thought indicates why they fit well into a view of role morality. The appropriate role for a public employee is, of course, continually at issue, but the concept of role morality tends to buttress a view that public employees internalise and apply the most basic values of public service not from fear but from an acceptance of their role.

If the reservoir of ideas and arguments suggested by these strains of thought can be characterised as 'a vision of public service', that vision shares much with the challenge posed to public employment law by whistleblower protection. They both take a broad view of employee loyalty, reject unity of command, support employee freedom of expression, encourage participation in agency decision-making and recognise a central role for public employees in preservation of the rule of law and in democratic accountability. Therefore, as powerful as is the challenge posed by whistleblower protection, the connection of that challenge with this vision of public service magnifies its effect.

## The Distinction between Public and Private Employment Law and Whistleblower Protection

The differences, or lack of them, between the protection of public and private sector whistleblowers probes the commonly drawn distinction between public and private employment law. Doubts about the validity of the distinction are part of a much more lengthy, and more generally articulated, critique of the distinction between what is public and what is private. These doubts also draw on the observation that the regulation of public and private employment increasingly rests upon statutes. These statutes do not vary significantly from public to private employment. In this context, the brief discussion here only plays some larger, well developed themes; it is a discussion that illustrates more than it expounds these themes.

For the purposes of this chapter, however, a discussion of whistleblower protection in public and private employment offers insights into the general thesis of this chapter — that whistleblower protection relies upon principles and precepts that challenge important concepts in public employment law. The application of those principles and precepts to private employment law ironically provides the last challenge to public employment law.

In the United States, although states address whistleblowers in the public and private sector in the same statutory provisions, many states address them separately. The statutes of jurisdictions which address separately the protection of whistleblowers in the public and private sectors approach the protections differently. These differences, however, are more likely to respond to practical differences in existing procedures in public and private employment law than to significant differences in the rationale for protection. Because the public employment system is more likely to have generated a broadly applicable uniform personnel and grievance system, public sector statutes show a greater preference for administrative procedures than do the private sector ones which are more likely to prefer judicial or other remedies.[121] The preference for administrative redress also leads to a greater reliance on administrative remedies in public than private sector statutes. For example, it may be much easier administratively to discipline supervisors in a unified public employment disciplinary system than to do so in the more disjointed private sector.[122] In private sector statutes, discipline is more likely to be through private suit or criminal prosecution.

Public sector whistleblower statutes rest upon the importance of access to government information. Although this rationale does not apply in the private sector, the differences in protected disclosures are not great.[123] Private sector statutes may be less likely to show the same concern with waste of funds or abuse of authority but other grounds for disclosure are quite similar. Private sector statutes are more likely to require internal disclosure than public sector ones and perhaps this difference reflects a desire to limit government interference in the private sector.[124]

One could expect that the differences between public and private sector employment would create more dramatic differences between public and private sector whistleblower statutes. There simply does not appear to be substantial and dramatic differences in the ways in which these statutes conceive protection of public and private sector whistleblowers. The striking similarity in approach is also exhibited by the number of jurisdictions which protect public and private sector whistleblowers under the same statute.

The similarity of approach suggests that the principles of whistleblower protection which invest public employees with the obligation of preserving the public interest are also applied to private employment. Indeed, the first protections of private sector whistleblowers in the United States rested not on statute but on judicial decisions which created a public policy exception to the doctrine of at-will employment, a doctrine which otherwise permitted an employer to dismiss an employee for any reason.[125] The application of the principles of whistleblower protection to private employment produces some startling propositions, at least for lawyers in systems which apply different constitutional and legal protections to private employment. Like public employees, private employees have a loyalty to the rule of law in a democratic society beyond any loyalty to their employers. They have an obligation to protect public health and safety. In addition, anti-corruption provisions rest upon equally startling propositions; for, they rely upon private employees to disclose corruption of public officials. These disclosures not only vindicate the rule of law but also provide access to information about the performance of government necessary to democratic accountability. In another sense, whistleblower statutes protect certain speech against regulation not by the government but by private employers.

The Australian statutes appear to draw clearer distinctions between whistleblowers who are public employees and those who are private employees. This clarity, however, does not weaken the conclusions regarding the similarities of public and private employment, previously drawn based on state laws in the United States.

Commonwealth legislation provides an example of the distinction between public and private employment. The *Public Service Act 1999* (Cth) provides that agency officials must not either victimise, or discriminate against, Australian Public Service employees who report breaches of the public service code of conduct.[126] The *Workplace Relations Act 1996* (Cth) prohibits employers covered by that legislation, generally corporate employers but also the Commonwealth as employer, from terminating a whistleblower's employment because of 'the filing of a complaint, or the participation in proceedings against an employer involving alleged violation of laws or regulations or recourse to competent administrative authorities'.[127] These Commonwealth statutes can be characterised as ones that protect disclosures of the breaches of differing norms applicable to the employment relationships in the public and private sectors.

The laws of the Australian states, discussed previously, also vary in the coverage of employees in the public and private sectors. Some protect disclosures of official misconduct by any person in either the public or private sector.[128] Others protect disclosures only by public employees.[129] Those Australian statutes protecting disclosures by both public and private employees reflect a recognition of the overlap between the public and private sectors and of the difficulty of distinguishing between them.[130]

However, the distinctions that these laws draw between employees in the public and private sectors do not alter the challenge that whistleblower protection poses to the concept of a public as opposed to a private employment law. These laws address the same problem of official corruption. Arguably the statutes applying only to public employees are striking not because they reflect a difference between public and private employment but rather, unlike may anti-corruption laws, they connect disclosures to employment. Therefore, these laws confirm rather than weaken the conclusions based upon an examination of state whistleblower laws in the United States.

These propositions and principles impute to private employment many of the values associated throughout this chapter with public employment. In a practical sense, the insights provided by whistleblower protection provisions suggest a useful way to examine the issue of the privatisation of public functions. These insights should ease the task of regulating private employees in this context by using principles and concepts from public employment law.

An examination of how the principles and precepts of whistleblower protection challenge public employment law also exposes the similarities between public and private employment law. In discounting the distinctions between the two, whistleblower protection ironically poses perhaps its greatest challenge, a challenge to the very notion of a distinct public employment law.

# ENDNOTES

1 *Civil Service Reform Act of 1978*, Pub L No 95-454, 92 Stat 1111 (1978). See generally Robert G Vaughn, 'Statutory Protection of Whistleblowers in the Federal Executive Branch' [1982] *Illinois Law Review* 581.

2 See below text at nn 26-28.

3 A discussion of subsequent amendments is found in Thomas Devine, 'The *Whistleblower Protection Act of 1989*: Foundation for the Modern Law of Employment Dissent' (1999) 51 *Administrative Law Review* 531.

4 5 USC § 2302(b)(9).

5 See, eg, *Parrish v Civil Service Commission*, 425 P 2d 223 (Cal, 1967); *Harley v Schuylkill County*, 476 F Supp 191 (ED Pa, 1979).

6 See generally, Robert G Vaughn, 'Public Employees and the Right to Disobey' (1977) 29 *Hastings Law Review* 261, 286-93.

7 Robert G Vaughn, 'State Whistleblower Statutes and the Future of Whistleblower Protection' (1999) 51 *Administrative Law Review* 581, 582 n 3.

8 See below text at nn 47-55.

9 See below text at nn 56-65.

10 Australia: *Public Service Act 1999* (Cth) sec 16 (Cth); *Public Interest Disclosure Act 1994* (ACT); *Protected Disclosures Act 1994* (NSW); *Whistleblowers Protection Act 1994* (Qld); *Whistleblowers Protection Act 1993* (SA); *Public Interest Disclosures Act 2002* (Tas) and *State Service Act 2000* (Tas), s 10(5); *Whistleblowers Protection Act 2001* (Vic); *Public Interest Disclosure Act 2003* (WA) and *Corruption and Crime Commission Act 2003* (WA); Canada: *Employment Standards Act*, NB 1982, c E-7.2 s 28; *Public Service Act*, O 1990, c 47 s 28.11-42; New Zealand: *Protected Disclosures Act 2000* (NZ); South Africa: *Protected Disclosures Act 2000* (SA); United Kingdom: *Public Interest Disclosure Act 1998* (UK).

11 See below text at nn 67-78.

12 M Wilding, 'The Professional Ethic of the Administrator' (1979) 34 *Management Services in Government* 181, 183. See generally Robert G Vaughn, 'The Role of Statutory Regulation of Public Service Ethics in Britain and the United States (1981) 4 *Hastings International and Comparative Law Review* 341.

13 Council of Europe, *Criminal Law Convention on Corruption*, Europ T S No 173 (27 January 1999); Council of Europe, *Civil Law Convention on Corruption*, Europ T S No 174 (24 November 1999); *Inter-American Convention Against Corruption*, opened for signature 29 March 1996, 35 ILM 724 (entered into force 6 March 1997).

14 World Bank, *Standards and Procedures for Inquiries and Investigations* (draft revision 1.1, (30 May 2000); European Commission, *Reforming the Commission*, Consultative Document CG3 (17 January 2000).

15 See below text at nn 47-52.

16 *Civil Service Reform Act of 1978*, Pub L No 95-454, 92 Stat 1111 (1978).

17 *Whistleblower Protection Act of 1989*, Pub L No 101-12, 103 Stat 16 (1989).

18 See generally, *Executive Session Hearings Before the Select Committee on Presidential Campaign Activity of the U. S. Senate*, 93rd Cong 2nd Sess (1974).

19 See generally, Robert G Vaughn, *Principles of Civil Service Law* (1977) § 1.4.

20 *New York Times v US*, 403 US 713 (1971).

21 5 USC § 2302(b)(8).

22 5 USC §§ 1206-1207.

23 See generally Robert G Vaughn, *Merit Systems Protection Board: Rights and Remedies* (revised ed, 2001).

24 'Theory X' in public administration asserts that employees must be coerced, manipulated and disciplined in order for them to work effectively. 'Theory Y', however, holds that employees will exercise self-restraint in pursuing goals with which they agree. For a more complete discussion of relationship of the Civil Service Reform Act to public administration theory, see Patricia Ingraham and David Rosenbloom (eds), *The Promise and Paradox of Civil Service Reform* (1992).

25 Ibid.

26 5 USC § 1206(g).

[27] Another provision permits the Office of Special Counsel to pursue disciplinary actions for arbitrary and capricious withholding of information under the federal *Freedom of Information Act*, 5 USC § 1206(e)(1)(C) (1966).

[28] HR Con Res 175, 72 Stat B12 (1958).

[29] Because abuses of authority may rest upon internal delegations and practices not specified by law, rule or regulation, disclosures of such abuses may extend beyond those regarding violations of law.

[30] It is possible that a violation of law by a private party contracting with the government would so affect the mission of the government that disclosure of such a violation could be seen as addressing of violation of law by the government. As discussed below, specific and substantial dangers to public health and safety may concern the activities of private parties regulated by the government.

[31] *Freedom of Information Act of 1966*, Pub L No 89-554, 80 Stat 383 (1966).

[32] ALASKA STAT § 39.51.020.

[33] Hearings on S 1210 Before the Subcomm on Administrative Practice and Procedure of the Senate Comm on the Judiciary, 94th Congress, 1st Session (1975).

[34] 5 USC § 2302(b)(8).

[35] Vaughn, 'Statutory Protection of Whistleblowers in the Federal Executive Branch', above n 1, 637-641.

[36] Ibid. In one sense, the whistleblower provision may be more narrow than the First Amendment. The First Amendment protects opinions; the whistleblower provisions protect disclosures which reasonably evidence particular violations. Therefore, protected disclosures of whistleblowers must rely upon some factual grounds not required for the protection of opinion by the First Amendment. This difference may reflect the closer connection between whistleblower protection and access to government information.

[37] 5 USC § 2302(b)(8).

[38] Vaughn, 'Statutory Protection of Whistleblowers in the Federal Executive Branch', above n 1, 620-23.

[39] 5 USC § 1206 (b)(3)-(6).

[40] Vaughn, 'Statutory Protection of Whistleblowers in the Federal Executive Branch', above n 1, 620-23.

[41] *Huffman v Office of Personnel Management*, 263 F 3d 1341, 1351 (Fed Cir, 2001), citing HR Rep No 100-413, 12-13 (1988).

[42] Vaughn, 'Statutory Protection of Whistleblowers in the Federal Executive Branch', above n 1, 664-66. In these circumstances, the employee must disclose information acquired in the course of employment. This requirement suggests that other disclosures may rest upon information that the employee has otherwise acquired.

[43] Devine, above n 3.

[44] Ibid 554-55. The previous standard required that the protected disclosure be a substantial factor in the alleged retaliatory action.

[45] Ibid 556-58. The test is not whether the agency could have taken the personnel action absent the protected disclosure but whether it would have.

[46] 5 USC § 2302(b)(9).

[47] Vaughn, 'State Whistleblower Statutes and the Future of Whistleblower Protection', above n 7, 582 n 3.

[48] Ibid.

[49] Ibid 588 n 16. Most of these laws also protect disclosures regarding violations of rules and regulations.

[50] Ibid 589 n 17.

[51] Ibid 589 n 18.

[52] Ibid 592-93.

[53] Ibid 597.

[54] Ibid.

[55] Ibid 599 n 57.

[56] Ibid 600.

[57] Ibid 600-01.

[58] Ibid 602.

[59] Ibid 603 n 70.

[60] Ibid 604 n 75.

[61] Ibid 604 n 76.

[62] Ibid 608-09. Some states permit whistleblowers to carry this burden of persuasion through reliance on the presumption that an adverse personnel action that closely follows a protected disclosure is taken because of that disclosure: Ibid 609. In most jurisdictions, employers may overcome the whistleblower's case by showing that action an independent ground for the action. The statutes appear to differ as to whether it is sufficient to show that the action could have been taken without the protected disclosure or whether it is necessary to demonstrate that action would have been taken in any event. Usually, the employer need only prove this ground by a preponderance of the evidence and not by clear and convincing evidence: Ibid 609-10.

[63] Ibid 617 n 130.

[64] Vaughn, *Merit Systems Protection Board: Rights and Remedies*, above n 23 § 16.03.

[65] Vaughn, 'State Whistleblower Statutes and the Future of Whistleblower Protection', above n 7, 619-20.

[66] See above n 10, 13-14.

[67] *Public Interest Disclosure Act 1998* (UK) c 23 ('Public Interest Disclosure Act)'.

[68] J Mitchell, *Constitutional Law* (1964) 176; E Wade and G Phillips, *Constitutional and Administrative Law* (1974) 106.

[69] Civil servants were anonymous and politically neutral. 'Parliamentary supremacy and ministerial responsibility deny the civil servant an appeal to some independent authority as the basis for doing something contrary to the minister's instructions': Vaughn, 'Statutory Regulation of Public Service Ethics in Great Britain and the United States', above n 12, 380 (footnote omitted).

[70] Wilding, above n 12, 183.

[71] The Official Secrets Acts are several acts passed in 1888, 1911 and 1920. *Official Secrets Act 1911* (UK) c 28, s 2 prohibits civil servants and former civil servants from disclosing any government or government information to an unauthorised person.

[72] J Michael, *The Politics of Secrecy: The Case for a Freedom of Information Law* (1979) 6.

[73] These arguments are built around weaknesses in the convention of ministerial responsibility and stress professional standards and civil servants' obligation to the law as the basis of whistleblower protection. See Vaughn, 'Statutory Regulation of Public Service Ethics in Great Britain and the United States', above n 12, 382-84 (discussing examples in Britain setting out these justifications).

[74] *Public Interest Disclosure Act 1998* (UK), c 23, s 43K(1)(b),(c), amending the *Employment Rights Act 1996* (UK) c 18. Members of the intelligence services, the army and police officers are excluded (although special provisions apply to the police). In addition, a minister may certify that a particular employee has duties implicating national security.

[75] Public Concern at Work, *Annotated Guide to the Public Interest Disclosure Act* (2003) <http://www.pcaw.co.uk/policy_pub/pida.html> [August 2007].

[76] *Freedom of Information Act 2000* (UK) c 36.

[77] *Public Interest Disclosure Act 1998* (UK) c 23, s 43J.

[78] Public Concern at Work, *Annotated Guide to the Public Interest Disclosure Act* (2003) <http://www.pcaw.co.uk/policy_pub/pida.html> [August 2007] referring to Public Interest Disclosure Act, ss 43J, 43B(2).

[79] Ibid.

[80] Ibid, referring to *Public Interest Disclosure Act 1998* (UK) c 23, s 43B(1).

[81] *Public Interest Disclosure Act 1998* (UK) c 23, s 43C(1).

[82] *Public Interest Disclosure Act 1998* (UK) c 23, s 43F.

[83] *Public Interest Disclosure Act 1998* (UK) c 23, s 43G(1)(b).

[84] *Public Interest Disclosure Act 1998* (UK) c 23, s 43G.

[85] *Public Interest Disclosure Act 1998* (UK) c 23, s 43G(2).

[86] *Public Interest Disclosure Act 1998* (UK) c 23, s 43G(3)(a)-(d).

[87] Council of Europe, *Civil Law Convention on Corruption*, Europ T S No 174 (24 November 1999).

[88] Council of Europe, *Criminal Law Convention on Corruption*, Europ T S No 173 (27 January 1999).

[89] *Inter-American Convention Against Corruption*, opened for signature 29 March 1996, 35 ILM 724 (entered into force 6 March 1997).

[90] Organization of American States, *Support for the Implementation of the Inter-American Convention Against Corruption in Central America, Non-Reimbursable Regional Technical Cooperation*, No ATN/SF-6184-RG. That model law is broader in scope than many whistleblower laws. See Thomas Devine, Keith Henderson and Robert Vaughn, *Model Law Protecting Freedom of Expression Against Corruption: Section-by-Section Explanatory Notes*, (2001); Robert G Vaughn, Thomas Devine and Keith Henderson, 'The Whistleblower Statute Prepared for the Organization of American States and the Global Legal Revolution Protecting Whistleblowers' (2003) 35 *George Washington International Law Review* 857.

[91] *Corruption and Crime Commission Act 2003* (WA).

[92] *Corruption and Crime Commission Act 2003* (WA) s 4, definition of 'misconduct'.

[93] *Corruption and Crime Commission Act 2003* (WA) s 175.

[94] *Corruption and Crime Commission Act 2003* (WA) s 220. There is also protection from criminal liability (other than liability under the Act itself): s 220.

[95] *Protected Disclosures Act 1994* (NSW). Note the *Review of the Protected Disclosures Act 1994 Final Report*, November 2006, <www.parliament.nsw.gov.au/prod/PARLMENT/Committee.nsf/0/370027A06FBB2C77CA2572340012BDDC> [July 2007].

[96] *Protected Disclosures Act 1994* (NSW) s 3.

[97] *Protected Disclosures Act 1994* (NSW) ss 8-9.

[98] Disclosures may be made to the public agency affected by the misconduct or in varying circumstances to the Independent Commission Against Corruption, the Ombudsman, or to the Auditor-General: *Protected Disclosures Act 1994* (NSW) ss 10-12. Disclosures to the press or to members of Parliament are only protected in certain limited circumstances, after a previous disclosure of substantially the same information to an appropriate governmental body in circumstances that suggest that the allegations have been rejected or not timely considered: *Protected Disclosures Act 1994* (NSW) s 19. In addition, the employee must reasonably believe that the allegations are substantially true, and they are in fact substantially true: *Protected Disclosures Act 1994* (NSW) s 19(4), (5).

[99] *Whistleblowers Protection Act 1994* (Qld) s 8; *Whistleblowers Protection Act 1993* (SA) ss 3 (object) and, 4(1) 'public interest information' definition para (a)(iv) (also covers a substantial risk to the environment).

[100] *Whistleblowers Protection Act 1994* (Qld) s 10.

[101] *Whistleblowers Protection Act 1993* (SA) s 5.

[102] *Whistleblowers Protection Act 2001* (Vic) s 3(1); *Public Interest Disclosure Act 1994* (ACT) s 4.

[103] *Whistleblowers Protection Act 2001* (Vic) ss 6, 38; *Public Interest Disclosure Act 1994* (ACT) ss 15 (making a public interest disclosure) and 9 ('proper authorities').

[104] M R Goode, 'Policy Considerations in the Formulation of Whistleblowers Protection Legislation: The South Australian *Whistleblowers Protection Act 1993*' (2000) 22 *Adelaide Law Review* 27, 29.

[105] Ibid 43.

[106] Ibid 30-31.

[107] Given this characteristic of disclosures regarding corruption, it is surprising that a statute would limit protections to public employees: see, eg, *Protected Disclosures Act 1994* (NSW) ss 8-9.

[108] Vaughn, Devine and Henderson, above n 90.

[109] Thomas Sargentich describes three competing visions of administration — the rule of law ideal, the public purposes ideal and the democratic process ideal — that draw upon different strains of liberal political and economic theory: Thomas O Sargentich, 'The Reform of the American Administrative Process: The Contemporary Debate' [1984] *Wisconsin Law Review* 385. Gerald Frug relies upon critical legal theory to examine stories intended to assure us that bureaucracy is under control; these stories are the formalist model, the expertise model, the judicial review model, and the market/pluralist model: Gerald E Frug, 'The Ideology of Bureaucracy in American Law' (1984) 97 *Harvard Law Review* 1276.

[110] See generally Robert G Vaughn, *Conflict of Interest Regulation in the Federal Executive Branch* (1979) ch 1.

[111] For example, in US government-wide regulations prohibit any conduct which creates the appearance of using public office for private gain, giving preferential treatment to any person, impeding government efficiency or economy, losing complete independence or impartiality, making a government decision outside official channels, or adversely affecting the confidence of the public in the integrity of the government: 5 CFR § 735.201.

[112] Woodrow Wilson expressed this idea of unity of command in Woodrow Wilson, 'The Study of Administration' (1887) 2 *Political Science Quarterly* 197. Sargentich's analysis suggests that the rule of law ideal of administration places an emphasis on unity of command: Sargentich, above n 109, 397-407.

[113] Frug, above n 109, 1297-1300.

[114] Sargentich, above n 109, 410-415; Frug, above n 109, 1318-1323.

[115] See, eg, Herbert Kaufman, *Administrative Feedback: Monitoring Subordinates' Behavior* (1973) 62-79 (centralisation could prevent the detection of widespread patterns of noncompliance); Anthony Downs, *Inside Bureaucracy* (1967) 71-74 (loyalty to a single leader creates second-rate subordinates); Warren Bennis, *Beyond Bureaucracy* (1966) 19-20, 188 (collaboration and shared leadership required in a social system operating under conditions of chronic change); Vincent Ostrom, *The Intellectual Crisis in American Public Administration* (1974) 136 (arguing for a system of democratic administration in which public employees consider, among other factors, the legal constraints of constitutional and public law).

[116] John Rohr, *Ethics for Bureaucrats: An Essay on Law and Values* (1978) 59-76 (advocating the incorporation of democratic and constitutional values in administrative decisions).

[117] See generally David H Rosenbloom, *The Federal Service and the Constitution: The Development of the Public Employment Relationship* (1971).

[118] *Pickering v Board of Education*, 391 US 563 (1968).

[119] Sargentich, above n 109, 425-28.

[120] Harry Kranz, *The Participatory Democracy* (1976).

[121] Vaughn, 'State Whistleblower Statutes and the Future of Whistleblower Protection', above n 7, 624.

[122] Ibid.

[123] Ibid.

[124] Ibid.

[125] Nancy Modesitt and Daniel P Westman, *Whistleblowing: The Law of Retaliatory Discharge* (2004).

[126] *Public Service Act 1999* s 16 (Cth). Reporting alleged breaches is also protected in s 16.

[127] *Workplace Relations Act 1996* s 659 (Cth). The provision protecting whistleblowers adopts the language of the convention of termination of employment of the International Labor Organization: David Lewis, 'Employment Protection for Whistleblowers: On What Principles Should Australian Legislation Be Based?' (1996) 9 *Australian Journal of Labour Law* 135, 140.

[128] *Whistleblowers Protection Act 1993* (SA); *Whistleblowers Protection Act 2001* (Vic); *Corruption and Crime Commission Act 2003* (WA).

[129] *Protected Disclosures Act 1994* (NSW); *Whistleblowers Protection Act 1994* (Qld). (In the case of public interest disclosures, 'anybody' may make disclosures).

[130] Goode, 'Policy Considerations in the Formulation of Whistleblowers Protection Legislation', above n 104, 30-31. Not only were the lines between the public and private sectors blurred at the time of the passage of these provisions, but also were likely to become more so in the future with privatisation and contracting out.

# Chapter Seven

# Outsourcing and New Employer Entities: Challenges to Traditional Public Sector Employment

## Marilyn Pittard

Outsourcing is a contemporary business practice in both the private and public sectors. Typically outsourcing involves an organisation engaging under contract the services of another entity to carry out certain functions which that first organisation had performed itself. The Federal Court of Australia noted that whilst there may be varying details of the outsourcing arrangements in particular instances, outsourcing usually involves a contractor being engaged to carry out 'a function or operation, previously undertaken by the enterprise itself, in a more efficient way; perhaps by the use of more sophisticated equipment, perhaps by using specialised labour'.[1] The Australian Public Service ('APS') itself adopted a similar definition: 'Outsourcing refers to an arrangement whereby an APS agency has a function or service which was previously undertaken in-house performed by a private sector provider'.[2]

Various terms are applied to this outsourcing, including 'contracting out', but in the public sector the term 'privatisation' may also be used. Outsourcing or the privatisation of some APS functions commenced as far back as the early 1980s. However the real growth of outsourcing in the Australian public sector occurred from the 1990s and the pace accelerated in more recent years. In the fields particularly of information technology and human resources, there has been an enormous increase in outsourcing in the last five to ten years with implications for terms and conditions of employment of former public sector employees.

This chapter will explore first the nature and extent of this public sector outsourcing and the legal and administrative framework for that outsourcing. It then analyses the legal implications for public sector employment which occur as a consequence of the new interposed entity (which is the new employer) now performing functions previously undertaken directly by government. The question whether previous conditions of public sector employment continue to govern the terms of employment of the outsourced employees and bind the new employers will be examined, together with the concept of transmission of business and the effects of the *Workplace Relations Act 1996* (Cth) and the *Workplace Relations Amendment (Work Choices) Act 2005* (Cth) ('Work Choices Act'). Reducing labour costs as a type of cost cutting might be achieved primarily through avoiding the operation of particular industrial instruments; the freedom of association objectives in the *Workplace Relations Act 1996* (Cth) can act as a safeguard to ensure there is no avoidance of such obligations through outsourcing. This will be explored in the chapter.

Other implications also arise from outsourcing — for example, in terms of discrimination, equal opportunity and affirmative action issues; whether there is an obligation to abide by the APS Values and APS Code of Conduct by the outsourced employees or new employees taking over the former government-performed functions; the shift of government control to contract management and the rights and remedies of employees moving from administrative, statutory and public law regimes to those mainly under the contract of employment. These will be examined.

The first section of this chapter provides an overview of outsourcing in the public sector.

## Scanning the Landscape: Overview of Public Sector Outsourcing

The Commonwealth government's outsourcing, contracting out and privatisation activities became very significant in the 1990s.

The functions outsourced tended to be a part of the government function. In 1997, for example, the Commonwealth took the decision that IT infrastructure would be outsourced but subject to competitive tendering; it 'embarked upon one of the largest and most complex information technology outsourcing initiatives in Australia'.[3] Thus in December 1999, IBM Global Services Australia and the Australian Federal Government signed an agreement, the Health Group Agencies IT Outsourcing Agreement, in which IBM undertook to provide information technology and technology services worth $350 million over five years to the Department of Health and Aged Care, the Health Insurance Commission and Medibank Private. By December 2000, '23 departments and agencies in five groups had outsourced their IT infrastructure. This [represented] around half of the agencies in the Whole of Government Information Technology Outsourcing Initiative (the Initiative) and approximately $1.2 billion in contract value out of a total estimated $4 billion for the entire Initiative'.[4] Mindful of the risks, the government decided to set up a review of the IT outsourcing initiative — to review IT outsourcing and report on risks and the future — and appointed Richard Humphrey to undertake the review. The report, submitted in December 2000 and entitled *Review of the Whole of Government IT Outsourcing Initiative*, became known as the Humphrey Report.

The Humphrey Report described the Commonwealth government outsourcing of IT policy initiative as being 'ambitious and broad-ranging' with the purpose of 'complementing modern management practices within the Commonwealth Public Service and enhancing access to wider technical skills and technologies'.[5] Further, the aim was to achieve economies of scale and to decrease costs.[6] Although the policy reasons were clear, the task itself was enormous, bringing with it risks and concern by members of the public and others, including members of the opposition.[7] The Humphrey Report's comprehensive 105 pages focussed on the implementation risks and the transition from in-house provision to outsourcing.

Following the Humphrey Report, on 23 March 2001, two Commonwealth government departments, the (then) Department of Employment, Workplace Relations and Small Business and the Department of Education, Training and Youth Affairs, announced that they would pursue the outsourcing of the IT infrastructure and do this using a 'segment-by-segment approach'. Behind this decision was the consideration by the departments of the contents and recommendations of the Humphrey Report.

More generally, the government was conscious of the need to oversee the process of outsourcing. In the early 2000s, a section of the Commonwealth Department of Finance and Administration, the Competitive Tendering and Contracting Branch (CTC), oversaw the contracting out of the delivery of activities, previously performed by a Commonwealth agency, to another organisation. This form of outsourcing was described then as:

> a vital part of the government's reform agenda which is about making the public sector more responsive to the needs of government; and building a performance culture through devolved decision making, responsibilities and accountability.[8]

Competitive tendering and contracting processes were utilised in numerous areas, during this period, including in Centrelink; the Department of Defence; the (then) Department of Employment, Workplace Relations and Small Business; and the Department of Foreign Affairs and Trade.

Examples of functions which have been outsourced are somewhat varied. The Department of Foreign Affairs and Trade outsourced the Australian Passport Service and its passport interviewing and application processes. Clearly this had an implication for the jobs and nature of work of those staff who remained in the Australian Passport Service within the Department of Foreign Affairs and Trade. According to the Department:

> While work loads have increased due to demand and additional security requirements, staff levels have been steady as outsourcing allows staff to concentrate on policy matters and 'big picture' issues such as

improvements in customer service, instead of being focused on routine, simple processing activities, so providing greater job satisfaction.[9]

The Department of Employment, Workplace Relations and Small Business contracted out workplace services delivery to the states and contracted out its federal award and agreements inquiry and compliance services to two state governments.

Further examples of public sector outsourcing undertaken at various stages include:-

- The Department of Defence outsourced the delivery of port services and support craft for the Royal Australian Navy;
- The Department of Human Services and Health outsourced cost recovery process for medical services;
- The Department of Immigration and Multicultural Affairs outsourced the internal audit function to the private sector.

Parallels occurred in the states too where, for example, there were various models used in the outsourcing of the provision of public transport; and Tourism Victoria outsourced the core function of marketing.

In 2005, Commonwealth government agencies reported as follows:[10]

> Overall, 49 agencies (60 per cent) reported finalising new outsourcing contracts or contract extensions in regard to at least one aspect of an ICT or HR function or service during 2004–05 … Finalising or extending an outsourcing contract in relation to at least one aspect of ICT services occurred in 44 per cent of agencies in 2004–05, consistent with 47 per cent of agencies in 2003–04. However, there was a substantial increase in 2004–05 in the proportion of agencies that entered or extended an outsourcing contract in relation to at least one aspect of HR services (38 per cent in 2004–05 compared with 20 per cent in 2003–04).

The table below summarises the changes from 2002-2003 to 2004-2005 in respect of information and communication technology services and strategic planning and human resource services.

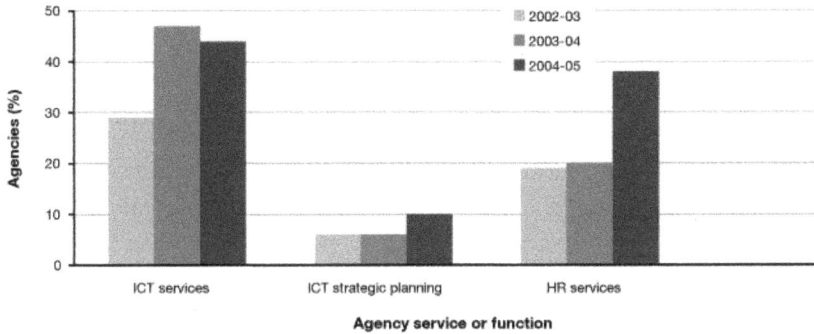

**Agencies' outsourcing activity, 2002–03 to 2004–05**

*Source: Agency survey* [11]

In 2005, too, in accordance with the requirements of the *Financial Management and Accountability Act 1997* (Cth), the Commonwealth Procurement Guidelines 2005[12] were promulgated for agencies to ensure value for money in procuring goods and services, as well as efficiency, encouraging competition, accountability and transparency, and effective and ethical use of resources.

It seems that there has been a significant expansion in outsourcing in the past few years. Whilst the Commonwealth's *State of the Services Report* itself acknowledges that it is not clear whether this change is cyclical, the point remains that outsourcing is significant.[13] Recent figures for outsourcing are not now available through the *State of the Services Report* because it was decided that it was no longer necessary to report that data. Hence the extent of current federal government outsourcing is now difficult to accurately ascertain.

## How Does Public Sector Outsourcing Compare to Private Sector Outsourcing?

In the survey *Changes at Work: 1995 Australian Workplace Industrial Relations Survey*,[14] according to the workplaces surveyed (both private and public sector) outsourcing was more prevalent among workplaces which had 200 or more employees. Workplaces with 200 or more employees reported 51 per cent contracting out compared to only 33 per cent of smaller workplaces. Outsourcing, even at that time, was more prevalent in the public sector, with 52 per cent, compared to the private sector, 32 per cent.

The services which were contracted out related mainly to cleaning (36 per cent), building maintenance (23 per cent) or parts of manufacturing or production processes (23 per cent). In terms of industries in which outsourcing occurred most strongly, figures are as follows:

• electricity, gas and water supply (67 per cent of firms);

- construction (61 per cent of firms);
- education (60 per cent of firms);
- mining (55 per cent of firms).

Similarly, the analysis set out in *Australia at Work: Just Managing* [15] shows that the main users of outsourcing were public sector organisations — government business enterprises (53 per cent), statutory authorities (56 per cent) and State public service departments (53 per cent), whilst less than one-third of private sector firms had engaged in outsourcing.

There is also an impact on employment; one review in 1999 concluded that: 'Public sector employment share in Australia has fallen dramatically over the past 20 years. A number of factors have contributed to this, significant among which has been the increased privatisation of functions at both Commonwealth and state levels of government'. [16]

Whilst both private and public sectors undertake outsourcing, it seems that, relative to the public sector, outsourcing in the private sector has become more global with functions including information technology, call centres, financial services and back-room office functions outsourced to countries such as India. [17]

## Framework for Outsourcing

In the Commonwealth public sector, an established legislative framework is relevant to decisions by the Commonwealth to outsource, as well as to purchase goods and services which do not involve outsourcing. This Commonwealth legislative and administrative framework includes: the *Financial Management and Accountability Act 1997* (Cth), the *Auditor-General Act 1997* (Cth), the *Commonwealth Procurement Guidelines and Best Practice Guidance* (September 2001) and, more recently, the *Commonwealth Procurement Guidelines 2005*. The Department of Finance and Administration has published a number of Guidance Notes to assist in compliance with the legislative requirements and the Guidelines. [18]

The Commonwealth Procurement Guidelines ('CPGs') provide that:

> 1.2 The CPGs establish the core procurement policy framework and articulate the Government's expectations of all departments and agencies (agencies) subject to the *Financial Management and Accountability Act 1997* (FMA Act) and their officials, when performing duties in relation to procurement. [19]

The CPGs thus apply to 'officials' who are persons in agencies (or part of agencies) and therefore include members of the APS. [20]

A decision to outsource the provision of a service or function (previously undertaken by members of the APS) necessarily involves responsibilities of officials under the *Financial Management and Accountability Act 1997* ('FMA Act') and the Regulations made pursuant to the FMA Act ('FMA Regulations'), since it involves the expenditure of public monies through contracts entered into between the Commonwealth and an external service provider. The impact of this regulatory environment on the work of officials has a number of facets.

A chief executive of an agency in the APS (eg. a department) is required to ensure the efficient, effective and ethical use of public monies.[21] The FMA Act then authorises a chief executive to issue 'Chief Executive Instructions' (to personnel in the relevant agency) to ensure that this objective is achieved.[22] Further, the FMA Act provides for the chief executive to delegate powers to other officials; that is, members of the APS.[23] To support this legal framework for expenditure, the FMA Regulations provide that the Chief Executive Instructions can deal with a number of matters, including making commitments to spend public monies.[24]

In addition, the FMA Regulations provide for the Minister for Finance and Administration to issue the Commonwealth Procurement Guidelines which an official must have regard to and, if the official takes action which is not consistent with the Guidelines, the official must record reasons for doing so.[25]

In respect of the duties of a member of the APS, the FMA Regulations provide that a proposal to expend public monies may only be approved if it is in accord with the policies of the Commonwealth and if it makes efficient and effective use of public monies.[26] An official must not approve a proposal to expend public monies unless he or she is so authorised.[27] Of most importance in relation to outsourcing is the requirement that an official cannot enter into a contract on behalf of the Commonwealth unless a proposal for the expenditure of public monies has been approved under FMA Regulation 9.[28]

There is therefore a range of sources of obligations of a member of the APS in respect of a proposal and a decision to outsource particular services or functions. Those obligations are enforceable not only through the ordinary contractual obligations of an employee but also through the APS Code of Conduct dealing with the obligation of members of the APS to comply with Australian laws (which of course include the FMA Act and the FMA Regulations).

In addition, individual departments may determine rules and procedures relevant to outsourcing through their rules dealing with procurement. It is also to be kept in mind that a particular official must have appropriate delegated financial authority to commit the Commonwealth to particular expenditure.

There is nothing specific in the FMA Act or the FMA Regulations which requires an official in making a proposal for, or in considering or approving, an expenditure of public monies associated with entering into a contract for outsourced services to take account of the terms and conditions of employment of the APS employees who may be affected by the proposal. Despite this, some aspects of the APS Values and the APS Code of Conduct themselves could arguably require that consideration be given to the impact of an outsourcing decision on members of the APS — for example, s 10(1)(i) and (j) of the APS Values extracted in the Appendix to this chapter, and the requirement in the APS Code of Conduct to uphold the APS Values.[29]

It follows that, in effect, decisions to outsource are not regarded in the basic legislative framework as being different in legal character to any other decision by the Commonwealth to enter into a contract, at least viewed from the perspective of the regulatory regime provided by the FMA Act and instruments made under it. As we have seen the regime does impose obligations on APS employees involved in implementing a government policy decision to outsource a particular function or activity.

## New Employing Entities, Same Public Service Employment Conditions?

Once a decision has been made to outsource a government function as outlined above, what is the status of public sector employment rights and duties in respect of the employees affected by the outsourcing? This aspect will be explored in this section of the chapter.

There are several safeguards in the *Workplace Relations Act 1996* (Cth) which endeavour to protect employees' entitlements when businesses are restructured and which may either constrain the new employer in terms of the conditions it is obliged to continue providing to the transferring employees or constrain the entity making the decision to restructure. As we will see these protections may be less certain in their operation where the restructure takes the form of outsourcing. These legal safeguards relate to:

- The transmission of business provisions in the *Workplace Relations Act 1996* (Cth) which provide that the new employer is bound by the former employer's award, collective agreement or Australian Workplace Agreement in certain circumstances including where there is a transmission, succession or assignment of the business;[30]
- the Freedom of Association provisions in Part 16, formerly Part XA, of the *Workplace Relations Act 1996* (Cth) which prevent an employer from undertaking conduct to avoid the operation of an award or industrial instrument.

The difficulty for a new company which takes over the business and successfully offers employment to some or all of the employees of the business is whether the transferring employees are covered by the *new* employer's awards, certified agreements or workplace agreements or the *former* employer's awards, certified agreements or workplace agreements. Fundamental to this is whether the outsourcing arrangements do indeed constitute a transmission, succession or assignment of the business (or part of the business).

These are not always easy matters, as the cases to be examined will show. As will be seen, attempts to resolve these issues in the application of the legislation have occurred through litigation and legislative change, including through the Work Choices Act. However, considerable uncertainties remain, particularly in the public sector, as there has been no further statutory definition or elucidation of the potentially — and actually — thorny problems of what is meant by a 'business', what is 'part' of a business and what constitutes transmission, assignment or succession in relation to a business or part of it. The consequence is that there are still unresolved employment issues in the current context of outsourcing in the public sector.

In addition, the statutory protection of conditions for employees who are employed by the outsourcing entity when there is a transmission of business does not generally include recognition by the new employer of entitlements arising from the period of service with the old employer (for example, a period of service for calculation of future severance benefits). Rather the statutory protection of conditions is concerned with protection, at least for a time, of the former terms and conditions of employment as determined by the application to the new employer of the relevant award, certified agreement (that is, a pre-Work Choices Act certified agreement) or workplace agreement made under the Work Choices legislation.

There has been a range of contexts in which outsourcing has been considered by the courts in relation to whether industrial awards or agreements 'transmit' from the old employer so as to become binding upon the new employer. Primarily, however, the contexts before the courts fall into the following categories:

a. outsourcing by the public service to a statutory corporation;
b. outsourcing by the public service to a Commonwealth–owned or state-owned private corporation (i.e. a corporation incorporated under the *Corporations Act 2001*, but whose shares are held on behalf of the Commonwealth or a state);
c. outsourcing from the public sector to a privately-owned corporation (whether its shares are listed on a stock exchange or not);
d. outsourcing by a private corporation to another private corporation.

As will be seen, the legislative changes and court decisions have not determined that the transfer of activities carried on by the Commonwealth or by a state to a privately-owned corporation necessarily constitutes a 'transmission' of 'business'; this issue remains to be resolved by case law or legislation. The case studies below illustrate the difficulties of determining when a transmission of business has occurred.

## Case Studies and Legal Questions

Four main case studies are discussed in this section, together with recent High Court rulings which may have an impact on the transmission of business question in the context of public sector outsourcing. These cases mainly occur in the environment prior to Work Choices. However they continue to be relevant. First, the Work Choices legislation did not attempt to change or clarify the law with respect to the meaning of 'transmission' of 'business'; rather the changes dealt with the consequences for employees' terms and conditions where there was a transmission of business. Secondly, the case studies provide illustrative examples of outsourcing arrangements and employment consequences, particularly in the public sector.

It is convenient to commence with a consideration of a case relating to transmission of business issues as between private employers because it sets the stage for consideration of relevant legal tests and contains significant obiter dicta relevant to government outsourcing.

## Approach in the Private Sector and Relevance to the Public Sector: *PP Consultants Case*

For some years, the St George Bank had operated in Byron Bay. In 1997, it decided to close this branch of the bank. Next door to the branch of the bank was a pharmacy (PP Consultants Pty Ltd) and St George Bank entered into an agreement with the pharmacy for the pharmacy to conduct some of the bank's functions on its behalf. In short, the bank decided to outsource certain activities to an external provider. The pharmacy owners would perform such functions as monitoring the operation of the ATM, collect deposits, open accounts, make loan referrals and transact withdrawals. Under the agreement, the pharmacy was to act as the bank's agent. The bank would provide at least one former bank employee to the pharmacy to assist in this work. As events turned out, two former St George Bank employees accepted offers of employment from the pharmacy.

The issue which came before the court in proceedings instituted by the Finance Sector Union of the Australia against PP Consultants Pty Ltd[31] was whether the employees should be governed by the St George Bank Employees Award.

### The Legislative Framework

The relevant provision in the *Workplace Relations Act 1996*, as it was at the time, was the section dealing with parties to awards, and in particular whether there has been a transmission of business. Section 149(1)(d) of the *Workplace Relations Act 1996* (prior to the amendments made by the Work Choices Act) provided, subject to any order made by the Australian Industrial Relations Commission, that an award becomes binding on an employer which is the successor, assignee, or transmittee of a business, or part of a business of an employer who was a party to the award. In particular, s 149(1)(d) provided that an award binds:

> (d) any successor, assignee or transmittee (whether immediate or not) to or of the business or part of the business of an employer who was a party to the industrial dispute, including a corporation that has acquired or taken over the business or part of the business of the employer.

Thus the question in this case was whether there had been a transmission by St George Bank of its Byron Bay branch operations to the pharmacy, whereby the pharmacy then became party to the award and was obliged to pay its employees (who were the former St George Bank employees) the same terms and conditions that they had enjoyed previously under the award applicable to St George Bank.

## From Federal Court to High Court

At first instance, Justice Matthews of the Federal Court concluded that there had *not* been a transmission of business by the bank to the pharmacy and noted that, although the pharmacy employed staff to undertake bank duties, 'to suggest that in doing so it is conducting part of the business of the bank is, in my view, extending the concept of a "business" beyond all realistic levels.'[32] Matthews J took the view that the pharmacy had not acquired any part of the bank's business as a going concern and that there had not been a succession, assignment or transmission of business. Whilst there was a substantial identity between previous activities of the branch of the bank and those that were carried on by the pharmacy on behalf of the bank, such substantial identity between two entities and activities was not enough to make out transmission of business under s 149(1)(d).

Following the union's successful appeal to a full bench of the Federal Court[33] in which the court decided that there was a high degree of similarity in the activities undertaken by the pharmacy and the bank and hence a transmission of business had occurred, the pharmacy appealed to the High Court. In *PP Consultants Pty Ltd v Finance Sector Union,*[34] the High Court overturned the full bench's decision but was reluctant to formulate any *general test* in order to ascertain whether one employer had succeeded to the business or part of the business of another[35] — it noted that the question of succession was a mixed question of fact and law and that the word 'business' was a 'chameleon-like word'.[36] However, the court did look at the business activities of the former employer and the business activities of the new employer and noted that if they were the same, usually there would have been a transmission of business.

Although the pharmacy did involve itself in banking activities, the High Court determined that it could not be said to be carrying on the business of banking;

the business it carried on was that of a bank agency. The bank had simply changed the way it conducted its business, rather than transferring or disposing of its business.

## Relevance to Public Sector Outsourcing

In the *PP Consultants* case, the joint judgment[37] of the High Court proposed a three-step process for deciding succession of business involving *private sector employers*:

> As a general rule, the question whether a non-government employer who has taken over the commercial activities of another non-government employer has succeeded to the business or part of the business of that other employer will require the identification or characterisation of the business or the relevant part of the business for the first employer, as a first step. The second step is the identification of the character of the transferred business activities in the hands of the new employer. The final step is to compare the two. If, in substance, they bear the same character, then it will usually be the case that the new employer has succeeded to the business or part of the business of the previous employer.[38]

The High Court in this instance was not being asked to consider whether there was a transmission of business from a government body of some kind to a non-government body. However the joint judgment did make some observations which pertain to outsourcing in the public sector where the transfer is between a *public sector employer* and *a private sector employer*:

> Whilst the notions of 'profit' and 'commercial enterprise' will ordinarily be significant in determining whether the activities of a private individual or corporation constitute a business, they play little, if any, role in identifying whether one government agency is engaged in the business of government previously undertaken by another government agency. In that situation, it is sufficient to ascertain whether or not the activities of the former are substantially identical to the activities or some part of the activities previously undertaken by the latter. That is because the word 'business' takes on a special or particular meaning in the expression 'the business of government'. It is not because, as a matter of ordinary language, 'business' means or includes activities undertaken in the course of business.[39]

Without explaining what it had in mind by the reference to 'government agency', the court further said:

> As already indicated, special considerations apply when one government agency succeeds to the activities of another. And there may well be other

considerations where a government contracts with a non-government body for the performance of functions previously carried out by a government authority.[40]

No doubt as the court did not need to elaborate these comments, it did not do so. On the face of these observations, nonetheless, the court appeared to have left open the possibility that some approach, other than the characterisation of the nature of the activities test, should be applied to situations in which transfers of activities occur from a government agency to the private sector; that situation is typically the case in public sector outsourcing arrangements.

## Outsourcing by Government-Owned Corporation of Call Centres

In *Stellar Call Centres Pty Ltd v CPSU*,[41] the question was whether Telstra Awards and certified agreements bound the new outsourced employer, Stellar Call Centres Pty Ltd ('Stellar'). The factual circumstances were that Telstra, a corporation with majority government ownership, had entered into an agreement whereby in essence an outside private organisation was to undertake some call centre activities by way of handling the overflow from Telstra's Call Centres, so that part of Telstra's functions were to be outsourced without Telstra relinquishing its main call centre activities. Telstra's agreement was by way of a joint venture with Excel Asia Pacific Pty Ltd, known as Stellar Call Centres, which was to provide services to Telstra by way of a call centre handling the overflow from Telstra's Centres of enquiries by Telstra customers (by telephone) in relation to billings, new products, and availability and connection of services.

The arrangement was to operate in such a way that Telstra customers would not be aware that they were not talking to an employee of Telstra. Under the terms of the arrangement, staff were not transferred from Telstra to Stellar, and there was no transfer of goodwill.

## Was There a Transmission of Business?

In the legal action brought by the public sector union, the Community and Public Sector Union, the legal question was whether there was a transmission of part of a business from Telstra to Stellar within s 149 of the *Workplace Relations Act 1996*. At first instance, Justice Wilcox of the Federal Court of Australia held that there was a transmission of business under the Act as there was substantial identity of the work between that performed by employees of Stellar and that previously performed by employees of Telstra.[42] Wilcox J stated:

> Stellar now performs work that otherwise would be done by Telstra itself. Contact with customers is a critical part of Telstra's business. No doubt it is burdensome and costly to provide that contact, but it is critical to do so. Without good marketing and attention to customer queries, the

business would quickly founder. The effect of the arrangement between Telstra and Stellar is that Stellar has taken on part of the burden of customer contact. In relation to the part of the burden transferred to it, Stellar is the "successor" of Telstra.[43]

## Substantially Identical Character of the Business

On appeal by Stellar, the Full Court of the Federal Court held that there was not a transmission of business and followed the High Court in the *PP Consultants* case, concluding that Stellar was not Telstra's successor.[44] Even though the businesses performed similar functions, and the employees also performed similar functions, the Federal Court took into account the activities performed by the new employer, by comparison to the business or part of the business of the old employer — in order for there to be a transmission there must be a substantially identical character of the business. That did not arise.[45]

It was not sufficient to focus on the similarities between the functions of the old employees and the functions they performed for the new employer. The answering of customer telephone calls was not a distinct part of Telstra's business and there was no transfer or assignment from Telstra to Stellar. This meant that the awards and agreements binding Telstra would not apply to Stellar Call Centres.

## The Approach to Outsourcing *within* the Public Sector: Outsourcing Health Services

In *North Western Healthcare Network v Health Services Union of Australia,*[46] the issue of transmission of business arose in the context of a public body taking over the functions previously performed by the public service, hence outsourcing occurred *within* the public sector, broadly defined. Traditionally, Victorian public mental health services had been directly provided by the Victorian government through staff engaged as members of the Victorian Public Service, that is, as public servants. The government decided that these services were to be outsourced, as part of the implementation of a major review of the mental health system operating in Victoria. The North Western Healthcare Network ('the Network'), a public hospital which was a body corporate established under State legislation, took over the operation of part of the Victorian mental health services. The question was whether the Network had become a 'successor, assignee or transmittee of part of the business' of the State of Victoria under s 149(1)(d) of the *Workplace Relations Act 1996* (Cth), thereby binding it to the following awards: the Health and Community Services (Nursing, Healthcare and Associated Group) Interim Award 1994 ('the 1994 Award'), and the Victorian Health and Community Services (Psychiatric, Disability and Alcohol and Drug) Services Award 1995 ('the 1995 Award'). These awards had applied to the employment of the relevant staff when they were employed as public servants in the provision of mental health services.

The Network took the view that the 1994 and 1995 Awards did not apply; rather the Network considered that another award, the Nurses Victorian Health Services Award ('the Nurses Award'), applied to the Network staff, including those staff now employed by it who had been previously employed by the state as public servants. The Health Services Union of Australia instituted proceedings, seeking penalties against Network for failure to pay employees benefits due under the 1994 and 1995 Awards in respect of employees who had transferred to the Network.

At first instance, Marshall J decided on 22 October 1997 that there had been a transmission of part of the business, so that the 1994 and 1995 Awards potentially applied.[47]

## Can a Government Function Be a 'Business'?

Critical to the argument was the question whether a government function could be a 'business'. The Network's argument was that provision of mental health services was not a 'business' within s 149(1) of the Act as such provision is a public function of government under statutory duties and powers, rather than a market-driven commercial venture; therefore the Network would not 'inherit' the Award binding the state government.

Marshall J rejected this argument, adopted a wide interpretation and concluded that the provision of mental health services was 'part of a business' of the State of Victoria within the meaning of the *Workplace Relations Act 1996*. Provision of mental health services had now been taken over by the Network, and the state had previously provided such services. Applying a 'substantial identity test', Marshall J concluded that there was a substantial identity of the services provided by the Network compared to those provided by the Victorian government. Whilst there were some changes in relation to management and relocation of some services as well as operational differences, these did not affect substantially the identity of the services provided.

## Applicability of Public Sector Awards to Non-Public Servant Employees

The Network also argued that the 1994 and 1995 Awards could not apply to it because they only applied to Victorian state public servants and, of course, the Network did not employ any such employees. Marshall J took the view that when the Australian Industrial Relations Commission (the Commission) made the Awards, there was no evidence that these Awards were intended to apply only to public service employees of Victorian state government.

## The Problem of the Clash of Awards

On the judicial reasoning to this point, the 1994 and 1995 Awards were transmitted to the Network. However, there was an additional problem in that the Nurses Award also seemed to apply. Justice Marshall declined to determine which award was more appropriate but stated:

> The situation where two Awards govern the terms and conditions of employment of certain employees, whilst relatively unusual is not an unknown one. In those circumstances, the employer is obliged to accord to its employees the better conditions in respect of the matters dealt with in the Awards, thus obeying all its obligations.[48]

## Full Court's Decision on Appeal

The Network appealed to a Full Court of the Federal Court which, in essence, upheld the decision of Marshall J.[49] On the question whether there could be a transmission of previously government-provided activity within the meaning of the Act, the Full Court decided that the fact that a government held legislative responsibility for providing health services did not prevent it from transmitting the business of providing those services to a third party; it is sufficient if there has been a transfer, as a matter of practice or reality, from one entity to another — there need not be a technical legal 'transmission' of a business. The Federal Court upheld the use of the 'substantial identity test' applied by Marshall J.

The Commission had not clearly and unambiguously stated that the 1994 and 1995 Awards were to bind public servants only and thus Network could be bound by these Awards. The Federal Court noted that the intention of the (then) *Workplace Relations Act* and its predecessor was that award conditions extend to all employers and all employees regardless of the 'public' or 'private' identity of the employer. To hold otherwise would mean that awards would have to be revised every time there was a change in employer.

In this instance, the Federal Court therefore determined that a public servant who accepted employment by a public hospital remained entitled to the benefit of awards applicable to him or her as a member of the Victorian public service, although he or she was now an employee of an employer outside the true public service.

## Privatising the Commonwealth Employment Service

The case of *Employment National Limited v CPSU* (*'Employment National* case')[50] arose out of the Australian government's decision to 'privatise' or outsource most of the work performed by the Commonwealth Employment Service (CES) and Employment Assistance Australia (EAA) from the Commonwealth to, amongst others, Employment National Limited (EN) and Employment National (Administration) Pty Ltd (ENA). The case before the Federal Court involved three different applications, but in essence, the issue to be decided was whether ENA was bound by four federal awards applicable to certain personnel in the Australian Public Service (which were part of the set of seven awards that themselves were consolidations of some 130 awards which applied across the Australian Public Service). The awards were:

- the APS General Employment Conditions Award;
- the APS Administrative Service Officers (Salaries and Specific Conditions) Award;
- the APS Professional Officers (Salaries and Specific Conditions) Award; and
- the APS Senior Executive Service (Salaries and Specific Conditions) Award.

There was also a certified agreement made between the Minister of State for Employment, Workplace Relations and Small Business and the Non-Senior Executive Service staff and certified in March 1998 — which was made during the process of privatisation.

## Background of Privatisation

The privatisation background was fully set out in the judgment of Einfeld J.[51] CES was established under the *Re-establishment Employment Act 1995* (Cth); it commenced operation in 1946 and remained until April 1998 as part of the Department of Employment and Workplace Relations (in its various names). Whilst the CES had statutory functions relating to maintaining high employment and providing services to those wishing to be employed, it actually served as a labour exchange providing job placement services, including screening of job seekers, assessing their needs, canvassing suitable employers and matching the two in order to place people in employment. It also conducted 'case management' for those who were long term unemployed, it provided its services free to the public (via as many as 300 branches around Australia), and in some limited cases it was paid a fee for service. The employees providing services to the CES were public servants employed under public service legislation. In 1994, the *Employment Services Act 1994* was enacted whereby EAA was established as a 'sister' organisation to the CES to take over individual case management of longer term unemployed. EAA used the services of up to 250 external contracted case managers on a fee-for-service basis, and the Employment Services Regulatory Authority was set up to regulate EAA case maintenance system.

In the August 1996 budget, the Australian government announced that there would be a change to the delivery of employment services and a process of 'outsourcing, mainstreaming or contracting out' of employment services was commenced. The services previously provided by CES and EAA were to be provided by contracted bodies who had to compete first for government tenders and, when won, then interview customers (job seekers). Contractors were to be paid according to their success in achieving various performance indicators and delivering outcomes set by the government. In essence, 'they would be paid by the Commonwealth according to how successful they were in placing people into jobs.'[52]  In 1996 a Ministerial statement 'Reforming Employment Assistance'[53] was issued which outlined proposed changes. The government was to retain some services, others were to be contracted out to the 'job network' of employment service providers and EN/ENA was to be established by the Commonwealth as one such employment service provider.

Pursuant to the *Commonwealth Services Delivery Agency Act 1997* (Cth), which created Centrelink, Centrelink became the service delivery agency as the government decided that the public sector should continue to provide, through this service delivery agency, a uniform national service for the registration of job seekers and so on. Centrelink provided some of the functions previously carried out by the CES, particularly the initial registration of unemployed persons. It also made available a self-help computerised search of a data base of employment opportunities. Centrelink was described in a Ministerial Statement as integrating some of the 'public contact services' of both CES and EAA. Its employees were engaged under the *Public Service Act 1999* (Cth). Amongst other things, it referred job seekers to Job Networks such as EN and administered the unemployment benefit scheme.

EN, incorporated in the ACT in August 1997 under the name Public Employment Placement Enterprise Limited, was wholly owned by the Commonwealth. The Commonwealth provided its start-up capital, the shareholders held all of the company's shares as representatives of the Commonwealth and EN engaged a Managing Director. ENA, a corporation established under the Corporations Law, was a wholly owned subsidiary of EN and employed over 1000 people. It was formed in September 1997 in order to provide services and employees to EN to enable EN to operate its business, which was, essentially, labour exchange services.

EN entered into two contracts with the Commonwealth:

- the first, in November 1997, was a transitional contract covering the conduct or management of the work of CES/EAA;
- the second, made on February 1998, the 'Employment Services Contract', was the principal contract obliging it to supply employment services to the Department.

There was also an agreement between EN and ENA whereby relevant services were provided by ENA to EN to enable EN to fulfill its obligations under the contract. EN, however, was not the only contractor providing services — following a competitive tender process approximately 310 providers, consisting of both private and public community organisations, were awarded contracts. The contracts were to last for 18 months whereupon the Commonwealth would call for new tenders. Performance would be monitored by the government and breaches of its code of conduct would result in cancellation of the contract. Payment would be in accordance with the contract.[54]

## Threshold Question

Justice Einfeld considered first whether the activities of the governmental entities constituted a 'business' for the purposes in s 149(1) of the *Workplace Relations Act 1996* (Cth). The judge adopted the broad interpretation of the term 'business' which the court had used in the *North Western* case. This included a notion that the term was neither technical nor a term of art; that 'business' related to the word 'activities', and that there was a long practice of interpreting the term in an industrial context by reference to the definition of 'employer'. Einfeld J said:

> As I see the position, there is no reason to consider that the activities of public servants which are capable of giving rise to an 'industrial dispute' to which the employer is capable of being a party, and which leads to an Award within the meaning of section 149, should not be construed as a 'business' for these purposes.[55]

He took the view that it would indeed be a strange result if a certified agreement or an award could be made under the *Workplace Relations Act* in respect of a business to which a government was a party but the business did not come within the meaning of s 149!

## Was ENA a Successor to the Business of CES/EAA?

The answer to this successor question depended on 'whether, as a matter of fact, there is "substantial identity" between the activities of respective entities (or of their employees whose activities go to make up what their employers do) in a corresponding business or part of the business. If so, transmission of the business will have occurred'.[56]

The judge looked at the principal contract providing 'Flex 1, 2 and 3', which denoted flexible labour exchange services. Flex 1 provided for job matching; Flex 2 provided for job search training and Flex 3 was a system whereby payments were made in stages to a person in need of considerable assistance, training or retraining to obtain and hold a job. The judge noted that an examination of the scheme, as set up under the principal contract, as well as the evidence of employees who were transferred from government to ENA revealed that substantially the same activities were undertaken by EN as previously were carried on by CES/EAA. The transferred employees (now called 'employment consultants') did not receive any new training, apart from one day of orientation to use a new information database.

According to the evidence in the case of a former Assistant Secretary of the Department, there were four significant differences between the business of CES and EN:

- first, the different framework within which the employees operated;
- secondly, EN was operating in a competitive, market-exposed environment;
- thirdly, the EN employees focused on 'employment outcomes';
- fourthly, there were different procedural guidelines for the respective employees - CES operated according to strict guidelines when referring persons to employers whereas EN consultants operated in a more flexible environment.

After hearing considerable testimony, Einfeld J said that the 1998 fundamental changes to structure did not alter the substantive activities of the employees providing labour exchange services. His Honour stated:[57]

> That the structural or organisational framework altered upon transmission from government to 'private' employers is undoubted but in my opinion this change did not in itself mean that the actual 'business' or activities were any different. There is no reason to believe that public service personnel were not 'substantially focused' on achieving the outcome of employment, and although obviously not as directly affected by actual placements as when success is linked to reward, individually they were surely required to perform in order to maintain their positions or gain advancement.

On the question of government employees being constrained by government procedure whereas private competition 'permitted more relaxed and discretionary practices,'[58] Einfeld J said that procedures required of EN employees were 'not relevantly different' and:

> Indeed the CES duty statement established that its employees were expected to respond creatively to the labour market, and were required to exercise 'discretionary and professional' skills, whatever the particular prescriptions governing their work. To borrow from the language utilised by EN in another context, the employees received only minor training on the adjusted *means* to carry out the same *functions* of providing labour exchange and case management services to the unemployed. That was the business transmitted.[59]

Further, the asset and stock previously used by and belonging to the government were transferred to EN and were used by EN employees — this included computers, telephones and furniture. Properties used by CES and leased by them were transferred to EN and EN took over much of the customer base of CES.

Einfeld J agreed that it was not necessary to establish a legal relationship between the old business and the new, although this could be done in this case. All that was necessary was that the notions of 'succession', 'business' and other terminology in s 149(1)(d) of the *Workplace Relations Act* be given a general, non-legal specific characterisation. The issue that the legislation raised was not whether the businesses were structurally different, but whether the workers were doing, and therefore the employer was delivering, the same or different work.[60]

The judge also described EN and ENA as 'emanations of the Commonwealth',[61] because, whilst they were run as fully competitive enterprises along commercial lines, they both provided services in accordance with departmental policy; the Commonwealth completely controlled the companies — it was the sole shareholder and also determined in a real sense the content of the companies' incorporation documents. In the words of the judge:[62]

> It is artificial to conceive of them as anything other than two Commonwealth corporate entities in the business of providing employment services to the community relevantly and indistinguishably from CES/EAA.

Einfeld J also rejected the argument by EN relating to the competitive framework that there should be a distinction between the functions of the department and its agencies, and the means of it discharging those functions. Just because EN might now compete with over 300 other providers did not add anything of relevance to the transmission question. Einfeld J stated:[63]

> ... I consider that the businesses themselves did not materially change. The ethos and legal framework changed so that the governing regime moved from a statutory base to a contractual base. However, EN is in the business of providing labour exchange and intensive or longer term assistance services, and these businesses were transmitted to it from CES/EAA. I find that a transmission of the businesses to which the awards and agreements related occurred on 1 May 1998.

## International Approach to Transmission of Business

Drawing an international comparison, the judge noted that the Commonwealth legislative scheme and the courts' approach to transmission of business were consistent with developments in the European Community. The European Court of Justice had placed an emphasis on 'substance over form' in deciding whether a business transfer had taken place 'in a manner reflective of the approach of this Court generally favouring transmission and the corresponding protection'.[64]

## Application of Award to Public Sector Only?

In rejecting the argument that the award applied to the public service only and could not be applied easily outside that sector, the Federal Court took the view that it is not relevant that an award is inconvenient or not ideally suited to the circumstances of the transmittee. Einfeld J said:[65]

> Indeed, the purpose of the transmission provisions of the Act is precisely to guard against an employer deciding of its own accord that the award conditions, which are part and parcel of the business to which it has succeeded, do not suit its wishes or operating conditions. There is adequate provision for the alteration of the content of an award after transmission where the employer has or perceives difficulties in observing its terms. If EN considered that the award was so APS-specific that it was totally unsuitable to its employees or employment environment, it could energise those processes. But as a matter of law the award transmission is unaffected.

Moreover, given that the transmission provisions operate to avoid any undermining of the industrial relations system, policy required the approach to apply equally to both private and public sector employees - 'all other things considered, the section must apply to public sector transfers of business or "outsourcing"'.[66] There are not any 'compelling circumstances' to construe the awards to 'allow for their frustration by the transmission of the relevant business to EN'.[67]

## Possible Limitations

Thus the Federal Court, in keeping with the *North Western* case, concluded that in substance the functions of government employees and the privatised service employees were substantially the same, and the application of the award could not be avoided by the change in identity of the employer and service provider. The process of coming to this decision necessitated much minute analysis of the considerable testimony as to the factual position relating to the entities, their structure and operation, thereby underscoring the complexities in making these determinations about transmission in the context of privatisation with its significant implications for public servants.

The High Court later handed down its judgment in the *PP Consultants* case (discussed above) in which it raised the question whether a different approach to transmission applied in the context of privatisation of government functions. Whilst the legal approach of Einfeld J in the *Employment National* case is compelling, it is not certain that the High Court would have reached the same conclusion.

## Implications for Commonwealth Outsourcing from Developments in the High Court

In March 2005, the High Court of Australia handed down its decision in *Minister for Employment and Workplace Relations v Gribbles Radiology Pty Ltd* ('*Gribbles* case')[68] in which it held (by majority) that Gribbles Radiology Pty Ltd (Gribbles) was not bound by the previous federal award binding Dell, as there was no succession or transmission of business when Gribbles took over the functions previously undertaken by Dell, including using the same premises. In this case, which involved private sector employees, the court held that:[69]

> ...to be a 'successor' to the business or part of the business of a former employer, the new employer must enjoy some part of the 'business' of the former employer... it will not suffice to show that the new employer pursues the same kind of business activity.

Whilst this case has been regarded as raising more issues than it resolved, it did not exclude the possibility that there could be transmission of business in similar scenarios where there was a transfer of tangible and intangible assets.[70] The particular facts and legal relationship must be examined. In practical terms, what this means for public sector employers or agencies which outsource part of their functions is that sometimes the outsourcing might give rise to a transmission of business and sometimes it might not.

The *Gribbles* case emphasised that the individual facts will be important, for example, whether there is transfer of assets. Nonetheless, in principle, the judgments in *Gribbles* and *PP Consultants* suggest that:-

- where the Commonwealth outsources activities to a private company (A), under a contract with A, it is not clear whether A will be a transmittee of industrial instruments binding on the Commonwealth;[71] and
- where company A's contract is later terminated or not renewed by the Commonwealth, and another private company (B) enters into the contract for the provision of the same services to the Commonwealth, company B will not be bound by company A's industrial instruments, even if some or all of company A's employees are recruited by company B so as to enable it to provide the services required under the contract.[72]

Even in the absence of the Work Choices amendments concerning transmission of business discussed below, based on the *Gribbles* case, there could be no question of transmission of industrial instruments from the Commonwealth to company B when it is awarded the contract in the circumstances above.

## Legislative Solutions

In an attempt to resolve some of the issues concerning the application of industrial instruments to transmittees of a business, a Bill was introduced in the

Commonwealth Parliament in 2001[73] and ultimately the *Workplace Relations Act 1996* (Cth) was amended to provide a procedure whereby application could be made to the Australian Industrial Relations Commission for an order that the certified agreement apply or not, or for a limited time, to the new employer of the transmitted business.[74] It had already been possible in the case of an award for the application of transmission provisions to be varied by order of the Commission.

Further, the legislation now sets out different provisions in relation to transmission of business and the applicability of an award, collective agreement or Australian Workplace Agreement. The *Workplace Relations Act 1996* (Cth), as amended by the *Workplace Relations Amendment (Work Choices) Act 2005* (Cth), provides in Part 11 for the application of old awards or agreements to the new employer.

Whilst there must still be a transmission of business, the old instrument — whether it is an award or certified or other collective agreement — will apply only so long as certain conditions are met; one significant condition is that the old instrument will apply so long as there are employees of the old employer still being employed by the new employer.[75] The transmittee employer is only bound by the transmitted award or agreement in respect of a transferring employee.[76] Thus, once there are no longer old employees of the former employer being engaged, the instrument ceases to apply and there will be a natural end to the application of it to the new employer. Furthermore, the transmitted industrial instrument only applies for a maximum period of 12 months from the date of transmission and can be superseded during that period by a new workplace agreement.[77]

Public sector employees who become private sector employees as a result of a privatisation or outsourcing, sooner or later, will cease to have the benefit of the public sector terms or conditions, even if there is a 'transmission' of business.

Generally the amended transmission of business provisions apply to workplace agreements made under the post-reform Act, as well as to awards, collective agreements and Australian Workplace Agreements made under the pre-reform Act (whilst those instruments still apply).[78] There is however one specific change in the transmission provisions (applicable to both pre-reform and post-reform instruments) which possibly is designed to provide a statutory foundation for arguments which failed in cases such as *North Western Healthcare Network*. In that case, it was argued that the public service awards were incapable of applying to the Network as it was a statutory corporation. That argument was rejected.[79] For the reasons set out below, this line of reasoning might now be at least an arguable proposition.

The Work Choices Act introduced into the Act a provision[80] which establishes the concept of a 'transferring employee in relation to an industrial instrument'. This provides that a transferring employee (that is, one who was previously employed by the old employer immediately before the time of transmission and who has become an employee of the new employer in the business being transferred) is a transferring employee *in relation to an industrial instrument* if:

a.  the instrument applies to the employee immediately before the time of transmission; and
b.  when the employee becomes employed by the new employer, 'the nature of the transferring employee's employment with the new employer is such that the instrument is capable of applying to employment of that nature'.[81]

In short, the industrial instrument will not apply to the employee, even if the employee is a transferring employee, unless the instrument is appropriate to the new employment. Ordinarily, the nature of the employment will not change merely because of the transmission of business. However this may not always be the case. For example, the nature of the work required may vary in the new employment compared to the old. More importantly, perhaps, the nature of employment in the new employment may not be the same — possibly where the employment is with a private employer rather than a public or government employer with its different characteristics (as exemplified by the specific Values and Code of Conduct applicable to employees in the Australian Public Service). If this is so, then the new provision may apply, so that the industrial instrument does not apply to the new employment. The possibly different approach to the concept of 'transmission of business' which the High Court in the *PP Consultants* case identified as requiring consideration in the context of government agency transfers to private employers (compared to private sector transmission) might not be necessary because of the new provision.

It is at least arguable that the nature of employment of a private sector employee (engaged by an employer who is a contracted provider of services to the Commonwealth) is different from the employment of a public servant in providing these services directly to the Commonwealth as a member of the APS. If this is so, then it will be potentially far more difficult for a former public sector employee to claim the benefit of agreements with the Commonwealth employer applicable to him or her, when he or she takes up employment with the new private sector employer in the transferred business.

It should be emphasised that the provisions under Work Choices have not shed light on the meaning of transmission of business generally; hence, in the context of Commonwealth outsourcing, there remain the uncertainties analysed in the discussion of the applicable legal principles in the sections 'Case Studies' and 'Implications for Commonwealth Outsourcing from Developments in the High Court'.

## Cost-Cutting Reasons for Outsourcing and Freedom of Association

One of the main motivators for outsourcing would undoubtedly be costs; if an external provider can provide a particular service to an organisation at a lower cost, an employer would often prefer to use such a provider, all other things being equal. When governments outsource to external providers, the potential providers generally are required to go through a competitive tendering process. One of the legal issues in this context is the role of freedom of association provisions under the *Workplace Relations Act 1996* (Cth), as shown in the case discussed below.

### *Greater Dandenong Council* Case

Illustrative of the pressure to reduce costs and legal issues raised by implementing outsourcing, albeit in the local government sector, is the case of *Greater Dandenong City Council v Australian Municipal Clerical and Services Union*. [82] The Greater Dandenong City Council ('the Dandenong Council') had decided to outsource its home and community care services that it provided to disabled, aged and frail persons within the community. It employed about 75 people in connection with home and community care services, and in March 1996 foreshadowed seeking tenders to provide home and community care services.

By virtue of the *Local Government Act 1989* (Vic), as amended by the *Financial Management Act 1994* (Vic), local government councils in Victoria were obliged to follow a regime of compulsory competitive tendering. This meant that in the financial year 1994-1995, councils were obliged to have competitive arrangements for 20 per cent of their expenditure, and in 1995-1996, this obligation increased to 50 per cent of their expenditure. Tenders could be provided by external providers but also by 'in-house' teams of council employees.

Tenders sought by the Dandenong Council in accordance with these compulsory competitive tendering processes — for the provision of community care services for the Council — closed on 23 December 1998. There were two bids, from:

1. Silver Circle; and
2. A Council in-house team.

The Silver Circle tender was for approximately $6.6 million and the in-house bid was for approximately $7.8 million. An evaluation committee appointed by the Council assessed the bids, looking at them from the view point of four criteria:

- financial stability;
- price;
- capability to develop and deliver specified outcomes; and
- management capability qualifications.

Both tenders passed in respect of financial stability and were competitive in relation to capability and management. Price, however, yielded a big difference. This was largely because Silver Circle employees were engaged under an award ('Silver Circle Award') which provided for lower wages and penalties than the Council employees received under an award and a certified agreement binding on the Council in respect of its employees. The in-house team had decided to put in its bid based on their current entitlements as Council employees to wages and conditions under the certified agreement and award.

On 22 February 1999, the Council considered the report of the evaluation committee and decided, by majority of seven to three, to accept the Silver Circle tender. There was extensive debate relating to the cost difference between the two tenders, arising for the reasons mentioned earlier.

The Council terminated the employment of its home and community care workers on the grounds of redundancy on 23 May 1999. Silver Circle had already indicated to the Council's employees that they could apply to work for Silver Circle. As a result, nearly 50 workers previously employed by the Council were engaged by Silver Circle. However, as noted by Madgwick J in the Federal Court at first instance: 'As a result, these workers were then paid significantly less for doing virtually identical work'[83] and for the same clients.

## The Legal Framework at the Time

The legal framework in the *Workplace Relations Act 1996* (Cth) which was then relevant to the *Greater Dandenong City Council* case were the provisions in Part XA of the Act dealing with Freedom of Association.[84] In particular, s 298K(1) provided:

> An employer must not, for a prohibited reason, or for reasons that include a prohibited reason, do or threaten to do any of the following:

> a. dismiss an employee;
> b. injure an employee in his or her employment;
> c. alter the position of an employee to the employee's prejudice;
> d. refuse to employ another person;
> e. discriminate against another person in the terms or conditions on which the employer offers to employ the other person.

'Prohibited reason' was further fleshed out in s 298L which identified conduct which constitutes a prohibited reason. The relevant conduct in this case was covered by paragraph (h) of s 298L[85] - that the employee 'is entitled to the benefit of an industrial instrument or an order of an industrial body'.

As it applied at the time, s 298V of the *Workplace Relations Act 1996* provided for a rebuttable presumption that the conduct was carried out for the particular reason alleged (in a proceeding against a respondent). In the context of outsourcing, this provision could raise some difficult issues for the new employer undertaking the outsourced functions when it was the respondent in proceedings alleging breach of the freedom of association provisions.

## The Courts' Decisions

In legal proceedings brought by the Australian Municipal Clerical and Services Union against the Dandenong Council, Madgwick J held[86] that the Council had contravened s 298K(1)(c) (on 22 February 1999) by resolving to contract out the home and community care services, and declared that the Council contravened s 298K(1)(a) in dismissing the employees on 23 May 1999. The judge ordered their reinstatement. Thus the judge found that the Council contravened the *Workplace Relations Act* by altering the position of the employees to their prejudice and by dismissing employees, in each instance on account of the prohibited reasons relating to the entitlement of employees to the benefit of a certified agreement.

In the appeal by the Dandenong Council, the majority of the Federal Court upheld the decision of Madgwick J.[87] Focussing relevantly on the ground of appeal relating to the interpretation of s 298L(1)(h), the differing reasons of the majority judges result in the decision on that point being less clear cut. Wilcox J, agreeing with the interpretation by Madgwick J of s 298L(1)(h) and his application of that section to the circumstances of the case, stated that:

> Section 298L(1)(h) does not apply only to conduct motivated by the **fact** that an industrial instrument or order applies to an employee. It applies, also, where the employer is motivated to engage in proscribed conduct because of the **content** of the instrument or order.[88]

Wilcox J also noted the implications of outsourcing in the context of the *Workplace Relations Act* as follows:

> Although the details vary from case to case, outsourcing typically involves the engagement of a contractor who carries out a function or operation, previously undertaken by the enterprise itself, in a more efficient way; perhaps by the use of more sophisticated equipment, perhaps by using specialised labour. It will generally be possible for an outsourcing employer, accused of s 298K(1) conduct for a s 298L(1)(h) reason, to negative that reason by proving other reasons for the decision to outsource. What makes this case unusual is that the functions to be undertaken by Silver Circle were exactly the same as previously undertaken by the council and would be performed by many of the same people and in virtually the same way. It was not suggested that new equipment would be used; the only envisaged 'efficiency' was a saving in costs by moving the labour force from the certified agreement to the [Silver Circle] Award.[89]

It was open to the judge at first instance, in the view of Wilcox J, to find that the Council had failed to establish that the reason for the dismissal or any other conduct was not because of the Council's workers entitlement to benefits of the certified agreement. Thus,

> a principal reason why it took that course was that, whilst employed by the council, the [health and community care] employees were entitled to the benefit of the award and certified agreement while employees of Silver Circle (even if they were the same people) would not be so entitled.[90]

Merkel J made the following significant comments:[91]

> An employer will have breached ss 298K(1) and 298L(1)(h) where the dismissal or other prejudicial conduct is for the reason that the employer is not prepared to pay the award entitlement of the employee. As an employer is obliged to pay award rates, the employer is expected to be capable of organising its business so as to be able to meet its award obligations. The mere fact that an award increase cannot be passed on or is inconvenient does not relieve the employer of the constraints of ss 298K(1) and 298L(1)(h). Thus, the section can extend to prejudicial conduct which is carried out for the reason that the award rates have made the employer's business less profitable.

Merkel J acknowledged that profitability could involve 'questions of degree' so that 'where the reason for the prejudicial conduct is that the employer is unable to pay the award entitlement or the employer's business is not capable of operating at a profit by reason of the entitlement, it is likely that the section will not have been breached'.[92] He noted that the same principles would apply to certified agreements or Australian Workplace Agreements.

Merkel J reasoned slightly differently and concluded that Madgwick J erred in the positive inference he drew about the reason for the dismissal of the employees but, nonetheless, the appellant Council had not established that there was an error in concluding that there had been a breach in the provisions of the Act when the councillors resolved to accept Silver Circle's tender. The Council had not established that it had rebutted the presumption of the reason for the conduct, so the judge correctly found a contravention of the Act. The Council might have been in a position, for example, to have brought evidence to show that a reason for accepting Silver Circle's bid was not because councillors took the view that the community care workers were unreasonably holding on to their award and certified agreement conditions in formulating their bid.[93]

## The Current Legal Framework for Freedom of Association

In conclusion, under the pre-reform legislation the freedom of association provisions provided a check to ensure that a purpose for the outsourcing was not to avoid the obligations of employers under awards or agreements, as illustrated in the *Dandenong Council* case. That degree of protection of employees has now been significantly undermined. In the amended *Workplace Relations Act* after Work Choices, s 792(4) now provides that the prohibited reason must be the 'sole' or 'dominant' reason for the employer's actions if the freedom of association provisions are to apply. Thus the safeguards in the *Workplace Relations Act* are now more limited. Outsourcing by the government for the reasons of cost-cutting by avoiding the operation of industrial instruments, even where the former public servants are doing the same job, may not involve a contravention of the Act.

## Public Sector Values

Whilst there is doubt about the 'transportability' of the public service agreement or award provisions through the transmission of business provisions, the question arises whether the values of the Australian Public Service in relation to employment are carried across to the new employers.

We have seen that the *Public Service Act 1999* (Cth) sets out the APS Values and Code of Conduct.[94] Several of the Values, which are set out in the Appendix to this chapter, relate directly to employment — employment decisions based on merit: (b); workplace free from discrimination: (c); workplace relations which value communication and consultation: (i); a fair and flexible workplace: (j); managing performance: (k); and equity in employment: (l). Arguably, some of these have counterparts in the private sector — for example through anti-discrimination legislation — but most are specific values to the public service, there being neither a general legal requirement that Australian workplaces be fair or equitable nor implied obligations in the contract of employment to generally follow fair practices.[95]

Government agencies could require, via the contract which outsources the function to the private sector, the new employer to comply with standards in employment that are equivalent to the APS values. Such decisions are in the province of the agency to determine to the extent that they are not directly regulated by the mandatory requirements in the procurement guidelines relevant to the contract.[96] In the absence of express contractual requirements, public sector values are not likely to be 'transferred' to the private sector outsourced employers.[97]

In addition, in s 13 of the *Public Service Act 1999*, there is some guidance as to implementation of the APS Values, through the APS Code of Conduct provisions as to how the employee should behave — with honesty, integrity, following lawful orders and so on. Many of these arguably are very similar to those duties implied by the common law in the contract of employment and would be imposed in this way on private sector employees. However, some of the public sector values and duties do not correspond with such implied duties — for example, the APS employee's obligation to treat everyone with respect and courtesy; to disclose any conflict of interest, real or apparent; and to behave overseas in way which will uphold the good reputation of Australia.

Arguably the standards imposed on the public sector employee are higher than those on the private sector employee. In particular the Values in the APS which together make up a bundle of values emphasising service and loyalty transcend simple employee loyalty to an employer, and are more akin to a loyalty to one's country 'to serve', that is, to perform a true 'public service'. These values could not easily be replicated in duties on employees working for private sector employers who have the main motive of profit for the business. Thus some values may inevitably be lost by transfer of government function to the private sector.

## Diminution of Public Remedies When the Nature of the Entity Changes: A Question of Contract

Although the *Public Service Act 1999* in respect of employment matters has to a degree expressly replicated, through the APS Code of Conduct, some obligations which are similar to those of an ordinary employee in the private sector which arise from the contract of employment itself, the change in the character of employment from public to private involved in outsourcing has significant implications for employees in matters of workplace conduct or performance or in relation to restructuring and redundancy.

A person holding office under statute, for example, may have certain public law (administrative law) remedies which are removed once the entity changes its nature. Even if the person is question is not the holder of an office, but is a public servant with the status of an employee, the change from public to private is not without significance. Formal inquiry and disciplinary processes under the *Public Service Act 1999* and prescriptions for the nature of remedies open to employers for employee breach, for example, of the APS Code of Conduct, are designed to protect the public servant from arbitrary or unreasonable action and have strong procedural as well as substantive protections. This is of course very different from the situation for employees of employers with 100 or fewer employees in the private sector; they have lost unfair dismissal protection under the *Workplace Relations Act 1996* (Cth) after the Work Choices Act.

In its degree of procedural and substantive protection the regime for Commonwealth public servants is more prescriptive than what might be regarded as the norm even for employers with 101 or more employees in the private sector, who remain subject to the unfair dismissal provisions of the *Workplace Relations Act* in respect of harsh, unjust and unreasonable dismissal.[98]

Thus the obligations of the new private sector employer will not include the previous procedural and substantive obligations under the *Public Service Act* in respect of the transferring employees. Moreover, the employee now engaged by the private sector employer does not have any public sector remedy that might previously available. Any rights are largely governed by contract, which might include any policy incorporated as terms of the contract of employment. Thus contractual rights assume major importance and, depending on the circumstances, may or may not provide the employee with any real relief. The procedures for fair promotion, a feature of public sector employment, will not generally be a facet of private sector employment, thus promotion appeal rights will be lost to the newly privatised workforce.

## Other Legal Issues Emerging from Private Sector Control

Other issues raised by the change to private control of employees can be identified. They are legal issues which may have an impact on the way employers operate or should operate, and which may later surface dramatically in ways which with hindsight may have been avoided.

## Public Service Career and Redeployment Opportunities

To the extent that outsourcing reduces the number of positions in the Australian Public Service then there is a lessening of redeployment opportunities where required, for example, after a workplace injury or illness. Firstly, the Commonwealth policy of endeavouring to provide suitable alternative employment for injured employees able to return to some form of work within the public service may not be able to be fulfilled where there has been a downsizing of the public service. As pointed out by the Administrative Appeals Tribunal in the case of *Gail Goldsmith v Comcare,* [99] the spirit of the *Safety Rehabilitation Compensation Act 1988* (Cth) which, 'envisages rehabilitation and return to work programs in lieu of compensation' is 'at odds with the reality of the public service environment and government policy at this time. The public sector is being downsized in favour of privatisation'[100] resulting in fewer offers of alternative employment.

Secondly, to the extent that individual departments and agencies with APS staff see themselves as operating as independent 'entities', it may become practically more difficult to arrange for redeployment of personnel between agencies. The agencies' operation as 'separate corporate entities' was alluded to by the AAT in the *Goldsmith* case as another factor in the intentions of the *Safety Rehabilitation Compensation Act 1988* (Cth) being 'thwarted by the realities of the public sector environment in which it is operating today'.[101]

The public service employees who have been transferred to a private sector organisation now performing the functions previously employed by the government will also lose the possibility they once enjoyed of being redeployed within the public sector. Similarly, they will lose the public service career structure. Whilst they may gain career possibilities within the private sector entity, these will be of a different nature to the public sector and they will certainly not include the possibility of moving between departments and within the public service in the way provided by the more traditional career public service.

## Discrimination, Equal Opportunity and Affirmative Action

Private sector employers who are constitutional corporations and Victorian employers[102] will be subject to the *Workplace Relations Act 1996* (Cth), and, irrespective of their legal status or place of activity, to the law relating to the contract of employment, anti-discrimination legislation and occupational health and safety laws. Clearly such private employers will not be subject to the *Public Service Act 1999*. It has been argued that they will not usually have to import the APS Values and the APS Code of Conduct in the arrangements in the private sector, although some of these may correspond to implied duties in the contract of employment.

The public service has equal opportunity and diversity policies imposed via the *Public Service Act* 1999 (Cth) and its Code of Conduct and Values, together with the policies developed by agencies at agency level. No such specific overarching policy applies at private sector, save for the anti-discrimination legislation itself[103] and, relevant specifically to employment of women, the *Equal Opportunity for Women in the Workplace Act 1999* (Cth).

However, consistent with policies for diversity in employment, employers of over 100 employees were obliged under the *Affirmative Action (Equal Employment Opportunity for Women) Act 1986* (Cth), the predecessor of the 1999 legislation, to develop an 'affirmative action program', to ensure that:

a.   appropriate action is taken to eliminate discrimination by the relevant employer against women in relation to employment matters; and

b.   measures are taken by the relevant employer to promote equal opportunity for women in relation to employment matters.[104]

The *Equal Opportunity for Women in the Workplace Act 1999* (Cth) now prescribes the equal opportunity programmes and reporting requirements for employers with a shift away from terminology about affirmative action.

Thus there is a difference in source and degree of equal opportunity policies and requirements on public and private sector employers.

## Access to Information about the Operation of the Service

At both Federal and state levels, freedom of information legislative provisions share the basic premise of providing for accessibility to government-held information, unless specific exemptions can be made out.

As freedom of information legislation has no application to private entities (including private employers), where provision of a service is outsourced the change in nature of the entity carrying out the service from public sector to private sector necessarily takes the private entity and employer outside the scope of the freedom of information legislation. It follows that the change in the nature of the entity has an impact on the entitlements of persons (including employees) to utilise this legislation in a number of different but practically significant ways.

This change in relation to access to information can have a significant impact on accountability of the way in which the services to the public are operated — for example, access by private organisations or individuals who are concerned to monitor the effectiveness of services is more limited and there is a diminution of material publicly available. These limitations in mechanisms for accountability in turn may affect the work performance of employees and may ultimately require other mechanisms to promote accountability of the services in private hands.

In the employment context, as a consequence of the change in the character of their employer from public to private, employees themselves are unable through freedom of information legislation to access information held by their private employer which might be relevant in a range of employment matters such as employment promotions, disciplinary matters, unfair dismissal proceedings and so on. However, had they remained members of the APS, they would be entitled to access at least to some information relevant to such matters from their employer through the utilisation of freedom of information provisions. This is not to say of course that such information may not be available through other mechanisms (such as discovery in litigation); rather it is to emphasise that the change in the status of the employer removes one significant means which would be available to the public employee to obtain information relevant to decisions concerning the exercise of their employment rights in such matters.

## Conclusion

Outsourcing has contributed to the shrinking of the public sector and the diminution of public sector rights and values in employment. Contract management is the new means of controlling the performance of the activities which were formerly conducted by government and subject to control through administrative direction. Whilst it is possible that contract management could extend to determining maintenance of employee conditions after outsourcing, in the cases studies considered this was not done.

Where there is genuine transmission of business in outsourcing, generally the new employer must abide by the former public service conditions under a transmitted award or collective agreement. The case studies show that there are considerable legal and factual complexities in determining whether a transmission of business has indeed occurred, resulting in uncertainties for employees and employers as to whether they remain under the public service conditions.

The amendments to the *Workplace Relations Act 1996* (Cth) by the Work Choices Act ensure that these public sector conditions cannot be maintained indefinitely, even where there is a transmission of business. Outsourcing taking place now will move the employees more rapidly to private sector conditions; consequently, there is a move to private sector employment remedies away from possible remedies under the *Public Service Act 1999* (Cth) and certainly no access to administrative law remedies. Amongst other implications which have been considered, there are implications for access by employees to information held by their employer as a consequence of the non-application of freedom of information legislation in the private sector. Furthermore, there are differential policies relating to equal opportunity between public and private sectors. It has been argued that many public sector values are inevitably lost by transfer of government function to the private sector.

The challenge to traditional public sector employment has come about from shifting, to the private sector, employees and functions previously performed directly by the public service.

## Appendix

In s 10 of the *Public Service Act 1999* (Cth), the Values outlined are as follows:

1. *The APS Values are as follows:*
    a. *the APS is apolitical, performing its functions in an impartial and professional manner;*
    b. *the APS is a public service in which employment decisions are based on merit;*
    c. *the APS provides a workplace that is free from discrimination and recognises and utilises the diversity of the Australian community it serves;*
    d. *the APS has the highest ethical standards;*
    e. *the APS is openly accountable for its actions, within the framework of Ministerial responsibility to the Government, the Parliament and the Australian public;*
    f. *the APS is responsive to the Government in providing frank, honest, comprehensive, accurate and timely advice and in implementing the Government's policies and programs;*

g.  *the APS delivers services fairly, effectively, impartially and courteously to the Australian public and is sensitive to the diversity of the Australian public;*

h.  *the APS has leadership of the highest quality;*

i.  *the APS establishes workplace relations that value communication, consultation, co-operation and input from employees on matters that affect their workplace;*

j.  *the APS provides a fair, flexible, safe and rewarding workplace;*

k.  *the APS focuses on achieving results and managing performance;*

l.  *the APS promotes equity in employment;*

m.  *the APS provides a reasonable opportunity to all eligible members of the community to apply for APS employment;*

n.  *the APS is a career-based service to enhance the effectiveness and cohesion of Australia's democratic system of government;*

o.  *the APS provides a fair system of review of decisions taken in respect of APS employees.*

2.  *For the purposes of paragraph (1)(b), a decision relating to engagement or promotion is based on merit if:*

a.  *an assessment is made of the relative suitability of the candidates for the duties, using a competitive selection process; and*

b.  *the assessment is based on the relationship between the candidates' work-related qualities and the work-related qualities genuinely required for the duties; and*

c.  *the assessment focuses on the relative capacity of the candidates to achieve outcomes related to the duties; and*

d.  *the assessment is the primary consideration in making the decision.*

# ENDNOTES

[1] Wilcox J in *Greater Dandenong City Council v Australian Municipal Clerical and Services Union* [2001] FCA 349 at para 81.

[2] *State of the Service Report 2004-5*, Australian Government, Commonwealth of Australia, 2005, Ch 12, 'Outsourced services' at 289.

[3] Ibid.

[4] *Review of the Whole of Government Information Technology Outsourcing Initiative, Report*, 4.

[5] Ibid.

[6] In the words of the Humphrey Report, ibid, the outsourcing of technology would 'introduce discipline in the use of technology to achieve economies of scale and reduce overall costs'.

[7] Ibid.

[8] On website 2001 <http://www.dofa.gov.au/ctc/ctc>.

[9] On website 2001 <http://www.dofa.gov.au/ctc/ctc/case_studies/dfat.html>.

[10] Agencies report only contracts in excess of $100,000.

[11] *State of the Service Report 2004-5*, Australian Government, Commonwealth of Australia, 2005, Ch 12 'Outsourced services'.

[12] <http://www.finance.gov.au/ctc/commonwealth_procurement_guide.html> accessed August 30 2006.

[13] 'Given the limited trend data available, it is difficult to determine whether this increase is cyclical representing many agencies renewing and/or extending their outsourcing contracts for HR services in 2004–05.': *State of the Service Report 2004-5*, Australian Government, Commonwealth of Australia, 2005, Ch 12 'Outsourced services'.

[14] A Moorhead, M Steele, M Alexander, K Stephen, L Duffin, *Changes at Work: 1995 Australian Workplace Industrial Relations Survey*, (Melbourne, Longman, 1997).

[15] Australian Centre for Industrial Relations for Research and Training, 1999.

[16] Research Note no. 29 2005–06, Tony Kryger, 'The incredible shrinking public sector', Statistics Section, 24 March 2006' at <http://www.aph.gov.au/Library/Pubs/ RN/2005-06/06rn29.htm> accessed August 2006.

[17] This information about the private sector being more willing to *globally* outsource is based on inferences from the data available on the destinations of outsourced functions.

[18] These can be viewed at <http://www.finance.gov.au>.

[19] See Guidelines at <http://www.finance.gov.au/procurement/procurement_ guidelines.html# CPGs-Purpose> accessed January 2007.

[20] See s 5 *Financial Management and Accountability Act* 1997 (Cth) (FMA Act).

[21] Section 44 ibid.

[22] Section 52 ibid.

[23] Section 53 ibid.

[24] Regulation 6, FMA Regulations.

[25] Regulation 8 ibid.

[26] Regulation 9 ibid.

[27] Regulation 10 ibid.

[28] Regulation 13 ibid.

[29] See generally chapters 2 [Weeks] and 3 [Nethercote] in this volume.

[30] In the *Workplace Relations Act 1996* (Cth), prior to the amendments of Work Choices, s 149(1)(d) governed the application of award in instances of transmission of business. Most of the transmission cases dealt with the application of the old award to the new employer. Similar provisions applied to certified agreements and Australian Workplace Agreements. In the *Workplace Relations Act* as amended by Work Choices, Part 11 now governs application of awards, collective workplace agreements and Australian Workplace Agreements.

[31] Initially *Finance Sector Union of the Australia v PP Consultants Pty Ltd* [1999] FCA 631.

[32] Ibid at para 38.

[33] *Finance Sector Union of the Australia v PP Consultants Pty Ltd* (1999) FCR 337; [1999] FCA 125.

[34] [2000] HCA 59; (2000) 201 CLR 648; 176 ALR 205; 75 ALJR 19.

[35] Ibid at para 14.

[36] Ibid.

[37] Gleeson CJ, Gaudron, McHugh and Gummow JJ; Callinan J delivered a separate judgment concurring in the outcome.

[38] [2000] HCA 59; (2000) 201 CLR 648; 176 ALR 205; 75 ALJR 19 at para 15.

[39] Ibid at para 13.

[40] Ibid at para 14.

[41] [2001] FCA 106 (Full Federal Court — Ryan, Lee and Branson JJ).

[42] *CPSU v Stellar Call Centres Pty Ltd* [1999] FCA 1224; 92 IR 224.

[43] Ibid at para 48.

[44] Stellar made application to Katz J of the Federal Court to stay the application of the decision of Wilcox J at first instance pending the appeal. Interestingly, Katz J held that Stellar would not be disadvantaged significantly by complying with the Telstra awards and certified agreements until the appeals were heard: *Stellar Call Centres Pty Ltd v CPSU* [1999] FCA 1236. By way of contrast, Wilcox J had concluded that the employees would be disadvantaged if the Telstra instruments were not applied because they would not be able to be retrospectively compensated for non-monetary benefits which were not given to them during the period of the appeal.

[45] [2001] FCA 106 at para 30.

[46] [1999] FCA 897 (2 July 1999).

[47] *Health Services Union v North Eastern Health Care Network; Health Services Union v Western Health Care Network* [1997] FCA 1084.

[48] Ibid in section 'Award Application Consequences'.

[49] *North Western Health Care Network v HSU of Australia* [1999] FCA 897.

[50] [2000] FCA 452 (11 April 2000, Einfeld J).

[51] This section is drawn from the judgment of Einfeld J ibid.

[52] Ibid at para 17.

[53] Ibid at para 18.

[54] Following this but not relevant to the judgment, some of the contracts with service providers were not renewed after the 18 month term.

[55] [2000] FCA 452 at para 38.

[56] Ibid at para 43 per Einfeld J.

[57] Ibid at para 62.

[58] Ibid at para 63.

[59] Ibid.

[60] Ibid at para 77.

[61] Ibid at para 78. The judge acknowledged these words of the CPSU.

[62] Ibid.

[63] Ibid at para 83.

[64] Ibid at para 95.

[65] Ibid at para 114.

[66] Ibid at para 119.

[67] Ibid.

[68] [2005] HCA 9; (2005) 222 CLR 194; 214 ALR 24; 79 ALJR 679.

[69] Ibid at para 35.

[70] The High Court stated in relation to tangible and intangible assets, ibid at para 39: 'The "business" of an employer may be constituted by a number of different assets, both tangible and intangible, that are used in the particular pursuit, whether of profit (if the "business" is a commercial enterprise) or other ends (if the activity is charitable or the "business" of government). In the case of a commercial enterprise, identifying the employer's "business" will usually require identification both of the particular activity that is pursued and of the tangible and intangible assets that are used in that pursuit. The "business" of an employer will be identified as the assets that the employer uses in the pursuit of the

particular activity. It is the assets used in that way that can be assigned or transmitted and it is to the assets used in that way that an employer can be a successor.'

71 This is based on *PP Consultants* case

72 This is based on *Gribbles* case.

73 See Bills Digest No. 123, 2000-01 Workplace Relations Amendment (Transmission of Business) Bill 2001, Parliamentary Library, <http://www.aph.gov.au/library/Pubs/bd/2000-01/01BD123.htm> accessed June 2006.

74 *Workplace Relations Amendment (Transmission of Business) Act 2004* (Cth).

75 *Workplace Relations Act 1996* (Cth) as amended by the Work Choices legislation: as to awards, s 595(2); as to collective workplace agreements, s 585(2); and as to Australian Workplace Agreements, s 583(2).

76 Ibid: awards, s 595(1); collective workplace agreements s 585(1); Australian Workplace Agreements, s 583(1).

77 Ibid: awards, s 595(2); collective workplace agreements, s 585(2); Australian Workplace Agreements, 583(2) as applied by s 580(4).

78 See Part 11 and Schedule 9 of the *Workplace Relations Act 1996* (Cth), as amended by the Work Choices Act.

79 *North Western Health Care Network v HSU of Australia* [1999] FCA 897.

80 *Workplace Relations Act 1996* (Cth), s 582 and Schedule 9.

81 Ibid s 582 (1)(b).

82 [2001] FCA 349.

83 [2000] FCA 1231 at para 81.

84 Freedom of association provisions are now contained in Part 16 of the *Workplace Relations Act* as amended by Work Choices Act 2005.

85 Now s 793 *Workplace Relations Act* 1996 as amended by the Work Choices Act 2005.

86 [2000] FCA 1231.

87 *Greater Dandenong City Council v Australian Municipal Clerical and Services Union* [2001] FCA 349. Wilcox and Merkel JJ were in the majority with Finkelstein J in dissent.

88 Ibid at para 81.

89 Ibid at para 80.

90 Ibid at para 91.

91 Ibid at para 162.

92 Ibid.

93 See, ibid, at paras 168 to 181.

94 See especially chapters 2 [Weeks], 3 [Nethercote] and 4 [Molloy] in this volume.

95 This general statement may be slightly qualified by the implied duty of mutual trust and confidence at common law. However this duty, even if accepted fully in Australia, would not go so far as to instil such values via the contract: see generally R Owens and J Riley, *The Law of Work* (2007). The proposed charter of employment rights may promote such values: see M Bromberg and M Irving (eds) *Australian Charter of Employment Rights,* (Australian Institute of Employment Rights, Hardie Grant Books, 2007).

96 See Australian Public Service A-Z Index, *APS Values and Code of Conduct in Practice,* 'Working with the private sector and other Stakeholders' <www.apsc.gov.au/values/conductguidelines8.htm>.

97 See R Mulgan, 'Outsourcing and public service values: the Australian experience' (2005) 71(1) *International Review of Administrative Services,* 55-70.

98 *Workplace Relations Act,* Part 12, Division 4 deals with termination of employment. See M Pittard, "Fair Dismissal: A Devalued Right", chapter in Teicher et al (eds), *Work Choices: The New Industrial Relations Agenda* (Pearson Prentice Hall, 2006).

99 [1998] AATA 830 (AAT 13394, decision of Administrative Appeals Tribunal on 21 October 1998).

100 Ibid at para 57.

101 Ibid.

102 'Constitutional corporations' are defined in s 4(1) of the *Workplace Relations Act 1996* (Cth) as trading, foreign or financial corporations. Also employers in the Territories which are not incorporated are covered by the *Workplace Relations Act,* as also is the Commonwealth as employer.

103  Also the *Workplace Relations Act 1996* (Cth) provides for unlawful termination of employment where there is dismissal for discriminatory reasons: Part 12.

104  Section 3(1) *Affirmative Action (Equal Opportunity for Women) Act 1986* (Cth).

# Chapter Eight

# 'The Politics of Partnership': The Evolution of Public Sector Industrial Relations in Victoria

## Peter Gahan

## Introduction

The Australian Labor Party ('ALP') unexpectedly won the Victorian State election in October 1999. The election win followed an extended period of conservative government in which the Victorian public service — and the public sector more generally — had undergone a dramatic transformation and restructure.[1] In many areas of government, the outcome of the process of reform, informed by the ideas associated with 'new public management', had challenged both the rationale for public ownership of certain assets and the delivery of services by public sector employees. Like many governments across the globe, Victoria had discovered 'privatisation', 'corporatisation', and 'public-private partnerships'.

Consistent with these developments, public sector industrial relations in Victoria also shifted significantly during the 1990s. These changes were to occur at both the peak level between central agencies and unions, as well as the workplace level, involving union representatives' dealings with management. At the peak level of government, unions found it increasingly difficult to engage central agencies in policy and workforce issues, and wage setting was decentralised to the Department/agency level. At the workplace level, unions were excluded from workplace change processes and management was encouraged to introduce individualised employment agreements as a substitute for collective agreements and awards. In the wider public sector, the Kennett government also sought to direct public sector organisations to introduce individual agreements and, following the passage of the federal *Workplace Relations Act 1996* (Cth), Australian Workplace Agreements ('AWAs'). Unions, not surprisingly, took on a more adversarial approach to dealing with both government and Department or agency-level management, using industrial muscle where it could be exercised. Inevitably these changes were associated with increasingly differentiated outcomes between Departments/agencies, both in terms of wages, approaches to industrial relations and human resource/employment practices. By the end of the 1990s, the relationship between public sector unions in Victoria and government was hostile and non-cooperative.

On gaining office, the Bracks Labor government stated its commitment to overturning the approach taken by the previous Kennett government. It immediately convened a summit ('Growing Victoria Together') which was intended to indicate, as many of its pre-election policy documents had done, the ways in which it would seek to distinguish itself from its conservative predecessors. The government remained committed to a strong focus on financial management and the maintenance of budget surpluses, but sought to differentiate itself in terms of its key policy priorities and initiatives designed to create an invigorated capacity for government to deliver value to citizens. This involved a commitment to creating a new public sector organisation and management.

As was the case for the Kennett government, the priorities were focussed on growth through improving the regulatory environment for business and investment attraction, but in contrast, the process of developing and implementing policy would be consultative, although not necessary consensual. This has led to an ongoing insistence that any policy proposals must not only go through a process of assessment for its economic impact, an 'Economic Impact Statement', but should also involve a period of 'community consultation' before the presentation of any actual proposals as bills before Parliament.

This 'consultative but not consensual approach' was also intended to be a hallmark of public sector industrial relations under a Labor government. Its purpose was to embark on a 'partnership' with unions to improve the delivery of services and, at the same time, build a strong relationship with public sector unions and employees through cooperation and consultation. The government moved quickly to reinstate a collectivist approach to industrial relations, directing Departments/agencies to discontinue the practice of engaging employees on individual agreements (AWAs). Proceedings before the Australian Industrial Relations Commission ('AIRC') were terminated and the government sought to negotiate a Partnership Agreement with the Victorian Branch of the Community and Public Sector Union (the 'CPSU'). This agreement, which was negotiated in a relatively short period of time, articulated an approach which sought to bring unions back into the process of reshaping public sector employment practices.

For all intents and purposes, the election of the Bracks government appeared to represent a counter-revolution against the 'new public management' and the general direction of industrial relations reform in Australia. Within the first 12 to 18 months, however, the government was required to negotiate a number of agreements on wages and conditions for significant groups of public sector employees. This process proved to be challenging for both government and unions and posed problems for any commitment to the 'partnership approach' of its own rhetoric. For government, it immediately brought into focus the tension between its fiscal objectives and public sector wages policy. For unions, it required a significant adjustment of their high expectations of a new Labor government following a long period of State government hostility towards unions.

The purpose of this chapter is to review the nature of this counter-revolution of public sector industrial relations in Victoria and assess the extent to which it generated a transformation of public sector industrial relations and workplace practices. This analysis will take account of a number of significant shifts in the context in which this new approach to public sector industrial relations has been implemented which have influenced the implementation of policy. These include:

- on-going wages pressures following a period of suppression and creation of inter-occupational anomalies;
- significant shocks in both the labour supply for key public sector occupational groups and the demand for public sector services;
- unexpected shifts in the budgetary pressures; and
- changed political circumstances.

The chapter provides a brief outline of the concept of 'new public management', which has informed key changes in public sector organisation and management practice over the last decade. Then there is an overview of the political and industrial context faced by the incoming Bracks government following its shock election win in 1999. The next section of the chapter outlines the key reforms in unions and wages policy that had occurred prior to 1999. The section 'Instituting a Partnership Approach' summarises the key elements of the Bracks government's public sector industrial relations policy that was introduced after the October 1999 election, most notably the idea of developing a partnership with public sector unions. The section 'Challenges to Partnership' considers challenges for the partnership approach posed by subsequent industrial relations outcomes and dynamics. 'Reforming the System' outlines the state of public sector industrial relations in Victoria generally in the period 2002-2006, while the concluding section provides an assessment of changes since 1999.

The overall assessment is that whereas the shifts in approach were significant, they represented an *evolutionary* development rather than a fundamental counter-revolution against the more radical ideas associated with new public management. While seeking to take a cooperative approach to wage negotiations, the government's policy framework provided for agreements to be negotiated within the same funding parameters applied by the previous government. The initial changes can also be judged to have met with mixed success, both industrially and in terms of creating a workforce to deliver government service priorities. The incrementalist approach reflected both the terms on which the government was elected and the subsequent challenges it has faced. By 2003, this (partial) transformation had emerged as a coherent alternative to the more extreme model to meet the emerging challenges in public sector industrial relations and workforce planning.

## The Concept of 'New Public Management'

The last two decades to 2006 have been associated with a fundamental shift in the principles of public sector management in all industrialised countries.[2] This had, in turn, been a product of a general reinvention of the role of government, its agencies, the means by which services are delivered, and employment practices within public sector organisations.[3] At its core, this has been associated with a move away from a traditional model of public administration towards variants of the 'new public sector management' model.[4]

The traditional model of public administration, based on the doctrine of the separation of powers, was associated with the delegation of a specific set of functions to public administrators in the implementation of policy and the expenditure of public funds.[5] A central principle associated with this model was the idea that public service employees were independent from the political process.[6] Their role was encapsulated by the maxim of providing advice 'without fear or favour'. This capacity for independent advice was assured through the idea of a career in the public service and explicit norms of behaviour and professional conduct.[7] It has also been presumed that public service employees were less likely to be motivated by extrinsic rewards, more likely to identify with value of service to the public and the provision of public goods, and have a strong commitment to principles of justice, fairness and equity in discharging their duties.[8]

This traditional model of public administration was associated with an expansive view of the role of government, which prevailed throughout much of the twentieth century. This view produced a significant role for government in regulating economic and social relations, owning productive assets and producing goods and services, in a range of areas in the period until the mid to late 1970s. From that time, the role of government and public sector organisations came under sustained scrutiny, with the result that governments privatised production of many goods and services previously seen as the natural domain of government, such as essential services; withdrew from the direct control of production of goods and services funded by the public purse through corporatisation and outsourcing; and encouraged the contestability of markets in which the government had previously been a monopoly producer.

This general reorientation of the role of government has been associated with changes to internal organisational attributes and management practices within public sector organisations. This 'new public management' has shifted the focus from public service to service delivery. The principles associated with new public management have been informed by the idea that public service needs to be more responsive to both the preferences of beneficiaries, citizens who pay for service provision through tax, and politicians who represent the collective will and make policy choices.[9] From this perspective, ministers are seen as analogous to customers,[10] and citizens to consumers.[11] New public management has been informed by economic doctrines that have advocated privatisation, contestability in the delivery of public goods and services and, where possible, the provision of these goods and services through the private sector.[12] For the core public service, this has also been associated with significant reforms to public employment systems and the norms of what constitutes professional public service.[13]

For Australian public service employees, this shift has involved the displacement of core legislative protections associated with independence by 'value statements' and 'codes of ethical conduct', along with protective legislation for whistleblowers.[14] More generally, this shift has occurred within the context of a decentralisation of managerial responsibilities for workforce planning and human resource management to individual departments and agencies. For middle managers, this has meant a significant increase in responsibility for both ensuring probity in managerial practice and dealing with the ethical issues and conflicts that arise in dealing with ministers and stakeholders, the responsible expenditure of public money and the fair and just delivery of services to the community.[15]

## The Political and Industrial Environment

In Victoria, the prescriptions associated with new public management were influential throughout the 1990s.[16] In September 1992, following an extended period of Labor government, a Liberal-National Party coalition government, led by Jeff Kennett, was elected in a landslide. In the period immediately prior to the change of government, Victoria experienced declining economic fortunes. In 1991-2, the state debt stood at 31.5 per cent of Gross State Product and the state's operating deficit was slightly more than $A 2 billion. In addition, the state faced significant unfunded superannuation liabilities and debts which resulted from a failed experiment in seeding industry development through the Tricontinental Bank.[17] The subsequent collapse of Pyramid Building Society based in Victoria's largest regional centre, Geelong, further depressed the state's economy and fuelled declining confidence in the government.

The incoming Kennett Government's agenda, which was outlined in its election manifesto,[18] involved a radical departure from the traditional public administration model that characterised the Victorian public service. In its place, an approach consistent with a strand of 'new public management' that Peters has labelled the 'deregulated state' was quickly implemented.[19] Broadly, these reforms can be summarised as follows:

- the separation of traditional policy development and regulatory functions from service delivery roles of government;
- a shift towards output based funding for Departments and Agencies;
- the introduction of contestability in the delivery of public services where possible to ensure consumers were provided with choice and agencies were responsive.

Consistent with these developments, the Kennett government, where possible, sought to contract out the delivery of services or to privatise.

To enable this new public management approach to government, the Kennett government also introduced significant changes in the structure and responsibilities of individual Departments. In particular, three reforms defined the changing character of public sector management and industrial relations in Victoria.

The first of these reforms involved the consolidation of the number of public service Departments. Departments moved from stand-alone portfolio administrative units to larger organisations clustered around groups of related portfolios. The number of Departments was reduced from 22 in 1992 to just eight in 1996.[20] At the same time, however, this consolidation was countered by a deliberate policy of horizontal disintegration aimed at creating smaller, more focused agencies, often with statutory roles.

Second, the streamlined Departmental structure enabled the introduction of new governance arrangements which defined the relationship between the executive branch of government and the senior bureaucracy. The new approach dismantled traditional governance arrangements and responsibilities, and introduced changes which resembled a standard private sector model associated with publicly listed corporations. The role of government was, under these arrangements, defined as analogous to a company's board of directors. The role of senior bureaucracy was viewed as paralleling that of a company's Chief Executive Officer and senior management team authorised to implement government's 'business strategy'. This relationship was facilitated through the introduction of the State Coordination and Management Committee ('SC&MC') in October 1992, which was comprised of Departmental Secretaries, the Chief Commissioner of Police and the Public Services Commissioner. This body, while not vested with any substantive decision-making power, reinforced the central role of the Secretary of the Department of Premier and Cabinet as the titular head of the public service. Its creation was intended to maximise the coordination of functions and decision-making between departments so as to give proper effect to government's policy decisions.

The third and final significant reform consisted of the diminution of central agencies' role in defining and determining public sector management practices and industrial relations outcomes. This was principally achieved through a concomitant devolution of responsibility to Departments and Agencies for employee recruitment and development, pay systems and performance management and the management of industrial relations. Key to these reforms was the *Public Sector Management Act 1992* (Vic). This legislation devolved responsibility for human resource management to Departmental Secretaries, including the powers to make employment decisions, determine the work value of jobs and promotion, manage disciplinary procedures, redeployment and redundancies. It also introduced fixed term employment contracts for executive officers and allowed for more widespread introduction of non-standard employment arrangements. Implicit within these reforms was that prime responsibility for workforce planning and development lay with Departmental Secretaries.

The Act also defined a limited role for the Office of Public Employment as central agency. Its primary responsibility was in the form of establishing guidelines relating to the discharge of statutory functions under the Act and monitoring adherence to them. The *Public Sector Management and Employment Act 1998* (Vic), which replaced the *Public Sector Management Act 1992* (Vic) and the *Public Authorities (EEO) Act 1990* (Vic), further diminished the role of the Office of Public Employment in prescribing employment and human resource management practices at the Departmental level. This legislation instead outlined key principles of public sector employment, and provided the Commissioner with the capacity to establish a Code of Conduct for Public Sector Employees.

These broad discretionary powers were further augmented in 1994 with the introduction of a broad-banded classification structure and salary scale for non-executive officers. This classification structure consisted of five classifications with no fixed salary points within them, compared with a structure consisting of around 120 separate pay and grading classifications.[21] Officers were appointed at a single point within a scale, and movement within the value ranges that defined a classification was based on performance assessments rather than annual increments or work value assessments. The additional costs associated with basing wage increments on performance were to be funded by Departments and Agencies rather than supplementation.

The extended discretion provided to Departments and Agencies was, however, proscribed by other developments. Most significant was the repeal of the *Industrial Relations Act 1979* (Vic) and its replacement by the *Employee Relations Act 1992* (Vic) (the 'ER Act'). For the first time, this Act placed public sector employees under the same arrangements as private sector employees. The ER Act restricted access to compulsory arbitration of industrial disputes and provided for the introduction of individual employment agreements, which took precedence over collective agreements. While not prescribed, Departments and agencies were strongly encouraged to adopt individual employment agreements.[22] A second stage of reform in 1994 involved the abolition of some 240 state Awards and their replacement with 19 industry sectors.[23] On application from either employees or employers, the State Employee Relations Commissioner was vested with the power to determine minimum wages for occupational groups covered by these industry sectors. On 10 November 1996, however, the Victorian Government repealed the ER Act and referred its industrial powers to the Commonwealth.[24] To counter the expected effects of the ER Act, the CPSU sought and gained an interim federal award in December 1996. Following the referral of powers in 1996, state public service employees continued to be covered by a federal award.

## The Transformation of Public Sector Unions and Wage Bargaining

The previous section described the institutional changes introduced after 1992 and before 1999. These developments represented a fundamental shift in the conduct of public sector industrial relations and wage-setting, the management of people and use of human resource practices, as well as and the institutional arrangements which governed them. By the time it was elected in late 1999, the Bracks government faced a highly decentralised industrial relations approach in the public sector, characterised by high (although varying) levels of individualisation of wage bargaining and conditions of employment, and significant differentiation in outcomes between Departments.

In addition to these institutional developments, other features of public sector industrial relations require consideration, notably the role of public sector unionism. Coverage in the public sector fell to a relatively large number of unions (see Table 1), although within the public service the main union remained the Victorian branch of the CPSU.

Following the September 1992 election, the Kennett government adopted a hostile approach to dealing with public sector unions. It refused to consult over public employment policy issues and encouraged Departments and Agencies to take the same approach in relation to workplace change issues. As noted above, individual Departments and Agencies were encouraged to utilise individual employment agreements — and later AWAs — as widely as possible. Automatic payroll deduction of union dues was prohibited for public service Departments and resulted in a significant decline in union membership. As part of the process of consolidation, and in response to the public debt crisis faced by the government, large scale workforce reductions were instituted over a relatively short period of time, further diminishing the capacity of the CPSU and other public sector unions to use industrial muscle to resolve disputes with government. (This was substantially less evident for some specific occupational groups, such as nurses).

## Table 1 Unions with coverage in the Victorian Public Sector, 1999

| |
|---|
| Association of Professional Engineers, Scientists and Managers Australia (APESMA) |
| Australian Education Union (AEU) |
| Australian Liquor, Hospitality and Miscellaneous Workers Union (ALHMWU) |
|    - Ambulance Employees Association of Victoria |
| Australian Medical Association (AMA) |
| Australian Services Union (ASU) |
|    - Local Authorities Division |
|    - Victorian Services and Supply Division |
| Australian Workers' Union (AWU) |
| Community and Public Sector Union (CPSU) |
| Media, Entertainment and Arts Alliance (MEAA) |
| Health Services Union of Australia, No.1 Branch (HSUA No. 1) |
| HSUA No.2 (Health and Community Services Union) |
| HSUA No.3 (Australian Health Professionals Association) |
| HSUA No. 4 (Association of Hospital Pharmacists) |
| HSUA No 5 (Health and Community Services Association) |
| National Tertiary Education Union (NTEU) |
| The Police Association (TPA) |
| United Firefighters Union (UFU) |

Along with a hostile approach to unions, the Kennett government's response to Victoria's fiscal crisis involved vigorous attempts to maintain wage increases at low levels and to break traditional relativities. This remained its approach for the entire period of its administration. The inevitable outcome was that some groups, particularly those with limited industrial capacity, had experienced a substantial decline in wage outcomes relative to other states and traditional comparators.

By the end of 1998, however, this policy had resulted in a number of emergent issues, which, arguably, would have required a significant change to the government's industrial approach had the Kennett government been re-elected. First, Victorian public sector unions had sought and gained federal award coverage for their members. This naturally created a greater tendency for outcomes which took account of interstate comparisons. Second, in a number of key occupational groups, most notably nurses and teachers, labour supply had become increasingly difficult to secure. In the case of nurses, the relatively inferior interstate wage was reinforced by an emerging global nursing shortage. Again this inevitably created wage pressure by the time the Bracks government had won office.[25] Third, and finally, the initial negative impact on public sector union membership had turned around, giving rise to a growing capacity to mobilise a willing membership and use industrial pressure in the process of wage negotiations. This was particularly true of nurses, teachers, police and other emergency services. Significantly, these groups make up the vast majority of the State Government workforce and wages costs.

By 1999, then, a vastly different public sector had been created. It reflected the core characteristics associated with the model of 'new public management' and 'marketisation' that had emerged in the United States and the United Kingdom during the 1980s;[26] its overall size had been substantially reduced by workforce reductions, outsourcing and privatisation; wage bargaining had become highly decentralised or individualised;[27] and the institutions governing employment practices had largely been recast to support a system intended to converge with private sector practice.

Not surprisingly, public sector unions held high expectations of the incoming Labor government's reform agenda. These expectations were not restricted to institutional issues such as reform of wage outcomes to restore interstate relativities, although these clearly had central importance. The unions also expected the government to take a more open and consultative approach to dealing with them over industrial issues, workforce development and planning and service delivery requirements which inevitably impacted on both of these. In the next section, I consider the new government's attempt to respond in this climate.

## Instituting a Partnership Approach

The unexpected election result of October 1999 did not provide the incoming Bracks government with a workable mandate capable of supporting the ambitious reforms that were demanded by unions. The government's majority in the Legislative Assembly was dependent on the support of three independents, while in the Legislative Council, it fell well short of a majority by 16 seats.[28] Its minority status severely restricted its capacity to give effect to its election agenda. In relation to private sector industrial relations, the government's initial intentions were to request the federal government to amend Schedule 1A provisions of the *Workplace Relations Act 1996* (Cth), which covered Victorian employees not otherwise covered by federal awards, in order to bring general conditions into line with that in other States.[29] However, following a refusal by the federal government to do so on terms acceptable to it, the Victorian government sought to withdrawal its referral of power to the Commonwealth and re-establish a State tribunal system. The Fair Employment Bill 2001 (Vic), however, foundered in the Legislative Council and no State system was able to be re-established.

In contrast to its stalled attempt to bring reform to arrangements covering private sector employees in Victoria, the Bracks government took immediate steps to reshape public sector industrial relations. Its capacity to do so reflected constitutional limits on the capacity of the Federal Government to directly regulate the employment conditions of state public sector employees,[30] and the general discretion of government to make significant changes within existing statutory provisions governing public employment in Victoria.

The Bracks government took two key decisions, which signalled public sector industrial relations reform was to be a key policy objective for government. First, it announced that all individual work agreements with public service employees would not be renewed and a collective agreement would be negotiated to cover the public service (see below). Second, it also established an Industrial Relations Subcommittee of Cabinet immediately following its election. This subcommittee was delegated the responsibility for the development and implementation of government's industrial relations policy framework, subject to full Cabinet approval. These decisions were also billed by government as the beginning of a new approach to managing industrial relations and workplace issues, based on partnership with unions. In broad terms, the intention was to bring unions into decision-making processes, to provide them with both adequate information about the parameters within which government needed to work and an opportunity to have input into the large policy issues affecting public sector employees as well as workplace change matters.

## The Partnership Agreement: An Example of the Government's Approach

This policy of partnership was given effect in a number of ways. To begin, the government withdrew from proceedings before the Australian Industrial Relations Commission (initiated by the Kennett government) that had followed a breakdown in negotiations between the government and the CPSU over the establishment of an enterprise agreement covering public servants. Following this, it quickly reached a Partnership Agreement with the CPSU.[31] The agreement was seen as a landmark development in that it attempted to give effect to three outcomes critical to re-establishing the government's relationship with public sector unions.

First, it recognised the CPSU as the major representative body of public service employees and required Departments and agencies to negotiate with the CPSU in setting wages and conditions. Clause 8 of the Partnership Agreement (the 'Agreement') stated that:

> The purpose of this [Agreement] is to create the framework enabling the implementation of Partnerships for High Performance. It creates the foundation and establishes the principles for subsequent... agreements... The purpose of this [Agreement] is to establish a partnership between the Victorian Government, its employees and the CPSU.[32]

The Agreement also sought to gain a union commitment to assist the government in resolving tensions which it faced in ensuring that public services were delivered on an on-going basis and in a fiscally responsible and sustainable manner. Clause 8 stated:

The parties acknowledge that:

- government policy is to be implemented;
- quality services are to be delivered; and
- fiscal responsibility is a high priority as is maintaining the integrity of Agency budgets.[33]

The parties committed themselves to responding to these challenges by working together to effect workplace change. Clause 18 of the Agreement required that the CPSU and employees were to be advised 'as soon as practicable' of any proposal to introduce workplace change, the rationale for the changes and the intended benefits.[34] It also required that, prior to implementing any major restructure or change to work practices, management would provide the CPSU with an opportunity to submit any alternative proposals. If the alternative were not accepted, the Agency was required to give just cause. Should a dispute ensue about the reasons given for this rejection, the Agreement sets a dispute settlement procedure to determine which proposal should proceed. In all, this clause provided the CPSU with an opportunity to participate in the decisions creating change.

The second major achievement of the Partnership Agreement concerned the relationship it established between Departments or agencies and central government. As was noted earlier, the *Public Sector Management and Employment Act 1998* (Vic), which was operating at the time, designated Departmental Secretaries as the 'employers' of public service employees and responsible for the determination of wages and conditions for departmental staff. This decentralised approach meant that each department or agency held primary responsibility for enterprise agreements. This in turn meant that, over time, wage movements for specific classifications varied from agency to agency. This formal responsibility was not altered by legislative amendment, but by agreement. The Partnership Agreement, which was reached with the unanimous agreement of (and formally signed by) all Department Secretaries, effectively introduced more centralised, or at least co-ordinated, wage bargaining between departments and agencies. Thus, while central agencies assumed some responsibility for concluding wage agreements, Departments and agencies were left to deal with implementing aspects of such agreements, negotiating productivity based wage increased within predetermined limits, and dealing with industrial matters specific to the agency.

This 'tight-loose' arrangement established by the bargaining framework was reflected in arrangements governing the management of industrial relations at the agency/workplace level. The framework continued to delegate responsibility for managing industrial issues within a Department to the Department Head. However, it also appointed Industrial Liaison Officers within Departments whose responsibility it was to ensure the core policy principles were reflected in Departmental practice.

The final change which the Partnership Agreement sought to give effect to was a reversal of the changes to the career structure instituted during the Kennett years. Given the potential budgetary implications, this issue was not directly addressed in this agreement. Instead, both parties agreed to establish a Career Structure and Work Organisation Review.[35] This review was to be completed during the life of the Partnership Agreement. The broad intention was to reintroduce elements of a independent career public service, which had been eroded over the previous decade. External consultants were commissioned to review the existing career structure, and a final report (the Wright Report) was provided to government in 2001.[36] A new agreed pay and classification structure, based on the recommendations of the Wright Report, was not implemented until 2003. This structure remains in place under the existing Victoria Public Service Enterprise Agreement (2006).[37]

## Challenges to Partnership

The achievements of the 2000 interim Partnership Agreement were, in retrospect, substantial. However, the arrangement left unresolved a number of important issues which, over the remainder of the first term of the Labor government, proved to present major challenges to the original intentions of the government's policy framework. These issues emerged quickly as the government faced the renegotiation of a number of major agreements in health, education, police and emergency services.

Most important among these issues were:

- unmet union expectations;
- an unsustainable demographic profile of public sector employment, and emerging labour supply shortages for key occupational groups, specifically nurses and teachers; and
- an adversarial approach to change at the workplace level.

## Union Wage Expectations

While the government sought to maintain a fiscally responsible position — which had been a hallmark of the previous administration — unions expected and sought to achieve a significant funding boost in their respective areas of coverage in the public sector, both in terms of employment levels and wage outcomes. It was also noted above that during the period of the Kennett Government, significant wage anomalies and pressures had emerged. These represented legacy issues which unions expected to be rectified. What subsequently emerged was a wage negotiation dynamic in which individual unions vigorously pursued their own wages and conditions in isolation. While most agreements were reached without extended industrial action, the government was forced to implement its wage policy principles inconsistently. Moreover, these agreements were not adequately integrated into a coherent approach that supported the government's public sector reform agenda or service delivery objectives.[38]

## The Demographic Profile of Public Sector Employment

The Victorian Public Service ('VPS') is made up of 20 organisations with around 28,000 staff, while the larger public sector comprises 240 organisations and employs around 185,000 persons. Of these, the health and education sectors account for around 80 per cent of the Government's total wages bill. Around two-thirds of all employees are female, reflecting the high proportion of women within the nursing and teaching professions.[39]

It was noted above that a key reform introduced during the Kennett government involved the creation of a broad-banded classification structure for public servants and other public sector occupations. The operation of this structure, in the absence of annual or work value-based increments, inevitably resulted in declining pay relativities. This, in turn, resulted in a number of predictable outcomes. As the VPS became increasingly unattractive as an employment option, agencies found it increasingly difficult to hire and retain staff.[40] This was, in turn associated with a break down of career paths and the traditionally strong internal labour market structures. Currently, approximately two-thirds of all public service appointments are made from external candidates A direct implication is that the VPS now spends significantly more resources on training and recruitment.

A further consequence is reflected in the age structure of the VPS, which is now heavily skewed to older workers: about 30 per cent of the Victorian public sector is older than 50 years; and the median age for males and females stands at 39 and 45 years, respectively.[41] Around 20 per cent of the female VPS employees are under 30 years of age, with a similar figure aged more than 50 years. In the case of men, 11.5 per cent of VPS employees are aged under 30, while around one-third of male VPS employees are now aged over 50 years.[42] This is reflected in developments in the broader public sector. In 2005, the average age of the employees in the Victorian public sector was 42 years; this compared with an average of 41.2 and 39.5 years in 2000 and 1998 respectively.[43]

These demographic issues create future labour supply issues for government and a potential wage blowout to attract large numbers to the public sector. In the broader public sector, labour supply shortages arose even earlier in significant ways in key sectors such as education and health. During the 1990s, a worldwide shortage of nurses had emerged and many Australian nurses were attracted to the United Kingdom in particular by the prospect of higher relative pay. The aging demographic profile of teachers, along with a declining capacity to attract young teachers into the system (particularly young men) had similarly posed an ongoing problem. In these areas, the government faced the prospect of either responding through agreement or having unions use the AIRC to prosecute their claims, as had occurred in other States.

## Adversarial Culture of Public Sector Industrial Relations

Relations between state governments and public sector unions have traditionally operated on a comparatively adversarial basis. As noted above, this dynamic was intensified during the Kennett period in which the CPSU and other unions were viewed as external parties. This has perhaps created a longer lasting effect on the way in which unions deal with agencies. Similarly, some Departments and agencies that for the first time in seven years have had to deal with unions found it difficult to adjust. The ongoing non-consultative approach deployed in some high profile instances has generated a low trust dynamic. Some agencies sought to continue the approach instituted by the previous government including the use of AWAs, common law contracts or non-union enterprise agreements made under the *Workplace Relations Act 1996* (Cth). This undermined the general principles of the government's policy direction. It also exposed the inherent tension in retaining a decentralised delegation of management responsibility, whilst seeking to impose centrally determined wages policy and industrial relations policy direction. Needless to say, it also created a source of ongoing tension between unions and government.[44]

## Reforming the System

### 2002-2004

The issues outlined above were emerging prior to the change of government in 1999, but were also reinforced during the first term of the Bracks government. This in part reflected the general fiscal conservatism inherited by the Bracks government and an overriding concern to avoid the problems associated with the Cain-Kirner years of Labor government. The Bracks administration was, understandably, guided by the overall aim of achieving improved service delivery outcomes in a fiscally responsible and sustainable manner. This concern has driven subsequent developments within the industrial relations policy framework. In order to achieve this, the original policy framework has evolved in a number of ways. This section focuses on describing the key elements which together constitute a revised policy framework implemented in the second term of the Bracks Government.

The core challenge for government was the need to take the partnership route, maximise its capacity to be an 'employer of choice' and, at the same time, realistically meet service delivery objectives within funding constraints. The policy and strategic planning hierarchy for meeting these objectives was:

1. the identification of the government's long-term policy priorities;
2. the determination of longer-term service delivery objectives;
3. the definition of consequent workforce requirements to achieve these objectives; and
4. the development and implementation of industrial relations strategy which facilitate the deployment of this workforce.

During the first year of the second term of the Bracks government (ie 2002-3), some key arrangements were established — they sought to align wages policy, workforce planning and development policy, and industrial relations policy in a way that reflected this policy hierarchy. Specifically, these arrangements included:

1. a Public Sector Industrial Relations Framework which linked enterprise agreement outcomes to service delivery and budgetary objectives, facilitated through high level communications between unions and government and, which sought to ensure that Departments and agencies have the capability to manage industrial relations change at the workplace level;
2. a strategic approach to workforce planning at the Department level, supported by a corporate workforce planning capability;
3. a Governance Framework for overseeing, planning and negotiating key enterprise agreements, including the establishment of a Subcommittee of the Expenditure Review Committee of Cabinet, to ensure central agencies and portfolio Departments work collaboratively to develop strategies in each sector that are conducive to the achievement of policy objectives; and
4. a wages policy which sets parameters within which portfolio Departments and agencies plan service delivery, workforce development and the management of workplace change and industrial relations to meet these objectives.

## Public Sector Industrial Relations Framework

In early 2002, the government endorsed the development and implementation of a revised public sector wages policy and industrial relations framework. This framework consisted of the following elements:

- a process for government and public sector unions to establish a working relationship within which industrial relations and workforce issues can be discussed on an on-going basis;
- a planned and differentiated approach to wage negotiations which links wage outcomes to service delivery objectives;
- a consultative approach to managing workplace change; and

- a review of current budget processes, to ensure that consideration of wage and workforce considerations and the annual review of Departmental budgets are complementary to each other.

The process for establishing a working relationship between unions and government at the peak level has been developed through the negotiation of a Public Sector Framework Agreement with public sector unions and, as part of that Agreement, the establishment of a Public Sector Industrial Relations Committee consisting of government and union representatives.

## Workforce Planning

In 2002, the Office of Workforce Development ('OWD') was established within the Department of Premier and Cabinet. The primary function of the OWD was to provide government with a corporate capability to identify key workforce challenges for the Victorian Public Sector and to assist Departments plan and develop workforce profiles required to achieve longer-term service delivery objectives. A key component of the OWD's activities centred on the development, negotiation and implementation of a revised VPS classification structure.

## Governance Framework for Negotiations in Key Sectors

In early 2003, the government endorsed a governance model for managing the planning and negotiation of Enterprise Agreements for key occupational groups (Public Service, Health and Education sectors). This model comprised the following:

1. The establishment of a Public Sector Industrial Relations Subcommittee of the Expenditure Review Committee of Cabinet to:
   - monitor and oversee the implementation of government's industrial relations and wages policy framework;
   - ensure structural arrangements and Departmental roles and responsibilities which maximise the government's capacity to plan strategically and manage industrial negotiations; and
   - ensure portfolio Departments strategically plan and manage negotiations in a manner that meets the government's expectations, addresses workforce development and service delivery objectives and wages policy objectives.
2. The establishment of Leadership Groups, chaired by the relevant Department Secretary and consisting of representatives from the relevant central agencies (ie the Department of Treasury and Finance, the Department of Premier and Cabinet and Industrial Relations Victoria) and relevant portfolio Departments, to oversee the Departmental level planning process and development of a negotiation strategy; and

3.    The formation of negotiation teams, led by the relevant Department, to carry out negotiations in a manner consistent with government policy and the approved negotiation strategy.

## Wages Policy Parameters

The 2003/4 Budget foreshadowed the introduction of a new funding model based on agreed output prices determined as part of the budget process introduced in 2004/5. As part of the 2003/4 budget process, the government also approved a transitional policy to apply to 2003/4. In outline, this transitional policy had three elements:

*   maintenance of real wages by providing supplementation at the projected rate of inflation (2.25%);
*   additional supplementation of up to 0.75% for tangible service delivery agreed to by government; and
*   further increases funded by Departmental productivity offsets/savings that are real and sustainable.

## Outcomes of the Revised Policy Framework

The revised policy framework was subject to the challenge of implementation during the process of negotiating major agreements in 2002/3. Three key agreements — covering public service employees, teachers, and nurses — have been renegotiated with only limited industrial action and recourse to arbitration. Nonetheless, it is not clear that the agreements have been reached without some compromise to wages policy principles outlined by government prior to negotiations. It is difficult to determine the extent to which all elements have been effectively implemented and, specifically, whether government has been able to successfully implement its stringent wages policy parameters. It will be some time before the effectiveness of these agreements can be fully assessed.

## Formalising the Reforms, 2004-2006

Despite this, a litmus test of the early success of the model, and the government's commitment to it, is evident in its willingness to formalise these reforms through legislative amendment. Following a review of the *Public Sector Management and Employment Act 1998* (Vic), this Act was repealed in December 2004. Its replacement, the *Public Administration Act 2004* (Vic), in effect refined and formalised many of the more evolutionary developments described so far.

Most importantly, it created the machinery to facilitate what was earlier described as a 'tight-loose' model of workforce planning and industrial relations. The most important reform has been the establishment of the State Services Authority ('SSA'), which subsumes the functions the Office of Public Employment and the

Office of Workforce Development (both of which were located within the Department of Premier and Cabinet). The SSA is charged with five related roles:

1. service integration and development;
2. standards and equity;
3. workforce development and planning;
4. establishing and overseeing standards for governance of public agencies;
5. maintaining an electronic register of the use of any instruments provided under the Act.[45]

In effect, the new arrangements provide a formal governance mechanism for organising and overseeing the machinery of government, including the responsibilities of workforce planning and management functions. It should however be noted that this does not imply a re-centralisation of public sector industrial relations and management functions. These responsibilities still remain with individual departments and agencies. These new arrangements, however, allow the government to conduct system reviews of organisational and workforce issues with Departments with a view to co-ordinating change across key areas of service delivery.[46] The arrangements also allow the SSA, at the request of the government, to review Departments or agencies and their activities, and if required, assume responsibility for them, and initiate reform before re-delegating responsibility back to the agency.[47] The Public Sector Standards Commissioner independently performs the function of promoting in the public sector high standards of integrity and conduct, with overseeing by the SSA.

## Conclusions

The aim of this chapter is to outline the implementation of an ambitious reform of the Victorian industrial relations and workforce planning framework covering public sector employees. The context in which these reforms were devised and implemented was an unexpected election win for the Bracks Labor Government in 1999. The previous government, led by Jeff Kennett, had introduced sweeping changes to public sector organisations, many of which challenged traditional principles of public sector administration.

These reforms were heavily influenced by a more radical version of new public sector management which, in turn, had been based on a free market ideology and an almost axiomatic belief that private sector organisation was a preferred model to carry out most public sector functions. Central to these reforms were changes in workplace organisation, management styles and industrial relations, including delegation of managerial responsibilities to the agency level, decentralisation of wage bargaining, and the wholesale individualisation of employment arrangements. These changes were associated with significant restructure in the organisation of public sector functions, as well as privatisation and outsourcing of service delivery previously undertaken by public sector employees.

While these changes have been associated with a number of positive outcomes, the manner in which the Kennett government pursued reform also created unsustainable pressures on employment arrangements, the capacity of public organisations to recruit and retain capable employees, and wage anomalies which did not reflect market conditions. This was particularly evident in relation to a number of key occupational groups where labour shortages had emerged due to demographic shifts in the workforce and worldwide shortages.

On gaining office, the Bracks government sought to re-orient industrial relations and wages policy significantly. In particular, it sought to implement what it termed a 'partnership approach'. In practice, this new approach involved a mix of both the Kennett reforms and a return to elements of the collective industrial relations deployed by previous state Labor governments.

This mix was evident in two key respects. First, while the new enterprise agreement (or Partnership Agreement) with unions covering public service employees reintroduced union recognition and institutionalised avenues for union involvement in wage bargaining and workplace change, it also sought to commit unions to recognise the inevitable tension faced by governments in balancing fiscal responsibility with its social objectives of providing appropriate employment conditions. Fiscal responsibilities and service delivery were to take precedence over those industrial obligations which unions felt a Labor government might have to their natural constituents. Second, the Bracks government retained the practice of delegating managerial responsibility to the agency level. This inevitably created tensions with a more centralised process of wage bargaining and dealing with industrial matters introduced after 1999.

The success of this process is, at this stage, difficult to fully appreciate or determine. This is so for a number of reasons. First, a number of legacy issues from the Kennett era remain points of contention between public sector unions and government. While many are still being 'worked through', some are unlikely to be resolved due to differences in views as to the appropriate way to proceed. Second, there remains a range of key issues which are in some respects difficult for state government to control or significantly influence, such as demographic changes in the general labour force, and shortages in key occupational groups, notably nurses and teachers. Improved wages and conditions alone are unlikely to deal with these problems.

Inevitably, all of this has meant that the partnership approach, which in its infancy seemed to be clearly articulated in key documents, such as the Partnership Agreement, has been subject to political forces and change. On the one hand, the prospect of a fiscal blowout remains a key concern and driver of government decision-making. This resulted in far more stringent wages policy parameters, which were implemented in 2002-3. On the other hand, however, it is not yet clear how effectively these parameters have been implemented, but it does appear that despite public rhetoric, the government has been willing to make concessions to avoid industrial unrest and in order to address anomalies. This pragmatism is hardly surprising. Nonetheless, the Victorian government's willingness to formalise the 'tight-loose' it has evolved to management of industrial relations and workforce management is perhaps an early indication of its success.

Unions have also found the new environment a challenging one. After a period of hostile government, it has not proved easy to work collaboratively with government at a central level, intent on avoiding the stereotyped view that Labor governments cannot manage budgets responsibly. Nor has it been easy for unions at the workplace level, dealing with managers who had previously been responsible for implementing government's policy of union exclusion and individualisation. The political response has been an attempt to bring unions into the fold through the development of a Memorandum of Understanding between government and public sector unions and the creation of a joint committee to work through issues of contention between government and unions. The most recent Agreement, which extends the 2004 VPS Agreement, again indicates that unions (and government) have proved capable of overcoming the inevitable political realities of the day and establishes a new partnership approach that enables the ever present tensions between fiscal responsibility and meeting union wage demands a manageable one.[48]

# ENDNOTES

[1] The 'public service' is defined as those public sector organisations directly involved in the production of policy advice and implementation of policy for the government of the day. The public service includes government departments as well as a substantial number of statutory agencies with specific responsibilities. These departments and agencies were covered at that time by the *Public Sector Management and Employment Act 1998* (Vic). The public sector, in contrast, is defined as the broader group of public owned or funded organisations involved in the delivery of goods or services. See now *Public Administration Act 2004* (Vic).

[2] See generally OECD, *Issues and Developments in Public Management: Survey 1997* (1997); Donald F Kettl, 'Public Administration at the Millennium: The State of the Field' (2000) 10 *Journal of Public Administration Research and Theory* 7.

[3] Michael Barzelay, *The New Public Management: Improving Research and Policy Dialogue*.

[4] Andrew Stark, 'What is the New Public Management?' (2002) 12 *Journal of Public Administration Research and Theory* 137.

[5] Kenneth Kernaghan and John W Langford, *The Responsible Public Servant* (1990).

[6] Christopher Hood, 'A Public Management for All Seasons?' (1991) 69 *Public Administration* 3, 8.

[7] Noel Preston, 'Public Sector Ethics in Australia: A Review' (1995) 54 *Australian Journal of Public Administration* 462.

[8] John Stewart and Kieron Walsh, 'Change in the Management of Public Services' (1992) 70 *Public Administration* 499; Brian Young, Stephen Worchel and David Woehr, 'Organizational Commitment Among Public Service Employees' (1998) 27 *Public Personnel Management* 339; Carole Jurkiewicz, 'Generation X and the Public Employee' (2000) 29 *Public Personnel Management* 55.

[9] John Alford, 'The Implications of "Publicness" in Strategic Management Theory' in Gerry Johnson and Kevan Scholes (eds), *Exploring Public Sector Strategy* (2001) 1; Paul du Gay, 'How Responsible is "Responsive Government?"' (2002) 31 *Economy and Society* 461; John Rohr, *Public Service, Ethics and Constitutional Practice* (1998).

[10] John Alford, 'Defining the Client in the Public Sector: A Social Exchange Perspective' (2002) 62 *Public Administration Review* 337.

[11] Kieron Walsh, 'Citizens and Consumers: Marketing and Public Sector Management' (1991) 11 *Public Money and Management* 9.

[12] Barzelay, above n 3.

[13] Andrew Dunsire, 'Then and Now: Public Administration, 1953-1999' (1999) 47 *Political Studies* 360; Rohr, above n 9.

[14] Preston, above n 7.

[15] Senate Finance and Public Administration Committee, Parliament of Australia, *Recruitment and Training in the Australian Public Service* (2003).

[16] John Alford and Deirdre O'Neill (eds), *The Contract State: Public Management and the Kennett Government* (1994); Mark Considine and Martin Painter (eds), *Managerialism: The Great Debate* (1997).

[17] Alford and O'Neill, above n 16.

[18] Liberal Party of Australia, Victorian Branch, *The Liberal — National Coalition Approach to Debt and Public Management* (1992).

[19] Guy Peters, *The Future of Governing: Four Emerging Models* (1996).

[20] Ciaran O'Faircheallaigh, John Wanna and Patrick Weller, *Public Sector Management in Australia* (1999).

[21] In addition to the VPS structure, a number of Department-specific classification arrangements were retained, but were also based on the same broad-banding arrangements.

[22] The Act also contained a number of statutory minima, including four weeks' paid annual leave, one week paid sick leave, 12 months unpaid maternity/paternity/adoption leave, long service leave, minimum periods for dismissal, and grievance and dispute settlement procedures. See Marilyn Pittard, 'Fundamental Transformation of Employee Relations in Victoria' (1993) 21 *Australian Business Law Review* 220; and Carol Fox, WA Howard and M Pittard, *Industrial Relations in Australia: Development, Law and Operation* (Longman, 1995) ch 12.

[23] *Employee Relations (Amendment) Act 1994* (Vic).

[24] This referral involved complementary legislation at both the State and Commonwealth level: the *Commonwealth Powers (Industrial Relations Act) 1996* (Vic) and the *Workplace Relations and other Legislation Amendment Act (No 2) 1996* (Cth). See Marilyn Pittard, 'The Labour Relations Power in the Constitution and Public Sector Employees', chapter in HP Lee and G Winterton (eds) *Australian Constitutional Landmarks* (Cambridge University Press, 2003) 355.

[25] Expansion of supply remains largely out of State Governments' control as the Federal Government is responsible for determining the number of places available in nursing programs at universities.

[26] Considine and Painter, above n 16.

[27] Peter Salway, 'Reform of Human Resource Management in a Public Service: The Victorian Experience' in Colin Clarke and David Corbett (eds), *Reforming the Public Sector: Problems and Solutions* (1999) 12.

[28] In the Legislative Assembly, the distribution of seats was as follows: ALP 44; Independent 3; Liberal/National Party 41. The distribution of seats in the Legislative Council was as follows: ALP 14; Liberal Party 24; National Party 6.

[29] Schedule 1A was enacted following a referral of industrial powers to the Commonwealth by the Kennett Government after the election of the Howard Government in 1996: see Marilyn Pittard, 'Victorian Industrial Relations: From Deregulation to Devolution' in Dennis Nolan, *The Australasian Labour Law Reforms: Australia and New Zealand at the End of the Twentieth Century* 172.

[30] See George Williams, *Labour Law and the Constitution* (1998).

[31] The 2000 Partnership Agreement was negotiated in a period of around six weeks, involved no industrial action, no recourse to the tribunal, and minimal legal cost.

[32] *Victorian Public Sector (Non-Executive Staff) Agreement 2001* clause 7.1-7.4.

[33] *Victorian Public Sector (Non-Executive Staff) Agreement 2001* clause 8.1.

[34] *Victorian Public Sector (Non-Executive Staff) Agreement 2001* clause 18.

[35] *Victorian Public Sector (Non-Executive Staff) Agreement 2001* clause 11.

[36] M Wright, *Classification and Pay Review — Non Executive Classifications Victorian Public Service* (2001).

[37] For details of the new classificatory system, see the current Victorian Public Service Enterprise Agreement 2006. This Agreement took effect from 1 March 2006 and replaces the 2004 agreement, which was not due to expire until 2007. Under the terms of the Agreement, the CPSU sought and obtained agreement to extend the existing agreement. There were a number of reasons for both parties to extend the agreement, not least of which has been the *Workplace Relations Amendment (Work Choices) Act 2005* (Cth) and the November 2006 state election. The terms of this Agreement are available at *Victorian Public Service Agreement 2006* (2006) BusinessVictoria <http://www.business.vic.gov.au/BUSVIC/STANDARD //PC_61258.html> [July 2007].

[38] A useful 'counterfactual' concerns the likely outcomes of these negotiations had no change of government occurred. Realistically, it could be argued that these wage pressures would have been present irrespective of the government in power.

[39] Wright (2001), above n 36. This remains the general level — see State Services Authority Fact Sheet No. 5 in Publications, December 2006 <www.ssa.vic.gov.au> [July 2007].

[40] The State Services Authority reports that turnover has increased steadily since the 1990s to around 7.5 per cent in 2005: <www.ssa.vic.gov.au/ResearchPublications>.

[41] State Services Authority <www.ssa.vic.gov.au/ResearchPublications>, [June 2006]; and State Services Authority Fact Sheet December 2006, above n 39.

[42] State Services Authority website <www.ssa.vic.gov.au/Research Publications>, [June 2006].

[43] Wright, above n 36. (for 2000 and 1998) and States Services Authority website <www.ssa.vic.gov.au/ResearchPublications>, [June 2006].

[44] This tension appears to have subsided over time, but in some areas remains a source of contention between Government and public sector unions.

[45] State Services Authority, *About the State Services Authority* (2006) State Services Authority <http://www.ssa.vic.gov.au/CA2571410025903D/ WebObj/Factsheet01/$File/Factsheet01.pdf> [June 2006]. See also State Services Authority Annual Report 2005-2006, <www.ssa.vic.gov.au> [July 2007].

[46] Peter Harmsworth, 'State Services Authority Launch' (Speech delivered at the State Services Authority Launch, 18 May 2005.

[47] See *Public Administration Act 2004* (Vic), particularly pt 4. See also Harmsworth, above n 46.

[48] The Victorian state government's responses to federal changes under the *Workplace Relations Amendment (Work Choices) Act 2005* (Cth) are addressed in chapter 11 in this volume.

# Chapter Nine

# Reconstructing State Employment in New Zealand

## Jane Bryson and Gordon Anderson

## Introduction

New Zealand, in common with much of the developed world, spent a decade or so deconstructing its traditional public sector structures. Throughout the late 1980s and 1990s the New Zealand public sector entered a brave new world of public management. These reforms were derived from the United Kingdom experience during the Thatcher years, where neo-classical economic ideals dominated. The reforms were therefore typified by the theories of public choice, agency and transaction cost economics. The application of these theories in New Zealand radically altered the systems of institutional, organisational and management control within the public sector, with the aim of creating a more efficient, transparent and performance oriented public sector. The New Zealand reforms have been widely noted as remarkable for their clarity of vision, comprehensive coverage and ideologically driven nature.[1] They catapulted 'a small country in a peripheral geographical location'[2] into a key destination on the public management visitors' tourist circuit. The reforms have been subject to a range of evaluations and scrutiny highlighting their advantages, disadvantages and unintended consequences.[3] Many commentators note that the reforms have resulted in major management and efficiency gains, but that they have not been without cost. Among those costs have been a number of downsides in the state sector employment environment. Given that the underlying structural reforms are now over a decade old, their longer-term consequences have become more apparent. Over recent years, and especially following the election of Labour governments in late 1999 and 2002, there has been an ongoing evaluation of the effects of reform and a move towards greater fine-tuning of the new system in the light of the lessons of that evaluation. This chapter is concerned primarily with the management and employment aspects of both the original reforms and of the current evaluation.

## The State Sector before Reform

New Zealand's modern state sector arrangements can be dated from 1912 when the *Public Service Act* of that year first established a coherent structure for state service[4] employment. Before 1912 the state service was disorganised, subject to political influence and patronage: a time described by one writer as 'an incredibly dark and dismal period for the career service, for efficient government and for personnel policies'.[5] The 1912 Act was intended to create a professional, unified career-based public service. Central to the Act was the creation of the office of Public Service Commissioner who stood between the politicians and the public service, who acted as the employing authority for the state service and who had overall responsibility for the efficient and economical operation of the service. The 1912 Act introduced a number of features which were to continue as the cornerstones of the state sector until the reforms of the late 1980s.[6] These included:

- The elimination of direct political influence on matters related to individual employment. This was achieved through the statutory delegation of responsibility for personnel matters to the Commissioner. The legislation included an obligation that the Commissioner 'in matters relating to decisions on individual employees... shall not be responsible to the Minister but shall act independently'.[7] This formulation is retained in s 5 of the current *State Sector Act 1988* for all state employers, which also makes it an offence to attempt to influence the employer in respect of such matters.[8]
- The introduction of a system of occupational classifications 'according to the nature of the duties required to be performed'[9] and the placement of state servants on the appropriate grade. This led to a detailed and rigid occupational structure operating across the state sector, subject to appeal and review.
- Detailed statutory personnel provisions covering appointments, promotions, transfers and disciplinary matters.
- A merit based appointment system but one which gave existing public servants priority over external applicants, who had to demonstrate 'clearly more merit' than an internal applicant.[10]
- An appeal system allowed for appeals against grading decisions, non-appointment, non-promotion and the like as well as disciplinary actions. The Appeals Board was chaired by a magistrate and had one member nominated by the Commission and two by the main service union, the Public Service Association (PSA).

Originally this structure made no provision for employee involvement in the determination of pay and conditions. State sector employees were excluded from access to the arbitration system, which allowed collective participation in the private sector, and had no bargaining rights with the Commissioner. This situation was remedied with the passage of the New Zealand *Government Services Tribunal Act 1948*. This Act and its successors set up a parallel system of industrial relations for the state sector. The system provided for the determination of the full range of terms and conditions of employment both generally and for occupational classes. The primary principle used in setting pay and conditions in the state sector was that of fair comparability with the private sector although a range of other factors were relevant. A system of compulsory arbitration through a Public Sector Tribunal was created to determine disputes relating to pay and conditions. The Tribunal was chaired by a Judge of the Arbitration Court and included both an employer and employee representative.

This system survived largely intact until the reforms of the late 1980s. The major changes occurred in relation to the Commissioner who became a three person Commission in 1946. This body was renamed the State Services Commission (SSC) in 1962. This first change seems to have been the result of the expanding activities of the state and followed an increase in the number of government departments in 1946 following the report of the Public Service Consultative Committee. The latter change, however, resulted from the recommendations of a Royal Commission into the state services and was intended to address the perception that the Commission had become preoccupied with personnel and industrial relations matters to the detriment of ensuring an efficient public service. Whatever the intention in practice,

> the SSC largely continued the tradition set by its predecessor. Personnel and industrial relations matters became its main concern. Indeed, considering the general volatility of industrial relations in New Zealand during the first twenty years of the SSC's life, it could hardly do anything else.[11]

Concern with the structure of the public sector continued to be expressed through the 1970s and reached a crescendo in the 1980s. An official, but retrospective, view was that prior to reform the public sector 'was seen to have a bloated workforce, rigid employment conditions, unclear objectives, and a dearth of consequences for failure to perform'.[12]

The theoretical and practical drivers leading up to the reforms of the 1980s are discussed in detail by Boston[13] and need not be discussed in detail here. The economic and political theories involved were not unique to New Zealand and lie behind public sector reform generally. Within New Zealand, theoretical and ideological pressures that stressed the need for efficiency and improved management and accountability structures were reinforced by a number of local political factors. These included perceived issues of political accountability. In particular, a belief had developed within the Labour Party, arising from its time in government in 1972-75, that the public service had become impervious to the views of elected governments. A combination of the public service culture and officials' policy inclinations was seen as having undermined policy objectives.[14] Another factor was that the state pay fixing system was outside direct political control, a situation that had important consequences for government expenditure, especially for a government determined to exercise tight fiscal control. Awards of significant pay increases during the early period of the 1984-90 term of the Labour government made it clear to the government that fiscal control required significant reforms to the pay fixing system.

## The Reforms of the 1980s

The reforms to the public sector came in three phases. The first involved the separation of central government functions from the wide variety of other government and quasi-government organisations covering various state functions, a reform implemented by the *State-Owned Enterprises Act 1986*. The second phase was the reform of the state sector through the *State Sector Act 1988* which repealed the *State Services Act 1962* and the *State Services Conditions of Employment Act 1977* and thus the structure that was established in 1912. The *State Sector Act* brought state industrial relations and employment largely into line with that of the private sector. Finally the *Employment Contracts Act 1991*, which applied to both the state and private sectors, allowed the introduction of significant industrial relations changes. On top of these reforms sat the *Public Finance Act 1989* which introduced new systems of financial management and accountability into the state services.

## State-Owned Enterprises Act 1986

The *State-Owned Enterprises Act* was passed to provide a new corporate structure for government trading activities and in particular to require them 'to operate as a successful business' and to be '[a]s profitable and efficient as comparable businesses that are not owned by the Crown'.[15] Although some government owned entities were already corporations (such as Air New Zealand and the Bank of New Zealand) this number greatly increased with and following the enactment of the *State-Owned Enterprises Act*.[16] Unlike traditional public service entities, State-Owned Enterprises (SOEs) were created as companies with boards of directors who, while responsible to the shareholding ministers, were held accountable on commercial criteria. From an employee perspective the consequence was that the state sector employment structure ceased to apply and much greater flexibility was introduced in setting terms and conditions of employment. Although SOEs were required by the Act to be 'good employer[s]'[17] this somewhat nebulous obligation had little substantive impact as the new SOEs sought to impose managerial control and implement new organisational structures and values.[18] Indeed, corporatisation was in many cases the first step toward privatisation, as an unstated object of the Act was to prepare such SOEs for sale. Major restructuring, usually associated with significant reorganisation and large-scale redundancies, preceded the privatisation of many of the new SOEs.

# State Sector Act 1988

The second, and most important, phase of reform came with the *State Sector Act 1988*. It was this Act that abolished the traditional structure for the state sector as a whole and which introduced a radically new vision of state sector employment in which the concept of a unified public sector was abandoned and replaced by one centring on individual departments. The main features of this Act were as follows:

- The role of the SSC was radically altered to focus on reviewing the machinery of government and the performance of departments and their chief executives. This body was itself abolished in 1989 and was replaced by a single State Service Commissioner as chief executive of the SSC.[19] The SSC retains some personnel and industrial relations roles but the main operational function is that of appointing chief executives.

- Individual departments were now headed by chief executives. Each chief executive is responsible for 'carrying out the functions and duties of the Department'; tendering advice to ministers; for the general conduct of the department and its 'efficient, effective and economical management'.[20] Political accountability is to the responsible minister but there is also management accountability to the State Services Commissioner through performance review mechanisms. Chief executives are appointed for a maximum term of five years although the term is renewable.

- The chief executive of each department became the employer of the department's staff with the power to appoint and remove employees and has 'all the rights, duties, and powers of an employer'[21] except as otherwise specified. The SSC, however, retains the responsibility for negotiating conditions of employment, although in practice this responsibility was, over time, largely delegated to chief executives. The SSC also retains responsibility for developing and promoting personnel and equal employment opportunities (EEO) policies. A similar division of responsibilities was introduced in the education sector where individual school Boards of Trustees became the employer.

- In conjunction with the new division of employment responsibilities the distinctive system for dealing with state sector personnel and industrial relations matters was abolished and the state sector was brought within the mainstream realm of private sector employment law. This included coverage by the then *Labour Relations Act 1987*, which governed collective negotiations and provided employment protection through the personal grievance provisions. In other areas the common law governing employment contracts applied. The main remnants of the previous system were a broad, but relatively vague, statutory obligation to act as a 'good employer'[22] and an obligation in making appointments to 'give preference to the person who is best suited to the position'.[23] Substantive appeal and review rights in relation to personnel decisions were, however, abolished.

## Employment Contracts Act 1991

The *Employment Contracts Act* was introduced with the objectives of providing a more flexible labour market and enhancing management power in its relationships with unions and employees. This Act had a number of impacts on industrial relations. Generally, the overall impact was a significant individualisation and de-unionisation of the New Zealand workforce.[24] The Act effectively abolished the previous system of collective bargaining on an occupational/industry basis at a national level and replaced it, where bargaining remained feasible, with one of enterprise-based bargaining. The introduction of voluntary union membership in combination with the restrictions on bargaining significantly weakened union strength in general. Although the Act applied to employees generally it played a major role in reshaping state sector employment. The Act came into effect only three years after the *State Sector Act* and at a time when chief executives were seeking direct control over collective bargaining in their departments. The Act provided the legislative environment which gave the SSC the confidence to delegate to chief executives and gave chief executives the powers to use that delegation in a pro-active and industrially aggressive manner.

## Public Finance Act 1989

This Act, while not directly concerned with state sector employment, is of central importance when considering the drivers influencing the changing characteristics of state sector employment. As noted by Boston, 'the State Sector Act and the Public Finance Act cannot be viewed in isolation from one another: they form an integrated whole'.[25] The *Public Finance Act* introduced a system based on inputs, outputs and outcomes. In essence, the government, having decided which outcomes (less crime, better educated workforce) it sought, then appropriated the necessary monies necessary to achieve those outcomes. These monies financed the inputs (resources such as labour, physical resources etc) to purchase the necessary outputs (policy advice, service delivery, administration of transfer payments etc) needed to achieve the desired outcomes. In order to operate this scheme, the Act also introduced new and more transparent financial reporting and management systems, as well as improved accountability mechanisms, to allow government and parliamentary monitoring. The responsibility for achieving the contracted outputs rested with the chief executive of the relevant department or agency who was accountable to the relevant minister. Chief executives were also accountable to the State Services Commissioner for the management of their department in terms of their individual performance agreement. The corollary of the new accountability mechanisms was managerial flexibility — if chief executives were to be accountable not only for the contracted outputs but also the 'efficient, effective and economical management' of their department they required the necessary managerial autonomy to achieve the contracted results. The *State Sector Act* and later the *Employment Contracts Act* provided the tools necessary for managing the employment dimension of the 'new' state sector.

## Redesigning the State Sector

The passage of these four key pieces of legislation described above provided the required platform for the reforms to the state sector envisaged in the Treasury's briefing paper to the Labour government re-elected in 1987.[26] This paper identified the key aspects of the reform programme as clarity of objectives, freedom to manage, accountability and effective assessment and information flows. While the reform process was implemented by Labour, it continued with equal vigour when a conservative National government was elected in 1990.

The legislative platform provided the catalyst for massive change throughout the state sector as the new freedoms accorded by the legislative framework allowed the key reform objectives of structural, infrastructural and cultural change to be implemented. The result was a radically redesigned public sector. One consequence was the formation of the three-tier state described below and, although the basic reform model was similar for all tiers, there were significant differences as a result of the functions performed by each tier.

## The Public Service

At the centre was the public service consisting of the core government departments such as Treasury, Ministry of Foreign Affairs and Trade, Ministry of Justice, Ministry of Education and so on. It is these bodies which carry out what most people would regard as the principal functions of government, in particular advice on the development of government policy and the implementation of that policy. Normally the chief executive is accountable directly to a minister and operates under close ministerial control. The employees of these departments are also those likely to have continuing direct contact with ministers. These departments are specified in the First Schedule to the *State Sector Act*. The chief executive of each department or ministry is appointed by the State Services Commissioner, although the government does have the power to veto an appointment. The chief executive is accountable to the Commissioner for the management of the department.

## Crown Entities

Crown entities were those bodies listed in Schedule 4 of the *Public Finance Act* and consisted of a wide and diverse range of bodies with an enormous variation in function and form that were subject to the provisions of the Act. Crown entities were created and funded by government to provide specific, but non-commercial, functions and are normally governed by a government-appointed board and managed by a chief executive. The exact status of Crown entities and their link to the central political structure was sometimes less than clear, often deliberately as ministers may prefer a 'hands off' policy and the maintenance of a high degree of political distance between themselves and the entity. Indeed, a healthy degree of political independence is often necessary for some Crown entities to work successfully. The two largest groups of such entities are in health (District Health Boards, which administer hospitals) and education (individual School Boards of Trustees), but they include a wide range of other bodies ranging from the Accident Compensation Corporation through to the Fish and Game Councils, the Human Rights Commission and the Trustees of the National Library. Apart from the education service, these bodies were not directly covered by the *State Sector Act* although the Prime Minister may authorise the Commissioner to carry out any of its statutory functions in respect of any part of the state services. The government ownership interest in Crown entities is monitored by related departments/ministries (for those entities other than Crown companies). The government ownership interest in the financial performance of those Crown entities classified as Crown companies is usually monitored by the Crown Company Monitoring Advisory Unit (CCMAU). This unit is a semi-autonomous body attached to the Treasury but providing independent advice to Ministers about Crown companies. CCMAU focuses on 'entity performance at a company level, while the Treasury focuses on the economic and fiscal implications of the Crown's investment'.[27] There are a few exceptions to the CCMAU monitoring regime. For example, monitoring of health sector ownership now resides with the Ministry of Health and the tertiary sector with the Ministry of Education, and the Accident Compensation Corporation is monitored by the Department of Labour. The CCMAU, however, takes the lead in developing best practice in the monitoring of ownership interest.

A significant amount of government work is conducted in Crown entities and they represent a major interface between the public and the government. Outside education and health however, they are the organisations about which government has known and cared the least. Structurally, their status and governance has been vague: '[i]n sum, the Crown entity regime has inadequate governance arrangements, patchy accountability, and significant legislative gaps and inconsistencies'.[28] Several politically embarrassing incidents, including inappropriate payments to board members and chief executives of some Crown entities, catalysed more serious review. Hence, detailed guidelines for Ministers, Crown entities, their boards, and public service departments were issued in 1999, and the SSC began working towards a legislative clarification of the roles of Crown entities. This was identified as 'one of the key initiatives designed to support the government's goal of improving trust in government organisations'.[29]

This, in combination with initiatives arising from the Review of the Centre (2001), finally resulted in the passing of the *Crown Entities Act 2004*, both of which are discussed below.

## State Owned Enterprises

The overall practical effect of the *State-Owned Enterprises Act* was largely to remove SOEs from the state sector employment system. As a side effect, however, the SOEs provided a managerial and employment model for the subsequent reforms to the remainder of the state sector. SOEs operate in a similar way to private companies and are driven primarily by the same commercial imperatives. Generally they operate independently of government, although from time to time political factors may become relevant. A recent example is government modifications to state-owned television charters to require a greater focus on local content which is likely to be at the expense of maximum profitability.

## Implementing the New Design

The redesign of the state sector, underpinned by the theories of new institutional economics, was based around the key principle of functional separation. This involved the separation of policy functions from operations and service delivery; of ownership from purchase; and of funding, purchasing and provision of services, with the intention of encouraging competition between service providers and creating greater focus, synergy and information.[30] Within the public service, it led to the breaking up of large government departments into separate policy ministries and service delivery departments. For example, the Department of Justice splintered into the small policy-focused Ministry of Justice, a Department of Corrections responsible for the prison and probation service, and a Department for Courts responsible for running of court services. Some other services from Justice were reallocated to other departments. The large Ministry of Transport was restructured into a small policy ministry with the regulatory functions being shifted to new Crown entities such as the Land Transport Safety Authority, the Maritime Safety Authority and the Civil Aviation Authority. These examples were typical of the comprehensive process of restructuring throughout the public service. Moreover changes to the form and status of organisations have remained an ongoing feature and the public service continues to be characterised by mergers, de-mergers, abolition and creation of new entities. For example, in 1995 the Ministry of Agriculture and Fisheries first de-merged to become a Ministry of Agriculture and a Ministry of Fisheries. Then in 1997, a merger with the Ministry of Forestry (which had been formed in 1987) created the Ministry of Agriculture and Forestry. Most employees in these organisations had experienced five restructurings in a ten-year period. Similarly, in 2003, the Department for Courts was merged back into the Ministry of Justice.

The wider state services also joined the restructuring merry-go-round. One of the most important examples was the health sector. A change of government in 1991 heralded a move to 'managed competition' through the implementation of a structural model separating the funder, the purchaser, and the provider. This saw 14 Area Health Boards (with community elected boards) transformed into 23 Crown Health Enterprises (with commercial boards of directors accountable under the *Companies Act 1993*) and with a legislated mandate to work for profit (*Health and Disability Services Act 1993*). The Act changed the role of the Ministry of Health to that of 'funder', created four new purchaser or contracting entities in the form of Regional Health Authorities, and established a Public Health Commission. In 1995 the Commission was abolished and its functions absorbed back into the Ministry of Health. The election of the Coalition government in 1996 saw the profit imperative removed from Crown Health Enterprises and replaced with an instruction to operate in a 'business-like manner'. In the interim, the numbers of Crown Health Enterprises reduced from 23 to 21 as financially unsustainable regions merged with neighbouring enterprises. Similarly, the four Regional Health Authorities were eventually merged in 1998 to form one purchasing agency, the Health Funding Authority. In 1998 the remaining 21 Crown Health Enterprises became 22 Hospital & Health Services entities (21 hospital regions and one blood service). Most recently these services have been reincarnated as 16 District Health Boards and the Health Funding Authority has been absorbed into the Ministry of Health.

These examples are the tip of the iceberg — structural change has been pervasive throughout the core public service and the broader state sector, and there is no state-funded organisation that has not been impacted. This structural change continues to this day, albeit at a less frenetic pace, and despite a centrally espoused preference not to restructure.[31] More recently the Commissioner has signalled a move from reform to development.[32]

## Restructuring the Employment Environment

As might be expected, one of the most important consequences of the reforms has been the immediate and longer term impact on managers and staff, and on systems of industrial relations and human resource management. These changes have fundamentally and irrevocably changed the employment experience of public servants. The reformed state sector was seen as requiring a new model of employment. This model had two main dimensions. The first, much greater control over state sector pay levels was, at one level, a result of the government's desire to control and reduce overall government expenditure. Greater control over industrial relations and especially pay outcomes was, however, also needed as part of the new state sector management model. If chief executives were to be accountable for their departmental budgets and required to operate within strict fiscal parameters, they required the power to control and manage labour costs. This, in turn, required the ability to assert the necessary bargaining strategies to achieve desired cost outcomes. The result was that a much more pro-active and aggressive approach to pay demands and employment generally was adopted both at central and departmental level.

The second dimension was that of a new approach to human resource management at departmental level as chief executives sought to impose a new culture of managerialism and to re-focus the employment relationship at the level of the individual department or agency rather than on the public service generally. The new public management system was reflected not only in the structure of the state sector but also in the management of its constituent organisations. The *State Sector Act 1988* removed administrative control from central agencies and devolved managerial responsibility to chief executives. As summarised by Pollitt: '[i]t shifted the role of SSC from that of employer and manager of the public service to that of employer of the Chief executives and advisor to the government on general state sector management issues'.[33] The previously centralised bureaucratic control of the public sector became devolved to organisation-specific employment relationships. Underpinning these changes was the drive to establish accountability. '[T]he principal concern was to be clear about accountabilities. This concern manifested itself in a simple proposition, namely that managers in the State sector could be held accountable only for things they could control'.[34] The accountability of government agencies was managed via a cascade of contracts: purchase agreements for specified outputs between the minister and the department, performance agreements and employment contracts between the chief executive and the State Services Commissioner and between the chief executives and their senior management, and similarly between management and staff.

## Industrial Relations

The abolition of the old public service pay fixing system and especially its centralised arbitration and negotiating system allowed much greater flexibility for the government in its approach to industrial relations. From the perspective of the government of the day, the most important change was almost certainly that its ability to control the fiscal outcomes of collective bargaining was massively enhanced. Under the previous system, governments were required to meet the costs of independently agreed settlements. Under the new system the culture changed as governments made it clear they would no longer automatically meet the cost of negotiated settlements and that the cost of any settlement would need to be met from existing funding. This approach led to a much more active bargaining stance by state employers, initially the SSC and later individual chief executives. As a result, the rate of state sector pay increases decreased significantly and fell behind increases in the private sector.[35] Initially, collective bargaining was tightly controlled from the centre, the SSC being the bargaining party for virtually all state pay negotiations. Over time, however, this control was relinquished and passed to individual chief executives with the SSC retaining only an oversight role and ensuring that government policy on state sector pay was implemented. Greater delegation was partly the result of pressure from chief executives seeking full control over this central part of their operation, but it was also the result of increasing experience within departments and greater confidence by the SSC that the new culture was 'in place'. Delegations increased markedly following the enactment of the *Employment Contracts Act*.

Within departments the new freedom was employed not only to limit the rate of wage increases, but also to reduce the range of employees covered by collective bargaining and to bring greater flexibility to employment contracts. Traditionally, state agreements had covered virtually all employees. However, with the new managerial emphasis, there was a largely successful, co-ordinated drive to remove senior levels of management from collective coverage, although these managers often then achieved considerably higher levels of remuneration under the new system. Individual contracts were seen not only as allowing greater accountability but also as encapsulating the new management ideology that held that managerial employees should not be unionised. Outside the education sector, where a combination of legislation and strong industrial pressure was required, there appears to have been little resistance to these moves. Other characteristic changes within the period saw specific pay scales replaced by ranges of rates, the abolition of automatic advancement, an increase in individual contracting and the like. In 1995, 17 per cent of employees in the core public service were on individual contracts. By 2001 that number had increased to 45 per cent.[36]

Given the impact of the *Employment Contracts Act* in the private sector, it is worth observing that the degree of change was much less in the state sector. There was, for example, little fragmentation of bargaining below departmental level so that bargaining units remained relatively large. Within the education sector in particular, bargaining continued to be largely at sector level although the traditional division between primary and secondary teachers remained. The ability of state sector unions to continue to bargain effectively was one reason that unions in the state sector fared considerably better than their private sector equivalents. Additionally, unlike private sector unions, state unions also had the advantages of a long tradition of voluntary membership and a membership centred in relatively large-scale, and hence organisable, units. The state unions never experienced the massive declines in union membership suffered by their private counterparts. The Victoria University union membership survey reported that the drop in union membership in the public and community services sector (primarily government employment) was 21 per cent between 1991 and 1999.[37] This figure is the lowest, by a substantial margin, for all industry groups. The report for 2003 states that bargaining density in the state sector was about 61 per cent compared with 13 per cent in the private sector.[38] The major union in the core public service, the PSA, survived and is the second largest union in the public sector and third largest in the country.[39] The major educational unions remained strong as did the professionally-orientated unions in the health sector. There was some union fragmentation, but this was limited and tended to be confined to particular areas of employment such as prisons, inland revenue and customs. Such unions were usually formed to represent dissatisfied PSA members who felt betrayed and unsupported throughout the extensive restructuring exercises of public sector reform. In some cases such members also tended to disagree with the PSA's policy of constructive engagement with management during the restructuring period.

## Human Resource Management

The new public management system reshaped systems of human resource management as responsibility was devolved first to departmental level and then, internally, to line managers. Individual line managers and human resource managers engaged in employment management practices that emulated those of their private sector counterparts. A variety of infrastructural mechanisms was used to bring about change. These included, most prominently, the assurance of accountability at various levels through new forms of employment contracts and performance management systems. These were coupled with a new focus on efficiency and the introduction of the language, systems and ideas of corporate human resource management. The consequence was, inevitably, a marked change in the employment experiences of state sector employees.

SOEs led the way throughout 1986–7 as corporatisation procedures changed them from monolithic government organisations to commercially focused businesses, embracing private sector practices in order to improve their business delivery capacity and as part of the lead-up to ultimate privatisation. Because of this restructuring and privatisation, the number of jobs in SOEs dropped from 84,000 to 22,000 between 1988 and 1997.[40] The SOEs' successful, no-expense-spared transformations provided a blueprint for the change and creation of Crown entities and the core public service. In the case of the core public service the key change signal was the enactment of the *State Sector Act* in 1988 and over the next year government agencies transformed themselves, both symbolically and practically, through an 'out with the old, in with the new' philosophy. This transformation included the wholesale disposal of the Public Service Personnel Manual and the assorted rules, delegations and supporting systems; staff sections were reborn as Human Resource Management (HRM) units; permanent heads and deputy secretaries transmogrified into chief executives and general managers; bureaucratic rules were replaced with 'high performance workplace practices'; and regulated transparency (such as publicly available pay scales and occupational classifications) was replaced by 'market related' employment flexibility (results of job sizing are not publicly available, and remuneration packages are individualised). Performance-based pay systems were introduced at senior management levels and staff levels, although in practice budget pressures at staff levels often rendered performance pay meaningless for many employees.[41]

Associated with these changes, and reflecting private sector HRM trends, government organisations flattened their levels of hierarchy and moved to business unit/single focus type structures, thus replicating functional separation imperatives at an organisational level. The approach of agencies to organising and acquiring their workforces changed with a move towards maximum flexibility characterised by a smaller core of permanent staff and increased reliance on a peripheral or transient staffing base of fixed term contractors and consultants.[42] Restructuring, lack of sector-wide focus, and flattened organisations, accompanied by significantly reduced numbers of permanent staff, contributed to a loss of career structures within organisations and across the public sector. At management levels this was exacerbated by the failure of the Senior Executive Service (SES) established under the *State Sector Act* with the intention of providing a core pool of sector-wide public service management expertise. The failure of the SES epitomised the tension within the Act between giving individual chief executives management autonomy and encouraging the collective entity of the public service as a whole. The success of the SES relied on chief executives relinquishing some of their newly found management discretion over the salaries and conditions of their senior managers. Not surprisingly this did not meet with resounding support with the result that by 2000 New Zealand had the smallest SES in the OECD with a membership of fewer than 30 managers.

A distinctive feature of the *State Sector Act*, which separates public management from private sector management, is the statutory obligation of state employers to be 'good' employers. These obligations are mainly written in general, and probably unenforceable, terms but they also include responsibility on chief executives for meeting the aims and aspirations of EEO target groups. Recent research reports that this legislative requirement has resulted in

> success in producing better EEO outcomes ... for target group members by affording them improved access to public service employment ... [W]ith respect to representation rates the public service consistently and comprehensively outperforms the general labour force. The representation rates found in the public service are nearly double those for the wider labour force.[43]

Target groups, especially women and Maori, fare much better in public service employment. However, although these groups are better represented in the public service, they are not better paid. This issue is not isolated to EEO target groups. The large disparity in pay rates between management and lower level staff has been reported to government as an issue of concern across the state sector.[44]

## The Consequences of Reform

State sector reform was just one, albeit highly visible, set of changes in the last 15 years. Economic reform, electoral reform, civil rights and social reform have all been implemented through various state mechanisms — primarily legislative and structural. All these changes have contributed to a changing culture affecting not only the workplace but also home life, and even the sports field. The changes to the state sector are only one element of these changes but they have nevertheless permeated and affected most New Zealand households.

Between 1987 and 1992 the core public service reduced in size by 47 per cent from 89,000 to 47,000 staff.[45] Fluctuations in numbers have continued so that by June 2001 there were just over 30,000 staff.[46] However, according to the SSC 'despite the reduction in the size of the core public service, the overall level of government activity in the economy has been relatively constant over the past 20 years'.[47] In some cases this reduction has come about through the transfer of core public service activities to the Crown entity sector.

As already noted, the economically inspired institutional separations, contracting out of activities, and devolution of managerial discretion led to the rapid disaggregation of the public sector. The reforms gave focus and flexibility but they also produced fragmentation and short-term behaviours. The collective interest ceased to be a salient consideration in the activities of public agencies as organisational and individual objectives and performance became the driving concerns. The introduction of the language and ideas of HRM reinforced this individualist perspective and helped to cement a changed culture.

Because 'the public sector set out to close the gap between public sector management and the best private sector management',[48] the clear drive throughout the reforms was for a more business-like corporate culture. This has been reflected not only in the introduction of the notion of management (as opposed to supervision or administration) and a new public sector management vocabulary, but also through the development of a carefully managed corporate image. This is seen in staff presentation, in public consultation documents, in advertising, in reports and not least, in the physical presence of government agencies. For instance, the interior decoration of many government agencies has provided a highly visible sign of a more modern, some might say more profligate, corporate culture. The most politically charged example of this was associated with the creation of Work and Income New Zealand (WINZ), the department responsible for the administration of welfare benefits and unemployment policies. The conspicuous and expensive rebranding of the department, various political scandals concerning the costs of corporate administration and the highly personalised image of the chief executive led to several years of political attack, a review of the department,[49] and eventually to non-renewal of the chief executive's contract. Even Treasury was not immune from this criticism when a scandal regarding the cost of the imported furniture in the chief executive's office attracted media attention. This corporate re-imaging, and assumed mirroring of the private sector, has however been at some cost and resulted in some loss of sight of the essential nature and fundamentals of the public service. Indeed, it could be argued that the desire to be different, more like the private sector, has led to direct (and indirect) denigration of the people, structures, systems and processes which were perceived to be too public service-like.

However much state sector managers may aspire to be like the private sector there are fundamental differences between the two sectors and in particular different accountabilities. In the final analysis, the state sector remains accountable to the government and through it to the public. Whatever the culture and whatever the formal structure, politicians remain politicians and are driven by political imperatives. One consequence of the changes outlined above has been to make the public sector more exposed to the vagaries of political life. Although formally chief executives are accountable for departmental performance to ministers, who are in turn accountable to and answerable to Parliament, the new structures have, in practice, had the result of shifting responsibility downwards. The focus on accountabilities has often had the effect of personalising particular issues. It is, for example, not uncommon for individual line managers, rather than their chief executive, to front the media over contentious issues in their units. Nor is it unusual now for members of Parliament and ministers to publicly point the finger at individual public servants.[50] Ironically, it seems that a lack of trust in government by its citizens has fuelled governments' lack of trust in its agencies. This, in turn, has at times strained relationships between ministers and chief executives, resulting in a number of recent high profile cases of a complete breakdown in the relationship.[51] The most high profile example concerned the chief executive of WINZ[52] but this case was not an isolated example.

The perception of a breakdown of public service ethos is no doubt a function of constant restructuring, downsizing, individualisation and loss of career that has led to perceptions of a culture in which there is less trust and less loyalty. Academics and cabinet ministers alike observe that the structuring of institutions and incentives has undermined individual loyalty and the public service ethos,[53] and the change, or loss, of this ethos as a consequence of the reforms has been widely rued by a number of commentators.[54] In keeping with obligations imposed under the *State Sector Act*, the SSC issued a Code of Conduct, and other publications to guide public servants generally and chief executives specifically in the public service ethos.[55] But in a devolved regime, with the multiple cultural and accountability pressures already discussed, these have had little impact.

In one annual report the State Services Commissioner noted that 'a few high-profile cases of public servants abusing their power, and the public's trust, has made me take these values less for granted'.[56] Similarly, he extended these concerns beyond the core public service (hence beyond the then SSC sphere of influence) to Crown entities. It was stated that '[t]he transfer of service delivery functions out of departments into separate legal entities that have adopted, consciously or unconsciously, different corporate cultures probably has contributed to the change in long-established Public Service values in these organisations'.[57] Various measures were taken to address these issues. In November 2000 a State Sector Standards Board, reporting annually to the Minister of State Services, was formed to provide an 'outside' perspective of state sector ethos. The Board's first report summarised a state sector environment in similar terms to that described in this chapter and noted the following as important influences on ethos: leadership, performance management, remuneration, governance, the role of the State Services Commission, and relations with politicians.[58] Significantly, many of the issues raised by this Board were incorporated in the subsequent Review of the Centre Report (2001), which has been highly influential on the future shape of the public sector.

The pursuit of flexibility, individualisation and focus on the individual business needs of each government agency led to inconsistent and short term human resource management practices across (and sometimes within) agencies.[59] Training provides a clear example of the resulting problems. Prior to the reforms there was, for example, a co-ordinated public service graduate recruitment scheme aimed at investing in and developing capability for the public service. Recent research, however, shows that there are now very few graduate recruitment strategies operated by government agencies and in some cases there is a distinct preference to recruit only experienced personnel.[60] Other research has found that organisations often have no training and development strategy and that opportunities for training are generally driven by individual staff initiatives. Consequently, there is limited connection to desired organisational capability.[61]

The lack of investment in developing the public sector labour market as a whole has come back to haunt all agencies and is now magnified by global shortages in skilled staff. As Walsh observed, early in the public sector change process, the reforms significantly reduced the internal labour market and hence its future survival was a subject of much interest.[62] By 1997 and 1998 SSC reports noted serious shortfalls in strategic HRM planning in (and across) government agencies, including a lack of forecasting of future skill demands and how to meet them. Famously, in 1999 one public service department (ostensibly due to lack of internal capacity) used consultants to prepare the departmental brief to the incoming Labour - Alliance Coalition government which during the election had stood on a platform of reducing the use of consultants in the public sector. These issues of human resource capability (and political embarrassment) have given rise to the recent fascination with organisational capability.

Many of the predicted impacts were comprehensively confirmed by the results of a public service wide survey of 'career progression and development'.[63] This found that while public servants want to progress their careers in the public service '[h]alf of public servants felt their opportunities for advancement were "Poor"'.[64] This was attributed to '[f]lat management structures, a lack of visible career paths, inadequate information about job vacancies, and a perceived preference for departments to source talent externally rather than to "grow" their own'.[65] The report noted that 'concerns about fairness and its impacts on career progression were a recurring theme ... especially related to selection processes and differential access to development opportunities'.[66]

## Trends into the Twenty-First Century

For the future, one thing seems certain. The experience of public sector employment in New Zealand will continue to change. The direction of that change has been signalled by recent initiatives which address mounting concerns about public management issues including: the perceived fragmentation and lack of coordination of the public sector as a collective entity; issues of skilled labour supply; issues of short term focus created by contract and accountability mechanisms; diminution of a public service ethos; issues of organisational capability; perceived lack of trust of government organisations; and issues of control in the health and welfare sectors.

Many of these concerns were targeted by the *Report of the Advisory Group on the Review of the Centre*, conducted for the Ministers of State Services and Finance.[67] The Advisory Group was made up of public service chief executives, external commentators and a PSA union representative. It proposed improvements to the public management system in three areas: first, integrating service delivery across multiple agencies; second, addressing fragmentation of the state sector and improving its alignment; and finally, developing a stronger culture, a better place to work and a focus on developing people. It was proposed that these improvements would be achieved through 'new ways of working'. These new ways included changes to the accountability and reporting system; 'structural consolidation' (ie reducing the numbers of government agencies), and a culture shift within the state sector. For example, it was proposed that cross-agency 'circuit-breaker' teams be established to solve intractable problems in service delivery and to enhance regional coordination of state sector agencies by building on existing models of local coordination. The proposed improvements to accountability and reporting systems hinged primarily around a better focus on outcomes through departmental Statements of Intent (SOIs). SOIs are planning documents that provide a better link between outputs and outcomes, and are discussed and signed by the minister and the chief executive to signal mutual commitment to ensuring the department's capability to deliver. The structural consolidation envisages fewer agencies and 'bigger, more "federal" departments comprising sub-units with compatible objectives'.[68] The review report discussed formation of between seven and ten 'super-networks' as a move towards 'substantial structural change'.[69] This vision extended to Crown entities, and advocated a reversal of the functional separation between policy and operations. In addition, it called for a review and subsequent legislative change to resolve confused governance arrangements in the Crown entities. This was expected to build on the work already completed in the Crown entities reform initiative.[70]

Perhaps the most significant proposal was the exertion of greater leadership by the central policy agencies of the SSC, the Treasury and the Department of Prime Minster and Cabinet. After a decade of dealing with Crown entities at arms length, this review applied its recommendations across the state sector. The Advisory Group advocated greater leadership by the central agencies, particularly the SSC, with regard to people and culture. To achieve this, it recommended amendments to the *State Sector Act* in order to extend the mandate of the State Services Commissioner to Crown entities, and suggested that

> [t]here would be benefit in the progressive adoption of common standards, the sharing of good practice, and the development of joint systems or programmes … [I]individual agencies' human resource planning [should] be done within the context of an overarching State sector human resources framework.[71]

Reassuringly, for chief executives, the review did not envisage any fundamental change from current employment arrangements, so that staff would continue to be employed by their own agencies. They did, however, 'see a case for more active nurturing of the State sector workforce'.[72] One important aspect of the new system was intended to be improved systems of training and development with a particular focus on leadership development. Together these activities signalled an expected change of priority and culture, and it was envisaged that they would promote state sector values and ethos. A further indication of commitment to strengthening state sector skills was New Zealand's involvement in the recently formed Australia and New Zealand School of Government which involved a partnership with the Australian federal government, some State governments and a group of leading universities in both countries.

Surprisingly, however, given current industrial relations legislation and the sector-wide nature of these initiatives, the recommendations in the review report are all expressed as being in the context of the PSA's Partnership for Quality

Agreement with the government. As was noted above, a number of other unions have emerged within the public service whilst, within the state sector generally, there are a number of large and well-established unions, especially in the education and health sectors. The review document, possibly because of the PSA representation and the public service experience of the Advisory Group, ignores the presence in the state sector of unions other than the PSA. There may also be a government preference for the more moderate and 'responsible' approach of the PSA partly because of experience with the partnership agreement which aims to better integrate the perspectives of staff in the operation of the state sector. In practice however, the government is unlikely to be able to avoid dealing with staff who have chosen to be represented by other unions. If nothing else, the 'good faith' requirements of the *Employment Relations Act 2000* require consultation and negotiations with all relevant unions.[73] It might also be noted that the report does not deal with representation of the significant number of state employees who have elected not to join a union.

This review gave a clear signal of the intended shape of the public management system for the early years of this century. It essentially proposed an exercise of reconnecting and recentralising that eschews aggressive change in favour of incremental change. In practice, however, the proposed changes are likely to have a very significant impact and one wonders if a perceived restructuring fatigue in the state sector has resulted in a 'let's not scare the horses' approach that adopts the language of soft, incremental capacity building in a plan that in reality would have a major impact on many state sector workers. The report specified the expected differences staff would experience within five years. They 'will receive more standardised training and education', 'will talk more proudly about their jobs, and the value of the State sector', 'will be working with other agencies more', 'may be working under different management or in a different organisation', 'will understand the overall vision and purpose better', 'will notice that their views get reflected in policy', 'will feel connected to Wellington', 'will see senior Wellington people at the frontline', 'will have more contact with people in other sectors', 'will find work more satisfying'.[74]

In other words, audacious incremental change! Indeed, for the observant, this so-called 'incremental' approach was exactly the thrust of a recent OECD symposium on the future shape of government reform.[75]

Indeed, many of the recommendations of the Review of the Centre have been put into effect. In mid-2003 a new senior leadership and management development strategy was launched for the public service. A key part of this strategy is an Executive Leadership Programme delivered through the Leadership Development Centre, a Centre sponsored by public service chief executives.[76] In mid-2004 the State Services Commission launched the Human Resources Framework which aims to be a new, shared approach to HRM for the public service in order to build people capability. The framework provides departments with tools and guidance in four key areas: human resource planning; people capability development; employment environment and conditions; and other special projects. It also established structured secondments within the public sector, a common set of public service induction modules for all departments to incorporate in their induction processes, guidance on recognizing previous service in public service jobs, a process for identifying remuneration pressures across the public service, and encouragement of the Partnership for Quality between departments and the PSA union. In 2005 the State Services Commissioner launched six development goals for the state services: employer of choice, excellent state servants, networked state services, coordinated state agencies, accessible state services, and trusted state services.[77] This is clearly a consolidation of the recommendations from the Review of the Centre.

A raft of legal changes, addressing concerns raised by the Review of the Centre, were brought about through the Public Finance (State Sector Management) Bill. The Bill, when enacted in December 2004, was split into four Acts: the *Public Finance Amendment Act 2004*, the *State Sector Amendment Act (No 2) 2004*; the *Crown Entities Act 2004*; and the *State-Owned Enterprises Amendment Act 2004*. These represent the largest legislative change in New Zealand public management in the last decade. The amendments to the *State Sector Act*, in combination with the *Crown Entities Act*, extend the mandate of the State Services Commissioner beyond the public service to the state services as a whole. This mandate includes providing advice on integrity and conduct to employees; advice on management systems, structures and organisations; and promoting senior leadership and management development, all to the wider state services.

The *Crown Entities Act* clarifies governance and accountability in order to achieve better alignment between agencies and government objectives. It also provides a framework for integrating Crown entities into the rest of the state sector for a strengthened whole-of-government. The Act creates distinct categories and types of Crown entity and establishes standard governance requirements for each category. These range in the proximity of their working relationship with the government: Crown Agents (eg District Health Boards) have the closest relationship and can be directed by the responsible Minister; Autonomous Crown Entities (ACE) (eg the Museum of New Zealand Te Papa Tongarewa) must have regard to government policy; Independent Crown Entities (ICE) (eg the Electoral Commission, the Human Rights Commission) operate at arm's length from the government; at even greater remove are Crown entity companies which are established under the *Companies Act* (eg the nine Crown research institutes), School Boards of Trustees, and Tertiary Education Institutions. In terms of accountability the Act ensures more balanced reporting of Crown entity intentions, actual performance and outcomes.

While some of the ongoing agenda of structural, infrastructural and cultural change is talked about and clearly identified, as in the Review of the Centre and the suite of public management legislative amendments, there are also other developments that appear to be passing largely unnoticed by central agencies and public management commentators. Again, these are likely to impact significantly on the employment experience in parts of the public sector. The reason for this lack of overt interest may be that the initiatives respond to areas in which managerialism and contractualism are not best equipped to adequately control or ensure the quality of service delivery. These areas include the health and welfare sectors where the response has been to use legislated professional control mechanisms. For example, the *Social Workers Registration Act 2003*, which impacts primarily on employees in the government-funded welfare agencies, sets and monitors competence levels for social workers, thus providing some assurance of professional judgement. Similarly, over the last decade there have been various changes in legislation pertaining to health professionals. These include the establishment of a Health and Disability Commissioner[78] to investigate public complaints relating to the health sector, as well as revamped competence standards for doctors and restructured disciplinary committees. Most recently the *Health Practitioners Competence Assurance Act 2003* has been introduced, significantly so-named to encompass a broad range of practitioners in health. It seems likely that this type of occupational legislation will continue to develop and impact on the employment experience of social workers and health practitioners, a significant number of which are employed in, or funded by, the government.

A final factor will be the impact of new employment legislation. The most significant change from the perspective of the state sector in the *Employment Relations Act 2000* is the ability to negotiate multi-employer collective agreements, a practice effectively prevented under the *Employment Contracts Act* as strikes in support of such bargaining were unlawful.

The impact of this change will be, and indeed has been, most marked in the health sector where the relevant unions have been able to negotiate national level agreements with the various separate District Health Boards. An indication of a more co-ordinated approach to the health sector was also seen in the enactment of a *Code of good faith for the public health sector*.[79] In addition to such matters as requiring provision to be made for patient safety during industrial action, the code contains a number of provisions relating to employment and professional relations in the sector generally. These include the nature of management-employee relations and extend to recognising the role of health professionals as patient advocates and recognising the right of employees to comment publicly on matters within their experience and expertise.

Other significant changes in the state sector are unlikely as the state sector remained both highly unionised and continued to bargain collectively throughout the era of the *Employment Contracts Act*. The new environment may have contributed to a more vigorous approach to bargaining by state unions that have gained the confidence to attempt to address the comparatively slow growth in income levels. This is particularly evident in the education and health sectors where teachers and medical professionals have been particularly affected by government fiscal restraints. Recently a combination of industrial militancy, the ability to negotiate multi-employer agreements under the *Employment Relations Act* and government recognition of the uncompetitive levels to which salaries had fallen has resulted in both nurses and teachers receiving increases substantially in advance of the general level of settlements.

Interestingly, the government may be more exposed to grievances by state employees because of the changes in 2002 to the *Health and Safety in Employment Act 1992* which added the management of stress in the workplace to employers' responsibilities.[80] This is because the construction of a leaner, more flexible state sector has arguably led to greater work intensification. The recent core public service career progression survey reported that three-quarters of public servants work more hours than they are employed for, and that heavy workloads were a recurring complaint.[81] This was reported to deter employees from seeking more senior positions and limited their ability to take advantage of development opportunities due to time constraints. The costs of failing to manage workplace stress have recently been brought home by a successful legal action against a government department.[82] The facts of this case provide a stark illustration of how centrally driven budgetary and performance concerns resulted in management largely ignoring clear warnings of increasing workplace stress. The case concerned a probation officer who resigned because of extremely severe stress-related heart problems caused by excessive workloads in an already stressful occupation. The problems, largely arising from staff shortages, were ignored by the department which saw shortages as a means to save money.

## Conclusion

The reforms of the late 1980s and early 1990s introduced a comprehensive legislative base as a catalyst of change, and as a reflection of the strategic direction of government. In the employment setting the role of law as a protector of rights was down-played. This chapter is being written at a time when there appears to be something of a turning point in the state sector reform process. The 'big' reforms have been achieved and are now firmly embedded, as is the legislative framework and the supporting culture. It did however, become apparent that those reforms had been at some cost. This cost included a level of deterioration in the capacity and capabilities of particularly the core public service to carry out the functions of government. This deterioration should not be overstated but there seems to be a realisation first, that private sector values and methodologies are not necessarily best suited to all the functions of government, and secondly that the public service had become unduly segmented with the result that there has been a loss of a broader public service culture.

This time, although the rhetoric is different, the mechanisms for achieving further reform in the state sector remain broadly similar — the law, structures, and culture. The degree of legislative change is smaller and less comprehensive, but still significant. For example the *Crown Entities Act,* the amendments to the *State Sector Act*, the *Public Finance Act* and *State-Owned Enterprises Act,* changes to the *Health and Safety in Employment Act* and other employment legislation including the *Employment Relations Act,* as well as the changes in professional/occupational legislation, will in combination have significant medium to long term repercussions throughout the state sector. The role of the law has ceased to be that of a catalyst for dramatic and bold change but has become more focused on achieving normative and cultural evolution within the state sector. The push for change will come from the 'structural' mechanisms: the committees, boards and project teams established to implement aspects of the Review of the Centre and the teams, networks and organisational consolidation that emerge as new ways of working. The cultural mechanisms are evident in an emerging new state sector lexicon around co-ordination, capability, sustainability, leadership, values and outcomes. Whether these will be reinforced in state sector workplaces, and across sectors, remains to be seen.

Indeed, as governments worldwide grapple with skill shortages, particularly in the health and education sectors, will a joined up/reconstructed state sector be enough to meet the potential labour market and employment relations challenges that face a small economy such as that of New Zealand?

# ENDNOTES

[1] Jonathan Boston et al, *Public Management: the New Zealand Model* (1996); Christopher Pollitt, 'The Implementation of Public Management Reforms in New Zealand' in Christopher Pollitt et al, *Public Management Reforms: Five Country Studies* (1997).

[2] Christopher Pollitt and Geert Bouckaert, *Public Management Reform: a Comparative Analysis* (2000) 252.

[3] See for example, Boston et al, *Public Management*, above n 1; Robert Gregory, 'Social capital theory and administrative reform: maintaining ethical probity in public service' (1999) 59 *Public Administration Review* 63; Steering Group, *Review of State Sector Reforms (Logan Report)* (1991); Pollitt, above n 1; Allen Schick, *The Spirit of Reform: Managing the New Zealand State Sector in a time of change* (report prepared for the State Services Commission and the Treasury, New Zealand) (1996); Allen Schick, 'Reflections on the New Zealand Model' (Lecture delivered at the New Zealand Treasury, August 2001).

[4] In this chapter the term 'public service' is used to refer to core government departments while 'state service' is used to refer to the wider instruments of the Crown and includes, for example, the health and education services. This usage reflects the definitions in s 2 of the *State Sector Act 1988*. The terms 'state sector' and 'private sector' are used in a broader descriptive context.

[5] John Robertson, 'Legislation and Industrial Relations in the Public Sector' in John Howells, Noel Woods and Frederick Young (eds), *Labour and Industrial Relations in New Zealand* (1974) 107, 108.

[6] The relevant Acts at the time of the 1980s reforms were the *State Services Act 1962* and the *State Services Conditions of Employment Act 1977* and the formulations below are from those Acts.

[7] *State Services Act 1962* s 10(1).

[8] *State Sector Act 1988* s 85.

[9] *State Services Act 1962* s 41(2).

[10] *State Services Act 1962* s 26(2).

[11] Boston et al, *Public Management*, above n 1, 56.

[12] State Services Commission, *Public Sector Reform in New Zealand: The Human Resource Dimension* (1998) 1.

[13] See Boston et al, *Public Management*, above n 1; Jonathan Boston et al (eds), *Reshaping the State: New Zealand's Bureaucratic Revolution* (1991).

[14] Boston et al, *Public Management*, above n 1, 56.

[15] Section 4(1).

[16] Boston et al, *Public Management*, above n 1, 65.

[17] *State-Owned Enterprises Act 1986* s 4(2).

[18] Pat Walsh, 'The Struggle for Power and Control in the New Corporations: the first year of industrial relations in the state-owned enterprises' (1988) 13 *New Zealand Journal of Industrial Relations* 179.

[19] Technically the previous government department had been the Office of the State Services Commission. This was renamed the State Services Commission with the Commissioner as chief executive.

[20] Section 32.

[21] Section 59.

[22] Section 56. The definition of a 'good employer' in this Act is more expansive than that in the *State-Owned Enterprises Act 1986*.

[23] *State Sector Act 1988* s 60.

[24] Gordon Anderson, 'Individualising the Employment Relationship in New Zealand: An Analysis of Legal Developments' and Sarah Oxenbridge, 'The Individualisation of Employment Relations in New Zealand: Trends and Outcomes' in Stephen Deery and Richard Mitchell (eds), *Employment Relations: Individualisation and Union Exclusion. An International Study* (1999) 204, 227.

[25] Boston et al, *Public Management*, above n 1, 268.

[26] Treasury, *Government Management: Brief to the incoming Labour Government* (1987).

[27] Treasury and State Services Commission, *Report of the Crown Company Monitoring and Advisory Unit Review Team: Phase II — Scope, Form and Location* (2000) 1.

[28] State Services Commission, *Crown Entity Reform: Overview* (2000) 3.

[29] Ibid 1.

[30] Graham Scott, *Public Management in New Zealand: Lessons and Challenges* (2001).

[31] Trevor Mallard (Minister of State Services), *Terms of Reference for Review of the Centre* (2001).

[32] State Services Commission, *Development Goals for the State Services* (2005).

[33] Pollitt, above n 1, 145.

[34] State Services Commission, *Annual report of the State Services Commission for the year ending 30 June 2001, including the annual report of the State Services Commissioner* (2001) 10.

[35] Boston et al, *Public Management*, above n 1.

[36] State Services Commission, *Human Resource Capability Survey of Public Service Departments as at 30 June 2001* (2001).

[37] Aaron Crawford, Raymond Harbridge and Pat Walsh, 'Unions and Union Membership in New Zealand: Annual Review for 1999' (2000) 25 *New Zealand Journal of Industrial Relations* 291, 297.

[38] Raymond Harbridge, Robyn May and Glen Thickett, 'The Current State of the Play: Collective Bargaining and Union Membership under the Employment Relations Act 2000' (2003) 28 *New Zealand Journal of Industrial Relations* 140, 143.

[39] The New Zealand Educational Institute covering primary teachers has a slightly larger membership. The New Zealand Nurses Organisation is the fourth largest. Department of Labour, 'Registered Unions' (2004) 16 (July) *ERA Info - The Report on Employment Relations in New Zealand* 2.

[40] State Services Commission, *Public Sector Reform in New Zealand*, above n 12.

[41] Jane Bryson et al, *Performance Pay Systems and Equity: An analysis in five New Zealand organisations* (Gender Earnings Gap Research Series) (1999); Robert Gregory, 'Getting better but feeling worse? Public sector reform in New Zealand' (2000) 3 *International Public Management Journal* 107.

[42] State Services Commission, *Public Sector Reform in New Zealand*, above n 12.

[43] Fiona Edgar, 'Equal employment opportunity: outcomes in the New Zealand public service' (2001) 26 *New Zealand Journal of Industrial Relations* 217, 224.

[44] State Sector Standards Board, *A Report to the Minister of State Services on: The Ethos of the State Sector* (2001).

[45] State Services Commission, *Public Sector Reform in New Zealand*, above n 12.

[46] State Services Commission, *Human Resource Capability Survey*, above n 36.

[47] State Services Commission, *Public Sector Reform in New Zealand*, above n 12, 7.

[48] Scott, above n 30, 224.

[49] Hunn Report, *Report of the Review of Work and Income New Zealand* (2000).

[50] State Sector Standards Board, above n 44.

[51] Colin James, *The Tie that Binds: The Relationship between Ministers and Chief Executives* (2002).

[52] See the Employment Court case of *Rankin v Attorney-General* [2001] 1 ERNZ 476.

[53] Gregory, 'Social capital theory and administrative reform: maintaining ethical probity in public service', above n 3; Trevor Mallard (Minister of State Services), 'Complying with the new government's priorities and plans for improving public sector performance and accountability' (Speech delivered in Wellington, 3 May 2000).

[54] Robert Gregory and Colin Hicks, 'Promoting public service integrity: a case for responsible accountability' (1999) 58(4) *Australian Journal of Public Administration* 3; John Martin, 'Ethics in Public Service: The New Zealand Experience' in Noel Preston (ed), *Ethics for the Public Sector: Education and Training* (1994); State Services Commission, *Annual report of the State Services Commission*, above n 34.

[55] State Services Commission, *Public Service Principles, Conventions and Practice* (1995); State Services Commission, *Responsibility and Accountability: Standards expected of Public Service Chief Executives: Key documents* (1997).

[56] State Services Commission, *Annual report of the State Services Commission*, above n 34, 8-9.

[57] Ibid.

[58] State Sector Standards Board, above n 44.

[59] Boston et al, *Public Management*, above n 1.

[60] State Services Commission, *Public Sector Reform in New Zealand*, above n 12; Pat Walsh, Jane Bryson and Zsuzsanna Lonti, '"Jack be nimble, Jill be quick": HR Capability and Organisational Agility in the New Zealand Public and Private Sectors' (2002) 40 *Asia Pacific Journal of Human Resources* 179.

[61] Walsh, Bryson and Lonti, above n 60; Robyn Rendall, 'A Framework for Measuring Training and Development in the State Sector' (Working Paper No 12, State Services Commission, New Zealand, 2001).

[62] Pat Walsh, 'Industrial relations and personnel policies under the State Sector Act' in Boston et al, *Reshaping the State*, above n 13.

[63] State Services Commission, *Career Progression and Development Survey, 2000: Results for the New Zealand Public Service: Highlights* (2002).

[64] Ibid 11.

[65] Ibid.

[66] Ibid 15.

[67] *Report of the Advisory Group on the Review of the Centre*, presented to the Ministers of State Services and Finance, November 2001.

[68] Ibid 27.

[69] Ibid 5.

[70] State Services Commission, *Crown Entity Reform*, above n 28.

[71] Report, above n 67, 29.

[72] Ibid 5.

[73] Section 4 imposes the obligation to deal in good faith on the 'parties to an employment relationship', which it defines to include the relationship between a union and an employer, and affirms that the obligation applies to the matters of collective bargaining and consultation between employers and employees.

[74] Report, above n 67.

[75] OECD, *Government of the Future: Getting from Here to There* (2000).

[76] <http://www.ldc.govt.nz> at 4 May 2006.

[77] State Services Commission, *Development Goals for the State Services*, above n 32.

[78] *Health and Disability Commissioner Act 1994*.

[79] *Employment Relations Act 2000*, sch 1B.

[80] *Health and Safety in Employment Amendment Act 2002*.

[81] State Services Commission, *Career Progression and Development Survey*, above n 63.

[82] *Attorney-General v Gilbert* [2002] 2 NZLR 342.

# Chapter Ten

# The Privatisation of the Civil Service

## K D Ewing

In 1953 the Scottish legal scholar, DM Walker published an article entitled 'The Legal Theory of the State'.[1] Professor Walker was concerned by the lack of 'an adequate legal theory of the State which takes account of modern social, political and economic developments as well as of the true legal position'.[2] Although there were many philosophical and political theories of the state, his aim was to develop a purely legal one. In developing a 'juristic theory of the State applicable to British conditions since 1947',[3] Professor Walker drew upon the private law concept of the corporation. According to Professor Walker, the state was 'a corporation aggregate' consisting of all people connected with the United Kingdom. He continued:

> This corporation has 'a managerial body' called the Government which comprises (i) an hereditary official variously called The Queen, the Sovereign, the Monarch, the Crown, and (ii) a body of directors chosen from the legislative assembly called variously the Government, the Cabinet, or the Heads of State. The managerial body acts in the interests of the persons who form the corporation through (a) a legislative assembly partly hereditary and partly elected by the adult members of the corporation, (b) a body of executive and administrative officials with departments and subordinate staff, and (c) a number of individuals empowered to adjudicate on disputes and apply to individuals the rules of law.[4]

For a distinguished private lawyer, the topic of Professor Walker's lecture seemed counter-intuitive. At a time of an expanding state and an expanding public sector, it seemed curious to locate a theory of the state in a private law model which at the time was politically contestable, with some of its commanding heights vulnerable to requisition by the state through nationalisation.[5] As social democracy was to expand in the years immediately after the article was published, it was to look even more curious. It now seems remarkably prescient.

The simile of the corporation now has a very contemporary ring in an era of active privatisation and outsourcing of state activity. But it also has a contemporary ring in terms of the changes that are taking place to the process of government and to the relationship between the government and the people, who 'have periodical opportunities to change the elected element in the legislative assembly and such changes may result in changes in the body of directors and in the policy of the board'.[6] Privatisation has been associated mainly with the sale of public corporations, notably the utility companies. But there has been a different kind of privatisation of central government itself, though here the privatisation has taken a different form. The privatisation of public corporations took the form of a series of events whereby they were sold to privately owned companies, albeit subject to public regulation.[7] In the case of central government activity, privatisation has been a continuing process. This process has seen the adoption of private sector attitudes in which the state is viewed as a corporation with many of the attributes of a corporation. The adoption of these private sector attitudes has had major implications for the role of the civil service within the structure of government, and coincides with a renewed emphasis on efficiency and delivery. The purpose of this chapter is to document the recent privatisation of the civil service, which has at least six dimensions. These relate to civil service focus, civil service structure, civil service values, civil service employment practices, civil service law and civil service regulation.

## Changing Civil Service Focus

The civil service occupies only part of the public sector. Public sector workers include those employed by local authorities responsible for roads, schools, fire, police, and rubbish collection and by bodies such as the National Health Service, said to be the largest employer in the world.[8] Workers employed by these authorities are not civil servants, a group who are employed directly by central or devolved governments. The closest we have to a legal definition is to be found in the *Crown Proceedings Act 1947* which defines a civil servant as 'a servant of the Crown working in a civil capacity', though there are a number of exceptions.[9] The civil service has thus operated beyond the scope of transparent legal rules, and to this day is governed by royal prerogative.[10] It is by virtue of the prerogative and not legislation that the Crown has authority to appoint, determine terms and conditions of employment, and has authority to dismiss at pleasure. But this is not to deny that there is also legislation (such as the *Official Secrets Act 1989*) which has a particular (though not exclusive) application to civil servants.[11] There are now about 500,000 civil servants in Britain, representing about 1.7 per cent of the labour force, with the public sector generally accounting for some 18 per cent of Britain's 24 million or so workers. The role of civil servants varies enormously, from direct contact with ministers, to the delivery of service in benefit offices, to the collection of taxes.

There is a growing sense in which the role of the civil servant is changing, though this may simply obscure the fact that civil servants have historically provided a range of functions.[12] At one end are the civil servants engaged in advice to ministers and the development of policy. To this end civil servants were supposed to be politically neutral in order to provide independent advice to ministers of any political party.[13] Although their legal status was one of great vulnerability, in practice civil servants enjoyed great security of tenure, designed to enhance this sense of the civil servant as a fearless provider of advice.[14] There are some who would argue that political neutrality was not the same as ideological neutrality, with political sociologists contending that civil servants were part of the institutional structure of the state and one of the great forces of conservatism. As explained by Miliband, '[s]enior civil servants in Britain constitute a formidable bloc of power, more cohesive and resourceful than any other element in the state, with the possible exception of the cabinet, but only if the cabinet is united, and determined to have its way'.[15] In recent years, many senior civil servants have become much more highly visible for a number of reasons related to the changes in the structure and organisation of the civil service. It is also the case that civil servants are now brought into the limelight as a result of investigations by parliamentary committees.[16]

It is perhaps curious to encounter concerns from the Left about the loss of civil service independence and impartiality. Yet there is a growing concern about the 'politicisation' of the civil service at the highest level, as revealed in the following exchange between the Cabinet Secretary (Sir Andrew Turnbull) and a backbench Labour MP. The occasion was a meeting of the House of Commons Public Administration Committee, one of the scrutiny committees of the House, and earlier in the proceedings Sir Andrew had denied that the civil service was becoming 'politicised'.[17] In what follows, neither side gave much ground, and in boxing terms we might say that the match ended in a draw. For the record it went like this:

> **Q133 Mr Hopkins:** If I could just turn to another article in *The Guardian* about the politicisation of the Civil Service. John Chapman, one of your former colleagues, wrote an article this week in *The Guardian* saying that the Civil Service is so politicised that its impartiality is just a myth. Do you think that is fair comment?

> *Sir Andrew Turnbull:* No, I do not think it is fair comment. I do not think things have changed. This implies that there has been some sort of sea change, that we now behave in some completely different way, but it does not feel like that. The kind of people who get to the top of departments are the same kind of people who used to get to the top of departments. Out there in the field in the work of Job Centre Plus, this whole politicisation debate just does not arise. They are getting on with their work. It is a Whitehall issue and I do not think that the change in the special adviser cadre is capable of producing the sea change that is described there.

**Q134 Mr Hopkins:** He goes on to describe how it works and how people have been gradually moved out and replaced, not by this broad range of views that you suggest, but actually by people whom he describes as minimalist free traders who believe in a very minimal role for Government. I think that would fit a description of your good self.

***Sir Andrew Turnbull:*** No. The Civil Service has been expanding over the last four years. The Government are not pursuing a minimalist policy. They believe that public services can do good for society and economic performance. I just do not see where this minimalist argument comes from. Most people argue that the Government are actually too intrusive. This does not capture the reality of what is going on.

**Q135 Mr Hopkins:** Can I just take you back to a question I asked at a previous meeting of the Committee. When you appeared before us before I asked about privatisation and contracting out of public services where, in future, the provision of these services would be done by people in the private sector. You said that this was the way of the world and that there were just a few remaining areas of Europe where social democracy still has a little bit of a grip. That was your view and you seemed to be quite enthusiastic about it. It certainly fits in with the Government view.

***Sir Andrew Turnbull:*** The Prime Minister has a slogan that what matters is what works and that the duty of the state is to see that certain services are provided. He adopts a quite pragmatic view of, who do we enlist to deliver on behalf of the state? If you look at what is happening in the Health Service, first of all the whole of primary care is done by enlisting private contractors. These are all self-employed people. Diagnostic and treatment centres are a mixture, some of them are profit-earning dividend-distributing companies, some of them are different kinds of NHS establishments. He is saying that, if someone will deliver education services, prison services or schools, we are prepared to look at them whether they are private sector, voluntary sector, local government or central government.

**Q136 Mr Hopkins:** We know the Prime Minister's view and the drift of Government. I am concerned about the Civil Service and what John Chapman is suggesting is that, over a long period, there has been a squeezing out of anyone who has fuddy-duddy social democratic views. He uses the example of one of his friends who was moved out and he never heard of him again. Indeed, later on, he himself was offered a regional job or resignation. It sounds like Mr Malenkov going to manage a small power station in Siberia!

*Sir Andrew Turnbull:* I do not know who Mr Chapman is and I cannot comment on it. My experience over 30 years is that ministers are looking for people who can make things happen, they are not interested in whether you have worked with a minister of a different political persuasion in the past or what your political view is. The question is, are you capable of delivering whatever the department —

**Q137 Mr Hopkins:** Yes but, if I may interject, lower down the Civil Service, these appointments are not made by ministers, they are made within the Civil Service. Is it not the case and has it not been the case over a prolonged period that an ideology has taken over the Civil Service which fits in very much with the ideology of recent Governments which is for the minimal state, for the privatisation and marketisation of public services, and that anybody who disagrees with that at a lower level is gradually being moved out?

*Sir Andrew Turnbull:* But that is an inaccurate description of the present Government's policies.

**Q138 Mr Hopkins:** I perhaps exaggerated slightly but not very.

*Sir Andrew Turnbull:* They do not believe in 'big state' either. They believe that public services contribute value in various ways to society. They have actually increased public spending. They have increased the number of civil servants and they have increased the number of public servants.

Although there are recent studies which indicate the continuing political influence of civil servants in the legislative process,[18] this is a function which is being challenged by a number of developments. The first and most important of these is the centralisation of government, the growth of so-called joined up government, and the reduced autonomy of individual government departments as a result.[19] In the words of Sir Andrew Turnbull,

> [t]he Prime Minister wanted to create a stronger centre and also make it a richer mix of special advisers as against civil servants. That is the interesting part of the constitutional change.[20]

Under New Labour we have seen a huge expansion of the Prime Minister's Department staff, some of whom were previously employed by the Labour Party. According to the current Cabinet Secretary, 'there has been roughly a doubling of the number of special advisers from 36/37 to 70-something', with 'most of that increase, 24 of the 36 increase' being accounted for by Numbers 10 and 11 Downing Street.[21] Number 10 now orchestrates the government's agenda and sets targets and priorities for every other department. In doing so it works with the Treasury, which initiated Public Service Agreements with individual departments.[22] These departments are required to identify their objectives and targets on a three-yearly cycle, with accountability to the Treasury for performance. Performance appraisals are published on departmental websites. According to the former Cabinet Secretary and Head of the Civil Service, Lord Butler, 'there is too much central control and there is too little of what I would describe as reasoned deliberation which brings in all the arguments'.[23] Related to this is the growth in the number of Specialist Advisers to ministers,[24] with uncertainty about the boundaries of their role: is it to advise and assist or do they operate as 'a layer at the top of the Civil Service between the minister and the rest of the Civil Service'?[25] Whatever the answer, this is a matter also addressed by Lord Butler who said that 'what happens now is that the government reaches conclusions in rather small groups of people who are not necessarily representative of all the groups of interests in government, and there is insufficient opportunity for other people to debate, dissent and modify'.[26]

These developments reflect the growing pre-occupation of government with delivery, particularly with the delivery of public services. Although associated with Blair, this is a feature of government that can be traced back to the Major years.[27] As Bogdanor explains:

> There came to be less concern with constitutional principles and procedures, the emphasis being placed instead on the effectiveness of the public sector, its output. Indeed, the dominant theme of the public management reforms of the 1980s and 1990s may be summed up in a phrase often used by John Major, the privatisation of choice. The aim was to give the consumer the same rights in respect of the public services as were enjoyed by the shopper at Marks & Spencer or Sainsbury's.[28]

There is a sense in which policy is developed by No 10 and the No 10 Policy Unit, and that the function of the civil service is more clearly related to delivery. This is reflected by the establishment of the Prime Minister's Delivery Unit in June 2001, with an 'over-riding mission' to 'ensure the delivery of the Prime Minister's top public service priority outcomes by 2005'.[29] According to the government, the Unit reports to the Prime Minister and

> works in partnership with the Treasury, No. 10, other parts of the Cabinet Office and stakeholder departments, to assess delivery and provide performance management for key delivery areas, and has a shared responsibility with the Treasury for the joint Public Service Agreement (PSA) target.[30]

It is important to note here the extent to which departmental activity is subordinated to 'ruthless prioritisation' and the enhanced focus 'on the Prime Minister's highest priority public service delivery areas'. According to Downing Street, a team of around 40 people, drawn from the public and private sectors, carry out the Unit's work. The Unit also draws on the expertise of a wider group of Associates with experience of successful delivery in the public, private and voluntary sectors.[31]

The influence of the private sector is one that is to be repeated as this story of change unfolds, but it takes place in an environment in which the Prime Minister is said to be 'operating as chief executive of ... various subsidiary companies'.[32]

## Changing Civil Service Structure

It would be fair to say that most of the preceding discussion has had little relevance for the great bulk of civil servants. They were never involved in policy development, and have always been engaged in service delivery, whether it be in job centres dealing with the unemployed or tax offices dealing with taxpayers. For them, the main change that has taken place relates not to the changing function of the civil service, but the changing structures within which they are employed. This too has implications for the senior civil service, and indeed it is at this level that the constitutional rather than the employment implications of the change are most keenly to be felt. The most important of these changes relates to the creation of the Executive Agencies following a seminal report, *Improving Management in Government: The Next Steps*, by Sir Robin Ibbs in 1988. But although it is the most important, it should be emphasised that the creation of these agencies was part of an overall strategy that saw the introduction of 'quasi–market structures into the public services', to be achieved by privatisation, market testing and contracting–out as well. Quoting another distinguished political scientist, WJM Mackenzie, Bogdanor claims that the basic case for these developments was 'the simulation of a business situation', before adding that the 'fundamental leitmotif of the reforms was that efficiency in the public services could be achieved by adapting the methods and practices of the private sector'.[33]

The key feature of the Ibbs Report was the recommendation that the civil service should be broken up into more manageable parts. The central civil service would continue to service ministers and manage departments, but other activity would be conducted by executive agencies that would be responsible for service delivery. Each agency would have a chief executive who would be answerable to the minister under the terms of a framework document which would be published. These recommendations were accepted with alacrity and by 2000 there were 137 executive agencies responsible for some 80 per cent of the civil service. They vary enormously in size from the Employment Service with 45,000 civil servants to the National Weights and Measures Laboratory with 45.[34] This delegation and decentralisation of function was designed to 'bring a new, more customer–focused approach to individual executive (service delivery) functions within government', leaving their parent departments 'to concentrate on policy development'. Executive agencies remain part of the Crown, and do not usually have their own legal identity, but operate under powers that are delegated from ministers and departments. They have a chief executive who reports to the minister against specific targets. Most agencies receive their funding from their parent department and, although they are required to publish and lay before Parliament separate accounts, these accounts also form a constituent part of their parent department's accounts.[35]

The delegation of function to the executive agencies has been seen to have a number of important constitutional implications, particularly in regard to the principle of ministerial responsibility. By virtue of this fundamental convention of the British constitution, ministers are responsible to Parliament for the conduct of their department, though quite what this means has always been uncertain. The principle is recognised judicially in the well known Carltona case where wartime regulations provided for the requisition of property under the authority of the Minister of Works. In this case, the letter of requisition received by the plaintiff company had been signed and sent by an official in the minister's department, and it was argued that the order was therefore invalid. But the claim was rejected by the Court of Appeal which held that 'constitutionally' the decision of the official was 'the decision of the minister'. In the words of Lord Greene,

> [t]he minister is responsible. It is he who must answer before Parliament for anything that his officials have done under his authority.[36]

The restructuring of the civil service has led to questions being asked about how this principle can operate when so much of the service delivery has been hived off to agencies. How can it now be said that the civil servants are acting under the authority of the minister when they are operating at arm's length from him or her, under the control of a chief executive? Although this may be a matter where there has been a tendency to exaggerate the practical nature of the problem, sensitivity arises because it raises matters of great constitutional significance, striking at the very heart of the fundamentals of the Westminster system of government.

There are in fact two constitutional dimensions to this question — the first is political and the second is legal. So far as the first is concerned, although ministers are responsible to Parliament for the conduct of their department, this has never entailed any sense of direct personal responsibility for departmental failures. It is only rarely that ministers have resigned because of departmental failures, and there is no sense of obligation to do so, provided the minister retains the confidence of the House. Most ministerial resignations have been for matters in a minister's private life rather than the incompetent management of their public duties. A good example is the resignation of the Right Honourable David Blunkett MP as Home Secretary amid claims that he had misused public office for personal benefit (or at least the benefit of his erstwhile mistress). Nevertheless, the creation of the agencies provides an opportunity for ministers to deflect responsibility to the chief executives, several of whom have been dismissed or have had to resign because of departmental failures. An early example of dismissal is the head of the Prison Service following a number of prison breakouts,[37] and a more recent example of the former is the resignation of the head of the Child Support Agency following 'widespread criticism' of the organisation.[38] Yet although the need for a scalp will make the chief executive peculiarly vulnerable to reduce the rising political temperature around the minister, it does not follow that the creation of the agencies wholly excludes any sense of responsibility to Parliament. Although not responsible to Parliament in the constitutional sense, agency chiefs are in practice accountable to Parliament through the medium of the select committees, while the minister is accountable to Parliament for his or her department, including all of its agencies.

These emerging patterns of accountability illustrate the diluted form that ministerial responsibility now takes: direct responsibility is deflected to the agency chief by virtue of his or her parliamentary accountability, while the responsibility of the minister has metamorphosed into a doctrine of accountability. But although accountability is a weaker form than responsibility, it may be that it more accurately reflects the practice not just since the creation of the agencies but since the 1950s, if not before. What is important is that ministers continue to be answerable (to use another term) for their stewardship of a department, even though that answerability may not mean a great deal when the government is supported by a large majority of mainly loyal MPs. Just as the constitutional convention has adapted at a political level, so it is likely that the creation of the agencies will be absorbed easily by the legal system. The *Carltona* principle is based on the civil servant acting with the authority of the minister. Although questions have been raised about agencies having the necessary authority, it is difficult to see why the agencies are not acting with such authority. But quite apart from the elasticity of the concept of authority and the ability of the courts to adapt to the dynamic nature of the constitution, such authority is surely to be found in the agency framework agreements. It is not to be overlooked that the *Carltona* principle extends a long way down the chain of command, so that, for example, it extends 'to cover the exercise of the [Home Secretary's] powers by an immigration inspector'.[39]

## Changing Civil Service Values

The civil service has traditionally been the subject of value systems that set it apart from many other forms of employment. The first are what might be referred to as the public service values which inform the relationship between the government and its staff, based on the nature of the employment in which the staff are engaged. These values reflect the unique nature of the role which many civil servants occupy, though it should be emphasised that the work of most civil servants has parallels in other parts of the public sector (most notably local government and the National Health Service). But alongside the public service values are what might be referred to as public employment values in which it was recognised that the state had a special responsibility as an employer to set an example to others as a model employer.[40] But not only did the government lead by example, it also led by coercion. So where the government acted not as employer but as contractor, it insisted that its contractors pay fair wages and recognise the right of their employees to trade union membership. The first Fair Wages Resolution was made in 1891, replaced by the Fair Wages Resolution of 1946, which set higher standards in terms of the duty of contractors to pay fair wages to staff, with fair wages being determined by prevailing collective agreements.[41] In recent years these public service values have been strengthened, while the public employment values have changed. Governments no longer lead the market, but are led by it.

So far as the public service values are concerned, some of these values are crystallised in the *Civil Service Code* which was published for the first time in 1996. This refers to the constitutional role of the civil service to serve governments with 'integrity, honesty, impartiality and objectivity', and the duty not to misuse their official position for private gain. These principles have been expressed elsewhere in the following terms:

**Incorruptibility** — Public policy and individual decisions made by civil servants are not influenced by considerations of personal gain, either while they are in the service or in the form of an outside appointment as a reward after they have left.

**Impartiality** — Successive Governments have come into office and found a Civil Service ready to put their policies and programmes into action from the start.

**Integrity** — Advice given to Ministers may be welcome or not, but it is the job of the Civil Service to see that the decision making process is as well informed as it can be.

**Independence** — Civil servants owe neither their jobs nor their prospects to the influence of political parties, lobby groups, business or other interests.[42]

It has also been said that civil servants must be adaptable in the sense that 'political priorities can change with events as much as with elections; civil servants must be ready to implement with the same vigour a radical change to previous policies'.[43] The *Civil Service Code* also makes clear that civil servants owe a duty to the Crown, not to the public. This means in effect to the government of the day: they 'owe their loyalty to the Administration in which they serve'.[44] This duty was brought into sharp focus during the Falklands war when a senior civil servant, Clive Ponting, disclosed government papers to a Labour MP about the sinking of the Argentinian ship, the *Belgrano*.[45]

Ponting was prosecuted under the *Official Secrets Act 1911*, s 2 (now repealed). This provided that it was an offence to make an unauthorised disclosure of government information unless the defendant could show that it was his duty in the interests of the state to disclose the information. Although Ponting was found not guilty, this was despite an instruction from the trial judge that the interests of the state were the interests of the state as determined by the government of the day and not by individual officials.[46]

Although s 2 of the 1911 Act has now been repealed, the sentiments expressed in the *Ponting* case remain intact. This was revealed most tragically in the inquiry into the suicide of Dr David Kelly, the government scientist who took his life shortly after an unpleasant grilling by the House of Commons Foreign Affairs Committee. Dr Kelly was thought to have made claims to a BBC journalist about exaggerations in the government's published case for invading Iraq. In his report into the circumstances surrounding the death, Lord Hutton made clear that Dr Kelly had exceeded his authority by briefing the BBC in the way that he did. In doing so Dr Kelly had breached the terms of the *Civil Service Code* which prohibit the unauthorised disclosure of official information obtained in confidence.[47] Dr Kelly was perhaps the most high profile example of this reinforcement of public service values; others were to find the criminal law in the form of the *Official Secrets Act 1989* mobilised against them.[48] In these ways the strengthening of public service values paradoxically operates to the disservice not only of the individual official but also the public.

Turning to the changing of public employment values, this has taken place gradually over a number of years, as more and more emphasis has been placed on the contradictory goals of service and delivery on the one hand, and efficiency and value for money on the other. Alongside the public service values, we find the rejection of public employment values and the creep of private sector values into the lexicon and practice of civil service employment. In these ways we see the emergence of private sector management practices, private sector legal forms, and private sector problems. This is a process which is calculated to increase, being cemented in a recent *Cabinet Office paper on Civil Service Reform — Delivery and Values*, where the business simile is used frequently: government is a business providing services to customers to whom the civil service must respond. Thus:

- There is a need to bring people in from the private sector to provide necessary business support:

  The Civil Service has already opened itself up and must continue to do so, both by bringing in people with skills we are lacking and by making sure that we train and develop more of our own people in those areas. This is particularly true of subjects such as project management, financial management and human resources. For too long we have failed to recognise the importance of fully professional skills in these areas, but they are central to any successful *business* and are too important to leave to chance — especially when the demand is rising sharply.[49]

- There is a need to review the concept of a job for life and to replace it with employment policies based on the requirements of the business:

  But in all employment sectors, the traditional concept of a career for life is fast disappearing. What matters now is the performance and potential of the individual, matched against the needs of the *business*. No one has a lifetime right to be a civil servant, irrespective of their abilities or the requirements of the department. But anyone who has the abilities needed by the *business*, or can stay ahead of a changing environment, can be confident of being valued and employed over a long period.[50]

- There is a need for new employment practices designed to improve productivity and performance of those employed in the business:

  The Civil Service has been historically poor at giving people honest, constructive feedback about their performance and ensuring that everyone, no matter how able, has a personal plan for improving this. We want a culture in which everyone is self-aware and is constantly learning new ways of doing things better.

  In particular, we need to get better at addressing performance which is consistently below the potential of the individual or the full needs of the *business*, but falls short of being a disciplinary matter. It has always been easier to pass the problem on, rather than to address it directly.[51]

But it is not only the emergence of business principles which now compete with or complement public service values. Also relevant is the emergence of private sector concerns. These include the greater use of outsourcing of 'large scale process functions',[52] for which the Fair Wages Resolution has been conveniently rescinded. They also include the better management of staff. Thus, there is a need for greater operational flexibility of staff to improve the performance of the business in which the government is engaged:

  One implication of this is that while the Civil Service will remain a distinct entity within the public sector, we should expect much more movement between civil servants and their public sector colleagues responsible for delivery. Experiencing and understanding the pressures on each side of the policy/delivery equation is critical to an effective linkage between the department as service leader, and the operational *businesses* that deliver the outcomes.[53]

There is also a need for greater business efficiency, both in terms of the overall numbers of staff and their location:

> This drive for efficiency is not a one-off event. We need a continuous process of self-generating improvement, with departments keeping up an internal process of reviewing their efficiency against the scope for improvements in the way they do their *business*.[54]

By 2007–08, some 84,000 posts will be lost. Yet this hunt for efficiency is not just about losing posts. It might also include new '[r]eward structures and performance review systems',[55] as well as — as we have seen — 'addressing performance which is consistently below the potential of the individual or the full needs of the business, but falls short of being a disciplinary matter'.[56] So far as the latter is concerned, there are some for whom the following passage may have made particularly chilling reading:

> 5.23 Although managing weaker performance is something that we want to improve across the Civil Service, we are leading from the top with a new approach starting this April for Senior Civil Servants. We will pay particular attention to the performance and development issues raised for those individuals who, relative to their peers, fall into the lowest 20 per cent of performance effectiveness in their current responsibilities. But the objective is support for improvement, not blame for the past.

> 5.24 The first task will be for managers and staff concerned to identify the causes of the performance weakness, and then to work out the best means of addressing them. This may be about the skills or training necessary for a particular post. It may be about an individual's range of experience and how it could be broadened: a highly competent policy maker may be unable to adapt successfully to commanding a large operational activity, or vice versa. The answer might lie in training, in opportunities elsewhere in the Civil Service, or perhaps in secondment to another organisation that helps deliver the department's objectives.

> 5.25 And there will always be cases where, whatever the abilities people may have been recruited with, either they or the organisation have moved on in ways which mean there is no longer a role they can fulfil effectively. For these people it is unhelpful and unfair to pretend otherwise: the individual should be supported to find work elsewhere. But the values and capabilities of civil servants are highly regarded in other sectors, and we should expect to see people moving more freely in and out of the Civil Service as a normal working pattern.

5.26 Identification as being in the lowest 20 per cent means that there is an issue to be addressed in comparison with the performance of peers. It is a relative judgement, not an absolute measure. That is why the new policy properly applies to everyone in the Senior Civil Service, from the most newly promoted Deputy Director to Permanent Secretaries.

## Changing Civil Service Employment Practices

Changing public employment values has coincided with changing public employment practices. The legal authority for determining pay and conditions is found in the Civil Service Order in Council of 1995, a prerogative instrument. This provides that:

> The Minister may from time to time make regulations and give instructions... providing for the number and grading of posts in the Service, the classification of all persons employed therein, their remuneration, expenses, allowances, holidays, hours of work, part-time and other working arrangements, retirement and redundancy, the reinstatement and re-employment of persons in the Service, the re-deployment of staff within the Service and the conditions of service of all persons employed in the Service.

It was the predecessor to this measure which formed the basis of the instruction to the trade unions in the famous GCHQ case, itself a symptom of the changing attitude of government in terms of its role as an employer. The then Minister for the Civil Service gave instructions that staff employed at GCHQ would no longer be permitted to join or remain in membership of a trade union. It was not until 1997 that trade union rights at GCHQ were partially restored. A legal challenge at the time was rejected by the House of Lords on the ground that the decision had been taken in the interests of national security,[57] and an application to the European Commission of Human Rights was rejected.[58] However, this high profile event should not obscure the fact that since 1925 a national pay bargaining system has been in operation for civil servants, based on the recommendations of the Whitley Committee in 1917.[59]

Until the 1990s the system of collective bargaining was based on national agreements setting terms and conditions which would apply across the sector to workers in the same grade, regardless of the department in which they were employed. Indeed this was consistent with the longstanding principle of a unified civil service. (This is not to say that there were not concerns about civil service management style in this earlier era. Apart from the GCHQ case already referred to, *Cresswell v Inland Revenue Commissioners* [60] was another case to reach the High Court around the same time. In this case the court held that the Inland Revenue was entitled to push forward with the introduction of new technology without the consent of the staff unions. In its view, employees were under a duty to adapt to new methods of working, provided that the new method did not involve 'esoteric' skills.) These collective bargaining arrangements were changed in 1992 by legislation that provided for the delegation of pay determination to the departments and agencies themselves. This was done by the *Civil Service Management Act 1992* which gave little clue as to its purpose by enacting that '[a] Minister of the Crown in whom a function to which this section applies is vested may, to such extent and subject to such conditions as he thinks fit, delegate the function to any other servant of the Crown'.[61] The 1992 Act was the harbinger not only of departmental pay determination, but also the break-up of the national bargaining arrangements. Mimicking the decentralisation of collective bargaining in the private sector from sector to enterprise, there has been a decentralisation of collective bargaining in the civil service, with bargaining now taking place in a large number of individual bargaining units.

The process began in 1996 when the then government withdrew from the national bargaining arrangements then in force. It has been explained that '[r]esponsibility for pay bargaining was delegated to individual government departments, agencies and related bodies: there are now over 170 pay systems, meaning 170 different pay scales, minimums, maximums and vastly differing terms and conditions'.[62] But it has also been explained that this is not a real delegation, as 'the negotiated departmental pay structures were tightly constrained by the un-negotiated decisions made at the centre'.[63] The point is made clearly by the *Civil Service Management Code* which states that departments and agencies 'have authority to determine the terms and conditions relating to the remuneration of their own staff outside the Senior Civil Service'.[64] But, as the Code also makes clear, this is a rather meaningless facility given that

> [d]epartments and agencies must develop arrangements for the remuneration of their staff which are appropriate to their business needs, are consistent with the Government's policies on the Civil Service and public sector pay, and observe public spending controls.[65]

There are also concerns about the pointless inefficiency of these 'devolved' arrangements:

> While centralised pay negotiations used to be carried out by some 40 people in the Treasury, the Civil Service College has now trained over 2,000 civil servants.

> Bargaining units vary in size from the Department of Work and Pensions with 115,000 staff, to the Queen Elizabeth II Conference Centre which is required to develop its own fully-fledged pay system and to conduct pay negotiations for just 50 staff.

Clearly, we have lost the economies of scale and of administrative time which were available when there were national negotiations on the core aspects of pay and conditions of service. Yet, since 1996, the Treasury has not carried out any cost/benefit analyses of delegation. This is remarkable given the considerable costs of:

- setting up new pay units in delegated areas,
- extra staff directly employed,
- staff time in delegated negotiations,
- administering the process of pay delegation and of pay remits,
- the use of consultants in establishing new pay systems, pay and grading reviews,
- job evaluation.[66]

The decentralisation of pay bargaining also has huge implications for industrial action by civil servants, which is subject to the same rules as apply to workers in other employment. The industrial action immunities apply only if the action in question is preceded by a ballot. But the balloting legislation is predicated on the basis of enterprise bargaining and enterprise disputes. This causes difficulties for national action, such as that which may be organised by the civil service unions protesting against job cuts. At a conference in November 2004, the General Secretary of the largest civil service union, the Public and Commercial Services Union (PCS), explained that 'we had to hold 160 separate ballots across the civil service and we still had to defend a legal action by the Learning and Skills Council'.[67] Industrial action is becoming an increasing feature of civil service employment. Indeed on 5 February 2005 the radical daily newspaper the *Morning Star* screamed from its front page headline: 'Biggest strike for decades'. Although carried not quite so provocatively or so prominently, the story was not neglected by other newspapers. Even *The Times* picked it up (albeit on page 24) with a scarcely more reassuring headline: 'Million-strong strike gets closer'. These headlines told us about a proposed public sector strike, to be led by 330,000 civil servants but to include local government workers and firefighters, all to be co-ordinated to take place on the same day, 23 March, just weeks before an anticipated general election.

At the heart of this particular dispute was a decision by the government to raise the retirement age of civil servants and to replace their final salary pension scheme with one based on average earnings. But the dispute itself was simply a symptom of a deeper problem in the civil service, following as it did industrial action by civil servants in 2004 about government proposals to relocate jobs from London to the provinces. Civil service employment is changing, and far from being a model employer, the government is now condemned by civil service unions. The condemnation is not only for its unilateral management style, but also for the fact that the civil service is now an area of low pay and gender pay discrimination. It is this question of pay which highlights that the public employment changes affect outcomes as well as procedures and institutional arrangements for pay determination. According to the PCS: '[l]ow pay in the civil service is a serious problem which is getting worse'. It is claimed that:

> There is a 27 per cent gap between the median salaries of male and female full-time workers in the civil service. Men earn an average of £20,380 per annum; women earn an average of only £14,810 per annum. Women are approximately twice as likely as men to be low earners — i.e. full-time staff on a salary below £15,000 per annum.

> Much of this pay gap arises from the fact that, while more than 50 per cent of civil servants are women, the majority work in the lower grades. Whilst there are 2,610 men in the Senior Civil Service, there are only 780 women; in Grades 6 & 7 there are 14,750 men and 5,290 women. Of the 1,000 staff earning above £70,000 per annum, only 170 are women. However, even within the same grade women earn only an average of 95 per cent of men's wages.[68]

These are problems which in the view of the unions can only be resolved by a return to some kind of national pay bargaining, establishing a National Pay Framework. So far as the gender pay gap is concerned, the union claims that 'the current system of delegated pay, grading and conditions of employment is part of the problem'.[69]

## Changing Civil Service Employment Law

The final step in the emergence of private sector values is the privatisation of civil service employment law. As we have seen in the era before modern employment law, civil servants were treated differently from other employees mainly because of the source of the authority by which they were employed. Civil servants had no contracts, they could not sue to recover unpaid wages, and they could be dismissed at pleasure. Indeed the impact of Crown employment went beyond its impact on the staff themselves, as revealed in *Mulvenna v Mulvenna* [70] where it was held that a wife could not attach (or in Scotland arrest) the wages of her husband to deal with defaulting aliment payments. These common law disabilities were ameliorated by the collective bargaining which took place within the civil service and gradually by the extension of employment legislation to Crown servants. Although the first wave of such enactments (dealing with minimum notice periods before dismissal and redundancy payments) had no application to civil servants,[71] the practice since 1971 has been to extend the burgeoning body of legislation to Crown employment, though there are exceptions.

The position of civil servants was potentially transformed, however, by the developments in judicial review and by the ruling by the House of Lords in 1984 that the exercise of prerogative power was no longer beyond the jurisdiction of the English courts, provided that the prerogative power in question was justiciable (as the employment power would almost certainly be). In *Council of Civil Service Unions v Minister for the Civil Service* [72] the decision to ban trade unions from Government Communications Headquarters failed not because it had been taken under prerogative power but because it had been taken in the interests of national security. The holding in that case that prerogative decisions could be reviewed opened up the possibility that civil servants might be able to seek judicial review to challenge decisions taken against them by their employer, whether it be discipline, dismissal or any other matter relating to their employment. It is true that at the same time as the Lords were ruling on the reviewability of the prerogative, the Court of Appeal was ruling in another employment case (this time involving a nurse employed by the National Health Service) that judicial review was not an appropriate forum for dealing with employment matters (even against public authorities).[73] But civil servants were different: unlike their colleagues in the National Health Service they were employed under prerogative.

The reluctance of the courts to entertain employment disputes in judicial review proceedings was nevertheless soon to affect civil servants. Here the courts were helped by the Cabinet Office which from 1985 began to assert the opposite from what they had asserted in the past, namely that civil servants were employed under contracts of employment after all.[74] Faced with this argument in 1988, the Divisional Court accepted that there was 'nothing unconstitutional about civil servants being employed by the Crown pursuant to contracts of service'. Indeed, such a position would be 'wholly consistent with a modern and realistic view of the position of civil servants vis-a-vis the Crown'.[75] That being the case, the relationship between the civil servant and the Crown suddenly metamorphosed into an relationship in private rather than public law. So in *R v Lord Chancellor's Department; Ex parte Nangle*,[76] it was held that the civil servant could not under judicial review proceedings challenge a decision to discipline him for sexual harassment: 'if the applicant can establish breach of contract by failure to comply with the express or implied provisions of the disciplinary code which has resulted in loss, he can sue for damages for breach of contract'.[77] But even if judicial review was applicable, the court went on to say that it was not prepared to entertain an action for what was wholly domestic and informal and not appropriate for judicial review.

So here we have the privatisation of public sector employment law: civil servants are now employed under contract, a journey that it now recognised at various points in the *Civil Service Management Code*. This now claims that '[b]ecause of the constitutional position of the Crown and the prerogative power to dismiss at will, civil servants cannot demand a period of notice as of right'.[78] In other words, although the courts now recognise the existence of a contract, the Crown continues to claim a power to dismiss without notice. To the extent that there is a prerogative power in relation to the employment of staff this would be it: the power to dismiss at pleasure. It is not clear whether the courts would accept this power claimed by the Crown, and it is noted that the Supreme Court of Canada has rejected similar (though not identical) extravagant claims by the Crown.[79] Here it was held that '[e]mployment in the civil service is not feudal servitude',[80] that senior civil servants are engaged under a contract, and that the Crown was bound to pay substantial damages for the premature termination of a contract. It is to be pointed out, however, that although the Crown in the United Kingdom claims a legal right to terminate an employment contract at pleasure, the *Civil Service Management Code* provides minimum notice periods which 'in practice' departments and agencies 'will normally apply'.[81] These generally track the minimum periods in legislation from which the civil service is excluded.

The effect of privatisation is to remove unequivocally any protection they might have under judicial review, which is likely to be much greater than that provided by contract, both in terms of the grounds for review and the remedies where a complaint is successful. We thus have not just the privatisation of civil service *values* and the privatisation of civil service *employment practices*, but also the privatisation of civil service *employment law*. By extending the law of contract and enhancing the status of civil servants, we are paradoxically weakening their legal protection by denying access to administrative law. But it should be noted that the extension of contract is purely formal: although civil servants now have contracts, the term of the contract is that they are employed at the pleasure of the Crown. This means that they have no common law remedy in private law for wrongful dismissal, though they may have a statutory remedy for unfair dismissal. The existence of the latter has provided another opportunity for the courts to refuse judicial review in dismissal cases brought by civil servants. Dismissed civil servants can appeal to a body called the Civil Service Appeal Board, a body set up under prerogative power.[82] Although the courts have accepted that the decisions of the Board are subject to judicial review (and have compelled it to give reasons for its decisions),[83] they have shown little desire to scrutinise its decisions in judicial review proceedings.[84] The last judicial review case was in 1991.

## Changing Civil Service Regulation — A Civil Service Act?

In these different ways the civil service is in a process of change. Also part of this process are proposals for the introduction of a Civil Service Act or a Public Service Act. The idea here is that the position of the civil service should be placed on a firm statutory basis, a proposal first made in the seminal Northcote-Trevelyan Report in 1854. This is a proposal which has been made in more recent years from a number of sources: the Public Service Committee of the House of Lords, the Public Administration Committee of the House of Commons, and the Committee on Standards in Public Life.[85] It also has academic support and indeed the idea was first seriously articulated in academic quarters.[86] But how — if at all — does this proposal support the thesis of this paper? The answer is that it does so, but only as a general indicator of the trends identified: it will move the base of regulation away from a peculiarly public law source (the royal prerogative) to one which is a mixed public and private law source of regulation. As Professor Hennessy told the House of Lords Public Service Committee: changes to Orders in Council were easily made and seldom noticed, but 'if it is in the form of primary legislation and you do want to make a change you have to be honest about it because only primary legislation can override primary legislation'.[87] It is true that the government appears only to be a late (and if the lack of progress is any guide, reluctant) convert to the idea of a Civil Service Act.[88] But that alone is not enough to diminish the contribution of the proposal to the process of privatisation that is underway, even if on this occasion it is not an unwelcome contribution.

The main concern of the reformers is with what we have referred to as protecting public service values rather than public service employment practices. But it is not clear that there is any great desire to change those values beyond what is already set out in the *Civil Service Code* which is seen to be a good statement of principle. This applies particularly to the following provision:

> The constitutional and practical role of the Civil Service is, with integrity, honesty, impartiality and objectivity, to assist the duly constituted Government, of whatever political complexion, in formulating policies of the Government, carrying out decisions of the Government and in administering public services for which the Government is responsible.[89]

Attention has also been drawn to the *Ministerial Code* which also contains a good section on the civil service and its relationship with ministers:

> Ministers have a duty to give fair consideration and due weight to informed and impartial advice from civil servants, as well as to other considerations and advice, in reaching policy decisions; a duty to uphold the political impartiality of the Civil Service, and not to ask civil servants to act in any way which would conflict with the *Civil Service Code*; a duty to ensure that influence over appointments is not abused for partisan purposes; and a duty to observe the obligations of a good employer with regard to terms and conditions of those who serve them. Civil servants should not be asked to engage in activities likely to call in question their political impartiality, or to give rise to the criticism that people paid from public funds are being used for Party political purposes.[90]

As the House of Lords Public Service Committee made clear, the main concern is to acknowledge the constitutional autonomy of the civil service and to protect it from politicisation. Thus:

> within that constitutional framework the position of Ministers, Parliament and the courts is acknowledged, assured and understood; but the same cannot be said of the Civil Service. If Ministers were to decide that Civil Servants had no role in identifying and explaining the public interest, that would be that. The Civil Service would, in effect, become a private service for Ministers and neither the Civil Service, Parliament nor the courts would be in any position to do anything about it.[91]

The purpose then seems to be to draw a line in the sand and to protect the values already established from further erosion. This becomes clearer on examination of the specific proposals for what a Civil Service Act would contain. The most fully developed proposals are those of the House of Lords Public Service Committee, which recommended that there should be legislation despite concerns from some high profile witnesses about the impact of legislation restricting the flexibility of the civil service. These witnesses included Lord Nolan (the first Chairman of the Committee on Standards in Public Life) who argued that good standards come from within and not from primary legislation, of which there was already enough. Nevertheless, the Committee envisaged legislation that would do the following:

- specify which public bodies come within its ambit; it would define the civil service and give statutory force to a Civil Service Code of the kind which was promulgated in 1996;
- clarify whether civil servants have any duties over and above their duties to Ministers and whether they owe independent duties as an organ of the constitution; it would set out the duties of Ministers in relation to civil servants;
- give uniform and clear guidelines on the recruitment and management of civil servants as servants of the Crown; it would define what changes to the ambit of the civil service could be effected only by primary legislation;
- specify a mechanism by which civil servants could in the public interest report breaches of the provisions of the Act, which they might otherwise be prevented from doing by their obligations of obedience and confidentiality;
- indicate the grounds upon which application may be made by those seeking judicial review of the action of civil servants or Ministers.[92]

There have in fact been several Civil Service Bills produced and introduced into Parliament, while the government dragged its feet. The fullest of these was the Bill introduced into the House of Lords in 2004, given a second reading but lost before the end of the parliamentary session.

The government has, however, now proposed action with the publication of its Draft Civil Service Bill in November 2004. The accompanying consultation document invited comments by 28 February 2005, and it was clear that even if the comments were all favourable, further progress would be interrupted by a general election later in the year. Nevertheless the Draft Bill contains a number of important proposals to put much of the civil service on a statutory footing. The Civil Service Commission would become a statutory corporation (clause 1), empowered to produce a recruitment code to ensure open competition for appointment to much of the civil service (clause 10). Separate provision is made in the Draft Bill for open competition (clause 8), for some time a fundamental principle of recruitment to the civil service, and essential to avoid the abuse of patronage. Commissioners would be appointed by the Prime Minister, who must consult the Scottish First Minister and the First Secretary of the Welsh Assembly, as well as the leaders of the main political parties. The management of the civil service is also to be placed on a statutory footing, with clause 4 proposing to vest 'management powers' in the Minister for the Civil Service. These are powers of a wide and varied kind, from the number of civil servants, to their grading and classification, to their remuneration and working conditions. There is no sense, however, that civil servants will enjoy any special treatment, with the accompanying consultation paper making clear that any Civil Service Act should 'leave civil servants subject to general employment practices', albeit with 'very similar statutory employment rights to other employees'.[93]

The other main provisions of the Draft Bill deal with ethical issues. The Minister for the Civil Service is to use his or her statutory management powers to publish a Civil Service Code, which must be laid before each House of Parliament (clause 5). The Code would require civil servants to carry out their duties for the assistance of the duly constituted government whatever its political complexion (clause 5(7)), and require civil servants to carry out their duties efficiently, with integrity and honesty, with objectivity and impartiality, reasonably, without maladministration, and according to law (clause 5(8)). It is specifically proposed that ministers must not impede civil servants in their compliance with the Code (clause 5(10)). The provisions of the Code — which do not apply to special advisers — are to form part of the terms and conditions of service of civil servants (clause 7). A separate code is to be published for special advisers (clause 6), for whom special provision is made in the Draft Bill. The government's intention is that the Draft Bill should make clear what special advisers can do (advise and assist ministers) and what they cannot do (exercise executive power). The Prime Minister may, however, designate two special advisers to authorise the expenditure of public funds, exercise statutory power, and exercise management functions over the civil service (clause 16). This power of appointed officials is justified as being 'designed to give the Head of Government a small degree of freedom in how he or she chooses to organise the centre of government'.[94] But it is likely to be highly controversial, as is the refusal of the government to put a statutory cap on the number of special advisers who may be appointed.[95]

## Conclusion

We began this discussion with an account of an argument presented in 1953 in which an attempt was made to draw similarities between the state and the corporation. We conclude with the thought that this argument may be more relevant and sustainable 50 years after it was first presented. This is so, not because the state has adopted the corporate form, but because corporate values have penetrated the public sphere. This is seen in what has been referred to as the privatisation of the process of government, not in the sense of government being sold or outsourced to the private sector, but in the sense of government embracing private sector similes, private sector values and private sector methods. We also see the adoption of private sector legal forms which remove some of the unfavourable legal treatment to which civil servants are exposed by virtue of their employment under the royal prerogative. Paradoxically, however, the extension of the contractual model to civil servants actually involves a dilution of rights, as it has the effect of ensuring that judicial review is not available to civil servants alleging an abuse of power by their employers. Having suffered years of legal disadvantage, it appears to have been thought to be a step too far to endow them with legal advantage. Any move in the direction of statutory regulation of the civil service is likely to ensure that any such privilege is avoided. This could be achieved by the simple expedient of providing that employment under the new arrangements is under contract and not otherwise. As we have seen, the government has already signalled that a move in this direction will confirm rather than reverse the trend of assimilating the position of civil servants with that of other workers, which in many cases is one of considerable insecurity and uncertainty.

The prospect of a Civil Service Act is perhaps another example of the privatisation of government and the civil service. Although — as suggested — it is not a compelling indicator of a move in the direction of privatisation, it does nevertheless indicate a move away from regulation by means of the royal prerogative, a peculiarly public law source of authority. Although a Civil Service Act may provide the basis of a greater degree of parliamentary scrutiny of government conduct towards the civil service than the regulation by the royal prerogative, it is unlikely to make much practical difference or to reverse the trend of recent developments. It is not to be overlooked that civil servants performed best when operating under public service employment values underpinned by public service legal rules which gave maximum power to the state as employer. The halycon days (if they ever existed) for the civil servant were ones in which there was little law and few enforceable rights — days in which the Crown claimed 'the right to change its officers' conditions of service at any time'.[96] In the days when the prerogative was at its purest (in terms of hiring and firing), collective bargaining was at its most effective. With governments having so enthusiastically embraced private sector methods and values, there are many obstacles to encounter before returning to such an era. But it is a nice lesson about the difference between public and private sector values and practices, and about how formal legal protection is more necessary where the latter rather than the former prevail. The current unrest in the civil service is also an indication that in a modern private sector regime such protection is never likely to be an effective brake on the abuse of power by the state as an employer.

# ENDNOTES

[1] (1953) 65 *Juridical Review* 255.

[2] Ibid 255.

[3] Ibid 258.

[4] Ibid 258–9.

[5] This was the era of large-scale nationalisation, on the form of which, see Lord Herbert Morrison, *Government and Parliament: A Survey from the Inside* (3rd ed, 1964) ch 12.

[6] Walker, above n 1, 259.

[7] For an account, see Anthony W Bradley and Keith D Ewing, *Constitutional and Administrative Law* (13th ed, 2003) ch 14.

[8] For a general account of public sector employment, see Sandra Fredman and Gillian Morris, *The State as Employer* (1989).

[9] *Crown Proceedings Act 1947* s 2(6). Compare Draft Civil Service Bill 2004 (UK) sch 1. Other provisions of the Draft Bill are discussed below.

[10] On which see Sir William Wade and Christopher Forsyth, *Administrative Law* (9th ed, 2004) ch 3.

[11] The impact of the *Official Secrets Act 1989* (UK) was revealed in *R v Shayler* [2003] 1 AC 247 in which it was held that the Act's restrictions on the disclosure of official information did not breach the *Human Rights Act 1998* (UK).

[12] See Vernon Bogdanor, 'The Civil Service' in Vernon Bogdanor (ed), *The British Constitution in the Twentieth Century* (2003) ch 7.

[13] *Civil Service Management Code* (UK) section 4.4.

[14] See Bob Hepple and Paul O'Higgins, *Public Employee Trade Unionism in the United Kingdom* (1971).

[15] Ralph Miliband, *The State in Capitalist Society* (1968) 104.

[16] The *Freedom of Information Act 2000* (UK) (which came into force in 2005) will also contribute to the growing transparency about the identity of civil servants and the advice they give, though at least one department is refusing to identify civil servants by name: David Leigh, 'MoD says staff names are secret', *The Guardian* (UK), 19 February 2005.

[17] Public Administration Select Committee, *Minutes of Evidence*, House of Commons, Paper No 423–i, Session 2003–04 (2004).

[18] Edward Page, 'The Civil Servant as Legislator: Law Making in British Administration' (2003) 81 *Public Administration* 651.

[19] Some of these developments are traced in highly readable terms in Peter Hennessy, *The Prime Minister* (2001) ch 18.

[20] HC 423–i (2003–4), above n 17, Q63.

[21] Ibid.

[22] See Bradley and Ewing, above n 7, 356.

[23] Boris Johnson, 'How Not To Run A Country', *The Spectator* (UK), 11 December 2004.

[24] This is a matter of considerable concern: see Public Administration Select Committee, *Fourth Report. Special Advisers: Boon or Bane?*, House of Commons Paper No 293, Session 2000-01 (2001).

[25] HC 423–i (2003–04), above n 17, Q64 (Kelvin Hopkins MP).

[26] Johnson, above n 23.

[27] See John Major, *The Autobiography* (1999) 250, 684.

[28] Bogdanor, above n 12, 262.

[29] Prime Minister's Delivery Unit, Cabinet Office, <http://www.cabinetoffice.gov.uk/pmdu/> at 8 February 2005.

[30] Ibid.

[31] Ibid.

[32] The Rt Hon Jack Straw MP, then Home Secretary, quoted by Hennessy, above n 19, 523.

[33] Bogdanor, above n 12, 260.

[34] Bradley and Ewing, ibid n 7, 273.

[35] See <http://www.civilservice.gov.uk/other/agencies/agencies_and_non_ministerial_depts/index.asp> at 5 July 2006.

36 *Carltona, Ltd v Commissioner of Works* [1943] 2 All ER 560, 563.

37 See Bradley and Ewing, above n 7, 275–6.

38 See David Batty, 'CSA problems mount as boss quits', *The Guardian* (UK), 17 November 2004.

39 *R v Secretary of State for the Home Department; Ex parte Oladehinde* [1991] 1 AC 254, 302 (Lord Griffiths).

40 See Fredman and Morris, above n 8, 1.

41 The leading account is Brian Bercusson, *Fair Wages Resolutions* (1978). The 1946 Resolution was revoked in the 1980s.

42 Cabinet Office, *Civil Service Reform — Delivery and Values* (2004) [4.2].

43 Ibid.

44 *Civil Service Code* (1996) [2].

45 See Clive Ponting, *The Right to Know: the Inside Story of the Belgrano Affair* (1985).

46 *R v Ponting* [1985] Crim LR 318.

47 See Lord Hutton, *Report of the Inquiry into the Circumstances Surrounding the Death of Dr David Kelly CMG* (2004) [259].

48 David Shayler (above n 11), a former MI5 agent, was convicted of breaching the Act by making disclosures to a national newspaper, including allegations of incompetence. There is also the case of Kathryn Gun, who was arrested and charged with leaking information about clandestine US surveillance of UN Security Council members before the UN votes on the invasion of Iraq, though the case against her was eventually dropped.

49 *Civil Service Reform*, above n 42, [3.2] (emphasis added).

50 Ibid [5.3] (emphasis added).

51 Ibid [5.21]–[5.22] (emphasis added).

52 Ibid [7.3] (emphasis added).

53 Ibid [6.6] (emphasis added).

54 Ibid [7.3] (emphasis added).

55 Ibid [5.19].

56 Ibid [5.22].

57 *Council of Civil Service Unions v Minister for the Civil Service* [1985] AC 374.

58 *Council of Civil Service Unions v United Kingdom* (1988) 10 EHRR CD269. For discussion, see Gillian Morris, 'Freedom of Association and the Interests of the State' in Keith Ewing, Bob Hepple and Conor Gearty (eds), *Human Rights and Labour Law: Essays for Paul O'Higgins* (1994) ch 2.

59 See Fredman and Morris, above n 8, ch 5.

60 [1984] ICR 508.

61 The purpose of this provision is explained at United Kingdom, *Parliamentary Debates*, House of Commons, 5 November 1992, col 451.

62 Public and Commercial Services Union, *Fair Play on Pay: A Civil Service National Pay Framework* <http://www.pcs.org.uk/Templates/Internal.asp?NodeID=882722> at 8 February 2005.

63 Ibid.

64 *Civil Service Management Code* section 7.1.

65 Ibid section 7.1.2.

66 Public and Commercial Services Union, *The cost of delegation* <http://www.pcs.org.uk/Templates/Internal.asp?NodeID=882797> at 8 February 2005.

67 *Morning Star* (UK), 15 November 2004.

68 Public and Commercial Services Union, *Action on Equal Pay* <http://www.pcs.org.uk/Templates/Internal.asp?NodeID=882805> at 8 February 2005.

69 Ibid.

70 [1926] SC 842.

71 See Hepple and O'Higgins, above n 14, 25–26 and *Redundancy Payments Act 1965* (UK) s 16(4)(b).

72 [1985] AC 374.

[73] *R v East Berkshire Area Health Authority; Ex parte Walsh* [1985] QB 152. For a re-assessment of this decision, see Gillian Morris, 'The Future of the Public/Private Labour Divide' in Catherine Barnard, Simon Deakin and Gillian Morris (eds), *The Future of Labour Law* (2004) ch 7.

[74] See Mark Freedland, *The Personal Employment Contract* (2003) 69–70.

[75] *R v Civil Service Appeal Board; Ex parte Bruce* [1988] ICR 649, 660. See also *McClaren v Home Office* [1990] ICR 824.

[76] [1992] 1 All ER 897.

[77] Ibid 905 (Stuart-Smith LJ).

[78] *Civil Service Management Code* section 11.1.1.

[79] *Wells v Newfoundland* [1999] 3 SCR 199. See also the discussion of the Australian position in this volume, Ch 2, Weeks, in section 'Dismissal at Pleasure'.

[80] Ibid [29] (Major J).

[81] *Civil Service Management Code* section 11.1.

[82] Ibid section 12.1.

[83] *R v Civil Service Appeal Board; Ex parte Cunningham* [1992] ICR 816.

[84] See especially *R v Civil Service Appeal Board; Ex parte Bruce* [1988] ICR 649.

[85] See respectively Public Service Select Committee, *Report*, House of Lords Paper No 55, Session 1997–98 (1998); Public Administration Select Committee, *A Draft Civil Service Bill: Completing the Reform*, House of Commons Paper No 128, Session 2003–04 (2004); United Kingdom, *Ninth Report of the Committee on Standards in Public Life*, Cm 5775 (2003).

[86] Norman Lewis, 'A Civil Service Act for the United Kingdom' [1998] *Public Law* 463.

[87] HL 55 (1997–98), above n 85, [411].

[88] See United Kingdom, *A Draft Civil Service Bill — A Consultation Document*, Cm 6373 (2004).

[89] *Civil Service Code* (1996) [1].

[90] *Ministerial Code* (2005) section 3.1. The same provision was made in the 1997 and 2001 versions of the Code.

[91] HL 55 (1997–98), above n 85, [407].

[92] Ibid [415]–[418].

[93] *A Draft Civil Service Bill,* above n 88, [20].

[94] Ibid [39].

[95] Ibid [41].

[96] *Cresswell v Inland Revenue Commissioners* [1984] ICR 508, 521.

# Chapter Eleven

# Challenges Ahead: Workplace Relations Legislation and the Future

## Marilyn Pittard

In Chapter One of this book it was stated that:

> The contributions in this book weave together the themes of, and influences on, public sector employment in contemporary Australia, whilst exploring parallels and differences between public sector employment in the United Kingdom and New Zealand, with some discussion of whistleblowers' legislative protection, including developments in the United States.

These themes embrace developments over time and up to the early part of the twenty-first century. What of the period beyond? What influences are emerging? What is likely to occur in public sector employment? What challenges are ahead?

In these concluding pages, some issues are explored and questions raised. They include the new influence ahead of the regulatory framework for industrial relations and the APS; state responses to the new regulatory framework in relation to state public servants; the challenges of employment diversity in terms of women, Indigenous Australians and people with disability; challenges associated with an ageing workforce; the influence of the private sector; the potential for clashes of market forces and APS codes and values; and the role of policy and guidelines. Finally, the work of Dr Peter Shergold, in forecasting the future in Australia to the year 2035, is examined.

## Workplace Relations Framework at Federal Level

One of the significant changes in recent times has been the enactment of the *Workplace Relations Amendment (Work Choices) Act 2005* (Cth) ('Work Choices') and the *Workplace Relations Amendment (A Stronger Safety Net) Act 2007* (Cth) ('Stronger Safety Net Act'). These Acts, which amended the *Workplace Relations Act 1996* (Cth), have radically changed the regulation of workplace relations in Australia. Utilising mainly the corporations power in the Constitution, section 51(xx), as the legislative authority for enactment, the Work Choices legislation of 2005 and the further legislative amendments in 2007 have overhauled the legal framework for collective and individual workplace relations in Australia, and hence the context in which Australian public sector employment operates. The new framework has:

- abolished compulsory arbitration;
- reduced the role of the Australian Industrial Relations Commission ('the Commission') in conciliation;
- generally removed that Commission's award-making role (except in limited circumstances);
- abolished the role of awards as a safety net (except as a standard for comparison in a limited way where the new fairness test brought in by the Stronger Safety Net legislation applies to agreements);
- generally shifted the role of the safety net in respect of wages to the new minimum rates set by the Australian Fair Pay Commission and the minimum conditions standards in the legislation (known collectively as the Australian Fair Pay and Conditions Standard);
- encouraged individual bargaining and collective bargaining resulting in Australian Workplace Agreements or collective agreements respectively, with the removal of former mechanisms of scrutiny (either the Australian Industrial Relations Commission or the Employment Advocate); rather workplace agreements are now lodged with the Office of the Workplace Authority (formerly the Office of the Employment Advocate) to be operational upon lodgement (it being noted that, in the case of collective agreements and those AWAs which meet specified remuneration levels, to be valid, such agreements must satisfy a 'fairness test');
- removed the protection from unfair dismissal for employees engaged by employers with staff of 100 or less, and for all employees, regardless of employer size, where there is termination of employment for operational reasons;[1]
- further controlled industrial action, through measures such as compulsory protected action ballots.

The impact of this legislation has been referred to in this book in the context of the framework for public sector employment, the making of collective and individual agreements and the impact of the transmission of business provisions, to name but some of the issues addressed in the chapters of the book. However one of the very significant aspects of the Work Choices legislation is the enactment of a single national system of workplace relations. The new system essentially applies to all corporate employers which are 'constitutional corporations' (that is trading, foreign and financial corporations), the Commonwealth and Commonwealth authority employers, and their employees.[2] It no longer rests on the employers and unions initiating an interstate industrial dispute and thereby obtaining award coverage through this mechanism or a collective agreement for settlement of such a dispute.

The implications for the Australian public sector are yet to emerge fully and to be analysed. However, many of the developments occurring in the Australian public sector previously had occurred against the backdrop of the compulsory arbitration system with award safety nets, the possibility of collective bargaining and the then new emphasis on individual agreements (AWAs). The new environment for workplace matters suggests that much of the impact will be felt in wage rates, wages differentials, gender (in)equality and less public disclosure of terms of agreements (particularly given the policy for use of AWAs at Commonwealth level) as well as in the content of agreements. It is far from clear how the changed legal framework, and the consequences for the private sector, will directly and indirectly affect workplace conditions for APS employees.

## State Public Servants

The introduction of the national system based on the corporations power has implications for the role of state systems. Essentially they remain in operation and of influence for employers outside the corporate sphere, that is employers who are not 'constitutional corporations'. It means that corporate employers which perform government functions (or perform functions under contract to state governments) at state level are embraced by the new unitary national system. Employers which are incorporated statutory authorities under state law will usually meet requirements of being trading, financial or foreign corporations and so be caught by the federal legislation.

The impact on state public servants is also very significant. As a general rule, too, employees of local government will be covered by the new Work Choices legislation as will employees of corporate employers which perform government functions. But what about employees who are members of a state public service and work in state government departments? Apart from Victorian government employees who are generally covered by the federal legislation as a consequence of Victoria's referral of powers to the Commonwealth, employees who are engaged in the state public services will not be employed by an entity which satisfies the definition of 'constitutional corporation' and will not be covered by the federal legislation. Likewise, a body which is established by the state law to perform some government functions may or may not constitute a 'constitutional corporation' and, if not, will not therefore be covered by the federal system.

State governments have been concerned at the possible ramifications of the new federal law on their own employees. A variety of responses has been undertaken by the states. In New South Wales, legislation was enacted to transfer employment of employees of corporate authorities to employment by the state in order to avoid the possibility of these employees being covered by the new federal law.[3] Similar legislation was introduced in South Australia and Western Australia.[4] Victoria has enacted legislation to enshrine public sector conditions by requiring agreements to meet a 'no disadvantage' test approved by the Victorian Workplace Rights Advocate before those agreements can be lodged federally and to enshrine, and provide for, additional rights, for example, in relation to unfair dismissal.[5]

Use of procurement contracts has been another vehicle whereby state governments attempt to maintain fair labour conditions for employees within the state. The mechanism used for example in New South Wales and South Australia is the imposition of contractual requirements on successful tenderers.[6]

## Diversity Issues

In addition several issues are emerging as important in the employment sphere. The ageing workforce is of concern not only to the private sector but also to the public sector. The need to maintain diversity of ages as well as diversity in race and sex and a full range of under-represented employees is vital to the goals and aims of the workforce. In the case of the APS, the *State of the Service Report 2005-6* indicated that women's representation in the APS increased over the previous five years from 46.6 per cent to 55.8 per cent of ongoing categories in employment, but women still tended to be engaged in lower classifications than men. By way of contrast, women made up a higher proportion of non-ongoing categories (62.8 per cent) but they were likely to be younger women and employed at lower levels.[7] The problems of representation in the APS of Indigenous Australians and people with disability are also acknowledged challenges[8] to fulfilment of the APS values of providing 'a workplace that is free from discrimination and recognises and utilises the diversity of the Australian community it serves'.[9]

## The Commonwealth as Employer, Market and APS Values

The public sector employer as the 'model employer' was formerly a role which was the subject of some note. Now the state as employer is decreasing its role as direct employer, due to factors including privatisation of functions and outsourcing.[10] Coupled with this is the revival of the market as the main determinant of wages and conditions of employment in the private sector — and leading the way in the revival is the Commonwealth itself. Its preparedness to put service delivery, efficiency and competitiveness ahead of model employment roles will no doubt force a further re-thinking of the role played by the Commonwealth as employer in the era of the Work Choices legislation. The new regulation of workplace relations will no doubt transcend the thinking in the public sector — vestiges of the Commonwealth as the model employer are likely to be eroded or at least challenged. However one of the challenges for the APS is acknowledged to be positioning the APS as the 'employer of choice', especially in tight labour market.[11]

The values and code of conduct applicable to APS employees may also be at odds with the new market-type regulation of employees of corporate employers. For example, the *APS Values and Code of Conduct in Practice: Guide to Official Conduct of APS Employees and Agency Heads* sets out in chapter 5, 'Working with the public', the relevant values and elements of the code of conduct. These have an overlay of administrative law requirements in administrative decision-making. To what extent do remuneration and reward systems for employees sit comfortably with the obligations of employees under legislation? Greater flexibility in remuneration is encouraged by the *Workplace Relations Act 1996* (Cth), such as remuneration related to work performance. How far can this be achieved in systems where there are express duties to third parties? More tightly governed schemes may be necessary to avoid a potential conflict between incentive to the employee and the employee's obligations to the public.

In this context, some differences between private sector employment and the public sector emerge. Whilst the private sector may have employment largely governed by industrial instruments and the contract of employment, the role of employment policy is increasing. Most large employers will have a bank of policies to control, explain and limit employees' exercise of discretion and conduct. Whilst the source of these policies is not legislative, the force and effect of them may be binding when they are incorporated expressly as a term of the contract or where they are implied as a term or otherwise constitute a source of legitimate instructions from the employer to the employee. More attention is devoted to the applicability and binding nature of such policies at common law, as we see for example in the case of *Goldman Sachs J B Were Services v Nickolich*[12] where the Federal Court upheld a decision of Wilcox J that the policy of the employer to provide a safe workplace and so on was regarded as having been incorporated into the contract of employment. It is more usual for cases to focus on the *employee* being bound by such policies.

These policies have their parallels in the public sector — the APS code of conduct and values, with individual policies fleshing these out as guidelines. Arguably the policy constraints are greater in the public sector and may always be so. The problem of differential conditions as between career public servants and short term contractors providing services to the Commonwealth may also be a challenge.

The public sector and private sectors have been closer together, when there was a high degree of tenure in the public sector and when the unfair dismissal laws provided a tight control on fair dismissal for private sector employees covered by the provisions. Since the 'attack' on public sector tenure, particularly at agency head level (as discussed in Chapter 2 of this volume) and the demise of unfair dismissal protection at federal level under the Work Choices legislation, arguably the two sectors are not so far apart on this measure of unfair dismissal protection. However, the statutory protection providing for fair processes for most public sector employees elevates that sector to one with fair safeguards for dismissal.

## Fast Forward — 2035

What is the vision for the public sector and employment in the next two to three decades? Dr Peter Shergold, as Secretary, Department of Prime Minister and Cabinet, undertook a 'forecast' in a speech entitled 'The Australian Public Service in 2035: Back to The Future'[13] in which he made a number or predictions about the Australian Public Service. These included:

- The decline in the size of the public services would continue. He predicted the APS would decline to a workforce of about 100,000 employees in 2035.
- Innovations in technology would enable more to be done with less.
- The development of 'a blended, multi-dimensional workforce' in which full-time and part-time employees would work with contract providers and consultants 'bound together by the work they do, not their working conditions'.[14]
- The problem of relativity of pay between the private and public sectors would remain. The Australian Public Service Commissioner, Lynelle Briggs, has also referred to 'the generally lower level of remuneration of APS staff compared with equivalent staff in the private sector'.[15]
- Women would represent approximately 75 per cent of the APS - and would be represented across all levels of the service.
- The career public service would remain.
- All APS employees would be graduates. In Shergold's words:

  "Managing an all-graduate service will present new challenges. The process of dismantling hierarchy as the basis of authority will have continued, driven by similarities in the education level of the workforce, workplace aspirations, flat job structures and communications technology. Employees will all, in a real sense, be managers — managing knowledge, contracts and projects to develop and deliver policy for the government of the day. They will all be expected to behave as leaders."[16]

- The influence of technology will be uncertain and difficult to envisage. However, Shergold stated:

  "I do not think it will all be for the better. Dealing with the wicked complexity of public policy will be as slow and difficult as ever but the flow of information and responses to it will be ever more immediate ... Governments and their public services will find it increasingly difficult to meet the expectations of citizens as to what government action can achieve and how quickly ... *The job of public servants to identify and promote a national interest may have become even more challenging.*[Emphasis added]"[17]

Some things will remain largely unchanged, in his view. For example, the nature of the public service itself — he was of the view that the merit-based and apolitical public service envisaged by Stafford Northcote and Charles Trevalyan, as discussed in Chapter 3 of this volume, would remain of relevance well into the twenty-first century.[18] Moreover, Dr Shergold said, 'The civil service that they sought, existing as an institution in its own right within the executive arm of government, will have survived'.[19]

The Australian Public Service Commissioner, however, noted that decisions would need to be made about the balance between in-house and external work. In her words:

> As public servants, we need to identify where collaborations with external stakeholders will add the most value and where work should be done in house. We also need to think about how we can try to loosen some of our controls and guidelines to facilitate more flexibility, innovation and effectiveness on the ground, while retaining high standards of accountability. The more we reduce unnecessary red tape, the better our arrangements will be for everyone.[20]

Perhaps it is fitting to conclude with the predictions of Dr Peter Shergold:

> A professional administrative class, willing and able to serve successive governments in a non-partisan manner, accountable through ministers for ensuring that decisions are taken and implemented in a lawful manner and responsive to the directions set by elected government — these, I suggest, are values which will retain their virtue in the decades ahead.[21]

# ENDNOTES

1. See generally the issue of volume 19 of the *Australian Journal of Labour Law* devoted to analysing the Work Choices legislation published in 2006.

2. Other employers are covered — eg maritime, waterside worker and flight crew officer employers; employers, corporate and non-corporate, in Victoria and the Territories.

3. The *Public Sector Employment Legislation Amendment Act 2006* (NSW) amended the *Public Sector Employment and Management Act 2002* (NSW) in March 2006.

4. See *Statutes Amendment (Public Sector Employment) Act 2006* (SA); and the Public Sector (State Employment) Statutes Amendment Bill 2007 (WA).

5. See *Public Sector Employment (Awards Entitlements) Act 2006* (Vic) and the *Public Sector Acts (Further Workplace Protection and Other Matters) Act 2006* (Vic). For analysis, see G Smith, 'Understanding and Implementing the New Workplace and Industrial Relations Guidelines-A Public Sector perspective' (2006) 12 *Employment Law Bulletin* 61.

6. See C Hartigan and A Kaviani Johnson, 'State Responses to Work Choices' (2007) 13 *Employment Law Bulletin* 13 and G Smith above, n 5.

7. *State of the Service Report 2005-6*, November 2006,

<www.apsc.gov.au/stateoftheservice/0506/index.html> [December 2006].

8. See *State of the Service Report 2005-6 at a Glance*, section in Challenges for the APS, <www.apsc.gov.au/stateoftheservice/0506/ataglance.pdf> [December 2006].

9. See APS Values, *Public Service Act 1999* (Cth), s 10.

10. In 2005, Commonwealth public servants accounted for 1.3 per cent of the entire workforce as compared to 2.7 per cent in 1976: 'The Incredible Shrinking Public Sector' Research Note, 24 March 2005, Parliamentary Library, <www.aph.gov.au/linrary/pub/RN/2005-06/06rn29.pdf> [July 2007]. See also Geoff Winter, 'Whither Public Sector Employment?', Research Note 17, 1997-98, Parliamentary Library, <www.aph.gov.au/library/Pubs/rn/1997-98/98rn17.htm> [August 2006].

11. See *State of the Service Report 2005-6 at a Glance*, section in 'Challenges for the APS' <www.apsc.gov.au/stateoftheservice/0506/ataglance.pdf> [December 2006].

12. [2007] FCFA 120 [12 August 2007].

13. Dr Peter Shergold, Secretary, Department of Prime Minister and Cabinet, 18 May 2005, speech to the CPA Annual Conference, Melbourne.

<www.pmc.gov.au/speeches/shergold/aps_2035_back_to_the_future_2005-05-18.cfm> [July 2007].

14. See Dr Shergold speech above, n 13.

15. 'Looking to the Future — Directions in Public Sector Reform', speech, Crawford School Alumni. Address by Lynelle Briggs, Australian Public Service Commissioner, 8 November 2006 <www.apsc.gov.au/media/briggs081106.htm> [July 2007]

16. Above at n 13.

17. Above at n 13.

18. Above at n 13.

19. Above at n 13.

20. Above n 15.

21. Above at n 13.

# Table of Cases

*Huffman v Office of Personnel Management*, 263 F 3d 1341, 1351 (Fed Cir, 2001), citing HR Rep No 100-413, 12-13 (1988): 185

*Jarratt v Commissioner of Police for New South Wales* (2005) 221 ALR 95: 2, 9, 32, 52

*Kaye v Attorney-General for Tasmania* (1956) 94 CLR 193: 47, 48, 52

*Keely v State of Victoria* [1964] VR 244: 46

*Kodeeswaran v Attorney-General of Ceylon* (170) AC 1111: 46

*Lucy v Commonwealth* (1923) 33 CLR 229: 13, 46, 48, 120

*M v Home Office* [1994] 1 AC 377: 52

*Macrae v Attorney-General for New South Wales* (1987) 9 NSWLR 268: 52

*McClaren v Home Office* [1990] ICR 824: 307

*Minister for Arts, Heritage and Environment v Peko-Wallsend Ltd* (1987) 15 FCR 274: 52

*Minister for Employment and Workplace Relations v Gribbles Radiology Pty Ltd* (2005) 222 CLR 194: 211, 226, 227

*Mongan v Woodward* [2003] FCA 66: 52

*Mulvenna v Mulvenna* [1926] SC 842: 297, 306.

*National Gallery of Australia v Douglas* [1999] ACTSC 79: 18, 48

*National Wage Case — March 1987* (1987) 17 IR 65: 120

*New South Wales v The Commonwealth* [2006] HCA 52: 124

*New York Times v US*, 403 US 713 (1971): 184

*North Western Healthcare Network v Health Services Union of Australia* [1999] FCA 897: 202-4, 210, 212, 226, 227

*O'Halloran v Wood* [2004] FCA 544: 51

*Parrish v Civil Service Commission*, 425 P 2d 223 (Cal, 1967): 184

*Perkins v Cuthill* (No 2) (1981) 3 ALN N88: 48

*Pickering v Board of Education*, 391 US 563 (1968): 188

*PP Consultants Pty Ltd v Finance Sector Union* (2000) 201 CLR 648: 199-201, 210, 211, 213, 226, 227

*Public Service Board of New South Wales v Osmond* (1986) 159 CLR 657: 48

*R v Civil Service Appeal Board; Ex parte Bruce* [1988] ICR 649, 660: 307

*R v Civil Service Appeal Board; Ex parte Cunningham* [1992] ICR 816: 307

*R v East Berkshire Area Health Authority; Ex parte Walsh* [1985] QB 152: 307

*R v Lord Chancellor's Department; Ex parte Nangle* [1992] 1 All ER 897: 298, 307

*R v Ponting* [1985] Crim LR 318: 306

*R v Secretary of State for the Home Department; Ex parte Oladehinde* [1991] 1 AC 254: 306

*R v Shayler* [2003] 1 AC 247: 305

*R v Toohey; Ex parte Northern Land Council* (1981) 151 CLR 170: 52

*Rankin v Attorney-General* [2001] 1 ERNZ 476: 277

*Re Australian Industrial Relations Commission and Arends; ex parte Commonwealth of Australia* (2005) 145 FCR 277

*Ryder v Foley* (1906) 4 CLR 422: 47, 48, 52

*Schmohl v Commonwealth of Australia* (1983) 74 FLR 474: 49

*Scott v Commonwealth* (1982) 64 FLR 89: 17, 47, 49

*Stellar Call Centres Pty Ltd v CPSU* [2001] FCA 106: 201-2, 226

*Stevens v Brodribb Sawmilling Company Pty Ltd* (1986) 160 CLR 16: 120

*Sullivan v Secretary, Department of Defence* [2005] FCA 786: 52

*Suttling v Director-General of Education* (1985) 3 NSWLR 427: 17-18, 47

*Twining v Australian Public Service Commission* [2005] FMCA 1738: 52

*Wells v Newfoundland* [1999] 3 SCR 199: 299, 307

*Williamson v Commonwealth* (1907) 5 CLR 174: 46, 47, 120

# Table of Statutes

**Codes**

**Regulations**

# Index

Merkel J, 217
Miliband, Ralph, 283
Moore-Wilton, Max, 29
Mulgan, Richard, 23, 41, 42

natural justice, 17, 19, 32, 33, 38, 40
New South Wales Court of Appeal, 16–18, 32
New South Wales Supreme Court, 14
New Zealand Public Service, 1, 6, 8, 56, 68, 253–76
Niland, John, 128
Nixon, Richard, 157, 158
North Western Healthcare Network, 202–3, 204, 207, 210, 212
Northcote, Sir Stafford, 63, 315
Northcote-Trevelyan Report, 55, 63–4, 69, 299

O'Connell, Shane, 148
outsourcing, 5–6, 86–7, 101, 189–223, 232, 233, 312
    Victoria, 192, 202–3, 204, 214, 215, 216, 217, 218, 229, 234, 238, 247–8

Peters, Guy, 233
Podger, Andrew, 67
Pollitt, Christopher, 263
Ponting, Clive, 291
Postmaster-General's Department, 59, 74
PP Consultants, 198, 199–200, 202, 210, 213
prime minister, 36–7, 38, 39, 40, 58, 60, 63, 67, 105, 106
Privy Council, 16, 18
Public Service Act Review Group. See McLeod Report

Reith, Peter, 25, 143
Remuneration Tribunal, 37, 60
Repatriation Commission, 59
Reserve Bank of Australia, 59
Rogers J, 14

Shann, Sir Keith, 66, 67
Shergold, Peter, 67, 137, 147, 309, 314–15

South African Public Service, 155
St George Bank, 198, 199–200
Stellar Call Centres Pty Ltd, 201–2

Telstra (Telecom), 59, 201–2
Trans-Australia Airlines, 59
Trevelyan, Sir Charles, 63, 315
Turnbull, Sir Andrew, 283–5

unfair dismissal, 12, 13, 17, 19, 28, 29, 32, 86, 105, 108, 111, 219–20, 310, 312, 313–14. See also dismissal at pleasure; Australian Public Service
unions, 7, 57, 63, 66, 72, 74, 75, 76, 118, 132, 138, 139, 239, 241, 243, 244
    bargaining, 7, 85, 86, 88, 89, 91, 105, 110, 116, 128, 129, 133, 135–7, 139, 141, 142, 229, 248
    disputes, 91, 142, 143–4, 145, 310
    marginalisation, 4, 74, 89, 108, 110, 116, 118, 127–8, 132, 135, 136–7, 139, 140, 142–3, 146–7, 148, 236, 237
    membership, 111, 112, 137, 141, 142, 143–4, 147–8
    public sector, 4, 5, 62, 71, 72, 73, 93, 97, 127–8, 129, 130, 131, 135–6, 137, 140, 146, 149, 230–1, 236, 237, 238, 239, 243, 244, 245, 248, 249
United States Civil Service, 42, 238. See also whistleblowers

Vardon, Sue, 143–4, 145

Walker, D. M., 281
Walsh, Pat, 269
Wanna, John, 41
Weller, Patrick, 40, 41
Wheeler, Sir Frederick, 66, 67
whistleblowers, 5, 156–7, 178–80. See also corruption
    Australia, 155, 174, 175–6, 182–3, 233
    international, 156, 170, 174, 177
    United Kingdom, 155–6, 170–4, 177
    United States, 155, 156, 157, 158–70, 171, 172, 174, 177–81, 183
    Victoria, 175

www.ingramcontent.com/pod-product-compliance
Lightning Source LLC
Chambersburg PA
CBHW061242270326
41928CB00041B/3362